SOCIAL POLICY IN MODERN BRITAIN

General Editor: Jo Campling

FOUNDATIONS OF THE WELFARE STATE

Pat Thane

LONGMAN
London and New York

Longman Group Limited
Longman House, Burnt Mill, Harlow,
Essex CM20 2JE, England
and Associated Companies throughout the world.

*Published in the United States of America
by Longman Publishing, New York*

First published 1982
Eleventh impression 1994

British Library Cataloguing in Publication Data

Thane, Pat
  The foundations of the welfare state.
  1. Great Britain – Social conditions –
  19th century   2. Great Britain – Social
  conditions. – 20th century
  I. Title
  303.4'84'0941   HN389

ISBN 0-582-29515-7

Library of Congress Cataloging in Publication Data

Thane, Pat.
  The foundations of the welfare state.
  (Social policy in modern Britain)
  Bibliography: p.
  Includes index.
  1. Great Britain – Social policy.   2. Welfare
state.   3. Great Britain – Economic policy.
I. Title. II. Series.
HN385.T43   361.6'1'0941   81–11727
ISBN 0–582–29515–7 (pbk.)   AACR2

Produced by Longman Singapore Publishers Pte Ltd.
Printed in Singapore.

CONTENTS

EDITOR'S PREFACE

This series, written by practising teachers in universities and polytechnics, is produced for students who are required to study social policy and administration, either as social science undergraduates or on the various professional courses. The books focus on essential topics in social policy and include new areas of discussion and research, to give students the opportunity to explore ideas and act as a basis of seminar work and further study. Each book combines an analysis of the selected theme, a critical narrative of the main developments and an assessment putting the topic into perspective as defined in the title. The supporting documents and comprehensive bibliography are an important aspect of the series.

Conventional footnotes are avoided and the following system of references is used: superior number ([6]) in the text refers the reader to the corresponding entry in the references at the end of the chapter. A number in square brackets, preceded by 'doc' [docs 6, 8], refers the reader to the corresponding items in the section of documents which follows the main text.

Unlike most existing textbooks on the history of social policy this book does not focus narrowly on social legislation and pressure groups, but argues that social policy can only be understood in the context of broader social, economic and political structures and changes. In particular, Pat Thane stresses that social policy must be discussed in close association with analysis of the economy and of economic policy. She also looks briefly at the experience of social policy in other countries. This is done partly to demonstrate that the British experience has not been uniquely progressive, but also in the belief that such comparative analysis is necessary if we are to understand what are the leading pressures for, and constraints upon, further redistribution through 'welfare' measures.

Jo Campling

AUTHOR'S PREFACE

Many of my friends have groaned audibly at the prospect of yet another survey of the history of social policy. I have happily ignored them for two reasons: firstly in the past decades many new studies have been published of aspects of social policy in the previously neglected period between 1918 and 1945. I felt that it was time for them to be synthesised and made available to a wider audience. Secondly, too often the development of social policy is examined within too narrow a framework. Like other aspects of government activity it cannot be fully understood by examining legislation alone. Social legislation is the product of structures, pressures and values in society, politics and the economy as a whole. I have tried, however inadequately, to place the study of social policy in this wider context. Also, to evaluate changes in social policy within one society, it is desirable to compare them with changes in other societies in order to discover what is and what is not particular to the British experience. This has been done with regrettable brevity to avoid producing too unwieldy, or too costly, a book.

The book begins in 1870 because it is concerned with state welfare and I believe that it was around that time that important demands began to arise for the state in Britain to take a permanent, as distinct from a temporary and residual, responsibility for the social and economic conditions experienced by its citizens. Although the scope of these state responsibilities gradually widened, it was not until after the Second World War that a government formally acknowledged that the welfare of the mass of its citizens was a major component of its activities and announced the dawning of a 'welfare state'. The books ends with this beginning. The requirement of the series of which it forms part was that I should end in 1945. I have overstepped this date a little, since so much of the legislation of the post-war years is inextricably linked with the post-war discussions and proposals, but in order not to tread too far into the territory of later books in the series I am aware that my treatment of post-war legislation has been all too inadequate.

My final justification for writing the book is that I hope it will fulfil a need among students required to study this period and among others interested in how and why British social policy took the form it did after 1945, a form which has remained the basis for much state social provision since then. At a time when the post-war 'welfare state' is actively being dismantled there is perhaps an especial need to understand the forces which can oppose, promote or defend state measures to meet social needs.

Pat Thane

ACKNOWLEDGEMENTS

Many people have helped, sometimes unconsciously, in the making of this book. With apologies for any distortion of their ideas, I am particularly grateful to Jose Harris, Roy Hay, Eric Hobsbawm, Joe Melling, Pat Ryan, Steve Schifferes and my students over many years at Goldsmiths College. I am also grateful to Robert Fox and an anonymous reviewer for their suggestions. To Jo Campling, Jane Harris-Matthews, John and Lucy Thane my thanks for their patience.

We are grateful to the following for permission to reproduce copyright material:

George Allen and Unwin for an extract from *Full Employment in a Free Society* by W. Beveridge: Cambridge University Press for an extract from *Wages and Income Since 1860* by A. L. Bowley; Hutchinson Publishing Group Ltd for an extract from *The Home Front* by Sylvia Pankhurst; Macmillan, London and Basingstoke for an extract from *The Middle Way* by Harold Macmillan; Macmillan, London and Basingstoke, the Royal Economic Society and Cambridge University Press for an extract from *How to Pay for the War* by J. M. Keynes.

To the memory of my grandparents,
who lived through much of this

Part one
CHANGES IN SOCIAL POLICY 1870–1945

Currently the British 'welfare state' faces a critical assault and the first determined attempt since the Second World War to cut it back. It is argued that government social expenditure has grown to a level and in a fashion which is both economically and socially undesirable; that it excessively distorts the functioning of the economic market and provides disincentives to effort. These very arguments were invoked against the initial growth of such expenditure in the half century before the First World War, and in the period of economic crisis in the 1920s and 30s. In both periods the arguments were found wanting and the 'welfare' activities of the state grew. The central purpose of this book is to ask why this was so.

History does not precisely repeat itself. Our understanding of the present may be distorted if we expect it do so. The value of history lies in helping us to understand the nature of present structures; what imperatives lay behind their introduction? We may more usefully defend or criticize the 'welfare state' if we understand more clearly why it came into being. To interpret its growth simply as a manifestation of altruism, of a desire to remove poverty and other social evils, renders mysterious the fact that much poverty remains, that those in greatest need have often gained least and that their gains have been hedged around with restrictions designed, for example, to keep benefits below normal wages. Public and official discussion of social policy has rarely been solely or even centrally about redistribution for the elimination of poverty, any more than it is at present. Equally or more important at various times have been questions of political and social order, of increasing the efficiency of the workforce, of international conflict and competition, of methods of increasing demand in the economy or of increasing central government control over economy and society.

Arguments derived from pure economic or social theory, or from humane revulsion against deprivation, even when plausible in themselves, have often conflicted with one another or been over-ridden by perceived political imperatives.

Consequently the analysis of social policy is complex. It is difficult to understand if it is abstracted from the context of social conditions, the structure of the economy and of power, of ideas and expectations from which policies and legislation have emerged. Conversely, the study of social policies tells us much about the society from which they derive. This is precisely because their discussion necessitates consideration of fundamental questions about the relationship between rich and poor, between government and citizens and about whether, or by which means, the achievement of economic growth or stability can be reconciled with the achievement of a stable and/or civilized society.

POVERTY AND SOCIAL CONDITIONS

For most people living standards rose in the later nineteenth century. The prices of essential goods were stable and those of food actually fell. Within this general pattern, however, there were major and persistent differentials among social groups and among geographical regions which barely began to narrow before 1900.[1] It is hard to give a precise picture of the extent of poverty in 1870, since no reliable statistics exist. Dudley Baxter's statistics of income distribution in 1867 may help place the discussion in context.[2] This maldistribution of income had changed little by 1900.

How many of those at the lower end of this scale could be described as 'poor'? This only became clear when serious large-scale efforts to define and quantify poverty began in the 1880s. Charles Booth between 1886 and 1902 surveyed, first, poverty in East London, and then in London as a whole. He did not conduct a house-to-house survey, nor did he construct a clearly defined 'poverty line'. He collected systematically the impressions of school board visitors, who were closely acquainted with poorer families, as to the number of families living in discernible poverty. This was not an unreasonable procedure at a time when poverty was startlingly evident in clothing, household goods – or lack of them – in undernourished faces or rickety legs. Booth then cross-checked these impressions with those of other local people such as clergymen, and with the observations of his own investigators after a period of residence in a poor community. Beatrice Webb, then Miss Potter, for example, lived among and observed the Jewish community of East London. Booth also collected household budgets from thirty families. The seventeen volumes of his survey provide a remarkable survey not only of poverty but of employment and religious observance in London.

Table 1   Income of Great Britain 1867

Upper and Middle Classes	No. of Assessments	% occupied population
Class I Large incomes:		
(1) £5,000 and upwards	8,100	0.07
(2) £1,000–£5,000	46,100	0.4
Class II Middle incomes:		
£300–£1,000	163,900	1.4
Class III Small incomes:		
(1) £100–£300	947,900	8.6
(2) below income tax– under £100	1,159,000	10.5
Total:	2,200,000	20.07

Manual Labour Class		
Men's average wages:		
Class IV Higher skilled labour and manufacturers – £50–£73	1,260,000	11.4
Class V Lower skilled labour and manufacturers – £35–£52	4,377,000	39.9
Class VI Agriculture and unskilled labour – £10.10s.–£36	3,270,000	29.8
Total	8,907,000	81.2
Grand total	10,960,000	

Total population of Great Britain 1867 (est.): 24,152,000

Source: R.D. Baxter *National Income* (1867) p. 64.

On this basis, Booth classified the population of London according to their degree of poverty or affluence. He found 30 per cent of the inhabitants of London to be living 'in poverty or in want'. Poverty, he defined as 'having no surplus', i.e. having the bare essentials much of the time, but nothing to spare to provide for a crisis such as unemployment, sickness or death in the family. According to Booth 8.4 per cent of the people of London lived in the worst condition of being 'at all times more or less in want', 'ill-nourished and poorly clad'. In East London where poverty was most heavily concentrated the figures were respectively 35 per cent and 13.3 per cent[3]

This level of poverty might be thought to have been peculiar to London, which was believed by contemporaries to have a greater concentration of poverty than elsewhere. However, when Seebohm Rowntree carried out a study of York in 1899, defining and measuring poverty more precisely than Booth had done, his findings were startlingly similar.

Rowntree's family were the largest local employers in York. The city was he believed, rightly enough, 'fairly representative of the conditions existing in many if not most of our provincial towns', providing a range of industrial and service employment with average pay and employment levels. He investigated the city at a time 'of average prosperity'. Rowntree tried to devise an objective definition of poverty based upon the minimum income required to maintain individuals in a state of 'physical efficiency'. This included an amount sufficient to buy food adequate for energy needs at various ages. This calculation was made possible by the recent discovery by nutritionists of the relationship between diet and health. Rowntree's poverty line was drawn up, however, on the assumption that food was 'all purchased at the lowest current prices. It only allows for a diet less generous as regards variety than that supplied to able-bodied paupers in workhouses. It further assumes that no clothing is purchased which is not absolutely necessary for health and assumes too that it is of the plainest and most economical description.' Other essentials such as rent, light and fuel were included, also at minimum prices. 'No expenditure of any kind is allowed for beyond that which is absolutely necessary for the maintenance of merely physical efficiency'.[4] On this basis, the minimum income necessary for a family consisting of father, mother and three children was 21s. 8d. per week.

Rowntree set investigators to survey every working class household in York (11,560) to establish family income and expenditure and to record their impressions of living conditions. Rowntree's stringent poverty line produced remarkably similar results to those of Booth. Ten per cent of the population of York lived in families with earnings below the poverty line. Rowntree described these as living in 'primary' poverty. Another 17.93 per cent he found to be living in 'secondary' poverty, i.e. their income was above the minimum but Rowntree's investigators described them as 'obviously living in a state of poverty, i.e. in obvious want and squalor'. Comparing his York findings with Booth's in London, Rowntree concluded that 'we are faced with the startling probability that from 25 per cent to 30 per cent of the town population of the United Kingdom are living in poverty'.[5]

If this was so, and it *was* 'probable', what of the rural population? Little public attention was paid to rural poverty before Rowntree undertook a survey in 1912. Yet in some rural areas there were even greater concentrations of poverty, visible to fewer passers-by, hidden sometimes behind outwardly more picturesque facades than the urban slums, but just as grim to experience. The proportion of the population living in the countryside had been declining throughout the century. It fell still more sharply from the mid-1870s as a result of severe agricultural depression due to a decline in demand for British produce, and increased imports of cheap food from abroad. The resulting fall in food prices was beneficial for wage-earners, but it caused unemployment in the countryside and emigration abroad and to British towns. Unemployed unskilled rural migrants added to the already overlarge pool of labour in many towns. Since this migration was primarily of young people, the age structure of many rural areas shifted towards a predominance of old people. This in itself increased the proportion of rural poor.

The impact of agricultural decline varied regionally, but tended to hit hardest regions which were already poorest in the 1860s. Throughout the period the lowest wages in the United Kingdom were in the rural areas of East Anglia, South-West England (where Cornwall was further hit by the decline of tin mining from the 1870s), the highlands of Wales and Scotland. Much of rural Ireland remained desperately poor. The rural poor were not compensated by lower prices or by the greater availability of jobs for wives and children. There was perhaps compensation in the possibility of supplementing income by gathering firewood, poaching, or growing produce, although the real possibilities of this kind can be exaggerated. In the rather fresher air of rural areas the poor were healthier and lived longer than the urban poor, who suffered from the ravages of urban atmospheric pollution, overcrowding and unhealthy working conditions.

Rural housing density was lower, but the houses themselves as overcrowded and unsanitary as in towns. It is probably true that, indeed, 'in this period there is no major occupational group more worthy of compassion than the rural labourer'.[6]

Nevertheless, urban poverty especially in London, attracted more attention and alarm than that in the countryside, and poorer rural areas were last to receive adequate schooling, housing, sanitation or other services – not to mention adequate wages. After Joseph Arch's short-lived attempt to organize agricultural labourers in the 1870s, they were also slow to unionize, and the countryside was politically more quiescent than the towns from the mid-1880s.

The overwhelming causes of poverty in rural areas were low pay and to a lesser extent old age and widowhood. The latter was everywhere a cause of severe poverty. Widowed mothers of young children had a poor chance of supporting their families adequately given the conventionally lower pay (by half to two-thirds) of women compared with men, even when a job could be found.[7]

The causes of poverty were much the same in towns. One of Booth's first discoveries from his study of East London was the extent of poverty in old age. He found 38.8 per cent of all inhabitants over 65 to be recipients of poor relief. However, his surveys as a whole suggested that 'low pay' and 'irregular work' were the major reasons for poverty. Rowntree, once more, was more precise. He found that 51.96 per cent of those in 'primary poverty' were so because the chief breadwinner was 'in regular work but at low wages'; 22.16 per cent of primary poverty was due, in modern terminology, to 'child poverty', i.e. the family had more than four children and insufficient income to support so large a family; 15.63 per cent to 'death of chief wage-earner'; 5.11 per cent to the illness and old age of chief wage-earner; 2.83 per cent to 'irregularity of work'; 2.31 per cent to unemployment. Both latter categories suggest the relative stability of the York economy in 1899. London, with its notoriously large casual labour market, for example on the docks, suffered more 'irregularity of work', and other towns at certain times experienced severe unemployment.[8] National unemployment figures for this period are seriously deficient but it was undoubtedly high at certain times, regionally and nationally, notably in 1867–69, 1878–79, 1884–87, 1893–94.

Rowntree made a further contribution to the analysis of poverty by pointing out that 'the life of a labourer is marked by five alternating periods of want and comparative plenty'. He or she was poorest when a child when the maternal family had most dependents, in early middle life after marriage and the arrival of young children and again in old age. This implied that the proportion of the population experiencing poverty at some point in their lives was higher than that suggested by the surveys.

Rowntree was less precise about the causes of 'secondary poverty'. This occurred, he believed, despite the household's 'sufficiency of income' and therefore could not be attributed to the same causes as 'primary poverty'. He asked why some families, but not others, lived in squalor on incomes which, although low, were sufficient for necessities. He had no doubt that a major reason was drink or, sometimes, gambling. He pointed out, however that these

are themselves often the outcome of the adverse conditions under which too many of the working classes live. Housed for the most part in sordid streets, frequently in overcrowded and unhealthy conditions, compelled very often to earn their bread by monotonous and laborious work and unable, partly through limited education and partly through overtime and other causes of physical exhaustion, to enjoy intellectual recreation.

Also important, he believed, were

larger questions dealing with land tenure, with the relative duties and powers of the state and of the individual towards legislation affecting the aggregation and the distribution of wealth. While the immediate causes of 'secondary' poverty call for well-considered and resolute action its ultimate elimination will only be possible when these causes are dealt with as a part of and in relation to, the wider social problem.

Hence a major factor predisposing urban and rural families to poverty was the low pay of men and the still lower pay of women, whilst they were in regular work. Irregular employment and unemployment were also important, more at some times and places than others. Statistically less significant but no less painful conditions were old age, disability, widowhood, or desertion by the husband, which was sometimes permanent, sometimes temporary if, like so many working men of the period, he tramped away in search of work. There were significant numbers of one-parent, female-headed families in this period. This was due not so much, as now, to divorce or separation (the former was expensive and rare, though not unheard of, among the labouring poor; the latter came into legal existence in 1876) as to death and desertion. Men, especially poor men, had a significantly higher death rate than women in their middle years.

Most of these causes of poverty had, however, been broadly constant for generations, although the growth of towns and of industry and of urban service occupations had changed the conditions in which they were experienced. In the last decades of the nineteenth century certain new trends of long-term importance began to emerge. A falling mortality rate led to a gradual increase in the proportion of the aged in the population. At the same time increased competitive pressure on British industry from expanding economies, such as those of Germany and the United States, caused employers to seek means of increasing productivity. One of these was a gradual trend towards laying off workers in their early sixties in the belief that age made them less efficient, and the introduction for the first time of fixed retirement ages. Hence not only were there more old people, but more of them became unable to support themselves at earlier ages.

The birth rate also began to fall from the 1870s, initially among the professional middle class. By the 1900s it was discernible though not yet dramatic among most working-class groups. Also in the 1900s the infant mortality rate began to fall with the result that some poorer families faced the cost of raising more children until they were old enough to work. The period of costly childhood dependency was further lengthened by the introduction of compulsory education from 1880.

ATTITUDES TO POVERTY

These causes of poverty were far from clear to observers in the 1870s. They had been long debated, but it should be emphasized how few individuals at this time believed that poverty could actually be eliminated, except perhaps in the very long run. Poverty had always been, and remained, the normal condition of a substantial proportion of the population in all known societies. Almost certainly it was less severe in Britain in 1870, the most industrialized and urbanized society in the world, than in any other country, or in Britain at any previous time. But it required a considerable imaginative effort to conceive even of Britain without a significant amount of poverty. Hence thinking tended to be directed towards minimizing both poverty and associated problems, such as those of economic growth and public order, rather than towards its elimination.

The debate on these issues continued throughout the last three decades of the nineteenth century, but with certain changes of emphasis. This change is often described as being from a general tendency to blame the fecklessness and idleness of the poor for their poverty, to recognition that the fault lay in the structure of the economy; from a 'moral' to an 'economic' diagnosis. From this change, it is said, followed another change, from prescribing as the cure more self-help and hard work among the poor, to recognition of the need for government intervention to support the poor in an economic situation over which they had little control; from 'individualism' to 'collectivism' as it is often put. A change is also detected from a mid-nineteenth century optimism that a free economy left to itself would eventually generate sufficient wealth to solve many problems, to pessimism about whether the British economy was capable of such sustained progress.

These generalizations contain some truths but oversimplify and to some degree distort a complex process of change. There was increasing recognition of the complexity of the causes of poverty and increased understanding of how the economy functioned. But the belief that it was necessary not simply to lessen poverty but to improve the moral standards of labourers and also of capitalists remained central to the debate. Most reformers in 1900 wished to achieve both, though they differed upon definitions of desirable behaviour.

Advocates of state 'collectivism' very rarely wished government action to take the place of self-help, philanthropy and the duty to work, but rather to supplement and reinforce these attributes. Furthermore there was considerable pessimism among mid-century political economists about the future development of the productive forces of capitalism, and marked optimism among later economists and reformers about a future in which the economy was better understood, the population better educated, and greater co-operation among classes would emerge.

Since the beginning of the nineteenth century there had been voiced a range of analyses of, and solutions to, poverty. Some, such as Robert Owen, among socialists, and conservatives such as Thomas Carlyle, had argued from the beginning of industrial capitalism in Britain that the source of the unequal distribution of wealth, income and power lay in the competitive, individualistic nature of the new economic system and the values it perpetuated and strengthened: the emphasis upon individual rather than co-operative effort, upon self-help for all rather than upon mutual obligation, such as the responsibility of the rich to help the poor in return for their labour.

In the 1830s and 40s alternative ideas such as those of Owen for the substitution of co-operation for individualistic competition lost the struggle for ideological hegemony to ideas of liberal *laissez-faire*, although they survived among groups of radical working people and among some philanthropists. The dominant view among those with economic, political and social power – employers, politicians, civil servants, clergy – was that embodied in the Poor Law Amendment Act of 1834 – described vividly by Engels as 'the most open declaration of war by the bourgeoisie upon the proletariat'.[9] In principle, after 1834, those who were physically capable of work were left no option but to support themselves. Public aid was given only to those – the aged, the disabled, etc. – who could be supported neither by their own labour nor by that of their families. Hence, it was believed, the economy would attain maximum growth, to the benefit of all: hard work, self-reliance and respectability – which were in theory demanded of all, including employers – would benefit both rich and poor, morally and materially.

This view rested on an optimistic assumption that there was employment enough in the economy for all if labour was sufficiently mobile, but it was impossible to test this assumption in the 1830s and 40s. In addition it was assumed that if there were insufficient jobs in Britain, other economies, such as those of America and Australia, were waiting for labour for their own development. The *laissez-faire* economy was conceived of as international, and indeed from the 1840s to the end of the century thousands emigrated from Britain. This view left room for considerable differences of opinion as to the means by which the labouring poor should be encouraged to work – by coercion or persuasion; as to the degree to which those who worked *could* provide for all their needs, such as their children's education, housing, sickness, old age, widowhood, or required support from the state in some or all of these circumstances; and as to the degree of culpability of those who did not provide for themselves.

Between the 1830s and 1860s there was no unanimity on these issues. Many employers and social observers recognized the existence of involuntary unemployment and inadequate pay. Even those who believed that poverty was largely self-inflicted did not always adhere to policies strictly consistent with this view. Poor Law administrators in practice operated with considerably varying degrees of harshness or generosity. Some, contrary to the spirit of the Act of 1834, supplemented wages and gave outdoor relief to the unemployed, recognizing that on occasion jobs were not to be found; others offered only the workhouse.[10] Central and local government began on a small but growing scale to put resources into education, factory reform and public health.[11] Some employers were crudely exploitative, others offered their workers shorter hours, better conditions, improved housing and medical care, from a mixture of philanthropy and conviction that the carrot was a more effective means of increasing productivity than the stick. The rapid growth of private charity in these years also gave rise to institutions demonstrating a variety of approaches to the palliation of poverty. Much of this philanthropy was fuelled by religious conviction, especially by the realization of evangelical Anglicans and Nonconformists that to save souls it was necessary first to remove the poverty which so consumed lives that the poor had no time for God.

Free market principles were not carried to their logical conclusion in the mid-nineteenth century. They were not, however, modified according to any consistent principle, but by a variety of *ad hoc* remedies. And, broadly, it continued to be accepted that the key to improvement lay in dedication to competitive enterprise, hard work and self-help, and that those unable to practice these virtues should be helped by their families or by voluntary charity. From the 1860s, however, growing numbers of those who had no desire to question or to alter the nature of the economic system became uneasy about the prevailing diagnosis of the causes of and cure for poverty. There was more persistent questioning of the assumption that the market could indeed provide enough work for all who deserved and sought it, either at home or in the colonies, at wages which enabled the worker to provide adequately for himself and his family. Members, for example, of the National Association for the Promotion of Social Science, the leading forum for the discussion of ideas concerning social reform, recognized in the late 1860s that the London labour market, at least, was overstocked leading both to low pay and irregular employment at the lower end of the working class.[12]

This had been obvious to Henry Mayhew in his vivid survey of *London Labour and the London poor* in 1856.[13] The Lancashire 'cotton famine', due to the cessation of cotton supplies during the American civil war of 1863–66 which caused severe unemployment and poverty, demonstrated most clearly that unemployment could be due to causes over which workers had no control; it also demonstrated the peaceful fashion in which the labouring poor could behave in such circumstances.[14] Despite rare incidents such as the 'Sheffield outrages' of 1866 there were no riots or upheavals to match those of the 1830s and 40s. The extension of the franchise to urban workers in 1867 was preceded by an agitation which was considerably more decorous than that before 1832. Working-class 'self-help' institutions such as Friendly Societies and savings banks proliferated.[15] Respectable workers were rewarded with the vote, and in 1868 the Royal Commission on Trade Unions recommended the extension of legal protection for trade unions, which was achieved in the Trade Union Act of 1871 which for the first time gave legal protection to Trade Union funds and the Criminal Law Amendment Act of 1875 which legalized peaceful picketing.

The apparent social harmony of the mid-century could be attributed to Britain's economic success in these years. However, from the early 1870s the British economy was beginning to face serious competitive pressure for the first time from the expanding economies of Western Europe and the United States. The prospects for future economic growth sufficient to contain if not to solve mass poverty seemed less certain.

From the early 1870s discussion of provision for the poor was influenced by the new facts that some of them had deserved the vote and that the economy faced certain difficulties. This did not automatically lead all in influential circles to conclude that there was a need for provision for the poor by the state. Rather, many contemporaries were impressed by the growing capacity of some at least of the working class to practice self- and mutual-help and they sought ways of encouraging its further development. They also wished and expected charitable effort to grow. They identified two distinct social problems: the 'low, loafing class', the 'residuum' at the bottom of society, the very poor and irregularly employed who constituted a permanent problem; and the élite of respectable labourers who suffered occasional problems of poverty due to unemployment, sickness and old age. These two sections of the working class were seen to require separate treatment.[16]

Disraeli, much influenced by the desire to secure the support of the new working-class voters (mainly better-off skilled men), introduced measures during his conservative government of 1874–80 to improve the status of trade unions, public health, education and housing. In doing so he emphasized that if leaders of society were to maintain the allegiance of the masses they must demonstrate their responsibility for them, sustaining the aristocratic tradition of obligation towards the poor. His legislation, however, was designed to provide the conditions in which self-help and independence could be attained rather than to redistribute wealth and opportunities from rich to poor. His ministry did little for the more difficult problem of the 'residuum'.[17]

Booth's conclusion from his great survey was, reassuringly, that although poverty was severe it was diminishing, and the capacity for self and mutual help among the masses was improving.[18] He advocated state support only for the minority who could not be self-helping because they were too old or disabled for work or because there were insufficient jobs available; and he accepted the need for punitive treatment of the undeserving at the base of society.

Alfred Marshall, the leading economist of the last decades of the nineteenth century, provided new tools for analysing the economy and demonstrated that involuntary unemployment could occur. He was deeply concerned about the need to improve social conditions; but he concluded that the economy had the capacity for recovery and expansion to create more and better jobs and argued that government intervention was more likely to harm than to assist that process.[19]

Liberal politicians led by Gladstone remained convinced that state action posed a danger to individual freedom, and would rarely assist economic growth or social or moral improvement. Liberal theorists such as T. H. Green argued in the 1880s and 90s that poor social conditions hindered the desirable growth of moral and communal responsibility among the poor, but Green also looked to improvement from increased voluntary exercise of responsibility and regarded state intervention only as a last resort.[20]

Although opposition to state action to alleviate poverty remained strong to the end of the century, countervailing pressures were growing. The findings of Booth, Marshall and Green in their differing spheres were susceptible of different conclusions, and the actions of the poor themselves began to force these to the surface. In the 1880s there was agitation, though of a peaceful nature, for further extensions of the vote. It was conceded for rural workers in 1884. Economic depression in 1878–79 and 1884–87 was marked by demonstrations of the unemployed in London, the North East and elsewhere. It was difficult in the 1880s to ignore the fact that some at least of the working class were becoming increasingly active on various economic and political issues, were less acquiescent than previously and that organizations were being formed to defend and further their interests. In 1884 both the Fabian Society (favouring gradualist reform but for unquestionably socialist ends) was founded and the revolutionary Social Democratic Federation (SDF) adopted a more radically redistributive programme. Both organizations added to the ferment of discussion about social problems, offering new ideas, reviving in new forms long muted arguments that capitalism itself created poverty and hence that capitalism could not be 'moralized' but must be eradicated.

The Fabians, Sidney and Beatrice Webb in particular, devoted themselves to the analysis of social and economic conditions. They were convinced of the incapacity of the free market significantly to diminish poverty and inequality. They placed their faith instead in social ownership, economic planning and extensive measures by central and local government to provide institutional and other relief to prevent and cure poverty due to unemployment, old age, sickness and other causes of need. The Webbs devoted themselves to pressing these ideas upon leading politicians and civil servants.[21]

The SDF and others further to the left also argued that capitalism must be abolished, but by revolutionary means if necessary. They were also, however, profoundly suspicious of proposals for state welfare, which they identified as a means of diminishing working-class control over their own lives and as palliative substitutes for the workers' just demands for control over the means of production, high wages and full employment.

Although the organized activists were not on the whole the very poor, the poorest joined the demonstration. After the relative quiescence of the working class since the late 1840s these new manifestations engendered fears that respectable workers might become less co-operative if their real grievances were not palliated. Working-class activity took a new form at the end of the 1880s. A period of prosperity and relatively full employment gave unprecedented bargaining power to the chronically underemployed and brought successful strikes among this previously unorganized lower stratum of workers, including the semi-skilled gas workers, Bryant and May match girls, and the casually employed dockers of London. These workers were of, or close to, the very poor, from the slums of East London; they were led by more secure workers and by intellectual socialists. Well-organized, they achieved maximum publicity for their demands. And in the face of some of their claims traditional assumptions were difficult to uphold. The dockers demanded an increase in pay from 4*d*. to a still paltry 6*d*. per hour. They paraded the smart streets of West London, displaying their meagre weekly rations. Manifestly they were very poor. Equally clearly they were workers, not loafers, and they conducted the strike and the demonstrations peacefully and respectably. These strikes were successful in achieving their immediate aims and led to the formation of permanent unions of previously poorer workers, although as yet only a small proportion of them.[22]

In the face of such evidence it was a little difficult for at least some of the non-poor to accept that such conditions should continue and that free enterprise could bring them to an end largely unassisted. It seemed that Britain was wealthy enough for some redistribution to be possible, as, arguably, it had not been in the 1830s, and that voluntary effort had achieved little in this respect.

The events of the 1880s moved some, such as Charles Booth, to detailed investigation of poverty, others to philanthropy or to pressure for government action. Concern about social conditions was both reflected and reinforced by a mass of polemical writing, in newspapers, such as the radical *Pall Mall Gazette*, in pamphlets, such as Andrew Mearns' *Bitter Cry of Outcast London* (1883), describing and attacking poverty especially in the London slums. The *Bitter Cry* was a vitriolic, moving and widely publicized polemic against the 'pestilential human rookeries...where tens of thousands are crowded together amidst horrors which call to mind what we have heard of the middle passage of the slave-ship'.[23]

Writing about slum life for middle- and upper-class consumption was not a new *genre* in the 1880s. Dramatic and colourful vignettes of urban 'low life', lacking any serious analytical purpose, had had a considerable fashionable readership in the 1850s and 60s. However, the prevailing tone of the work of the 1880s was different, critical of slum conditions, whereas previous writing had been descriptive, detached, rather anthropological in tone, as though describing alien barbaric tribes whose life was remote from that of the readership. It did not demand change. On the whole the writing of the 1880s did demand change and assumed that the privileged readers had such change within their power. The poor themselves were presented more realistically, whether as sources of threat or as objects of pity.[24]

Among politicians Joseph Chamberlain, a successful Birmingham manufacturer, had throughout his adult life been involved in Nonconformist philanthropy. Between 1873 and 1875 he was notable, as Liberal Major of Birmingham, for combining effective social reform with sound business principles. Slums were cleared, water supplies improved, municipalized and made profitable, an impressive city centre built. He was a Liberal Cabinet Minister until he left the Liberal party in 1886; he joined a Conservative Cabinet in 1895.

Chamberlain split from the Liberal party largely on the issue of Irish Home Rule, which he opposed, but also due to impatience with Gladstone's resistance to social reform. From the early 1880s he was conscious of the need for reform both for its own sake and to check the potential threat from labour to the political *status quo*. He was 'convinced that my fellow politicians unnecessarily exaggerate the influence of labour . . . it can easily be overcome by a political leader with genuine sympathy with the working class and a practical programme'. The 'programme' he developed from 1883, though most fully during his years outside the Cabinet. It included government-sponsored contributory old-age pensions, and eight-hour day and improved working-class housing.[25]

Social and economic change and political and industrial movements had by the end of the century made 'the social question' a more central political and intellectual issue than it had been in 1870. In influential circles there was greater knowledge of the nature and extent of certain social problems and stronger demands, for a variety of reasons, for government action to lessen poverty. But the new 'consciousness of sin' as Beatrice Webb called it, still affected relatively few of the sinful classes.[26] Political fear of the working class was not acute enough to bring about a widespread demand to conciliate the workers; rather the 1890s saw attempts to suppress trade unionism through the law courts, lock-outs and the use of 'blackleg' labour. Trade union membership declined slightly in the depressed years of the mid-1890s, especially in the new general unions.[27] Despite the foundation of the small national Independent Labour Party in 1893, Labour did not appear to present an irresistible threat. Sympathy with the conditions of the poor did not necessarily lead to a desire for reform by the state but for further voluntary action. Strong opposition remained to the growth of state interference.

'SELF-HELP' AND SURVIVAL

How, then, did the poor survive? In 1870 and still in 1900 support from agencies of either central or local government was the least sought and usually the last resort. The family was almost certainly the first resort. All members of poor families picked up work whenever possible from the earliest ages – a means of survival which was easiest in the big cities where the largest number of casual jobs could be found such as cleaning, running errands and child-minding. Mayhew gives a vivid picture for the 1850s of the variety of means by which the London casual poor scraped a living [doc 1]. When such means failed the extended family gave support most often in the form of food or of caring for some children of the family until a crisis was over, or permanently if it was sustained. This was done from affection or duty or in the certain knowledge that those who helped would someday need similar help themselves – as a form of insurance.[28]

The family might be too poor to help, or not available due to death or emigration. This was often the case with the aged who made up a high proportion of workhouse residents. It was found, time and again, that they were not, as moralists feared, abandoned by unfeeling children, but either had had no children or the children were dead, far away, or too poor to feed another family member.

In cases of temporary distress there is much contemporary testimony that the local community could be an important source of support. Eleanor Rathbone, for example, from her wide experience of charitable work in Liverpool pointed out:

In so close a community there are many and varied sources of help . . . One unfailing source is that of neighbours and friends. They know the circumstances of the family as no outsiders can hope to know them and time after time come to the rescue, helping with food and shelter, clothing, attendance as the case may require. It is to this source that application is made in any slight difficulty and it is only in the most serious pressure that help is asked either of the clergyman . . . or to one of the numerous charitable societies that distribute relief in food or clothing.[29]

The pawnshop also played an important role in enabling families to survive from week to week – setting their meagre possessions to work to provide some security. Shopkeeping itself, often on a very small scale in the home, enabled some women to supplement family incomes. Shopkeepers helped families out in bad times by giving credit.[30]

When family and community resources were exhausted, application to charity was, as Eleanor Rathbone suggested, the next step. The scale of private charity expanded remarkably in the mid-nineteenth century and offered considerable protection to the poor against the rigours of the Poor Law. A very large sum indeed was thus redistributed from rich to poor annually. Unfortunately it is impossible to say how much. Charities were many and multifarious: some long-lived, some short, some financing institutions such as Dr. Barnardo's homes (founded in 1869) or old people's dwellings, agricultural colonies for unemployed workers, homes for fallen prostitutes, or hospitals. Some charities combined pressure-group activity with practical action, such as the National Society for the Prevention of Cruelty to Children, founded in 1884. Some tried to help the poor by removing them from their environment, others aimed to change that environment and to help families and individuals within it. Some gave handouts in cash or kind, sometimes to specific groups such as widows, orphans, the unemployed or to Jews who converted to Christianity, sometimes to anyone in visible need. Sometimes need had to be proved, sometimes not. In London every magistrates' court and police station had a collecting box and proceeds were dealt out to the needy, often those appearing on charges. In times of special crisis at home and abroad such as severe unemployment in East London, or famine in India, the Lord Mayor of London, and mayors of other towns, opened relief funds which often attracted large subscriptions. Booth described the large number of charities established by religious bodies in London in increasing numbers from the 1860s. From 1865 William Booth, founder of the Salvation Army, grounded his East End missionary work in the belief that to save souls it was essential to save bodies; he did not discriminate between 'deserving' and 'undeserving' poor.

From the 1880s the richer members of the Jewish community made extensive and largely successful efforts to provide for the influx of destitute refugees from the Russian pogroms. The Jews settled in fairly clearly defined areas of larger cities, especially in East London, Manchester and Glasgow. They suffered considerable prejudice and criticism, adding as they did to the already excessive pool of surplus urban labour, though in practice they concentrated in trades, such as tailoring, in which there was relatively little competition. Jewish charity, in particular the Jewish Board of Guardians which relieved the destitute, and Jewish schools, such as the Jewish Free School of East London, were designed to mollify criticism and anti-semitism by providing for Jewish needs without recourse to the funds of the host community.[31] Roman Catholic charity and the work of priests and nuns provided similar services for the large poor Irish communities which were especially numerous in parts of London, Liverpool, Manchester and Glasgow.

However, the largest single inspiration to charitable effort, also religious in character, was that of evangelicalism, following the evangelical revival in the British Isles in the mid-nineteenth century. About three-quarters of voluntary charities established in the second half of the nineteenth century were evangelical in inspiration, including such charities as Barnardo's and the YMCA. The bulk of financial support for evangelical charities came from well-to-do middle-class families, although they also received much from lower income groups.[32]

The variety of religious motivations was not always conducive to harmony among philanthropists. The continuing conflict between evangelicals and Roman Catholics at times amounted to undignified scrapping over the souls of the proletariat. Although Catholics in theory regarded poverty as a holy state, they recognized that too much of it was not conducive to spiritual contemplation. Catholics and evangelicals indeed had much in common in regarding spiritual regeneration as the true end of philanthropy. Conflict arose because each wished to convert the poor – indeed the whole of society – to different forms of Christianity. Such disharmony at least stimulated competitive charitable effort.

Some places fared better for charity than others, the towns probably better than the countryside. East London was especially fortunate due to proximity to the largest concentration of wealth in the country, the remainder of London. In general the availability of charity varied with the existence or not of a resident bourgeoisie with a surplus to give, although a considerable amount was given by those with little to spare. For example, the 'Hospital Saturday' or 'Sunday' funds based on regular contributions of 1*d*. or 2*d*. collected weekly, on Saturday or Sunday, among workmates or in working-class neighbourhoods contributed to the funds of voluntary hospitals. However, charity was highly localized. In Newcastle, which had a resident middle class, it was widely available; in nearby largely working-class Gateshead it was not. There was a similar contrast between Manchester and neighbouring Salford.[33]

Larger endowed charities were registered with the Central Charity Commissioners, many others were not. Many left no records, hence the difficulty of assessing the importance of charity locally or nationally. One summary of London charities in 1861 estimated that 640 existed, with an annual income of £2.5 m. – which exceeded Poor Law expenditure in London. This survey omitted many small charities and individual gifts.[34]

The size and variety of charitable effort and the absence of universal or consistent principles underlying such activities was a major reason for the foundation of the Charity Organization Society (COS) in 1869. Its aim was to persuade charities to co-ordinate and concentrate their considerable resources so that they distributed systematically to those best able to make use of them, according to clear principles. These were the encouragement of 'self-dependence' by helping only those who were deemed capable of becoming self-supporting. The COS pioneered in England the practice of 'case-work' operating in some German towns. They enquired carefully into the backgrounds of their clients. If they were found worthy they were given help, including cash and the tools to carry on a trade, help in finding a job and regular visitation and advice until they could 'stand on their own feet'. Those whose 'condition is due to improvidence or thriftlessness and there is no hope of being able to make him independent in the future' were left to destitution or the Poor Law. The response of the COS to recognition that a proportion of poverty was due to the overstocked state of the labour market was to try to ensure that the available jobs went to the respectable and self-helping, who would serve as an example to others. They had no solution to the possibility that even they might sometimes fail to find permanent employment at a living wage.

The 'case-work' approach had much to be said for it in that it entailed a serious attempt to analyse the nature of the problem confronting the individual or family and to achieve a lasting solution without removing the clients from their familiar environment. Families who wished to emigrate and girls looking for domestic jobs were referred to two societies affiliated to the COS, the East End Emigration Society and the Metropolitan Association for Befriending Young Servants. The difficulties of this approach were that it was slow, time-consuming and could help very few. Between 1886–96 the COS assisted only 800 'cases' in London to find jobs. Also, the systematic scrutiny of an individual's character and private affairs was almost as objectionable to independent workmen as receipt of poor relief. Not all of the 'helpable' were willing to be helped by such means. These difficulties were the source of much of the conflict among philanthropists, between those who preferred to give thorough-going help to a few and those who believed that the scale of destitution was such that wholesale relief was necessary at least in times of high unemployment, to palliate serious destitution and to prevent social disorder. The approach also diverted attention from the broader causes of poverty.

The Society was substantially unsuccessful in its aim of persuading other charities to adopt the same methods. Their success was greatest, though very limited, in London, and far from complete elsewhere. Leaders of the COS argued that many charities were encouraging the 'demoralization' of the poor by handing out benefits in cash and kind too readily and with no attempt to ensure long-term improvement in the client's condition. The harmonizing of charities already locked in theological conflict presented problems of its own. Conflict between the COS and the evangelicals was almost inevitable given the view of the latter that *any* soul was worthy of salvation. It was indeed waged at times with a bitterness and pettiness which did the COS no credit.[35]

Many who subscribed to COS principles in theory found it difficult in practice to abandon to destitution or the Poor Law many who were in desperate and immediate need. Dissatisfaction with the COS led to some new approaches in voluntary effort, such as the Settlement House Movement, which pioneered, in effect, modern 'community work' as distinct from the case-work approach of the COS. In 1884 Samuel Barnett became warden of the newly established Toynbee Hall settlement in East London whose foundation he had inspired. Barnett had been a founder of COS in 1869 but, largely due to his experience in a desperately poor Whitechapel parish, he had become convinced that the COS did not understand the meaning of poverty and the helplessness which it bred. He came to believe that in order to help the poor and to achieve social harmony both the state and charity should work to improve living and working conditions. He also believed, as did Green, Marshall and many others, that it was equally essential for the rich to cease to patronize and exploit the poor. As he put it, 'not until the habits of the rich are changed and they are again content to breathe the same air and walk the same streets as the poor will East London be "saved"'. Only when the rich treated the poor as equally worthy human individuals would class harmony as well as material improvement be achieved.

Toynbee Hall was designed as a residential settlement to be inhabited by young university graduates, who were to work among the poor in their spare time – offering art, music and education as well as material help and advice – with the aim of achieving mutual knowledge and respect between the classes. By the end of the century thirty houses had been established on the model of Toynbee Hall, almost half in provincial cities, notably in Liverpool, another centre of desperate poverty.[36]

Recognition of the truth of criticism such as Barnett's, and fear of losing the initiative in the organization of charity, led the COS under C. S. Loch, its powerful secretary from 1875–1913, by 1890 into greater changes in its approach than it was always willing publicly to admit. Members recognized the great difficulty of distinguishing 'deserving' from 'undeserving' poor. They began to recommend the development of new industries, and of temporary work-creation schemes strictly for those capable of finding work in normal times. They were opposed, however, to any such action by central or local government; it was, in their view, the work of charity. The role of government, they believed, was to provide for the unhelpable residuum.[37]

Loch's somewhat high-handed attitude towards many public or philanthropic efforts contributed much to the lack of harmony within the philanthropic movement. He achieved for the COS, however, a degree of influence in government circles which was rather greater than the Society's contribution to philanthropy. Throughout his period of office the COS was represented in government enquiries into social problems and pressed their principles upon government, often to the exclusion of others.

Conflicts of interest among philanthropic groups originating in differing social or religious theories frustrated constructive action in certain fields. However, at the root of the conflicts lay the size or intractability of the problems concerned. This perhaps was most evident in the approach of the charities to the problems of unemployment and housing.

A major source of charity for the unemployed were the *ad hoc* funds raised by public subscription, such as the Lord Mayor of London's Mansion House funds, opened regularly in times of exceptional distress. In addition there were many, usually small and local, often ephemeral, societies for the relief of unemployment.

In the periods of high unemployment of the 1880s and 1890s the Mansion House fund, with COS support, introduced work-creation schemes for the London unemployed. However, the largest of these in 1892 set to work only 253 out of 716 applicants in West Ham, converting wasteland to allotments at 6*d*. an hour for 45 hours work per week. Similar charitable schemes outside London were equally ineffective, yet still the COS and its associates refused to co-operate with local authorities in establishing larger schemes, despite the capacity and willingness of the latter to put the charitable funds to more effective use in such necessary activities as road-building.

Another type of charitable relief of unemployment was 'home colonization'. Frequently this took the form of removing men, or sometimes whole families, from the towns for training in agricultural work in organized land settlements. The aim was to transform them into permanent subsistence farmers or labourers. This was not a new idea, but it attracted increasing support from the 1880s, due partly to the failure of alternative solutions to unemployment and to the apparent unlikelihood of more work being generated in the towns. During the 1870s agricultural depression had led to land and even rural jobs lying vacant. There was an attractive simplicity to the notion of moving the starving from the cities to become self-sufficient on otherwise wasted agricultural land. By this means some hoped that it might also become possible to reduce Britain's dependence upon imported food – similar colonies had been tried elsewhere in Europe with apparent success. Not all proposals for land colonies embodied this rather idyllic hope of regenerating the long dead English peasantry from the bones of the urban residuum. Sometimes they were envisaged as semi-penal institutions for the unregenerated poor.

Marshall, Charles Booth and Loch supported the less punitive form of colony. Some were established: by the London Congregational Union in 1886, by the Salvation Army from 1891 (in addition to their workshops for destitutes within East London) in England and America for emigrant British workers, and by the Church Army. Others were established under the Poor Law. Once more, however, they provided only for small numbers and their success even in establishing this few in permanent work or independence appears to have been small.[38]

Similar frustrations, though fewer conflicts, attended provision of working-class housing. Much charitable effort was devoted to this cause on the assumption that improved housing conditions, by removing some of the degradation from the lives of the poor, would give them more hope and greater enthusiasm for the struggle for self-help and survival.

In general, housing was built by private enterprise, since local authorities were unwilling or unable to provide it from their income from rates. Not until 1879 did the government offer local authorities low interest loans for housebuilding and little action followed until the 1900s. Government subsidies for housing were introduced only in 1918. A few philanthropic or canny employers provided housing – most notably, from 1888 W. H. Lever built a spectacular model village for his employees at Port Sunlight and from 1895 the Cadbury family developed Bournville as a garden suburb for Birmingham workers. But such efforts touched few and generally better paid workers.

The problem of the poorest was that they could not afford such rents as would bring an adequate return for builders and property-owners, unless they were crammed at very high density in property which received minimal repair. The problem was worsened in the big city centres by the inflation of land prices from the 1860s as demand for shop, office and factory building mounted. City land available for house-building was further reduced by the building of railways and roads which often swallowed up not only building land but also existing working-class housing. Resistance to road- and house-building in richer areas often diverted such develop- ments to more vulnerable districts. In addition local authorities such as the LCC in the 1890s drove new roads through notorious slums in order to demolish them. New Oxford Street and Victoria Street in central London were built partly for this pupose. Many of those displaced were not rehoused but moved on to multi-occupy neighbouring districts. Urban populations continued to grow. The poorest could least afford to travel from homes in the suburbs to work in city centres. Indeed those dependent upon casual labour had to live close to docks and factories if they were to be on hand for work as it became available.

All of these factors contributed to a major housing crisis in all cities and especially in London, Liverpool and Glasgow by the 1880s. A pioneer of philanthropic attempts to solve this crisis was Octavia Hill. For forty years from 1864 she initiated the building of low-cost apartments for poor families. She was a founder member of COS and managed her property in accordance with similar prin- ciples. Her tenants were poor but carefully selected in accordance with their apparent potential for self-improvement. Once installed, tenants were regularly visited by voluntary lady rent-collectors whose task was to advise tenants on the management of the house- hold or other aspects of their lives – how to sweep their floors, wash their children and clothing and to conduct themselves with propriety. The result was indeed improved if, of necessity, very basic housing, at a rent low enough for the very poor to pay. Resi- dence therein entailed rather intensive supervision: outside doors were locked at night; those whose behaviour did not meet the strict standards of the lady visitors were evicted. Many were unwilling to accept such intrusion in their lives even for the sake of better hous- ing. Others were more resigned or compliant, if only because clean low-cost housing in cities was otherwise almost impossible to obtain. Octavia Hill was an energetic propagandist and played an important role in bringing the appalling problems of filthy, over- crowded slum dwellings to the attention of government and of phi- lanthropists. One result was a considerable amount of low-cost tenement building by philanthropic associations in the cities from the early 1880s. Organizations such as the Peabody Trust and the

East End Dwellings Company designed and built tenement housing, which Nicholas Pevsner has rightly called 'truly humanitarian in its pretensions, yet depressing in its results' – solidly built, but, for reasons of economy, ugly and providing shared water-supplies and sanitary facilities. The buildings were subsidized by charitable donations but required rent-income for their upkeep, and the problem remained that the poorest could not afford the rent necessary for adequate housing. Many of these housing companies were known as '5 per cent philanthropy' companies. Contributors invested in them as they would in any commercial building company and their philanthropy lay in accepting a return which, at 5 per cent, was lower than they would expect on the free market.

Efforts of this kind, considerable though they were, could not solve the immense housing problem. Indeed, they were unable to get to the heart of providing for those who did not work regularly and hence could not pay regular rent or, often, any rent at all. They continued to live in conditions of severe overcrowding, rent arrears, 'moonlight flits' from one insalubrious dwelling to another, usually within a small area of the town or city. The problems of rural housing went almost untouched. It was increasingly obvious that government action of some kind was essential for the improvement of the housing situation. Charity could not solve fundamental problems of housing and unemployment.[39]

Clearly, the motives for giving to charities of all kinds were as various as the gifts. As Derek Fraser has suggested, they were of four main types: 'a fear of social revolution, a humanitarian concern for suffering, a desire to improve the moral tone of the recipients and a satisfaction of some psychological or social need', i.e. a desire for the confirmation of social status and superiority which came from giving to those poorer than oneself, and perhaps basking in their gratitude.[40] The growing numbers of underemployed middle- or upper-class women, for whom unpaid charitable work was one of the very few socially acceptable occupations, supplied a willing and almost endless supply of volunteers for such activity, such as has been available at no other period of British history.

Those with a surplus gave to the English poor with the same mixture of motives with which donations are now made to Oxfam. As we have seen, a religious motive was more often important then than now. The complexity of the charitable impulse led to the highly confused picture presented by nineteenth-century philanthropy.

The recipients also varied in their response. 'Scroungers' did exist, irresistibly when many were poor and charity was to be had sometimes merely for attending a church service; and then as now there was a flourishing mythology of great sums inveigled from charity by shrewd layabouts. Many poor people were grateful for anything which lightened their burden, others were resentful of patronage which went with it.

Above the level of the desperately poor, those who could *were* self-helping to a degree which should have gratified those who for so long preached the doctrine. The chief forms of 'self-help' available were saving or insurance, by which means workers, as the Charity Organization Society urged, strove to have something 'put by' for illness, unemployment, old age and other contingencies.

Commercial savings banks, used primarily but by no means exclusively by the working class – they attracted many lower-middle-class savers – expanded rapidly in the mid-nineteenth century. To encourage such savings further, partly on Gladstone's initiative, the Post Office Savings Bank opened in 1863. By 1891–95 it had average total deposits of £83 m. – an average individual deposit of £14.75.

Savings banks, naturally enough, attracted only those workers with a surplus to save. The most popular form of insurance – burial insurance – was, however, almost universal. It might be thought odd that the desperately poor spent hard-earned pence on providing for a ceremony they would never see. But a pauper burial was the final degradation of a miserable life, a respectable funeral a means of demonstrating self-respect to the end and hence of immense psychological importance. Burial insurance was bought also for children, and, given the high infant death rate, parents were accused of using the probability of a child's death as a means of accumulating a small nest-egg. If this was a common practice, and it was never proven, it was hardly deeply culpable. The weekly contribution for burial insurance was 1*d*. or 1½*d*., bringing about £7 10*s*. at death, sufficient to pay for a very modest funeral. The contributions were paid weekly to door-to-door collectors.

Insurance against other contingencies, chiefly sickness, and increasingly also old age, was available primarily through Friendly Societies. These offered up to 10*s*. per week sickness benefit plus the services of a doctor in return for a contribution of between 4*d*. and 8*d*. per week. They were established in increasing numbers from the 1830s and were of varying size and kind. Some were local, some national, some (the least popular) established for the working class by clergy and other philanthropists, others by workers themselves. All of them, but especially the independent working-class organizations, were unlike commercial insurance companies in holding popular, convivial meetings, often in pubs (although some societies were temperance organizations and met in places uncontaminated by drink) and in their sense of comradeship and obligation among members. Many even of the larger societies were in temporary financial difficulties by the 1880s due to their willingness to pay long-term sick benefit as an effective old-age pension to aged members past regular work. Past contributions had not been calculated to cover such expenditure, but societies felt an obligation to protect faithful members from ending their days on poor relief. They saw their role as providing for mutual help among the working class in a situation in which individual self-help was impossible for so many of them. The Friendly Societies were indeed the largest exclusively working-class organizations in Britain by 1900. They had around 6 million members in 1904; there were 1.3 million trade unionists at the same date.

In the last decade of the century commercial insurance companies providing sickness and burial insurance were growing rapidly, especially among younger people. As the available range of leisure activities expanded such people were less interested in the convivial aspects of Friendly Society membership and more concerned with safe insurance, which Friendly Societies had not always been able to guarantee. Nevertheless, Friendly Society membership continued to expand, and most had a sound financial basis by 1900.

Friendly Society membership throughout the period, however, came almost exclusively from the more secure, respectable stratum of the male working class, those who earned enough and regularly enough to contribute. Among such men membership was almost universal and membership was itself a mark of a respectable workman. There were, however, many rural societies and branches of larger societies, whose members were agricultural labourers, who often had the advantage of regular if not of high wages; and the high fall-out rate of membership of most societies testifies to the numbers who aspired to the security provided by membership but could not maintain regular payments.

Few societies admitted both men and women. This was partly because few labouring families even among the better paid could afford double contributions and in such families the needs of the man took priority. Few women earned enough to pay their own contribution. When, however, some women did wish to join the larger societies in the 1870s, the societies found their doctors unwilling to treat women unless they paid higher contributions than men, on the grounds that women were more often sick and would make heavier demands on their services, which thus would be of greater benefit to poorer women. Some societies established separate women's branches, with higher contributions, but with little success. Only in Lancashire were there flourishing women's societies, since Lancashire had better paid and more regular work for women, in the textile factories, than any other part of the country. Elsewhere working women and the wives of working men lacked access to this elementary form of private social security.

Lower-paid, unskilled and casual male workers joined, when they could, the only substitute for a Friendly Society open to them – an annual 'dividing-up' club, 'slate club' or 'tontine' – the name varied regionally. Often based in a pub, members paid weekly contributions, received small benefits when sick, and the sum remaining in the fund was divided among all members at Christmas. Such clubs were vulnerable to untrustworthy treasurers' misappropriation of funds and gave members none of the benefits of an interest bearing fund. They could not provide doctors' services or for old age. But they were well adapted to the insecure lives of poorer workers; if due to unemployment or other crisis they had to cease contributions they could lose no more than one year's contributions. Women were rarely allowed to nor could afford to join such clubs. For medical treatment they and their children depended upon the Poor Law or, mainly in the cities, medical charities, or upon the charity of doctors, some of whom treated poor families free of charge or ran medical clubs of their own to which poorer patients could make small contributions.

Certainly, and not surprisingly, the higher stratum of more secure workers and to a lesser extent their families had access to better health and also housing provision in this period before the state played a significant role in either area – at least for as long as they remained in fairly regular work. They were also the first to join permanent trade unions. By the 1880s most of these provided not only bargaining machinery but health, old-age and unemployment benefits for their members. Initially these were organized rather haphazardly with little serious attempt to match contributions to prospective claims on the funds. After criticism from, among others, the Royal Commission on Trade Unions of 1868, these arrangements were improved.

The 'new' unskilled unions formed in the late 1880s initially provided no such benefits, partly because their low-paid members could not afford the resulting higher contributions. They were motivated also by the determination of the militant leadership not to be diverted by such activities from the pursuit of better wages and working conditions for their members. These, rather than private insurance or public 'welfare', they saw as the real key to diminishing poverty. They feared that if the union fund was too heavily committed to payment of 'friendly benefits', insufficient would remain in the fund to finance industrial action.

However, as their memberships declined in the less favourable atmosphere of the 1890s, they began also to provide 'friendly' benefits. Members who had no other form of 'social security' available to them desired the benefits. Trade unionists also discovered that provision of benefits were an effective means of retaining members between periods of industrial militancy.

'Superior' workers were also the chief beneficiaries of other manifestations of working-class mutual help in this period. Building societies, for the finance of house building or purchase, grew rapidly and by the end of the century attracted many small investors, but their appeal was rather to tradesmen and the lower-middle class than to manual workers.

The Co-operative movement was a form of mutual aid with a wider working-class appeal although it also largely excluded the poorest. Co-operative stores provided relatively cheap, good quality foodstuffs or other essential consumer goods to members, dividing their profits – 'dividends' – among members. They were rarely situated in poorer districts, required a membership fee of up to £1, which the poorest could not afford, and did not allow 'tick' or sales in the very small quantities of foodstuffs (½ oz. tea, 2 rashers of bacon, etc.) which the poor were forced by low or uncertain incomes to buy.

A determined attempt to extend the benefits of Co-operative trading to the poor was made from soon after its foundation in 1883 by the women of the Women's Co-operative Guild. This impressive organization, the bulk of whose members were working women or the wives of working men, led by their secretary Margaret Llewellyn-Davies, advocated shops in poor districts with reduced subscription, selling in smaller quantities. Against the opposition of respectable male co-operators the women set up a number of successful shops of this kind. The Guild also encouraged women to be active in local government, to criticize or improve the administration of the Poor Law, education, housing and public health.

By this combination of means both 'respectable' and, with much greater difficulty, the 'residuum' survived periods of distress with varying degrees of success.[41]

By the end of the century larger business firms were developing company welfare schemes which added to the complex web of social provision. Some employers since the beginning of the nineteenth century had provided company housing, schools and other facilities either from philanthropic motives or in order to attract scarce labour. After 1870 rather larger numbers of companies were providing a wider range of provision, including in some cases, old-age pensions and health care. Partly this was because there were greater numbers of large firms able to afford such benefits. Also, in the atmosphere of greater international competition of this period employers were increasingly aware of the need to increase productivity and realized that more secure conditions of life could promote higher output. Company pensions enabled them to lay off older and less productive workers with a clear conscience and health care directly promoted more efficient production. In addition such provision promoted stability in the workforce, since workers were reluctant to leave jobs which provided benefits unobtainable elsewhere. Some employers, too, felt paternal concern for the welfare of their workers and were, like the Ouaker Cadbury family, active philanthropists in other fields. In general, employers were more likely to provide for their better-paid skilled workers who were less easily replaced than the unskilled labourers.

THE POOR LAW

Central and local government provided in most circumstances a residual 'safety net' when all else failed, chiefly through the Poor Law. The total number of paupers (i.e. recipients of poor relief was never in this period over 5 per cent of the population of England and Wales in any one year. We have seen that the proportion in severe poverty was considerably higher. Most paupers receiving workhouse or out-door relief from the Poor Law were children, their mothers, the aged, sick or disabled. The Poor Law had been most effective in forcing all those who could to be self-helping. It had not succeeded in eliminating their poverty.

The Poor Law was the most comprehensive official source for the relief of poverty, administered in England and Wales as laid down by the Poor Law Amendment Act 1834 and a succession of later amendments, in Scotland and Ireland according to different statutes and rather different principles. The Poor Law for England and Wales was supervised by central government through the Poor Law Board (established in 1847) until 1871. In 1871 the Local Government Board (LGB) was established to supervise all the growing functions of local government, including the Poor Law. Central supervision of the Poor Law operated both through the regional inspectorate who supervised the locally elected administrators, the Boards of Guardians of each Poor Law Union, and submitted annual reports to the LGB, and also through circulars or memoranda to the Boards of Guardians.

Local Guardians were elected triennially. Until 1892 generally only those paying rates on property with a rateable value of £40 p.a. or more were eligible for election as Guardians. This excluded virtually all manual workers and most women. After considerable labour pressure the qualification was reduced to £5 in 1892 and abolished in 1894. The only remaining qualification for office and for voting was twelve months residence in the area covered by the Union. The changes also applied to elections to municipal and county councils so that the electorate was now composed of all ratepayers, excluding recipients of poor relief.

On contentious points of policy Guardians and Officers could consult the LGB. The LGB had indeed only *advisory* powers over local Boards. If a Board chose to follow a generous policy, for example of paying outdoor relief to the unemployed, and could persuade local ratepayers to finance it, the central authority had some difficulty in stopping such action unless corrupt use of the money or the raising of excessive loans could be proved. A major restraint upon such generosity was, however, the opposition of ratepayers. The small tradesmen or shopkeepers who made up most Boards of Guardians throughout the period were unlikely to resist such pressure since their elections to the Boards depended upon the ratepayers. Turnouts in Guardian elections were extremely low (perhaps 10–15% of registered electors) and Guardians who offended influential ratepayers were easily ousted. Too grim a policy of refusal of poor relief was, however, restrained by the fact that Poor Law authorities had a fundamental obligation not to allow the destitute to die from starvation – in such cases the Relieving Officer could be indicted for murder. The poor rate was the largest direct tax paid by most rate payers at a time when income tax was levied only on incomes above £150 p.a. and was paid by all householders, many of them themselves poor.

Rates were locally assessed and the amounts payable varied

considerably from place to place. There was no provision for richer districts to subsidize poorer, hence unions with large numbers of poor persons could not tap the resources of those with few or none – a source of increasing resentment among Guardians of some poorer unions. For London alone from 1867 a Metropolitan Common Poor fund was established, to which all London Unions contributed for the building and maintenance of workhouses throughout London. Out-door relief continued to be financed by the rate yield of individual London Unions and continued to be a source of grievance among Guardians of poorer Unions.

The result was that by the late 1860s the Poor Law was locally highly anarchic. Expenditure rose by 40 per cent between 1850 and 1870, faster than the rate of population growth.[42] The response was a tightening up of Poor Law policy from 1871. The President of the Local Government Board, George Goschen, issued a memorandum urging that wherever possible out-door relief should be cut back; 'deserving' applicants for relief were to be referred to charities, the 'undeserving' to be placed in workhouses. Poor Law administrators were to encourage the co-operation of Boards of Guardians with charities operating on COS principles. The new policy was an attempt to integrate public and voluntary action on principles similar to those of the COS[doc 2].

Throughout the 1870s inspectors advised Guardians on means of cutting expenditure: in particular there was to be more stringent investigation of applicants for and recipients of out-door relief. Additional relieving officers were to be appointed to keep close watch on paupers, to enquire of neighbours and relatives as to whether they had undisclosed earnings or, in the case of single women, regular male friends capable of supporting them. Mothers on out-door relief were to be encouraged or forced by the threat of withdrawal of relief to send some or all of their children into the workhouse, so that the mothers could support themselves by work.

Previously the central Poor Law Authority had not insisted that women should work. An LGB circular of 1871 proclaimed that out-door relief should not be given to single women unless they proved their inability to find other employment by performing a daily labour task, officially termed a 'labour test', such as cleaning, in the workhouse, returning home at night.

Some Guardians pursued the new policy more vigorously than others. The result was a fall in the numbers receiving out-door relief. The change of policy hit women especially hard since they had greatly outnumbered men as recipients of out-door relief. In

January 1871 there were 166,407 female out-door paupers in England and Wales; in January 1891 only 53,371, despite the fact that the policy was pursued less vigorously in the 1880s than in the preceding decade. The policy of the 1870s was relaxed due to awareness of the hardship inflicted – those reduced to the extreme of applying for poor relief even in 1870 were those with no other resort, and their numbers could be further reduced only by increasing their hardship. Charity was not sufficient or evenly enough distributed to take over from out-door relief. The economy was not expanding in such a way as to absorb them in work, even if mothers of young children, children themselves, the aged and the disabled who made up the bulk of out-door paupers, had been able to take advantage of such expansion.[43] The unemployment of the mid-1880s contributed to the difficulty of sustaining the policy – workhouses were not large enough to hold all of the unemployed in the hardest hit district and out-door relief had to be given by many Guardians, though normally only in return for a daily 'test' such as stone-breaking in the workhouse yard – the task most favoured by Guardians for the male unemployed.

The attempt to impose a consistent out-door policy throughout England and Wales was effectively a failure. The election of radical working men to Boards such as those of Poplar and West Ham in London and of philanthropic women to some Boards after the abolition of the Guardians' property qualification, increased the tendency of some urban Boards to treat applicants with rather greater generosity than the LGB intended. In particular West Ham and Poplar and a handful of other Boards with active Labour members went as far as their resources permitted in providing out-door relief and improved workhouse conditions even for the unemployed, even though they faced considerable opposition from the LGB.[44]

The strict out-door relief policy of the 1870s did not lead to a fall in total Poor Law expenditure. This was due to the other important aspect of central policy from 1871, the improvement of institutional relief. The destruction of the prevailing form of institution, the 'general mixed workhouse,' was encouraged. Instead, Edwin Chadwick's aim of 1834 to give separate specialized care to deserving children, the aged, sick and lunatic was to be implemented. These were groups in need of institutional care and whose need could not always be attributed to their own fault. Nevertheless, Guardians were encouraged to 'classify' inmates according both to cause of poverty and to 'character'. Hence the old, the young, the sick and the mad were to be separated, and within each group those of better behaviour were to be rewarded with better diets or more 'comforts'. Since this encouragement was not accompanied by subsidy from central government, the outcome was locally various. Some ratepayers, especially in larger towns and cities, were persuaded to finance the building especially of workhouse infirmaries separate from the main workhouse building, where standards of treatment and nursing gradually improved – the room for such improvement being considerable.

Infirmaries were popular improvements since in many towns few free or cheap alternatives existed and the capacity of medicine to cure a wider range of illnesses was increasing. The increased use of antiseptic techniques, the isolation of bacteria and recognition of their role in disseminating disease, and the gradual spread of improved nursing under the inspiration of Florence Nightingale, all led to improvements first in voluntary then in Poor Law hospitals. Joseph Chamberlain as Chairman of the Local Government Board in 1885 was responsible for the Medical Relief (Disqualifications Removal) Act which removed the pauper stigma – disfranchisement – from inmates of Poor Law infirmaries who made no other demands on poor relief and increased both use of the infirmaries by respectable working people and their willingness as ratepayers to finance them. After 1885 infimaries continued to improve, though fastest in the big cities, but still, at the time of the Royal Commission on the Poor Laws of 1905–09, local provision varied considerably. Some still by that date did not have trained nurses but employed untrained workhouse inmates. Maternity wards were notably slow to improve, largely due to their popularly believed, if apparently unfounded, association with prostitution.

More slowly, separate institutions of a new kind were also provided for children, the emphasis shifting from the large sometimes disease-ridden 'barrack schools' in which they were accommodated in the mid-century, to the more intimate 'scattered homes' pioneered by the Sheffield Guardians in the 1890s, and 'cottage homes' on the model established by Barnado. Though still rather austere, the city and suburban villa 'scattered homes', housing between twelve and twenty children and their attendants, were a considerable improvement on the vast institutions still operating elsewhere in the country. As education became compulsory from 1880, children from such homes could attend schools with other children.

The development of such institutions resulted partly from the dissemination of beliefs in the importance of a child's environment upon personality, and of realization that children brought up in large institutions found considerable difficulty later in adjusting to non-institutional life. In 1870 the PLB had also, rather grudgingly, allowed some Guardians to adopt the Scottish practice of 'boarding out' (fostering, in modern terms) pauper children with working-class families, sometimes their own relatives. This practice was not adopted enthusiastically by the LGB, partly due to fears that its cheapness would encourage Guardians to send children to unsuitable homes – fears which were justified by some unfortunate and tragic incidents of maltreatment and exploitation of child labour. There was also a shortage of staff to supervise placements, and some opposition to the placing of pauper children often in more desirable homes than those of families of independent labourers. However, in 1885 a lady inspector, Mrs Mason, was appointed to supervise 'boarding out' throughout the country, a task later shared with two other lady inspectors.

The aged, too, were increasingly placed in separate institutions, or more commonly in separate wards of the old workhouse. LGB circulars of 1895 and 1899 recommended that out-door relief should be granted more readily to the aged poor. (In practice Boards of Guardians, especially in rural areas, had tended to show more generosity towards the aged than to any other group.) The circulars also recommended that those respectable aged who, for reasons of infirmity or lack of friends or family to care for them, required institutional care, should be allowed greater comforts in the workhouse. Such 'comforts' included the wearing of their own clothes rather than pauper uniform, permission to give or to receive outside visits, for aged husbands and wives to share rooms, for men to smoke, women to receive additional rations of tea and to eat other than the prescribed diet. The nature of the privileges suggests the rigour of the previous regime, which was still slow to change in many unions.

This changed treatment of the aged poor derived partly from the wider trend towards the improvement of institutional care. It was also the result of mounting pressure from the late 1870s for more humane treatment of the aged. Charles Booth and Joseph Chamberlain were among those who in the 1880s and 1890s pointed out that old age was a significant cause of poverty and pauperism. They argued that it was often non-culpable since even the most respectable workers could not always save sufficient to provide for old age – a hazard which not all could expect to live to experience and whose length was uncertain. Too many of the respectable labouring poor ended their lives in the workhouse or on out-door relief – 50 per cent of those reaching the age of sixty, according to Joseph Chamberlain in 1891. Others died in destitution for fear of the shame attached to a pauper funeral. Both Booth and Chamberlain argued that the state should provide old-age pensions of between 5s. and 10s. per week to enable those over sixty-five to live and die respectably, free from the stigma of pauperism.

The debate about pensions continued into the 1900s. In the preceding generation it contributed to the general discovery of the complex and various causes of poverty, and to considerable public discussion of the problem of the aged poor. A series of government investigations were held into the question of pensions and the conditions of the aged poor, in 1885–87, 1895, 1896 and 1899. Their sole effects upon the lives of the aged, before old-age pensions were introduced in 1908, were the LGB circulars of 1895–99.[45]

The central principle of Poor Law policy in this period was that a clear distinction could be made between the deserving 'helpable' and the 'residuum', who were to be coerced into more socially acceptable behaviour. This assumption arose from greater understanding of the complex causes of poverty, but this remained incomplete. A punitive approach to the poorest survived the accumulation of indications that much even of the worst poverty was not self-inflicted, but derived from the inability of the market to provide sufficient homes, jobs or adequate incomes.

GOVERNMENT ACTION OUTSIDE THE POOR LAW

Central and local government activities outside the strict limits of the Poor Law expanded, much of it guided by the principles which ruled poor relief. As a result of social investigation there was greater recognition than before of the causes of unemployment, in particular of the distinction between the chronic underemployment of the casual poor of big cities and the recurrent temporary unemployment of large numbers of superior workers in periods of depression. This owed much to analyses of the labour market by H. Llewellyn Smith, of the Board of Trade.

Fears of militancy resulting from unemployment and the inadequacy of voluntary efforts to relieve it led to some recognition that charity could not provide sufficiently for either type of unemployment. In Parliament in 1886, Liberals and Conservatives advocated publicly-funded 'public works' – prison, road, harbour and house

building – as a constructive means of relieving the temporarily unemployed.

Leading members of the labour movement advocated both an
eight-hour day, as a means of permanently increasing the regularly
employed labour force (a nine or ten hour day, six days a week
being then normal), and public works, despite some fears that
under private enterprise such sharing of work could lead to depression of wages.

In March 1886 Joseph Chamberlain, as President of the Local
Government Board, responded by issuing a circular to local authorities urging them to schedule necessary public works for periods of
depression, and to co-operate with the Poor Law by providing
paid, non-pauperizing work for those who applied for poor relief
due to temporary unemployment.

The circular gave formal acknowledgement to a practice already
employed by some authorities and which continued thereafter to be
ignored by others. Chamberlain was explicit about his motives in a
letter to Beatrice Webb: 'It will remove the great danger, viz, that
public sentiment should go wholly over to the unemployed and
render impossible that state sternness to which you or I equally
attach importance. By offering reasonable work at low wages we
may secure the power of being very strict with the loafer or confirmed pauper.' The circular was almost entirely ineffective. The
government offered no special finance for public works, and made
no attempt to enforce implementation. Once more, the poorest districts could least afford provision from their own funds. Most of
such work was unsuitable for operating in winter when unemployment was highest and when carried out with an untrained
labour force it was expensive or inefficient, and failed to attract the
temporarily unemployed artisans for whom it was intended. They
felt stigmatized, as skilled men, by taking unskilled work, and it
left them no time to search for work at their trade. The casually
underemployed benefited most.

Amid demonstrations of the unemployed in the depression of
1892–95, local authorities in districts where the problem was worst
established public works and opened labour bureaux, i.e. labour
exchanges for the simultaneous registration of the unemployed and
of available work. These also were largely ineffective because the
numbers of the unemployed, again largely casuals, far outnumbered the jobs notified. The central government took no further
action – although select committees investigated the problem in
1895 and 1896. Poor Law Guardians were still prohibited from

giving out-door relief to the unemployed except in return for 'test' labour.[46]

In the 1880s and 90s the state moved a little more decisively into the fields of housing, factory reform, and public health. With respect to public health, legislation in 1871 at last covered the whole country with sanitary authorities obliged to appoint such permanent staff as medical officers of health with powers to inspect and enforce eradication of such nuisances as polluted water supplies and inadequate drainage. The Public Health Act of 1875 further clarified the duties of sanitary authorities. A Public Health Acts Amendment Act in 1890 enabled every urban authority to introduce by-laws enforcing minimum standards of construction of sanitation and ventilation, etc., for new housing and provision of means of access for refuse removal.

Public health had been one of the first major areas of government social intervention, beginning with the Public Health Act of 1848. It was early seen as a public responsibility, since the individual could not be expected to control such large-scale enterprises as water supply and sewerage. Lack of control over these had led to health hazards for the entire population, rich and poor. It was an area in which competitive private enterprise in the supply of water had early and clearly been shown to be deficient.[47]

Education, arguably, could be provided through private enterprise, by the family. It also, however, had come to be seen as a cause of public concern. Concern for the religious and moral habits of the labouring poor and associated fear of public disorder among the uneducated masses had combined with philanthropic belief in the intrinsic value of education to bring the government to subsidize and later to supervise private provision, beginning in 1833. An educated population, it was hoped, would be God-fearing, industrious and respectful of the law.

To these motives for public intervention in education was added, from the 1860s, a growing belief in the need for an educated workforce if Britain was to outface foreign industrial competition of increasing technological sophistication. Britain remained, to the end of the century, slow – compared for example with Germany – to provide advanced technical education. The emphasis was rather upon providing children with basic skills. Children were inefficient contributors to the kind of workforce now required and also a smaller proportion of the entire population than in the early years of the century. The economy was felt to need their education rather than their work. In addition the spread of the franchise necessitated an electorate able to evaluate political issues, preferably in a manner acceptable to the existing controllers of politics. Private enterprise had failed to provide school places for all children and the state was required to fill the gaps.

The Education Act of 1870 set out to provide elementary schools for children up to a minimum age of ten throughout the country. It also established elected school boards to supervise school building and education. Education became compulsory in 1880 and free in 1891 – previously it had cost a small sum each week, with exemption for the very poor.

Many children continued to evade school. In many rural districts provision was still patchy and enforcement of attendance sporadic. Attendance officers were more active in towns and cities but, at least initially, met some resistance from parents. This was not necessarily because parents failed to recognize the value of education for their children. But the very poor could not afford to lose their children's wages or their care of younger children whilst mothers worked. This posed a real dilemma for administrators. Anne Besant, as a socialist member of the London School Board in the 1880s, was acutely distressed by the problems she saw of 'gaunt hunger-pinched men and women . . . decent folk who didn't want to keep their children ignorant, but sometimes there were no boots, sometimes there was a baby to feed, sometimes there were no food.' It appeared to be an almost insoluble dilemma.

Legislation further restricting the employment of children reduced the contribution they could make to the family economy. Many, however, continued in casual jobs which escaped legal regulation – running errands, minding market stalls, caring for younger children – and schools in poorer districts had high truancy rates. Some schools, e.g. in East London and Liverpool, adjusted their hours to take account of the needs of poorer children both for earnings and education, beginning or ending the school day later or earlier than was the custom, enabling schoolchildren to work before or after school. Clearly such arrangements were not ideal – they could be exhausting for children and were at best a compromise among the law, the need for education, and the reality of poverty. It was found in 1902 that perhaps 50,000 children in England and Wales were working more than 20 hours a week in addition to 27½ hours at school, some of them working between 30 and 50 hours a week.

By 1900 free education existed in principle for all children in England and Wales to the age of at least eleven. Curricula remained largely confined to 'the three Rs' and to rote-learning, although more adventurous, again mainly urban, school, boards, especially those of London, were beginning to widen their curricula and to provide 'higher elementary' education for older children.[48]

In other respects, also, the state became involved more closely with the care of children. From the 1870s there was a discernible shift from the traditional notion that children were the responsibility of their families and that none should intervene between parents and child, a shift associated with wider changes in attitudes towards both children and the family. The evangelical belief, much disseminated in the mid-nineteenth century, that children should be protected from the rigours of the adult world and educated and assisted to be morally good adults, was joined by the end of the century by a belief in the economic and military importance of building, from birth, a strong and stable race.

Evangelicals and others in the mid-nineteenth century still placed the central responsibility for the upbringing of children upon the family. They also, however, supported voluntary effort and legislation, such as the Factory Acts, to help children who lacked adequate family support. In 1889 the Prevention of Cruelty and Protection of Children Act for the first time outlawed proven cruelty to children and allowed children in certain circumstances to be removed from their families to a place of safety, usually a charitable institution such as Barnardo's. They might also be legally adopted by Poor Law Guardians. The Custody of Children Act 1891 gave judges discretionary powers to reject applications for writs of *habeas corpus* from parents of children removed due to ill-treatment. The emphasis of the legislation, as of philanthropic effort, was upon the removal of the child from a corrupting environment, rather than upon improvement within that environment which was still seen as too intractable a task.[49]

The state was as reluctant to intervene in the housing market, despite its manifest deficiencies. Partly, this was due to the deep-rooted belief in the importance of all forms of property being held in private hands, and partly to the potentially enormous cost of solving the housing shortage, as well as to rather vain hopes that increasing prosperity and improved public transport would enable poorer urban dwellers to move to cheaper suburban accommodation. Nor was it seen as of such immediate economic or political importance as public health, education or unemployment. There were no riots concerning bad housing; indeed, the SDF made entirely unsuccessful efforts to organize rent strikes.

Nevertheless, the crowding together of the poor in slums was seen to be dangerous – debilitating to health and facilitating possibly seditious communication of the kind which had led to the riots in Trafalgar Square in 1886. The crisis and propaganda of the 1880s persuaded the Conservative government in 1885 to establish a Royal Commission on the Housing of the Working Classes. This declared that there was a serious shortage of adequate houses in many areas, but recommended no legislation. Housing Acts in 1885 and 1890 eased local authority borrowing for housebuilding, and as a result £4.5 m. was borrowed for this purpose between 1890 and 1904.

The bulk of this expenditure was by the London County Council, formed in 1888. At last London became, for administrative purposes other than the Poor Law, a single unit, able to initiate or finance large projects. The first elected council contained such active and progressive members as Sidney Webb, eager to encourage housebuilding for the working classes. A distinguished department of architecture was established by the LCC which pioneered attractive low-cost housing design. From the early 1890s the LCC built the first large modern housing estates in the country. Other authorities followed slowly and on a smaller scale. Sheffield, Manchester, Liverpool and Bradford, all under strong labour pressure, were among the more active, especially as the number of working-class councillors increased from the early 1890s. In comparison with the size of the problem, however, such activities achieved only very small improvements by 1900.[50]

Factory and workshop legislation regulating hours and conditions – including safety at work – were gradually extended until by 1891 they in theory covered even smaller workshops laundries and docks. Many employers did little more than comply with the bare regulations. Enforcement and supervision of conditions was especially difficult in smaller establishments. The Factory Act of 1901 laid down enforceable standards of space, cleanliness and sanitation in workplaces, and of methods of payment. It ordered the fencing of dangerous machinery and forbade the cleaning of machines while they were running. Women were forbidden to work at night in any industry (a move opposed by some feminists). Enforcement remained a major difficulty.

A serious problem concerned the fate of workers injured at work. The rate of accidents, even of deaths, at work was high, especially in the mines, railways and docks and in the merchant navy. In 1902–06 fifty seamen, twelve miners and eight railwaymen per year were killed at work. In Birmingham it was common to see women with hands mutilated from mishaps in the metal workshops. Often employers acknowledged no liability, blaming the carelessness of the worker, who might if the injuries were serious be thereafter unemployable. The workman had to prove, by costly legal processes, that the employer had been negligent. The Workmen's Compensation Act 1897 made employers liable for accidents at work and obliged them to insure against such events and to compensate the worker, almost regardless of cause. Seamen, farm workers and domestic servants were initially excluded from the legislation.[51]

The Act of 1897 was partly the result of trade union pressure. The growth of unions and the serious industrial conflicts of the mid-1890s led the government into systematic intervention in labour relations. In 1896 a labour department of the Board of Trade was established, composed partly of trade unionists. Its role was partly arbitration and conciliation in industrial disputes and investigation of labour conditions. Under H. Llewellyn Smith the department also became an important source of investigation of the numbers and condition of the unemployed.[52]

Overall, by 1900 central government action concerning recognized social problems was greater than in 1870 but still slight in contrast with the magnitude of those problems and of the range of demands for action. In the 1880s and 1890s there was an impressive number of official investigations into problems – the Royal Commissions on Labour (1893–4), Housing of the Working Classes (1884–5), Aged Poor (1895), on the Depression of Trade and Industry (1886), Sanitary Laws (1871), Factory Acts (1876), select committees on Distress from Want of Employment (1895), National Provident Insurance (1885–7), Old Age Pensions (1896 and 1899), The Sweating System (1890), on Poor Law Relief (1888), on Artisans and Labourers Dwellings Improvements (1881), to name a few. The results were few, due partly to continuing powerful ideological opposition to government intervention.

There were other important inhibiting factors, one of which related to sources of government finance. Direct action by central government would necessitate substantially increased expenditure and therefore revenue. Low taxation was as dear to the Liberal heart as minimal government intervention. Direct taxation was indeed low, at a flat rate of 1s. in the pound on incomes of £150 or above. Minor changes, necessitated by increased expenditure on naval building and on education after 1870, brought from Conservative MPs pleas for no further change lest lower-middle-class voters be alienated. Those with earnings just above the tax threshold bore the heaviest burden of the flat rate tax as a proportion of income. The Treasury, under the control throughout this period of orthodox Gladstonians, was committed to the belief that the income tax was a temporary expedient to be removed as soon as possible.

One possible alternative means of raising revenue, a graduated income tax, was advocated largely by socialists and as such tainted in the eyes of the main political parties. The first attempt to tax the very rich a little more heavily was the introduction of death duties in 1889, by which duty was levied on estates exceeding £10,000 in value. A more substantial graduated tax on property left at death was introduced in 1894.

By 1900 about half of government revenue was raised from income tax and from death duties. The remainder was the yield on various customs and excise duties levied primarily on beer, spirits, wines, tobacco, cocoa and other 'luxury' items which varied a little from budget to budget. There was mounting working-class pressure against increasing such taxes which, it was argued, were contributed disproportionately by those least able to pay, whilst the rich paid a tiny proportion of their wealth and income in taxation.

Joseph Chamberlain proposed to solve the revenue problem by the introduction of tariffs on imported industrial goods which would, he argued, help industry, increase employment and finance desirable social reforms. Both political parties and the Treasury were, however, committed to free trade and opposed to tariffs, and the working-class movement feared that tariffs would lead to increased prices.

In the absence of other acceptable proposals or of the will on the part of government to override opposition to such proposals as existed, shortage of revenue remained an obstacle to central government action and was acutely worsened by the high cost of the Boer War which opened in 1899.

An alternative strategy for the government in these circumstances was to place the burden of financing social provision upon local government. The Poor Law was already almost entirely financed by local poor rates; rates contributed over one-third of total educational expenditure (£8.8 m. in 1900) and the major part of the cost of public health, housing and other measures.

For much of the nineteenth century this strategy was attractive to local government because it enabled localities to maintain to a large degree their prized autonomy. They believed, with some justice, that local authorities were better able to provide for variable local conditions than remote central authorities. However, local provision was constrained by ratepayer pressure against costly expenditure and led to considerable local variations in provision according to the willingness and ability of ratepayers to pay, and the imaginativeness or concern for local problems of local representatives. Also, by 1900, and more acutely later, the demands made by central government upon local rates were causing local authorities to protest against further demands being made upon them, for example to build working-class housing. The Local Government Board itself was also reluctant to take on yet further responsibilities in addition to those incurred since its foundation in 1871, with the growth of housing and public health legislation and the increasingly complex activities of the Poor Law. LGB opposition to extensions of social legislation was increased due to the reluctance of the Treasury to provide what the Board regarded as adequate staffing.[53]

Some local authorities made good use of their autonomy. The actions of Chamberlain in Birmingham, of Sheffield in introducing 'scattered homes' for children, of the LCC, together with Sheffield, Birmingham and Bradford, in housing, have already been noted. In towns where the labour movement was strong, trades councils and women's co-operative guilds put pressure on councils to improve housing and other facilities. The election of more working-class councillors after the Local Government Act of 1894, often with the support of trades councils and other organizations, acted as a further stimulus in some districts. Bradford was especially notable for its provision of clinics for infant and maternal health care and the provision of free milk for babies.

Many authorities pursued an active policy of 'municipalization'. This taking into municipal ownership of a variety of undertakings had various aims for those of differing political persuasions. Chamberlain had seen it as an ideal way of combining the efficient running of Birmingham with improving its water supplies, housing and city centre. The profitable running of such undertakings as water, gas, electricity and public transport could yield income either to relieve the rates or to provide other social services such as public baths or libraries. In many cities prominent businessmen encouraged and financed city centre improvements, the building of art galleries, museums, universities, for very pride in their city or town, to enhance its national and international reputation.[54]

˙ The Fabians, notably the Webbs, were also active advocates of municipalization. They shared Chamberlain's passion for efficiency but, unlike him, were in principle opposed to private ownership of the economy. They saw municipal ownership and its efficient management as a means of improving public services and as a first step towards public ownership of the entire economy, and improved administration to prevent or cure social ills. Many others in the labour movement, including many members of the Independent Labour Party (ILP), held similar views.

Some socialists but not on the whole the Fabians saw the continued decentralization of government to the municipalities as a desirable feature of future socialist society, providing a permanent check upon the growth or abuse of central authority. This view had much in common with the continuing liberal preference for strong local government for a similar end, although liberals preferred the ownership of the economy to remain in private hands.

The outcome of these parallel strands of support for municipalization was a growth, especially from the early 1890s, of municipal ownership of public utilities such as gas and water supplies and public transport, and municipal provision of such services as libraries, museums, baths, washhouses and improved street lighting and refuse disposal. It was extensive in Glasgow, and grew rapidly in London after 1888 and in many smaller towns. Municipal autonomy and initiative indeed reached a peak by 1900, thereafter, as we shall see, enthusiasm fast diminished and central government authority advanced.

Already by 1900 central government was under pressure to provide finance for such items as old-age pensions and subsidized working-class housing. Such pressure was, however, still limited and the coming of the costly Boer War put a temporary halt to such hopes.

REFERENCES

1. E. H. HUNT, *Regional wage variations in Great Britain 1850–1914*, Oxford University Press (1979).
2. R. DUDLEY BAXTER, *National Income*, Macmillan, London, (1868).
3. C. BOOTH, *Life and Labour of the People of London* (1902) 17 vols.
4. B. S. ROWNTREE, *Poverty – a Study of Town Life*, Macmillan, London (2nd Edition 1902) p. 297.

5. *Ibid.*, p.117.

6. E. H. HUNT, *op. cit. passim.*

7. P. THANE, 'Women and the Poor Law in Victorian and Edwardian Britain', *History Workshop Journal*, 6. Autumn 1978.

8. G. STEDMAN JONES, *Outcast London*, Oxford University Press (1971) Part 1.

9. F. ENGELS, *The Condition of the Working Class in England in 1944*, Blackwells, Oxford (1958) p. 320.

10. S. AND B. WEBB, *English Poor Law History* Part II, Vol. I, Longmans, London (1929); D. FRASER, *The New Poor Law in the Nineteenth Century*, Macmillan, London (1976).

11. U. R. Q. HENRIQUES, *Before the Welfare State*, Longman, London (1979).

12. G. STEDMAN JONES, *op. cit.*, Part 3.

13. H. MAYHEW, *London Labour and the London Poor* 1856, London. Reprinted Dover Publications, New York, (1968) 4 vols.

14. G. STEDMAN JONES, *op. cit.*, Part 3.

15. P. GOSDEN, *Self-Help*, Batsford, London (1973) *passim.*

16. G. STEDMAN JONES, *op. cit.*, Part 3.

17. P. SMITH, *Disraelian Conservatism and Social Reform*, Routledge & Kegan Paul, London (1967).

18. E. P. HENNOCK, 'Poverty and Social Theory', *Social History*, Vol. 1. No. 1, Jan. 1976.

19. W. J. BARBER, *A History of Economic Thought*, Penguin, Harmondsworth (1967), pp. 168–97.

20. R. BARKER, *Political Ideas in Modern Britain*, Methuen, London (1978) pp. 14–18.

21. A. McBRIAR, *Fabian Socialism and British Politics*, Cambridge University Press (1962).

22. J. LOVELL, *British Trade Unions 1875–1933*, Macmillan, London (Studies in Economic and Social History) (1977) pp. 20–9.

23. P. KEATING (ed.), *Into Unknown England 1866–1913, Selections from the social explorers.* Fontana, London (1976) pp. 91–111.

24. *Ibid.*, pp. 11–32 and *passim.*

25. P. FRASER, *Joseph Chamberlain*, Cassell, London (1966).

26. B. WEBB, *My Apprenticeship*, Penguin Harmondsworth (1971) p. 191.

27. J. LOVELL, *op. cit.*, pp. 30–1.

28. M. ANDERSON, *Family Structure in Nineteenth Century Lancashire*, Cambridge University Press (1971) Part 3.

29. E. RATHBONE, *The Condition of Widows under the Poor Law in Liverpool*, Liverpool University (1913).
30. E. ROBERTS, 'Working class standards of living in Barrow and Lancaster 1890–1914', *Economic History Review* (1976).
31. V. D. LIPMAN, *Social History of the Jews in England*, Watts & Co., London (1954).
32. K. HEASMAN, *Evangelicals in Action*, Geoffrey Iles, London (1962); G. WAGNER, *Barnardo*, Weidenfeld & Nicolson, London (1979).
33. N. McCORD, 'The Poor Law and Philanthropy' in DEREK FRASER (ed.) *The New Poor Law in the Nineteenth Century, op. cit.*
34. D. FRASER, *The Evolution of the British Welfare State*, Macmillan, London (1973) pp. 114–15.
35. C. L. MOWAT, *The Charity Organization Society 1869–1913*, Methuen, London (1961); G. STEDMAN JONES, *op. cit.*, Part 3.
36. B. B. GILBERT, *The Evolution of National Insurance in Great Britain*, Michael Joseph, London (1966) pp. 41–5.
37. J. HARRIS, *Unemployment and Politics 1886–1914*, Oxford University Press (1972) pp. 109–10.
38. *Ibid.*, pp. 102–44.
39. E. GAULDIE, *Cruel Habitations*, Allen & Unwin London (1974); W. ASHWORTH, *The Genesis of Modern British Town Planning*, Routledge & Kegan Paul, London (1954); J. TARN, *Five Percent philanthropy*, Cambridge University Press (1973); J. KELLETT, *The Impact of Railways on Victorian Cities*, Routledge & Kegan Paul London, (1969).
40. D. FRASER, *op. cit.*, pp. 115–21.
41. P. GOSDEN, *op. cit.*
42. M. E. ROSE, *The Relief of Poverty 1834–1914*, Macmillan, London, (Studies in Economic and Social History) (1972); S. AND B. WEBB, *op. cit.*, pp. 245–468.
43. P. THANE, *op. cit.*, pp. 33–5.
44. P. A. RYAN, 'Poplarism 1894–1930' in PAT THANE (ed.) *Origins of British Social Policy*, Croom Helm, London (1978).
45. M. A. CROWTHER, 'The Later Years of the Workhouse' in PAT THANE (ed.) *op. cit.*; P. THANE, 'Non-contributory versus insurance pensions' in PAT THANE (ed.) *op. cit.*; J. HEYWOOD, *Children in Care*, Routledge & Kegan Paul, London (1959) pp. 67–93.
46. J. HARRIS, *op. cit.*, pp. 51–101.
47. U. R. Q. HENRIQUES *op. cit.*, pp. 136–53.

48. P. W. MUSGRAVE *Society and Education in England since 1800*, Methuen, London (1968) pp. 42–76; D. RUBINSTEIN, *School Attendance in London in the 1890s*, University of Hull, Occasional Papers in Economic and Social History 1, (1969).
49. J. HEYWOOD, *op. cit.*, pp. 94–113.
50. E. GAULDIE, *op. cit.*, pp. 239–310.
51. J. R. HAY, *Origins of the Liberal Welfare Reforms*, Macmillan, London (Studies in Economic and Social History) (1975).
52. J. HARRIS, *op. cit.*, pp. 100–101; R. DAVIDSON, 'The Board of Trade and Industrial Relations', *Historical Journal* (1968).
53. R. MCLEOD, *Treasury Control and Social Administration*, G. Bell & Sons Ltd. London (1968).
54. A. BRIGGS, *Victorian Cities*, Penguin, Harmondsworth (1968); H. DYOS AND M. WOLFF, (eds) *The Victorian City*, Routledge & Kegan Paul, London (1973).

Chapter three
1900–1914

CONDITIONS AND STANDARDS OF LIVING

The distribution of wealth and poverty were examined more systematically between 1900 and the first world war than ever before. Such investigators as Rowntree, A. L. Bowley and L. Chiozza Money[1] demonstrated that the disparity between rich and poor and the proportion of the population living in severe poverty changed little over the period. There was a slight narrowing of regional differences in income and experiences but, broadly, the countryside remained poorer than the towns.[2] After the stability of prices in the later nineteenth century, prices of essential goods began to rise from 1902 causing decline in real wages until 1914. This contributed to the notable growth in trade union membership from 1902 and the industrial unrest of 1910 to 1914. Trade unionism enabled some workers to obtain wage increases in line with price rises, but such gains, and trade unionism itself, were most marked among the more regularly employed and better-paid workers. Some low-paid groups, such as agricultural workers, succeeded for the first time in establishing permanent unions although they remained relatively low-paid up to and beyond 1914. The problem of serious underemployment remained, as well as that of seasonal unemployment in many trades. Unemployment was high in 1902–05, and 1908–10, always reaching a peak in winter. The following table suggests how little the distribution of income changed between Baxter's estimate of 1867 and 1914.

In 1912–14 the statistician A. L. Bowley and his colleagues surveyed five representative English towns to establish whether Rowntree's findings in York were more widely applicable. For ease of comparability they used Rowntree's definition of poverty. They were fully aware, however, both of its stringency and its

Table 2

Occupational class	Nos. in thousands	% occupied population
Higher professional	184	1.03
Lower professional	560	3
Employers	763	4.16
Self employed	469	2.55
Managers and administrators	629	3.43
Clerical workers	887	4.83
Foremen, inspectors and supervisors	236	1.28
	3,728,000	20.34
Skilled manual workers	5,608	30.59
Semi-skilled manual workers	7,224	39.41
Unskilled manual workers	1,767	9.64
	14,599,000	79.65
Total	18,327,000	

Population of Great Britain in 1911: 42,861,000
Source: Guy Routh *Occupation & Pay in Great Britain 1906–60* (1965) p. 105.

limitations, for example the uncertainty as to what degree of physical efficiency his nutritional standard could obtain, or what standard of housing marked the upper boundary of deprivation. Clearly individuals could survive at a low standard of physical efficiency and in housing which to those accustomed to greater comfort was grossly overcrowded and substandard. In thus questioning whether poverty should be defined as existence in conditions below the barest subsistence minimum, or whether a higher minimum standard should be established in the interests of humanity and of aiming for high national standards of comfort and efficiency, Bowley and his colleagues raised for the first time some of the problems concerning the definition of poverty, which have remained at issue ever since. Bowley's work on this and other studies considerably advanced the scientific study of poverty. [doc. 3]

Bowley confessed himself unable to understand how any of those living at or slightly above Rowntree's minimum could be described, as Rowntree had done, as being 'neither ill-nourished nor ill-clad'. However, using Rowntree's definition, for the sake of comparability, in surveying the five towns of Northampton, Warrington, Bolton, Reading and Stanley (County Durham) he and his colleagues found:

	Percentage in each group below standard: working class only
All persons	12.6
All earners	6.9
All non-earners	17.2
All men (over 18)	7.2
All women (over 16)	9.4
All boys and girls over 14	10.5
Children (under 14)	21.6

They concluded that low pay and large family size were still the major causes of poverty.

From an adult male work force of around 8 m. Rowntree had estimated in 1900 that a family of two adults and three children required a minimum income of 20s. 6d. per week. By 1911 prices had risen. In 1911 Bowley estimated that 2.5 m. adult men earned less than 25s. per week while working full-time. These numbers, he pointed out, could have been considerably increased were it possible to assess the numbers working short-time, as occurred in almost every trade during some part of the year.[3]

It seemed indeed that the numbers of low paid unskilled jobs were growing with the advance of mechanization. Considerable concern was expressed, for example by R. H. Tawney, about the numbers of boys going from school into unskilled jobs with little prospect of advancement, from which they might be dismissed when they became old enough to qualify for higher adult earnings. Though it was little discussed, this was also a problem among girls. The marked growth of white collar employment in the period offered respectable, if not always highly-paid or secure, work to males and to unmarried women, generally to those from skilled manual working-class families. This may have prevented some children of artisans falling into poverty as a result of the decline of skilled occupations, but it did little for the lowest stratum who were always the most vulnerable to severe poverty.

Whilst Bowley and others investigated urban poverty, Rowntree became increasingly concerned about rural conditions and the drift from the land which he and others believed both increased urban problems and diminished the nation's capacity for self-support. He discovered from Board of Trade figures for 1907 that agricultural earnings varied from an average of below 16*s*. per week in East Anglia and Oxfordshire to above 20*s*. per week in the northern industrial counties, in Middlesex and industrial South Wales, although he found 'thousands' of families living on earnings below 14*s*. 11*d*. per week, sometimes as little as 10*s*. Rowntree's estimated minimum income of 20*s*. 6*d*. for a family of two adults and three children was derived from urban prices and, Rowntree pointed out, food prices tended to be higher in the countryside since the towns were the centres of food distribution. Also many families had more than three children. To supplement this wage data Rowntree sent his assistant, May Kendall, to collect budgets from a sample of forty-eight households representing low, medium and high wage districts.

Rowntree attempted no detailed quantification of rural poverty, in view of the wide scope of his inquiry. However, he emerged convinced of the extent of severe, if quietly borne, rural poverty, caused above all by low pay and compounded by large families and diminishing work opportunities for wives. Comparing the budget data with his York findings he found that only ten of the forty-eight households could afford food of sufficient energy value. Although rural diets could be supplemented by home-grown food this could rarely be produced in quantity and included little protein, since animals were more costly to rear than vegetables to grow. In any case, few men or women had sufficient time or energy after long hours of farm labouring or housework to devote to a garden or allotment. When meat was available it was given disproportionately, as in the towns, to the men; children received very little milk. Women and children suffered from underfeeding to a much greater extent than men. Sickness caused an 'appalling burden' of debt.

The lowest incomes were generally supplemented by charity and in many households women and children were also wage-earners. Very few families survived on a single wage. It seemed that those who augmented inadequate incomes by poaching or stealing food raised physically healthier families than the more law-abiding. Insufficiency of adequate housing was a serious problem.

Rowntree emphasized that such poverty was not due to idleness. Such conditions, Rowntree found, encouraged young people, often reluctantly, to leave the land, and created a brooding if often inactive hostility of farmworkers towards farmers and landowners. It meant that:

The be all and end all of life is physical efficiency. It means that people have no right to keep in touch with the great world outside the village by so much as taking in a weekly newspaper. It means that a wise mother, when she is tempted to buy her children a penny worth of cheap oranges will devote the penny to flour instead. It means that the temptation to take the shortest railway journey should be strongly resisted. It means that toys and dolls and picture books even of the cheapest quality should never be purchased; that birthdays should be practically indistinguishable from other days. It means that every natural longing for pleasure or variety should be ignored and set aside. It means, in short, a life without colour, space and atmosphere, that stifles and hems in the labourer's soul, as in too many cases his cottage does his body.[4]

Rowntree's moving account of rural poverty complemented Bowley's careful statistics, as did several similar painstaking, unsensational accounts of poverty in this period, all remarkably alike in the details of hardship they recounted. From 1909 to 1913 the Fabian Women's Group recorded the daily budgets of thirty families in Lambeth, published as *Round About a Pound a Week*, written by Maud Pember Reeves;[5] in 1907 *At the Works* by Lady Florence Bell surveyed the lives and living standards of the people of Middlesbrough. Eleanor Rathbone published her first studies of poverty in Liverpool. Beatrice Webb initiated a number of studies of aspects of poverty for the Royal Commission on the Poor Laws of 1905—09. [doc. 4] All of them made clear the extent to which poverty persisted even in households headed by a male working long hours, and when wives and children contributed to family income in all ways possible. Opportunities for wives and children to contribute to the household income varied from place to place, though they were everywhere low paid. The problem remained also of women who had no male to give them at least partial support, because they were widowed, deserted or never married; the census of 1911 counted 327,737 aged between 15 and 55 and thus likely to have dependent children.

The difficulties faced by these and by other women with dependent husbands or parents remained as great as before; neither higher wages nor action by the state came to their rescue. Women were,

Foundations of the Welfare State

as Eleanor Rathbone put it '. . . an inarticulate race. They do not strike or write to the papers, and they have no votes.' Only about 270,000 women were members of trade unions even in 1912 after the expansion of trade union membership after 1906, and it is likely that few of these had dependent children. Female access to other forms of working-class self-help also remained extremely limited. By 1911 only 2,235 married women were members of the four largest Friendly Societies.[6]

Further evidence of the extent of poverty in the period came from data of sickness and mortality. There continued to be striking regional and social class variations in infant mortality and in life expectancy at later ages. For example, in the notably poverty-stricken textile town of Batley in Yorkshire, the infant mortality rate was 172.5 per thousand, almost 1 in 6 of live births, compared with the national average of 127.3. Poor children who survived infancy were predictably shorter and thinner than others and the differential widened as they grew older. Between 1908 and 1912 the school medical officer for Batley found only 40.2 per cent of schoolchildren free from medical defects other than the endemic bad teeth.[7]

Despite the considerable evidence of continuing severe poverty, national adult death rates continued the trend of decline discernible from the 1870s, and infant mortality began to fall decisively, for the first time in British history, from an average of 152.2 per thousand live births in England and Wales in 1898–1902, to 131 in 1903–07 and 111.8 in 1908–12. The rate of decline was a little slower in Scotland.

Infant mortality is frequently assumed to be an especially sensitive indicator of severe poverty. However, as we have seen, there is little evidence that such poverty did decline in this period; indeed the survival of more mouths to feed may have increased it. The averages reflect a continuing social polarization, as one section of the population prospered and the condition of the low-paid and irregularly employed altered little. Nevertheless, the reasons for the striking decline in infant mortality in this period remain rather mysterious. It was perhaps partly attributable to medical and administrative change, in particular to new infant welfare services and supplies of cheap pasteurized milk. How much these changes contributed is unclear, since most of them began after the downward trend in infant mortality had become established. A possible alternative explanation for the trend is the improvement in the general health of many young females due to the improved living conditions of the late nineteenth century. As healthier mothers they were perhaps able to bear stronger infants. The birth rate also continued to decline, though most slowly among the poorest.[8]

ATTITUDES TO POVERTY

The purer strains of Liberal individualism were markedly less influential in the 1900s than in the previous generation. They did not disappear, but were more muted than before. A. V. Dicey's *Law and Public Opinion in England*, first published in 1905 with a second edition in 1914, was a distinguished lawyer's analysis of the growth of 'state collectivisim' since the 1870s and a warning (more insistent in the 1914 edition, after the Liberal reforms) that these developments were incompatible with democracy.

Hilaire Belloc's *The Servile State*, published in 1912 in response to the Liberal social legislation, was a trenchant restatement of the more radical style of liberalism which had long appealed to working people. He applauded those measures, such as Lloyd George's budget of 1909, which tended to diminish social inequality, but attacked all moves to increase state centralization and control over the individual. He described the National Insurance Act of 1911 as a 'vile enslaving measure' which compelled individuals to make contributions and to be registered with state agencics which diminished freedom and increased bureaucratic control. It did nothing, Belloc believed, to diminish social and economic divisions. Social justice, according to Belloc, could be attained only by destroying the concentration of power and wealth in the hands of a few, which bred inevitable contradictions between the values of self-respect and self-help preached in capitalist society and the material condition of the mass of the population which rendered it impossible for them to practice such principles. Belloc's ideal was the traditional radical vision of a roughly equal community of small producers. The considerable difficulty of achieving this transformation from a society in which wealth and power were becoming increasingly monopolistic diminished Belloc's appeal, although radical socialists supported his critique of state 'welfare'.

More orthodox Liberals moved rather towards a compromise between 'individualism' and 'collectivism', as was evident in the practice of the post-1906 Liberal governments. The foremost theorist of this view was L. T. Hobhouse, England's first Professor of Sociology, journalist and, briefly after 1906, Liberal MP. Hobhouse believed that the desirable spiritual regeneration of all classes in

Britain required state prevention of the accumulation of excessive wealth and of exploitation, through redistributive measures, and would be assisted by the encouragement of self-help organizations such as trade unions. By this means would emerge a general spirit of social responsibility, a strengthening of charity, self and mutual help, which would remove the need for long-term state intervention.

Hobhouse, like other 'new Liberals' such as C. F. G. Masterman, a Liberal MP who published in 1909 *The Condition of England*, an influential indictment of poverty and social inequality, went further in his demands for state action, especially for redistribution, than many contemporary Liberals were prepared to accept.[9]

But probably more important than works of social research or political theory in spreading belief in the need for some degree of state action, was both concern about the condition of the economy and the impact of the Boer War of 1899–1902. The latter initially diverted public attention from social issues. Newspapers were dominated by news of the war. The foremost advocate of social reform in the Cabinet, Joseph Chamberlain, was Colonial Secretary and responsible for the conduct of the war and hence had no time to pursue social issues. The costs of war enabled government to claim that they could not afford social expenditure. The war-time 'khaki election' of 1900 returned the Conservatives almost entirely on their war record with almost no discussion of social questions.

But it became increasingly obvious that Britain, the mightiest Imperial power, was having some difficulty in defeating a relatively small number of Boer farmers. This in itself was alarming. Then the news spread of large numbers of army volunteers (there was no conscription in this war) being rejected because they were physically unfit to fight. Some of these claims, spread energetically by certain leading military men, were almost certainly exaggerated, but they were none the less serious. They achieved even wider publicity and discussion when the ending of the war left time and space in the newspapers for such matters.

The impact of these discoveries was considerable because they reinforced other fears amongst individuals whose concern with social issues had not previously been notable. Britain's apparent relative industrial decline in the face of competition, especially from Germany and the United States, had caused concern in the 1890s. There were fears already of the likelihood of war with Germany, and the military performance in the Boer War caused new fears that Britain might face military as well as economic defeat at the hands of her chief rival. How to avert both these dangers became a major concern among employers, politicians and in the press, although optimism remained that solutions could be found. One solution was the improvement of administrative and managerial efficiency, but emphasis was increasingly placed upon the need to improve the physical and productive efficiency of the mass of the population, and to increase the size of that population. This gave a new urgency to discussions of the extent of poverty, sickness and physical disability. Equally disturbing was the fact that the birth rate was falling more rapidly than that of Germany and that the infant mortality rate remained high. The latter was even more distressing in view of the relatively higher mortality rate of male over female infants.

Such fears stimulated feelings of British nationalism. There was little doubt that Britain could continue to be successful, but certain adjustments were thought necessary to bring this about. National fears gave a minor stimulus to arguments for racial purity. Eugenicists advocated measures to restrain the mentally, and less determinedly the physically, weak from reproducing (by placing them in institutions, or, more radically, by sterilization). On the theoretical basis of the work of Karl Pearson and others, which proposed that mental and physical characteristics were primarily determined by genetic inheritance rather than by environment, such ideas enjoyed a minor vogue. They attracted the Webbs who advocated the segregation of the 'feeble-minded'. The socially undesirable characteristics which advocates of this movement felt were inheritable and should be eliminated were, as always, strongly influenced by contemporary social imperatives. They included, on occasions, 'work-shyness' and the predisposition to produce illegitimate children.

The debate, still active today, between the relative influence of heredity and environment upon attainment and personality had emerged in the later nineteenth century but began to be vigorously debated in this period. The emergence at this time of Freudian psychology, an important element in the international growth of this infant discipline in this period, offered one opposing perspective but was of insignificant influence in Britain before the First World War. This was perhaps partly due to distaste for all things Germanic but more to the greater strength of indigenous theories and to the much greater influence upon policy and administration of medical men, already strongly committed to the belief that the cleansing and improvement of the environment could substantially improve the condition and habits of the poor. The latter were more concerned with the tangible and apparently more readily eradicable physical conditions which they believed influenced behaviour than with the less tangible effects of infant emotional experience or of inheritance.[10]

Although eugenicist theories were influential within professional circles and attracted some who were concerned with wider social issues, their influence upon British thought and policy was limited. They offered some credence to the contemporaneous growth in anti-semitism: limited and localized though this was, Jewish migrants were criticized and condemned in very similar terms to those later invoked against post-Second World War black immigrants, and which in the nineteenth century had been raised against the Irish. Hostility reached a peak in the 1900s and restrictions were introduced upon Jewish immigration in the Aliens Act 1905.[11]

However, the search for methods of countering the national economic and military 'deterioration' after the Boer War was dominated by discussion of methods of improving the numbers and environment of the masses rather than of weeding out the unfit. Attention focused initially upon improving the condition of potential rather than actual members of the labour force and the armed services; on proposals and measures to diminish the infant mortality rate and to ensure that the surviving children grew up well fed and well cared for.[12] However, Britain's economic problems were immediate and the current generation of workers could not be neglected. Some employers became aware that the efficiency of the workforce could be increased not only by capital investment and technological improvement, but by 'increasing the efficiency of human capital', i.e. by improving working conditions and providing welfare benefits for workers, so that they were both physically stronger and psychologically more secure and hence able to work harder. Employers in this period were either providing from the resources of their businesses or demanding from the state such measures as pensions (which it was hoped would remove from workers worry about their future in old-age, and would enable employers to dismiss less efficient older workers with clear consciences), sickness benefit and medical care (which would enable them to recover more quickly and fully from sickness) and, more occasionally, unemployment benefit, which it was also hoped would increase the workers' sense of security.[13] In general they hoped, too, for considerable control over such measures and were unkeen about their falling into the hands of state bureaucracy.

Thus the experience of the Boer War combined with fears about the British economy to produce a demand for state and voluntary welfare measures designed to increase 'national efficiency', in the contemporary phrase, among influential social groups who previously had been hostile or indifferent to social issues. Fears about the economy also made some employers and politicians, as we shall see, a little more receptive to economic theories and proposals which promised to diminish the ill-effects of the swings of the trade cycle.[14]

A further stimulus to recognizing the urgency of social reform came from the growth of the labour movement and the increasing militancy of sections of it. Joseph Chamberlain's earlier recognition that working people could and should be seduced away from independent political action by state welfare measures was taken up by Lloyd George and Winston Churchill, as the need became more urgent due to the Labour success in the election of 1906 and to industrial militancy after 1909. As working-class demands and demonstrations for full employment and better pay became more insistent, they also became more difficult to resist without risking a more serious confrontation.

During the 1900s large sectors of influential 'public opinion' became more aware, and more afraid, of the claims of labour. The fear, given the absence of serious signs of undisputed support for revolutionary socialism, was not all-consuming. There remained grounds for believing that the mass of the working class could be persuaded to support a modified *status quo* and wider acceptance that the claims of labour for better conditions were either legitimate or, at least, necessitated some compromise to avoid a more threatening mass move to the left.

Hence there was a growing, if often reluctant, recognition that only the state had the resources to solve pressing social economic and political problems. A widespread insistence remained, however, that such action should be designed to stimulate and supplement self and mutual help and charity rather than to replace it. As a result the Liberal government elected in 1906, urged on by a clamorous radical wing but aware also of the doubts of many of its supporters, introduced new but moderate social measures. The Conservatives did not strenuously oppose them.

However, the labour movement was divided as to the extent and type of provision they desired from the state. Many still felt that the chief need was for full employment and adequate pay, which would enable the working class to provide for their own needs and to retain their independence of state control; though they were prepared to accept immediate state help for those whose needs could not be met in this way, such as the aged. Many also were prepared to accept state welfare reform if it was to be truly redistributive from rich to poor, rather than financed by taxes on the poor themselves. There was also widespread hostility to measures which entailed closer control over, and intrusion upon, the lives of the working class by those of other classes. There was considerable suspicion, for example, of health visitors, deriving from their reputation for criticism of poor mothers' conduct of their homes and families. School attendance officers were disliked for failing to take account of the need of some poor families for a child's income.[15] Understandably, welfare measures which gave benefits dissociated from any inspection or apparent evaluation of working-class character and habits appear to have been most popular.

Such opposition to bureaucratic intrusion drove a wedge between many working-class people and the Fabian socialists. The Webbs, in particular, placed their faith for the future in the efficient re-engineering of society by 'unassuming experts'. Well-intentioned though their desire was to make available to everyone the best information concerning hygiene, health care, child care, etc., and although they always placed such recommendations in the context of ensuring that everyone, through improved wages and benefits, would live at least at a 'national minimum of civilized life', the 'official interference' implied by their proposals was disliked as much by working people who would experience it, as by the Liberal bourgeoisie who were hostile to the principle.

Hence, there was considerable tension within the labour movement as to the desirability of state welfare. Many, however, came to accept it in the context of their hopes for future labour success: capitalist bureaucracy was undesirable, but when labour came to dominate Parliament, the bureaucracy would act in sympathy with the needs and condition of the working class and would no longer be regarded as an alien intrusion. In this context the Liberal reforms were acceptable as a first step towards greater, Labour-controlled, changes in the future.[16]

These growing hopes of political victory for Labour also contributed to a decline, though not disappearance, of support for municipal socialism in the 1900s. Once Labour controlled Parliament it was thought that it would no longer be necessary. It had also become clear that there were strict limits to its expansion in a capitalist state due to the reluctance of ratepayers to finance further municipal activities.

These divisions within the labour movement made it a less influential force on the side of social reform than is often thought. Fear of Labour remained the motive for the promotion of social reform among non-Labour politicians, but equally important were military and economic fears.

VOLUNTARY AND SELF HELP

Publicly-financed welfare grew at local and national levels but still by 1914 the very poor survived primarily by their own efforts and by the help of family and neighbours. This was stressed in all the social surveys of the period. These also noted the continuing importance of charity. However, although the large charitable institutions of the later nineteenth century continued, there are signs that many of them were finding increasing difficulty in raising funds and few significant new charities appear to have been founded. The reasons for this are unclear. In some districts it was due to the death of an older generation who were, often for reasons of religious belief, philanthropically disposed and whose successors lacked this combination of religious commitment (evangelicalism in particular had lost much of its mid-nineteenth century hold) and social responsibility. This century has seen a remarkably rapid secularization of British society (with the exception of Northern Ireland) which has had some effect upon the decline in voluntary action.

Roman Catholic organizations shared this experience of diminishing resources, Jewish institutions less so, perhaps in response to the mounting 'anti-alien' fervour of the first decade of the century. The activities of the Salvation Army and the smaller Church Army continued as before, but without notable expansion. Diminishing geographical and social contact between local business and professional elites and the poor of their towns, resulting from the growing size and suburbanization of towns, may have contributed to the slackening of voluntary effort. With rising prices the cost of maintaining a prosperous style of life also rose, and the growth both of the Labour party and of the trade unions perhaps destroyed hopes that charity could put an end to social and political divisions.[17]

The Charity Organization Society survived, its practice modified more than its principles; still, until 1914, dominated by C. S. Loch who remained a prominent public voice on matters of social policy. It was no more successful than before in controlling and 'organizing' the bulk of philanthropic activity.[18]

The settlement houses were as active as before but showed little sign of expansion, indeed Toynbee Hall found it increasingly difficult to attract residents. The main influence of Toynbee Hall lay in the numbers of civil servants and politicians later influential in the social policy field who gained early experience as residents, including Alfred Milner, later Governor-General of South Africa, and William Beveridge who was sub-warden of Toynbee Hall from 1903 to 1907. Beveridge and his contemporaries were much inspired by Canon Barnett, who by 1900 was firmly convinced of the economic as well as personal causes of distress and that more state help was needed for the destitute.

Beveridge himself, however, was sceptical of the value of much of the settlement's work. He regarded its main value as providing the opportunity for social research upon which the government could base more far-reaching changes. He had some reason for this view, since there was little sign that Toynbee Hall and the other settlements made any significant impact upon the East End. During his time at Toynbee, Beveridge became increasingly aware that local residents regarded its activities as patronizing, whether directed towards rescue or research.[19]

Local distress funds continued to be raised in periods and places of acute distress, although they came increasingly under government control. By the time, in 1909, the Majority Report of the Royal Commission on the Poor Laws and Relief of Distress recommended that the relief of poverty should remain primarily in the hands of voluntary organizations, such organizations were already beginning to decline from their late-nineteenth-century peak.

'Self-help' through mutual aid institutions remained crucial to the survival of all who could achieve it, with most such institutions expanding steadily. Trade unions offering welfare benefits, and commercial insurance firms, however, grew faster than traditional Friendly Societies.

STATE ACTION UNDER THE CONSERVATIVES, 1900–1905

The costs of the Boer War increased Treasury reluctance to countenance social expenditure by the state. However, under the post-war Conservative government they were under little pressure to do so. Balfour, as Prime Minister from 1902, and his Cabinet colleagues showed no passionate concern for social reform. Joseph Chamberlain resigned from the Cabinet and from active politics in 1903 after a serious accident. Tory philanthropy on the Disraelian model, if not dead, was not prominent.

The exception to Balfour's disinterest in social issues was education. The Education Act 1902 was largely the work of R. L. Morant, the chief civil servant at the Board of Education, one of a number of policy-innovating civil servants in his generation. But without Balfour's active support such a controversial piece of education reform would not have passed.

The Act abolished the separately elected school boards throughout England and Wales, bringing education under the control of the county and municipal councils. It allowed and encouraged these local authorities to extend provision of secondary education, after the minimum leaving age, either by giving rate support to voluntary grammar schools, or by establishing rate-financed grammar, technical and/or 'higher elementary' schools. They were also allowed for the first time to subsidize denominational primary schools. In return, local authorities were empowered to appoint the teachers in such schools for all subjects other than religious instruction.

The purpose was to improve and standardize educational provision. Rate support and local authority influence was expected to improve the often low standards of denominational schools, which made up a high proportion of existing elementary schools. Secondary education was to become more widely available, providing a more educated workforce to meet the more sophisticated needs of an economy under increasing competitive pressure. Furthermore, the abolition of the school boards was a first step towards reducing the number of overlapping, separately elected, local authorities which had emerged during the preceding seventy years; and importantly, in the eyes of Balfour and Morant, it would diminish the independence of local education authorities and the consequent considerable variation in the quality of provision, and also reduce the denominational influence upon local education. Both Anglicans and Nonconformists had successfully controlled many school boards since their establishment in 1870, assisted by the low turn-outs in school board elections.

The Church of England as the major provider of denominational schools felt amply compensated for this loss by the new rate subsidies. The Nonconformists, however, fought the Act bitterly. They resented the fact that it perpetuated a situation whereby in many areas, notably in Wales, the only available school was

Anglican, no alternative being provided for non-Anglican children. Non-conformist outrage at the Education Act was one reason for the Conservative defeat in the election of December 1905.

Another important effect of the Act was the growth of provision for secondary education. Since, however, local authorities were enabled to subsidize established voluntary grammar schools as well as to found their own secondary schools, social divisions in secondary education were reinforced. Voluntary grammar schools retained higher social status than the publicly financed 'higher elementary schools', which were stigmatized by their association with the entirely working-class elementary schools. The voluntary schools continued to charge higher fees and were socially and intellectually selective in their intake. (Fees were also charged for local authority secondary schools, though of lower amount.) Another social division also emerged between those, mainly day, voluntary schools which needed to accept rate subsidy in order to maintain and improve their standards, and the elite, mainly boarding, schools, which were able to survive and indeed in this period to expand, unsubsidized, on the financial basis of their income from fees, endowments and investments. The Act of 1902 reinforced divisions in education which had long existed but which had become more acute with the rapid expansion of both the private and public educational sectors since the 1870s.[20]

As regards other aspects of social policy, the government was under pressure to introduce measures to improve the physical condition of the working class. The post-war concern about population decline and the high infant mortality rate contributed to the introduction of the Midwives Act 1902. Demands for the training and registration of midwives, to prevent avoidable infant mortality due to inexpertly attended births, had emerged before the Boer War. This measure, whose public cost was negligible, was passed despite the opposition of thousands of untrained midwives who feared, reasonably enough, for their futures. The implementation of the legislation was delayed to enable some of them to acquire qualifications.[21]

The passing of the Midwives Act owed more to pre-war pressures and commitments than to post-war Conservative policy, although its passage through Parliament was assisted by the revelations during wartime of the poor physical condition of many of the working class. Also before the war, voluntary organizations as various as the SDF and the COS had provided free or subsidized meals for needy schoolchildren. In 1889 the London School Board concluded that

12.8 per cent of children attending London schools were permanently undernourished. By 1905 there were over 300 charitable feeding associations in the United Kingdom, most founded before 1900, most of them providing free meals. The high rates of sickness and mortality among infants in the later nineteenth century led voluntary organizations to provide advice on infant care and access to free or subsidized milk for poor mothers. Local authorities with substantial Labour or progressive Liberal representation, notably Bradford and Liverpool, opened the first mother and baby clinics in the 1890s.

'Hygienic milk depots' were set up by local authorities (the first in St. Helens in 1899) to provide sterile milk for bottle-fed babies, although the standard of hygiene even of this milk was sometimes dubious. In the 1890s many local authorities appointed lady health visitors, a practice begun on a voluntary basis in Manchester and Salford in the 1860s. In 1892, on the suggestion of Florence Nightingale, Buckinghamshire county council engaged full-time health visitors and other local authorities followed. They were not always welcomed by working-class mothers, who resented what they saw as intrusion into their lives and the sometimes patronizing advice on childcare from women who were often childless and who certainly had no experience of the difficulties of rearing children in poverty and in the inescapable dirt of poor homes with inadequate water supplies. Many mothers recognized that their childrens' health was endangered by unhygienic homes, by their own inability to buy sufficient food or milk, to breastfeed adequately, to obtain treatment for their sick children, but found that advice rarely met these real needs, which were the products essentially of poverty.

The socialist sisters Margaret and Rachel Macmillan were especially active, first in Bradford, then in London, in pressing through the school boards and municipal councils for more municipal and state provision for the health of infants. From the 1890s some members of the ILP were actively demanding the 'endowment of motherhood' (later known as family allowances) arguing that regular, unstigmatizing financial support from the state would enable poor mothers to rear healthy children. Such humane pressures were reinforced by concern about the political, military and economic implications of continuing to produce a physically substandard nation, and of the loss of population caused by the high and rising infant mortality rate.

Reports that almost one-third of volunteers for the army during the Boer War had to be rejected due to physical inadequacy (too short or too thin) or ill-health (in many case due to flat feet or bad teeth but frequently also due to heart and lung trouble or other serious ailments) were often exaggerated, but they strengthened such fears.

Such adult physical disabilities originated often in poor diet and medical care in early childhood, hence the increased pressure to improve the health and survival rates of infants and children. Medical Officers of Health and others were convinced that the chief causes of physical weakness and infant mortality were unsuitable feeding and lack of hygiene in the home which could, they believed, be improved by the education of mothers in childcare and domestic skills.

Hence, more intensively in the 1900s, MOHs and such voluntary organizations as the Women's Co-operative Guild and the Infant Health Society gave talks to women, issued leaflets, and established schools to train mothers in childcare and domestic skills. Domestic training became more prominent in the curricula of girls schools.

The government responded in September 1903 by appointing an interdepartmental Committee on Physical Deterioration. Its title, significantly, assumed the deterioration of the physical condition of the population from some presumed superior state in the past, of whose existence no proof existed. This committee of civil servants was to assess its causes and recommend remedies.

It interviewed Booth, Rowntree and most others prominent in the discussion of poverty: doctors, Friendly Society officials, military recruiting officers and others with relevant interests, such as factory inspectors, Poor Law officials and COS representatives. On its behalf the Medical Inspector of Schools for Lambeth, Dr Alfred Eichholz, undertook studies of children in a sample of London schools.

The Report of the Committee said nothing surprising to the interested or informed about poverty and malnutrition. It concluded that while actual deterioration remained unproven (medical witnesses in particular were sceptical about deterioration), working-class health and nutrition left much to be desired. Its fifty-three recommendations included the extension and enforcement of state regulation of environmental health conditions such as overcrowding, smoke pollution, provision of open spaces, control over the distribution of food and the handling of milk; work conditions should be improved, over-fatigue prevented; mothers should be taught proper childcare and girls instructed in cookery and dietetics; adult drinking and juvenile smoking should be curbed; the state should

encourage physical training and exercise; there should be an adequate system of school medical inspection and a state-sponsored
system of school feeding.

The Report included indeed a comprehensive set of proposals
for the prevention of child and adult ill-health. It said little about
care through improved health services. The recommendations concerning children attracted most attention among officials, politicians and the public. Though eugenicists found some ammunition
in the Report, of which they sought to take advantage, the medical
profession were equally responsive but more influential. The BMA
urged the extension of physical training and medical inspection of
schoolchildren. The government responded by establishing another
committee to investigate the carefully marshalled findings of the
interdepartmental committee on the issues that attracted most public attention. This interdepartmental Committee on the Medical Inspection and Feeding of Children Attending Public Elementary
Schools was appointed in March 1905 and was, in the words of the
minister responsible, Lord Londonderry, (President of the Board of
Education) not to be 'at liberty to make far-reaching proposals that
the Unionist party would decline to support'. Its Report, delivered
in November 1905, fulfilled this objective admirably. The Committee had been unable to decide how successful school feeding would
be, but suggested that local authorities should keep a close watch
upon voluntary experiments. It found that school medical inspection
was beneficial but that due to poverty or more often, they felt, to
apathy and indifference, defects discovered by medical officers
were often not remedied.

Pressure from the Conservative and Liberal backbenchers forced
the government to permit Poor Law Guardians to give relief in the
form of free school meals to necessitous schoolchildren, on application from a schoolteacher or school manager. This was the minimum possible gesture by the government towards the school feeding lobby. The parents of children receiving relief would still,
according to Poor Law principles, be disfranchised, the statutory
punishment for any head of a family who allowed a family member
to receive poor relief. Many parents refused to allow their children
to receive relief for fear of this stigma. Nothing was done about
medical care for children.[22]

The Boer War brought problems concerning children into
greater prominence but forced little action from the government. Public and official absorption in the war and its cost delayed
action on other measures, such as old-age pensions, which the

Conservative Cabinet had been seriously considering in 1899. Support for pensions revived after the war but met invincible Treasury and Cabinet opposition on grounds of cost.[23]

Unemployment was less easily ignored; it reached a peak in the winter of 1902–03 and remained high, especially in the winter months, throughout the Conservatives' period in office. There were demonstrations of the unemployed in London and elsewhere, organized by the SDF, the ILP and the Labour Committee for the Unemployed. A prominent part in this agitation was played by the Poor Law Guardians of Poplar through public statements by its leading Labour Guardians, George Lansbury and Will Crooks (both prominent Labour politicians).

In Poplar, as elsewhere in the winter of 1902–03, and in the still more severe distress of 1903–04, public funds were opened for the 'relief of distress', often sponsored by newspapers. They were used mainly to provide public works and made only a marginal impact upon the distressed: the Poplar workhouse was severely overcrowded in both winters. In 1903 the Poplar Guardians leased for one year a new workhouse specifically for the use of able-bodied men. In 1904 they opened the first Poor Law farm colony, in Essex, to provide work training for the unemployed.

The combination of high unemployment and the unprecedented unwillingness of some at least of the unemployed to accept their fate passively, demonstrated more starkly than before the absence of systematic public provision for the unemployed. The Poor Law had been designed to prevent rather than to relieve unemployment and relatively few 'able-bodied' men had ever resorted to it. The labour test was unattractive both to the many of the unemployed, because it impaired their skills and prevented their seeking work elsewhere, and to Poor Law administrators, because discipline was difficult to maintain in the stoneyards. When they had last been extensively used, in 1894 and 1895, able-bodied paupers in Bermondsey terrified the workhouse staff and played leapfrog in the stoneyard; in Poplar they formed a union and went on strike for a higher rate of relief. Borough Councils with their power to offer public works could, as we have seen, deal only very imperfectly with unemployment.

Even a Board of Guardians so unusually influenced by Labour as that of Poplar was reluctant to pay out-door relief to the unemployed. This was, of course, forbidden by Poor Law regulations unless paid in return for test labour. The Guardians in Poplar and other Unions with high rates of unemployment were constrained from paying out-door relief not only by the regulations but by the fact that such payments would have to be financed by the rate-payers of the Union, most of whom were low paid. Hence the Poplar guardians constantly but unsuccessfully pressed the government to introduce rate equalization.

The government was persistently unwilling to amend Poor Law principles to take account of the mounting evidence of extensive involuntary unemployment. Walter Long, President of the Local Government Board, was more sympathetic to the unemployed than many of his colleagues. His persuasion, combined with recurring unemployed demonstrations, moved them to introduce the Unemployed Workmen Act 1905. This enabled the establishment of 'distress committees' in all metropolitan boroughs and in all urban districts with a population of not less than 50,000. Elsewhere, they could be established at the discretion of the LGB when 'distress' was deemed to be suitably acute. In the provinces, distress committees were to be responsible for both the registration of applicants and the provision of work. In London they would register and investigate cases of distress, but the administration of relief was to be the work of a central body which would supervise and co-ordinate the work of committees throughout London. These committees included representatives of local councils, charities and Boards of Guardians and were financed by a combination of rates and voluntary funds.

Long failed to persuade the richer boroughs and the Cabinet to include a degree of rate equalization in the Act which was, however, important as an admission of government responsibility for relief to the unemployed. It remained, nonetheless, within the tradition of mobilizing voluntary in place of state action wherever possible. It was half-heartedly applied in many districts and this was effectively sanctioned by the obvious lack of government enthusiasm; it suffered from cumbersome and inexpert administration worsened by a shortage of full-time paid officials; from reliance on uncertain voluntary funding and, above all, from its central assumption that work could by these means be provided for those in need. Experience had shown that to be unlikely. Distress committees had no power to pay cash relief except in return for work. And the old problem remained that skilled men would neither be given suitable work nor time to seek it for themselves. The casual labour problem was too sizeable to be solved by these means and it was unsuited to the temporary needs of unemployed skilled men. Women were still ignored.

The Act was immediately attacked by the TUC. The number of unemployed demonstrations did not abate. On 6 November 1905, 3,000 working women marched silently from Walworth and Poplar to Westminster, after Lansbury's request that the Queen should receive a delegation of unemployed women was refused on the grounds that it was 'contrary to all custom and quite impossible'. This demonstration moved Balfour to urge more contributions to Queen Alexandra's funds for the unemployed.[24]

Labour was further incensed because Balfour's and the Cabinet majority's crowning blow to Long's hopes had been to ensure that the Act operated for only three years, the result of government's unwillingness to accept permanent responsibility for the relief of unemployment. The immediate pretext for limiting the period of the Act's operation was, it was announced, the need for a thorough review of the poor relief system before any major permanent change was introduced. Shortly before the Unemployed Workmen Bill became law, in early August 1905, Balfour announced the establishment of a Royal Commission on the Poor Laws and the Relief of Distress which would report on 'Everything which apertains to ... the problem of the poor, whether poor by their own fault or by temporary lack of employment.'

On one level this was a familiar delaying tactic from a government unwilling to respond more concretely to increasingly pressing demands for unemployment and other legislation. It was the more attractive because a general election was imminent and Balfour, at least, hoped to lose it, thus transferring the burden to the Liberals. Nevertheless, the case for a review of the poor relief system was strong. Unemployment was only one of a range of social problems for which the Poor Law's capacity to provide was, at best, controversial. The Poor Law was facing criticism from a range of sources. Many who had no wish to see the principles of 1834 modified were alarmed by the rise in poor relief expenditure. The measures of the 1870s had temporarily reduced it in relation to population size, but in the 1890s it had begun to rise and growth was dramatic after 1901. Expenditure in England and Wales was £7.8 m. in 1871; £8.1 m. in 1881; £8.6 m. in 1906. Some attributed the growth to the democratization of the Poor Law franchise in 1894. However, it was primarily the result of the gradual implementation of the LGB policy of improving institutional relief which, on average, cost four times as much per pauper as out-door relief. Despite rising expenditure, the ratio of paupers to total population continued to fall from the 1870s and rose only slightly during the depression of 1903–05. Poor Law expenditure per head of population in 1904–05 was 10 per cent lower than it had been in 1833–34, although real income per head had doubled in that period.

Among Poor Law administrators at all levels the change in LGB policy from the 1870s had created some confusion. Whereas previously it had sanctioned minimal provision for all paupers, since the 1870s it had insisted upon strict application of the principles of 1834 in the selection of paupers, and restriction of their numbers wherever possible, while at the same time insisting on relief 'adequate to meet need' in all cases. Difficult though 'adequacy' was to define, this meant in practice not only improved institutions but also that, contrary to much previous practice, out-door relief once given should be sufficient for 'decent living', whether granted in cash or kind. Out-door paupers should no longer be sent away with a sum of money obviously too little for survival. In the early 1900s, the Poor Law inspectors pressed the policy of 'adequacy' with notable enthusiasm, to the dismay of many Guardians and ratepayers, since it implied increased expenditure.

Arising equally strongly from the findings of the poverty surveys, and out of the labour movement, were criticisms of the principles of 1834 as being inappropriate for the conditions of the 1900s in which the existence of involuntary unemployment was becoming difficult to deny.

Hence, by 1905 the Poor Law faced criticism from all sides and the case for a review was strong.[25] The members of the Commission included representatives of all the conflicting points of view and all the most prominent of those publicly concerned with the 'social question': Charles Booth, Octavia Hill, Lansbury, Beatrice Webb, C. S. Loch and four other representatives of the COS, three representatives of the LGB and two of Boards of Guardians. Francis Chandler, Secretary of the Amalgamated Society of Carpenters and Joiners, was added belatedly in December 1905 after protests at the omission of a trade union representative. The chairman was the conservative MP (until the general election of January 1906) Lord George Hamilton. This formidable body did not report until 1909. Its investigations were important because the Poor Law continued to provide the institutional framework and principles for most publicly-financed welfare provision by the time of the election of December 1905.

STATE ACTION UNDER THE LIBERALS, 1906–1914

The 1906 election resulted in a victory for the Liberals, with a majority of eighty-four. It also saw the first major electoral success for Labour: twenty-nine Labour and Lib-Lab members were returned. Social issues were not prominent in the election campaign, with the exception of education, on which the Nonconformists waged a determined anti-Conservative campaign, and land reform. The Liberal government did not come into office committed to a clear social reform policy. However, the Liberal backbenches after the election contained a larger number than before of members known to be committed to social reform. Contemporaries regarded the party as one of reform, although probably a majority of Liberal members in the new Parliament still were radicals of the old Gladstonian kind, placing financial retrenchment and self-help before costly reform. Labour members, though generally more committed to old-age pensions, free school meals and redistributive taxation than Liberals and considerably more so than Conservatives, gave greater primacy in their election addresses to unemployment and hours of work, which they regarded as the major social issues.[26]

For their first two years in office the government acted very cautiously on social issues. This was partly for the reasons given above, but also due to the very large Conservative majority in the hereditary House of Lords, which soon rejected a Liberal attempt to amend the 1902 Education Act. This was the beginning of a long conflict between Conservative Lords and Liberal Commons which lasted until 1911. The Cabinet briefly discussed and rejected a dissolution and election on the issue and decided instead to try for a decisive election victory within three years. Social reform might assist such a victory, but it had to be of a kind which the Lords would not reject.

A further problem for the government was a serious shortage of government revenue, due partly to the costs of war and of peacetime defence measures, but also to the pressure of steadily increasing government expenditure upon relatively inflexible sources of revenue.

Children

In view of these constraints it is perhaps not surprising that the government was slow to propose concrete reform measures. Its first successful pieces of legislation were repayments to Labour for their support during the election: the Trade Disputes Act 1906, which reversed the Taft Vale decision and gave unions immunity from prosecution for non-violent acts in furtherance of an industrial dispute, and the extension of Workmen's Compensation, also in 1906. Its next major measure was forced upon it by Labour backbenchers. When William Wilson, Chairman of the Amalgamated Society of Carpenters and Joiners, introduced a Bill for the free feeding of schoolchildren by local authorities, early in the new session of Parliament, both the government and civil servants were unprepared, but in view of its considerable support in and out of Parliament, they agreed to support the Bill. The inability or unwillingness of many local Boards of Guardians and/or education committees to reach any agreement over the operation of the Conservative scheme, and the unwillingness of many parents to allow themselves to be pauperized by it, had made it largely ineffective.

The Education (Provision of Meals) Act became law in December 1906. It permitted, but did not, as Wilson had intended, require local authorities to provide meals for needy schoolchildren. These were to be financed by voluntary contributions, by charges on parents or, as a last resort, from public funds. However, parents who could not afford to pay for the meals were to be in no way penalized. The legislation was to be centrally administered by the Board of Education; it was in no way to be associated with the Poor Law.

This measure was important, first, because it was the first extension from the field of schooling into that of welfare of the principle that a publicly-financed benefit could be granted to those in need, free both of charge and of the disabilities associated with the Poor Law; second, it was a step towards recognition that parents were not necessarily culpable for the undernourishment of their children and that, with public support, needy children could be well cared for at home and did not require withdrawal into public or voluntary care. Although such measures had been and were still attacked, by the COS for example, for discouraging parental responsibility, it was equally arguable that they strengthened such responsibilities by making it possible for poor families to carry them out.

This was the unplanned beginning of a process whereby the Liberal government gradually withdrew provision for deserving groups from the Poor Law, at no cost to the Exchequer and as little as possible to local rates. It was, however, a slow beginning. By 1911–12 only 131 of the 322 education authorities in England and Wales had introduced the service. Of these, only ninety-five financed school meals out of rates, the remainder calling on voluntary contributions. In 1912–13 about 100,000 children were fed in London, 258,000 in the rest of England and Wales.

In 1914 the Board of Education initiated a new Education (Provision of Meals) Act which made this provision compulsory for all local authorities, provided an Exchequer subsidy, authorized feeding during school holidays and left the determination of need to the school medical officers who were to assess need purely on grounds of health rather than of parental income.[27]

The next major changes in social policy introduced by the Liberal government were also initiated outside the Liberal leadership. In 1906 an adverse report by the Board of Education's inspectors on infant education led to the Board for the first time limiting school provision for children under five – hitherto the normal age for the entry of working-class children to full-time education had been three. The higher age did not immediately become compulsory, due to the strain it would have placed upon the economy of working-class families.

In other respects the Liberals introduced few changes in education. However, from 1907 the Board of Education began to encourage the admission of working-class children to 25 per cent of the places in state-aided voluntary secondary schools. Their intention was to improve national literacy and technical skills: the provision of an educational ladder for brighter working-class children would increase the pool of highly-skilled manpower. Nevertheless, by 1911 there were only 89,000 12–14 year olds in such state-aided secondary schools, and 33,000 aged 15–18, few of them from the working class.

As with school meals, there had been pressure for a generation for free medical treatment of schoolchildren from doctors and philanthropists. There was by now considerable information as to the poor state of health of many elementary schoolchildren and the problem had become startingly visible as a result of the concentration of such children in schools after the introduction of compulsory education. Poor families could rarely afford medical insurance and treatment for more than one member, usually the father. Free treatment was available from voluntary hospitals and charitable dispensaries of which there were many in London and the large cities, but few elsewhere. Free treatment through the Poor Law was still avoided by the poor wherever possible. London appointed the first school medical officer in 1890. The second was appointed in Bradford in 1894. Bradford thereafter took the lead in the provision of medical inspection on a large scale and established the first school treatment clinic, developments which owed much to the energy of Margaret McMillan. Once again, however, it took the fears engendered by the Boer War to arouse widespread interest in the issue.

The Education (Administrative Provisions) Act 1907 included, buried among a number of routine administrative changes in the education service, a clause requiring local education authorities to 'provide for the medical inspection of schoolchildren' and 'to make such arrangements as may be sanctioned by the Board of Education for attending to the health and physical condition of children educated in public elementary schools'.

These provisions attracted little attention while the Bill was debated and passed, and the Minister, Reginald McKenna, was able to be vague on the important question of the source of finance, which was the local rates. The Act enabled Morant to establish a medical department at the Board of Education headed by George Newman, who was well-known for his commitment to improving health care for the working-class.

This department was responsible for the eventual establishment of school clinics throughout the country, but only slowly and after considerable controversy. Expansion of the service was Morant's intention. He was responsible for slipping the medical clauses unobtrusively into the Act of 1907, judging rightly that this was the only means to avoid public and parliamentary conflict about this extension of state action. It would not, however, have been possible without the support of McKenna and the Ministers who succeeded him.

Morant and Newman hoped gradually to develop a comprehensive free health service for children administered by local Medical Officers of Health, seeing this as the first step towards a free health service for all. They faced, however, opposition from doctors expressed by their professional body, the British Medical Association. Doctors feared that their own functions would ultimately be supplanted or controlled by local authority health services and their opposition slowed the development of the inspection and treatment of schoolchildren. The BMA strove to insist that local officials (medically qualified though they were) should merely inspect child health, leaving treatment to the independent doctors.

In the face of such opposition officials were unable to insist that children should receive full treatment, although in 1908 education authorities were advised to provide it where possible. A few local authorities established school treatment clinics staffed by salaried doctors. The BMA remained opposed to such appointments but with the national supply of doctors exceeding the amount of remunerative work available, in a society in which relatively few could afford to pay the full cost of treatment, doctors were found to fill such posts.

From 1912, almost unnoticed by Parliament, Exchequer grants were paid to education authorities providing medical treatment. Characteristically, Bradford had the largest scheme by 1910. By 1914, 214 (out of 317) local authorities were providing some form of medical treatment for children, mostly under the control of the local MOH. Elsewhere voluntary hospitals and charitable dispensaries were flooded with young patients, suggesting the extent of previously untreated ill-health among children. It became clear, however, that a serious obstacle to the formation of an efficient national health service was the determination of the BMA to prevent its members becoming salaried state officials.[28]

The considerable post-Boer War concern about children was reflected in the amount of legislative attention paid to them in the first years of the Liberal government. The Notification of Births Acts of 1907 and 1915 were further steps towards quantifying and analysing the causes of, and ultimately further diminishing, infant mortality.

The next major move was the Children Act 1908. This consolidated the legislation of the previous half century concerning the treatment of children by the law in both criminal and civil cases, and extended it in important ways. Since the mid-nineteenth century, minors under sixteen had been progressively withdrawn from adult forms of trial and punishment. The Probation Act 1907 established the form of probation still with us, as long urged by the Howard Association for Penal Reform. The Children Act established separate juvenile courts from which adults not concerned with the hearing were excluded. It brought closer Home Office control and local authority subsidy to reformatories for children for whom the first resort of probation had either failed or was thought inappropriate. Remand homes were established by Treasury grants, supervised by the police, to prevent any child awaiting trial joining adults in prison. No child under sixteen was to be placed in an adult prison for any purpose. It was said in Parliament that 'The courts were to become agencies for the rescue as well as the punishment of children.' The Act aimed to reinforce rather than to diminish parental responsibility by requiring the presence of parents in court and by increasing the courts' powers to require parents to pay fines for their children's offences.

Under the Act the Poor Law acquired the responsibility of visiting and supervising, in institutions or in their own homes, children who had been the subject of cruelty proceedings. Local authorities were given the duty of inspecting all fostered children under seven, appointing infant life protection officers, and inspecting voluntary children's homes. The Act imposed penalties for neglect of children, whereas previously only wilful cruelty had been penalized. It became an offence for anyone in charge of children to allow them to bet in public places or to enter brothels. Children were prohibited from smoking in the streets and the sale of tobacco to them became an offence.

The Act of 1908 was an important step in the extension of the state's responsibility for children, aimed above all at trying to prevent deprivation in early life leading to accidental death, criminal, or seriously disturbed, adulthood. It aimed to reinforce 'responsible parenthood', mindful of contemporary fears that state action would contribute to the destruction of family responsibilities; and it increased state control over voluntary childcare.

In 1909 the Local Government Board carried out its responsibilities under the Children Act by making boarding-out committees obligatory in each Poor Law Union. In 1911 it required that one-third of all boarding-out committees should consist of women, for their assumed superior sensitivity to children's needs, and that relieving officers should no longer supervise boarded-out children, thus removing such children from direct stigmatizing contact with the official administration of the Poor Law. The boarding-out committees were to appoint salaried female visitors to visit boarded-out children and widows with children receiving out-door relief, and to supervise the conditions in which Poor Law children were working in service or as apprentices. They also undertook life protection visiting under the 1908 Act. A superintendent women inspector was appointed by the LGB to supervise these activities.

Guardians were slow to appoint salaried visitors; only 80 unions had done so by 1913. However, the number of boarded-out children increased steadily, from 2,799 in 1885 to 11,596 in 1914 (14% of all children in care). By 1913 there were 8,206 children over three in workhouses (compared with 11,072 in 1906); 70,676 were in voluntary institutions in 1913, compared with 58,991 in 1906. In 1913 the Poor Law Institutions Order prohibited children between the ages of three and sixteen from remaining in a general mixed workhouse for more than six weeks. Children under three were to remain with their mothers. Hence by 1914 a large proportion of one of the largest groups traditionally provided for by the Poor Law had been substantially removed from direct association with it.[29]

These measures increased the sometimes petty and patronizing intervention of officials in poor families. There was still too easy an assumption of the incompetence of the poor at parenthood. Yet, given the reality that a number of children were deprived and neglected and the shortage of sympathetic officials, who could in any case have done little about the causes of such deprivation, it is difficult to known what alternative measures were available. One cause of deprivation among children and their mothers, marriage break-up, received attention in the Matrimonial Causes Act 1907. This consolidated previous legislation concerning maintenance payments to divorced and separated women but did not resolve their long-standing difficulties in obtaining these payments from recalcitrant or poor husbands. Payment could be enforced only by the courts, and would achieve little when poor husbands could not afford to pay. Support increased for the 'endowment of motherhood', cash support for all families regardless of the cause of their poverty.[30]

The amount of social legislation initiated by the Liberal government increased notably from 1908. Their relative slowness to act in their first two years in office was partly due to the continuing revenue problem. Asquith, as Chancellor of the Exchequer, concluded that a free trade government could solve this only by introducing a graduated income tax. The existing flat rate tax of 1s. in the pound could not, Asquith assumed, be increased without incurring hardship for those on lower taxable incomes. He overcame considerable opposition from within the Treasury, with the support of a favourable report from the Select Committee on Income Tax of 1906. Nevertheless he had to move cautiously, aware of the considerable prospective opposition from the remaining Gladstonians on his own backbenches, from the Conservatives, and from the Lords. Hence in the Budget of 1907 he took only a first step towards graduation by introducing into the tax system different rates of tax for earned and unearned income. He achieved this by the least painful means possible, by reducing the rate of tax on lower levels of earned income. He had thus established a principle upon which his successors could, and did, build. It did not, of course, increase the revenue. However, the absence of any immediate military threat enabled him to reduce naval expenditure in this and the succeeding Budget, thus leaving a small amount of revenue available for social expenditure.

More important in bringing about a change of direction in government policy were changes in the top government positions. In April 1908 Campbell-Bannerman retired due to ill-health, and shortly afterwards died. Asquith succeeded him as Prime Minister; Lloyd George took his place, entering the Cabinet for the first time, as Chancellor of the Exchequer. Another new Cabinet Minister, Winston Churchill, became, somewhat reluctantly, President of the Board of Trade. These changes shifted the balance of interests within the Cabinet by placing in key positions ministers who were, for different reasons, committed to social reforms. Asquith, like Campbell-Bannerman, was personally, if somewhat indolently, in favour of reform, but also like his predecessor was extremely cautious about pursuing it, for fear that it would lose as many votes from middle-class taxpayers as it might gain from others. He was, however, open to the persuasion that both Lloyd George and Churchill were prepared to apply.

Lloyd George had both a real desire to bring about social improvement and a shrewd appreciation of the gains it could, if carefully approached, bring both to the Liberal party and to his personal reputation. Churchill, for this period of his life, seemed also to have inherited something of his father Randolph's concern for social matters. He also felt strongly that a moderate reform programme was an essential means to destroy the menace of Labour and an essential prerequisite of military success and imperial expansion. [doc 5] He was also determined to turn the role of President of the Board of Trade (at this time a junior post well under the control of the Treasury) to his advantage by introducing striking social legislation. In this he was much assisted by an enthusiastic and expert collection of civil servants.

Old-Age Pensions

Asquith, meanwhile, recognized the necessity for some social legislation if the problem of the Lords was to be solved by another victorious general election for the Liberals. The chief measure which he had in mind was old-age pensions. Pressure for this was considerable and it appeared to have popular support.

For a generation a debate had raged concerning the form pensions should take. Pensions financed by a weekly contribution throughout working life, of the kind introduced in Germany in the

1880s, had been advocated by Chamberlain and others. They were, however, opposed by many working people on the grounds that those in need – low-paid workers, including most female workers – could not afford to contribute, and deserved after a life of labour a benefit paid from taxation rather than from their own pockets. The Treasury also opposed contributory pensions, objecting to the cost of setting up the machinery to collect contributions, to keep the necessary records and to make payments, in addition to the cost of paying pensions to those who were already aged and could make no contribution.

Asquith was persuaded by these arguments. He believed that the central problem was that of helping the existing aged poor who had suffered from the bad industrial conditions of the past, and that younger generations should be induced to save. He believed that they had greater capacity to do so than previous generations and hence would be less in need of support from the state when they reached old-age – there was therefore no need to establish complex insurance machinery. In the Liberal tradition, Asquith preferred to think of state welfare as a temporary measure which would be rendered unnecessary by the increasing capacity of the population to practice self-help.

Once Asquith had accepted the principle of state-financed pensions he had to decide to whom they should be paid. The labour movement, supported by Charles Booth, had long advocated universal pensions payable to all over sixty-five. Booth argued that any selective system would give rise to anomalies and would necessitate a costly system of selection. It also risked acquiring the stigma attached to the means-tested Poor Law.

However, the likely cost of universal pensions at sixty-five was £17 m p.a. The Treasury made it clear that they would allow no more than £7 m. This led Asquith to fix a pensionable age of seventy, despite the mass of evidence that most people who survived to old age ceased to be able to support themselves by work in their mid-sixties – sixty-five was the age adopted by most occupational and charitable pension schemes. Treasury stringency, however, left no option but to restrict the pension in this way. Raising the pensionable age, however, was not enough to meet the Treasury's requirements. Further means of limiting the number of pensioners were worked out by a Cabinet committee.

The Pensions Bill was guided through the Commons by Lloyd George the new Chancellor, although he had played no part in drafting the Bill. Although the pension was later popularly known as the 'Lloyd George' he did not strictly deserve the credit. The Pensions Act which became law in August 1908 granted a pension of between 1s. and 5s. per week to those over the age of seventy with incomes of between £21 and £31 10s. p.a., provided that they had not been imprisoned for any offence, including drunkenness, during the ten years preceding their claim, were not aliens or wives of aliens, and could satisfy the pension authority that they had not been guilty of 'habitual failure to work according to his ability, opportunity or need, for his own maintenance and that of his legal relatives'. This clause proved impossible to implement. Also excluded was anyone who received poor relief after 1 January 1908, although, as a result of a Commons Amendment, this clause was to be reviewed after two years and was removed in 1911. It was argued that it unfairly penalized those who worked throughout their lives until their mid-sixties, but were thrown onto the Poor Law before they qualified for the pension. Better-off workers could survive this period on Friendly Society or trade union benefits; the clause discriminated against poorer workers, including women, who had no access to such resources. Qualification for the pension was to be determined by newly-appointed district pensions committees.

It was a pension for the very poor, the very respectable and the very old, as progressive Liberal and Labour Members of Parliament pointed out. Their attempts to lower the age limit to sixty-five failed, but drove Lloyd George to protest that the measure was only an experimental 'beginning' in a new field of state action and beginnings needs must be cautious. Five shillings (2s. less than the lowest amount which, according to Rowntree, could support an individual for a week) was held to be too low. Lloyd George claimed that the pension was not intended to give full subsistence, merely an addition and an incentive to desirable private saving. The sliding scale of pension resulted from a Commons amendment, an attempt to minimize hardship for those narrowly above the income limit.

In its amended form the Bill passed easily through the Commons. The Conservative leaders expressed their preference for contributory pensions but did not restrain many of their backbenchers from voting for it. A minority of Liberals attacked the principle of state welfare, arguing that the state should rather encourage self-help and philanthropy. It was also passed, rather reluctantly, by the Lords. However, the number of defeated Commons amendments convinced Lloyd George and his Treasury civil servants that future pressure for costly extensions of the measure were inevitable. The civil servants belatedly regretted their refusal to set up contributory machinery which, though costly in the short run, would have shifted the cost of future changes in the scheme onto the contributors. They seem also to have underestimated the likely future increase in the cost of pensions due to the increasing numbers living into old age. The lack of enthusiasm for social expenditure in the Treasury produced a remarkable lack of foresight in such matters. Lloyd George became convinced that if need due to ill-health and other contingencies were to be met by cash benefits, as he believed that it should, the only financially and politically feasible means was the establishment of contributory insurance.

For all its inadequacies, when the first pensions were paid on 1 January 1909, 490,000 people qualified, a striking testimony to the extent of severe poverty in old age untouched by the Poor Law. A majority of them were women. The Act was welcomed by many old people because it gave them a regular income free from the taint of poor relief; though many, rightly, criticized it for giving 'too little too late in life', that little was more than had been given before. The historical importance of the measure was that it gave, for the first time, a publicly financed cash benefit to a group of the needy, free from the deliberately induced stigma associated with the Poor Law. However, it was granted on conditions of respectable behaviour not very different from those the Poor Law had been designed to induce. The introduction of pensions was an official admission that the respectable and hard-working could be poor through no fault of their own.[31] [doc 6]

National Health Insurance

Lloyd George saw ill-health as the next major problem to be tackled. It threw too many respectable people onto the Poor Law and caused the loss of many working days. Hence, almost immediately after the Pensions Act was passed, Lloyd George set off for Germany to investigate the longest established national insurance system. After his return in August 1908 from a packed five-day trip he set his civil servants at the Treasury to explore means of setting up a similar scheme for Britain.

He hoped initially to provide weekly cash benefits and some medical treatment for all earners beneath the income-tax limits, also maternity benefit – one more attempt to reduce infant mortality – widows' and orphans' pensions (which would remove a substantial group from the Poor Law) and an 'invalidity pension' for those unable to work due to permanent sickness or disablement.

During the process of discussion, Lloyd George's dreams were forced to contract. Widows' and orphans' pensions were not greeted with enthusiasm outside women's organizations, who supported them but had little influence. It appeared that they would require a higher contribution than many working men could afford, and they were dropped. For the same reason invalidity pensions were restricted by the Treasury to the severely disabled – an advance, but less than Lloyd George had hoped.

The day-to-day administration of the scheme which emerged – the collection of contributions and payment of benefits – was placed in the hands of organizations already experienced in such work: Friendly Societies, trade unions and certain commercial insurance companies. This placated their fears that national insurance would replace and destroy them and provided a ready-made and cheap machinery of administration. Workers who were too low or irregularly paid to be accepted by Friendly Societies and did not join a trade union, might contribute through the Post Office. The administration was placed under the general supervision of a central National Insurance Commission, established in 1912 under the control of Robert Morant. The Societies were assured that they would suffer no state intervention in their traditional business.

Insured workers acquired the right to full treatment by a doctor whom they could choose from a locally selected list, or 'panel'. The doctors were paid on a *per capita* basis. Contributors were also eligible for free treatment in TB sanatoria – TB being a major cause of ill-health and death among adults. They were not eligible for free hospital treatment for any other purpose – an evasion of the problem that fifteen million insured people, if actually treated for all their needs, would have overwhelmed the hotch-potch of voluntary and Poor Law hospitals.

When the National Insurance Act was introduced in 1911 it also provided sickness benefits of 10s. per week for men, 7s. 6d. for women (because their loss of earnings during sickness was lower than that of men) for the first thirteen weeks of sickness, although nothing was paid for the first three days, the aim being to help long- rather than trivial short-term sickness; 5s. per week was paid to men and women for the following thirteen weeks. The disability pension was 5s. A 30s. maternity benefit was to be paid to the wives of insured men.

Contributions for most within the scheme were 4*d*. per week from male employees, 3*d*. from the employer and 3*d*. from females. It covered those aged sixteen to sixty-five earning £160 p.a. or less. Arrangements were made to obtain contributions from employers of casual labour who might have more than one employer in any week. However, in view of the importance of even 3*d*. in the weekly budget of the poor, the inconvenience to, and lack of enthusiasm for the scheme of, employers and the absence of any machinery for ensuring that all workers earning under £150 p.a. were indeed covered, it is probable that many of the poorest workers (many of them women) were not in the end provided for.

The scheme, unlike that of Germany, was 'fully-funded', i.e. contributions were not as in Germany calculated on an annual basis to cover outgoings in each year, but supposedly accumulated at interest to pay the full cost of an individual's benefit, as in commercial insurance. The state subsidized older contributors. It gained the disposal of a large fund – a matter of some interest to a Chancellor short of revenue. It was argued that this arrangement would make the scheme more popular both with contributors and with advocates of self-help, since contributors would appear to be financing their own benefits, whilst experiencing a form of training in saving.

The measure met the qualified support of Labour in Parliament who argued, as always and reasonably enough, that the scheme gave too little. They were also aware of the considerable Labour criticism outside Parliament that the scheme was insufficiently redistributive in view of the high employee contributions and the fact that the 'approved society' machinery was also financed by working-class contributions. Again it was argued that the poor should not have to pay for their own 'welfare' out of hard-earned incomes. [doc 7]

The scheme met, if anything, a stronger assault from the right. Conservatives who had claimed to prefer contributory pensions in 1908 faced outraged complaints from their constituents about the growth of bureaucracy and the cost to employers. This became especially colourful as it dawned upon employers of servants that they would have to buy stamps for their cooks and skivvies. The indignation aroused by the granting of 'sickness benefits for serving girls' is one of the more enlightening moments in the history of class relations in Britain. Attempts to organize boycotts of contributions by employers of servants were apparently unsuccessful. However, once more, it is unknown how often silent evasion went undetected: the official machinery was not extensive enough to check on the activities of all small employers.

Nevertheless, the Bill passed easily through Parliament. Despite the reservations about the scheme of the BMA, which spoke mainly for the consultant élite of the profession, less prosperous GPS flocked to join the 'panels'.

⌈Benefits were paid from 15 January 1913. One of the most noticeable results was the unexpectedly high number of claims from women. Unsure whether this was due to a greater propensity to malinger or to a higher rate of ill-health among women, a committee of enquiry was set up in August 1913. This reported in July 1914. The committee was impressed by the testimony of doctors as to the unexpectedly high rates of previously untreated illness among women. Women had rarely previously been members of Friendly Societies, the extent of their ill-health had been unknown when the Act was framed, and administrators were unprepared for it.⌋[doc 8]

The Insurance Act was also followed by an increased demand for in-patient hospital treatment by men and women, which again suggests the extent of illness previously undetected. Such discoveries strengthened arguments for a comprehensive health service. The insurance scheme entirely neglected the health problems of contributors' dependents. Lloyd George was assured by his civil servants that a healthier male workforce would be better able to provide for their wives and children, and, contradictorily, that lower-paid workers would be unable to afford sufficient contributions to cover their families. Though the health problems of women were almost certainly greater than those of men, they were less visible and of less direct concern to advocates of economic efficiency. The legislation did most for the better-paid male workers, an increasingly crucial sector of the workforce both economically and politically.[32]

Taxation

Simultaneously Lloyd George tackled the pressing problem of government revenue. The controversial Budget of 1909 (initially rejected by the Lords and finally passed in April 1910 after a general election on the issue and amidst continuing constitutional conflict) took further Asquith's moves towards a graduated income tax. The basic rate of tax on earned income was raised to 1s. 6d. in the pound. A super-tax was introduced on incomes above £3,000 p.a. Death duties were increased on estates of over £5,000 and for the first time, and an especial cause of the controversy with the Lords, taxes were levied on land: 20 per cent of the unearned increment on land values, levied on sales of land. As a form of compensation to taxpayers with lower incomes and higher outgoings due to dependent families, Lloyd George introduced another new and lasting principle into the tax system: a £10 abatement of tax for each child under sixteen for taxpayers earning £500 p.a. or less. He also provided £200,000 for a development fund, to be devoted to increasing job opportunities by such measures as afforestation and the provision of smallholdings in the countryside. A small step in this direction had already been taken by the Smallholdings and Allotments Act 1908, a response to a long-standing Liberal interest in the land question. Immediately before the outbreak of war in 1914 Lloyd George was planning, in association with Rowntree, further measures to diminish rural, and to a small extent also urban, poverty, by the renewal of the countryside. Such action was prevented by the war.[33]

The Royal Commission on the Poor Laws

Also in the last months before the war Lloyd George appears to have been contemplating a more direct assault upon the Poor Law which had been almost unchanged by the Reports of the Royal Commission in February 1909. This Commission had undertaken an immensely detailed study of poverty and poor relief and had ended in conflict between the majority of its members and a minority composed of Beatrice Webb, George Lansbury, Frances Chandler and the Rev. Russell Wakefield, Dean of Norwich. This division to some degree reflected the pre-existing division of opinion on the Poor Law and its desirable replacement. However, the Minority and Majority Reports which resulted had more in common than divided them. It is likely that some degree of unity could have been achieved between them had not Mrs Webb become convinced that the division was irreconcilable and determined to make every effort to bring her proposals to fruition. She felt, rightly, that the majority would never share her belief in the efficacy of the expert and of efficient administration.

Both reports condemned the existing system and recommended the end of a separate Poor Law. Both believed that it was too locally various and too unsystematically administered at the local level. Whereas in London and other large cities workhouses had largely been replaced by more specialized institutions, in too many Unions the general mixed workhouse still operated. Both recognized that much involuntary poverty went untouched by the Poor Law and that Poor Law functions overlapped too much with those of other local authorities. Both accepted that the new system of relief should be based on rigorous classification of applicants and the further development of specialized services. Both emphasized the importance of prevention of poverty and of rehabilitation. Both supported the introduction of labour exchanges, and decasualization of labour although, as we shall see, they differed on other aspects of unemployment policy. Both favoured the raising of the school leaving age in order both to reduce the size and improve the quality of the labour market. The majority favoured raising the age to fifteen except among those entering a skilled trade; the minority recommended part-time education to continue to age eighteen. Neither Report recommended giving any free services except after detailed investigation of individual circumstances.

The Majority Report wished to replace the Guardians with public assistance authorities in each borough or county, consisting partly of members of the elected local authority and partly of coopted members of local philanthropic organizations, with the role of investigating and assisting poverty. Thus they hoped to coordinate public and privately financed welfare with the efficiency which the COS had sought throughout its existence.

The Minority, whose Report was drafted by the Webbs, felt that this proposal would bring insufficient change. They demanded dramatically, with an eye to its propaganda value, 'the break-up of the Poor Law'. They argued that since poverty was not one problem but a complex of many, each category of need (sickness, widowhood, old age, etc.) should be separately dealt with by a committee of the elected local authority, with the exception of unemployment, which as a national rather than a local problem should be dealt with by central government. Beatrice Webb believed that the retention of a voluntary element in the social services would render them inefficient at exercising the 'element of compulsion and disciplinary supervision' over the clients which she thought essential for their improvement. 'It is no use', she stated 'letting the poor come and go as they think, to be helped or not as the charitable choose.'[34] The Majority, whilst also favouring discipline for the poor, argued that voluntary workers would respond more flexibly to need than those limited by state regulations. They recognized, as the Webbs did not, the strength of popular opposition to bureaucratic intervention. The system proposed by the Minority would be co-ordinated by a registrar of public assistance empowered to investigate cases and levy a charge for services where the client was able to pay.

Both Reports assumed the existence of a ne'er-do-well class at the base of society, for whom punitive labour colonies or similar institutions would be required. As the Minority Report put it: 'The national Authority dealing with the able-bodied requires . . . what we might almost term a Human Sorting House, where each man's faculties would be tested to see what could be made of him; and a series of Training Establishments, to one or other of which the heterogeneous residuum of Unemployed would be assigned.' It is wrong to represent the Majority Report as standing on the side of 'reaction', whilst the Minority carried the red flag of progress. Arguably, many of the Majority recommendations were the more politically and financially feasible and more in tune with popular feeling at all levels. When the Reports were published the Webbs launched a propaganda campaign on behalf of their proposals, for which there was little sign of mass support. The Reports were published amidst a general expectation among informed opinion that the Poor Law would indeed be reformed or abolished. Leading Liberals, including Asquith, frequently asserted their desire for radical reform of the Poor Law and there is little reason to doubt their sincerity. Their actions, however, were inhibited by hostility to change from the civil servants of the Local Government Board, supported by their ineffectual President, John Burns, once the fiery socialist leader of the dockworkers, the first working man to enter a Cabinet but no longer a radical on social issues. Action was also held back by the need to reform local finance which both Reports recommended. Without a system of rate equalization, equitable provision of local services was impossible. This was, however, opposed by richer local authorities and by those, often the same ones, who prized their local autonomy. Poorer districts saw fewer virtues in autonomy. Government leaders might have welcomed a united report from the Royal Commission, which could have justified real reform of the Poor Law. Instead they dismantled the Poor Law from outside, by removing from it needy groups by means of legislation on issues such as old-age pensions and national health insurance.

Hence the Poor Law remained substantially unreformed by 1914. The failure of the Webbs' campaign to 'break up the Poor Law' was a disaster for their most sustained attempt to achieve reform by 'permeation' of the Liberal party. Consequently on their return in 1912 from a recuperative world tour, the Webbs began actively to support the Labour party.

As a result of the measures concerning children, the aged and the sick, the total number of paupers fell between 1910 and 1914 from 916,377 to 748,019. The fall was most dramatic among outdoor paupers.[35]

Employment and Unemployment

The other major set of issues dealt with by the Liberal governments after 1908 concerned employment.

By 1908 it was clear that the 1905 Unemployed Workmen Act had done little to ameliorate the problem. There were increasing demands for a national policy for the unemployed as distinct from central support of local efforts. Willingness to help the unemployed varied locally as much as the incidence of unemployment itself. The labour movement was demanding, and demonstrating in favour of, 'the right to work' (which meant public works schemes, paid at standard wages) and shorter hours in order to spread the available work more widely. There were, however, divisions within the Labour movement between those prepared to press for unemployment benefits and public works and those who argued that these were mere palliatives, and that shorter hours, higher pay and ultimately social ownership of industry should be the fundamental aims. The only group of workers to achieve shorter hours by legislation were the miners, who were granted an eight-hour day in 1908 after forty years' campaigning. Since it enabled employers to replace the two-shift with a three-shift system in the mines, it produced little real improvement in miners' living standards. However in 1912, after a series of strikes, a rather reluctant government granted the miners a statutory minimum wage. In 1911 Churchill, by then Home Secretary, introduced a Shops Act, the subject of a long campaign led by Sir Charles Dilke and female trade unionists, which established a half-day closing each week, thus reducing the very long hours worked by shop assistants but without increasing job opportunities.

From 1906 radical Liberals were demanding nationally organized and funded, and preferably profitable, public works schemes, rural development, and improved education to increase skill and efficiency. They were motivated partly by concern about the continuing extent of the problems and by a desire to prove that a free trade economy was compatible with social improvement.

All of these proposals were puny in relation to the size of the problem, and unlikely to change it fundamentally. More far-reaching proposals were made both by the Majority and Minority Reports of the Royal Commission on the Poor Laws, both much influenced by William Beveridge's analysis of the causes of unemployment. This distinguished between the temporary unemployment of skilled workers in periods of depression and the permanent underemployment of others in a labour market overstocked with workers with limited or no skills.

Both Reports proposed the establishment of national labour exchanges at which all unemployed workmen would be registered and to which vacancies would be notified. Decasualization of such occupations as dock labouring was to diminish underemployment. Programmes of public works were proposed by the Minority, to be planned on a long-term basis designed to forestall, as well as to relieve, depression. The Majority, having less faith in the virtues of economic planning, saw public works only as emergency measures in times of crisis. Both Reports proposed that the problem of juvenile labour could be lessened, as R. H. Tawney recommended, by compulsory part-time education. Mothers of young children were to be withdrawn from the labour market to be supported by allowances from the state and by their more fully employed husbands. Industrial re-training would be provided, in colonies for those who refused to work. The latter were proposed more enthusiastically by the Minority than by the Majority. The Majority favoured unemployment insurance, the Minority non-contributory benefits which would enable suitably respectable beneficiaries to be selected; training colonies were the alternative for the undeserving.

The government went some way towards implementing some of the measures the Reports proposed in common, due largely to Winston Churchill's initiative. Before he became President of the Board of Trade and before the Royal Commission Reports were published, he advocated a package of social reforms including labour exchanges, training of juvenile labour, decasualization, counter-cyclical intervention by the state in industry and military service to absorb some of the unemployed. Churchill's move to the Board of Trade in 1908 coincided with the return of acute economic depression. The Local Government Board refused to take any new action. Churchill investigated German local labour exchanges and within a year proposed to the Cabinet their introduction and that of unemployment insurance and the development of employment opportunities in the countryside. They were accepted by the Cabinet.

Churchill's ideas concerning unemployment had been much influenced by Beveridge's analysis of unemployment and by his proposals. In July 1908 he recruited him to the Board of Trade with the responsibility of making the proposals a reality. With the details of their organization worked out by Beveridge, labour exchanges were introduced in June 1909, after an easy passage through the Commons. They were to be established in all districts, financed by the Treasury, and would publish information about job vacancies. Registration at an exchange was not to be compulsory for the unemployed; their large numbers and the mismatch of many of them with the available jobs would have led the scheme into immediate crisis. The appointed management boards of the exchanges included worker representatives. They were established from the beginning of 1910. By February 1914 there were 423 exchanges in the United Kingdom registering over two million workmen a year.

In practice, not unexpectedly, they were of more value to the temporarily displaced skilled worker than to the chronically underemployed – the most intractable problem. Even among the former they failed to make a decisive impact upon the labour market before 1914, due partly to workers' suspicion of bureaucratic intervention in the labour market and to the indifference of employers, who had little difficulty in finding labour when they needed it. By 1914 the exchanges were filling 3,000 vacancies a day, but these would perhaps have been filled even in their absence. For every applicant who found a job between 1910 and 1914, three did not. The exchanges achieved least, predictably, in areas and times of high unemployment. Once the exchanges were established Beveridge and Churchill moved on to examine how to introduce unemployment insurance.

Meanwhile, however, Churchill introduced the Trade Boards Act 1909. This for the first time established boards representing employers and workers to fix minimum wages in the largely ununionized 'sweated' industries. These were low-paid, largely female, occupations mainly unmechanized and carried on in small workshops. The largest trade concerned was tailoring, but similar conditions prevailed in such occupations as cardboard-box-making, lace-making, and chain-making. Many women in these trades were also employed as out-workers in their own homes. A Select Committee on the Sweated System in 1890 had recommended the extension of factory legislation to these trades to improve hours and conditions of work. Women's labour organizations continually raised the issue, and the Women's Fabian Group took it up actively in

1905, with the support of the *Daily News*. One aspect of the growth of the women's movement in this period was increasing female agitation concerning the conditions of poorer women. The Fabian women organized an exhibition in Westminster of photographs and reconstructions of the working conditions of women in the sweated trades, with information about their hours and wages. This, combined with pressure from such organizations as the trades-council-based Anti-Sweating League achieved, first, a Select Committee on Sweated Labour in 1907, then the Act of 1909.

Equally important in bringing about this and other measures concerning the labour market was the active support of civil servants in the Labour Department of the Board of Trade. This department was particularly well suited to putting Churchill's ambitions into effect. Socially and educationally, its recruitment was more open than that of most civil service departments. A high proportion of its members were specialist economists and statisticians with knowledge of labour conditions; others were trade unionists. They devoted much time to the investigation and publication of wage rates (A. L. Bowley was recruited for this purpose) and investigation of labour conditions, including those in the sweated trades.

However, the effectiveness of the Trade Boards Act is uncertain since the capacity of the Board of Trade to inspect and supervise the large numbers of small workshops, still less the women outworkers, was extremely limited. The proliferation of 'sweated' workshops, and outwork had itself been in part an employer response to the closer regulation of factories during the nineteenth century, an attempt to evade these regulations. The 1909 Act attempted to close off this means of evasion. The Labour Department did its best with the resources available to implement the Act.

An unemployment insurance scheme was not seriously proposed in Britain until 1907 when suggested by Beveridge as a desirable complement to labour exchanges: it could replace poor relief and relief works, giving the unemployed a right to benefit while they sought jobs. At the Board of Trade, Beveridge, with Llewellyn-Smith, gave considerable thought to the problems of putting it into practice. The central problem was that the chronically unemployed could not be covered by insurance. They would require relief so frequently that their unemployment could only be covered by unrealistically high contributions.

Llewellyn-Smith proposed that insurance should be compulsory for all grades of workers in three trades; shipbuilding, engineering and building and construction. These were trades liable to seasonal and cyclical fluctuations, but where unemployment was neither so frequent as to be uninsurable, nor so low as to be unnecessary. Casual workers in these trades, who worked for more than one employer in a week, were to pay a whole week's contribution for each employment. This was intended to encourage decasualization. Llewellyn-Smith estimated that three million men would be covered. Each insured workman would make a contribution of $2\frac{1}{2}d$. per week, the employer $2\frac{1}{2}d$. After the first week of unemployment the claimant would receive 7s. per week for a maximum of fifteen weeks in any one year, paid at the labour exchange at which registration would be compulsory for insured workers. Payment would be made only if the unemployment was involuntary; disputed claims would be referred to newly appointed local committees consisting of representatives of capital and labour; workers would be entitled to refuse work under conditions inferior to the norm for their occupation. The total cost to the state was estimated at £1 m.

The scheme faced criticism from orthodox Liberals, who objected to compulsion, and from a variety of sources in the trade union movement. Some socialists felt confirmed in their belief that this was a further stage in the government's plot to regiment and direct labour, even to force the unemployed to break strikes. They argued that to avoid this it should be placed under trade union control. Others objected to the substantial working-class contribution to the scheme, arguing that it should be fully redistributive and extended to all workers. The Webbs objected that the scheme did not distinguish sufficiently between deserving and undeserving and that it included no measures for the prevention of unemployment.

In the summer of 1911 the proposed unemployment insurance scheme passed easily through Parliament as Part 2 of the National Insurance Act. The first contributions were paid on 1 July 1912, the first benefits on 1 January 1913. By July 1914 it covered 2.3 m. workmen (almost no women worked in the insured occupations) of whom 63 per cent were skilled. Most had not previously been covered by a trade union unemployment scheme. The two years before the war saw a return of prosperity, yet in the year before July 1914 over 23 per cent of insured men claimed benefit. This demonstrates the high rate of unemployment even in relatively favoured trades in good times.

Both Lloyd George and Churchill saw national insurance as a

necessary first step towards the prevention of unemployment, which they hoped to bring about by extending the principle of the Development Fund into a national policy to counter depression. Churchill, Beveridge and their colleagues recognized that insurance dealt only with the most tractable tip of the unemployment problem. It covered predominantly skilled and organized workers while the casual labour problem and that of juvenile labour was untouched. The clauses concerning casual workers were largely ineffective, employers having no interest in decasualization and workers fearing that the alternative was lack of work. As yet no better solution could be found to the problem that there were more 'workers' than work available. The Education (Choice of Employment) Bill 1910 inched towards the latter problem by enabling local authorities to provide vocational guidance for school-leavers; in the following year the Board of Education gave grants for this purpose. By mid-1912 only forty-one authorities had responded. Part 2 of the National Insurance Act authorized technical retraining schemes for adults, but this was not implemented until 1925.[36]

With the two sections of the National Insurance Act, however, Lloyd George and Churchill had introduced new approaches to two major social problems, which were of lasting importance. They had done so at little cost to the state or to the better-off taxpayer. National insurance was, as Lloyd George recognized, a most convenient device for a government short of revenue since it drew finance from workers and employers without the politically unpopular necessity to increase income tax. The amount of help poorer workers were giving to the Exchequer by 1912 was, in fact, considerable. In that year a family earning 18*s.* per week was paying 10.2 per cent of this small income in indirect taxes (7.1%), National Health (2%) and Unemployment Insurance contributions (1.1%) These percentages declined as incomes rose. A family earning the respectable artisan wage of 35*s.* per week was paying only 5.27 per cent in taxes and contributions, 3.65 per cent of this in indirect taxes. There was considerable substance in the complaints of Labour that national insurance added to as well as diminished the burdens of poorer workers.[37]

Housing and Town Planning

The Local Government Board, which had historically borne most of the responsibility for the treatment of poverty, had played very little part in the new measures of the Liberal government, except on occasion to disrupt them. The one large measure for which they were responsible was the Housing and Town Planning Act 1909.

The housing problem had improved little since the 1890s, although a few local authorities, notably the LCC, had taken advantage of the legislation of 1890 and 1900 to build the first large council estates. But still by 1910 the LCC housed less than 2 per cent of its population.

The concern about health and infant mortality led nationally to some recognition that both were worsened by overcrowded and insanitary housing and by limited access to fresh air in polluted city centres. This gave some stimulus to the movement for town planning which, inspired by Ebenezer Howard's advocacy of 'garden cities', pressed for the substitution of the continuing spread of overcrowded cities with new low-density communities in which homes and industry were segregated. It offered a semi-rural idyll to the most urbanized nation in the world, at a time when rural life was rapidly shrinking.

The only such city started before 1914, was Letchworth, in 1903, built by a public company. The concept had greater effect upon the building of suburbs, which became leafier and of lower building density than before. Such new suburbs were most attractive to the lower middle class, although Port Sunlight and Bournville were built on similar principles for workers, as were the LCC's first cottage estates. Pressure to limit unplanned high-density urban sprawl was the more acute because, in the fifteen years before 1908, 500,000 acres of land passed from agricultural to building use, mostly on the fringes of existing urban areas.

Pressures for more and better housing for the working classes led to the introduction of a succession of unsuccessful Bills into Parliament from 1901. John Burns had shown some interest in the issue as a member of the LCC and in Parliament before 1906. The 1909 Act which he introduced was important both for consolidating previous legislation and for certain initiatives. It removed the previous obligation upon local authorities to sell their houses into the private sector. The LGB acquired powers to prod local authorities into action both in building housing and in closing unsanitary dwellings. Between 1909 and 1914, partly as a result of the Act, partly in continuation of a preceding trend, loan sanction was given for significantly more houses to more local authorities than before. However, the number of closures of unfit dwellings also increased. Between 1910 and 1914 loans for the building of 6,780 houses were sanctioned while 7,427 were closed – a net loss to the housing stock.

The 1909 Act was more important in the long run for its encouragement of urban planning. It concerned only new developments and enabled local authorities for the first time to make town-planning schemes 'as respects any land which is in course of development or appears likely to be used for building purposes'. It aimed, as John Burns put it, at 'the home healthy, the house beautiful, the town pleasant, the city dignified and the suburb salubrious'. The purpose of the Act above all was that future developments would be on low-density garden suburb or garden city lines, primarily the former. Local authorities still could not, however, as in Germany, purchase land compulsorily for planning purposes, merely by agreement. By 1915, 74 local authorities had obtained permission for 105 schemes. The problems of overcrowding and homelessness remained as great as in 1900.[38]

Conclusion

The Liberal governments of 1906–14 introduced new principles of social policy which have been of lasting importance, but in accordance with no conscious grand design directed at Cabinet level. The effect of their legislative changes, however, was to initiate the dismantling of the Poor Law from without, by withdrawing from it the most obviously deserving groups, though in accordance with principles little different from those of the Poor Law. This was clear in the system of disqualification for old-age pensions; also insurance benefits were by definition available only to those who worked and hence contributed regularly. Benefits were kept sufficiently low to preserve the incentive to work and save, but those least able to work or save – the lowest paid, the irregularly employed and women – gained least of all.

REFERENCES

1. B. S. ROWNTREE, *Poverty – A Study of Town Life*, Macmillan, London (1901); A. L. BOWLEY, *Prices and Wages in the UK 1914–20*, Oxford University Press (1921); A. L. BOWLEY, *Wages and Income in the UK since 1860*, Cambridge University Press (1937); L. CHIOZZA MONEY, *Riches and Poverty*, Methuen, London (1905).

2. E. H. HUNT, *Regional Wage variations in Great Britain*, Oxford University Press (1973).

3. M. PEMBER REEVES, *Round About a Pound a Week*, Virago, London, repr. (1979).

4. B. S. ROWNTREE AND MAY KENDALL, *How the Labourer Lives*, Nelson, London, (1913) pp. 312–13.

5. M. PEMBER REEVES, *op. cit.*

6. P. THANE, 'Women and the Poor Law in Victorian and Edwardian England', *History Workshop Journal* 6 (1978).

7. F. FINNEGAN AND ERIC SIGSWORTH, *Poverty and Social Policy. An historical study of Batley.* University of York. Papers in Community Studies, (1978) vol. 19.

8. R. MITCHISON, *British Population Change since 1860*, Macmillan, London (Studies in Economic and Social History) (1977); J. LEWIS, *The Politics of Motherhood.* Croom Helm, London (1980).

9. R. BARKER, *Political Ideas in Modern Britain*, Methuen, London (1978).

10. G. SEARLE, *The Quest for National Efficiency*, Blackwells, Oxford (1971); G. SEARLE, *Eugenics and Politics in Britain 1900–14.* Noordhoff International Publishing, Leyden (1976).

11. B. GAINER, *The Alien Invasion. The Origins of the Aliens Act 1905.* Heinemann, London (1972); C. JONES, *Immigration and Social Policy in Britain*, Tavistock, London (1977).

12. A. DAVIN, 'Imperialism and Motherhood', *History Workshop Journal* 5 (1978); B. B. GILBERT, *The Evolution of National Insurance in Great Britain*, Michael Joseph, London (1966) Chs. 2 and 3; J. LEWIS, *op. cit.*

13. J. R. HAY, 'Employers and social policy in Britain: the evolution of welfare legislation 1905–14', *Social History*, Jan. 1977.

14. J. HARRIS, *Unemployment and Politics 1886–1914*, Oxford University Press (1972) pp. 334–47, 366–68.

15. J. LEWIS, *op. cit.*, Part 2; D. RUBINSTEIN, *School Attendance in London*, University of Hull, Occasional Papers in Economic and Social History (1969).

16. A. McBRIAR, *Fabian Socialism and English Politics 1884–1918*, Cambridge University Press (1962); K. D. BROWN, *Labour and Unemployment 1900–1914*, David & Charles, Newton Abbot (1971).

17. M. CAHILL AND TONY JOWITT, 'The New Philanthropy: The Emergence of the Bradford City Guild of Help', *Journal of Social Policy*, July 1980.

18. J. HARRIS, *op. cit.*, 102–14.

19. J. HARRIS, *William Beveridge*, Oxford University Press (1977) pp. 44–63.

20. P. W. MUSGRAVE, *Society and Education in England since 1800*,

Methuen, London (1969) pp. 67–76.

21. J. DONNISON, *Midwives and Medical Men*, Heinemann, London (1977) Ch. 8.
22. A. DAVIN, *op. cit.*; JANE LEWIS, *op. cit.*; B. B. GILBERT, *op. cit.*
23. P. THANE, 'Contributory *versus* non-contributory old age pensions' in PAT THANE (ed.) *The Origins of British Social Policy*, Croom Helm, London (1978); B. B. GILBERT *op. cit.*, Ch. 4.
24. P. S. RYAN, 'Poplarism 1894–1930' in PAT THANE (ed.) *op. cit.*; J. HARRIS, Unemployment and Politics, *op. cit.*
25. J. HARRIS, *ibid*; S. AND B. WEBB, *English Poor Law Policy*, Longman, London (1910) Ch. V.
26. A. K. RUSSELL, *Liberal Landslide – The General Election of 1906*, David & Charles, Newton Abbot (1973) Ch. 3.
27. B. B. GILBERT, *op. cit.*, Ch. 3.
28. *Ibid.*
29. J. HEYWOOD, *Children in Care*, Routledge & Kegan Paul, London (1959) Chs. 6 and 7.
30. P. HALL *et al.*, *Change, Choice and Conflict in Social Policy*, Heinemann, London (1975) pp. 158–60.
31. P. THANE, 'Contributory *versus* non-contributory old age pensions' *op. cit.*; B. B. GILBERT, *op. cit.*, Ch. 4.
32. B. B. GILBERT, *op. cit.*, Ch. 6.
33. J. HARRIS, *Unemployment and Politics, op. cit.*, pp. 334–47; F. SHEHAB, *Progressive Taxation. A Study of the Development of the Progressive Principle in the British Income Tax.* Oxford University Press (1953).
34. M. E. ROSE, *The Relief of Poverty*, Macmillan, London (1972), p. 46n.
35. S. AND B. WEBB, *English Poor Law History*, Longman, London (1929) Vol. 2, Part 2, Ch. V; J. HARRIS, *Unemployment and Politics, op. cit.*, pp. 245–63.
36. J. HARRIS, *ibid.*, Chs. V–VII; K. D. BROWN, *op. cit.*; J. TREBLE, 'Unemployment and Unemployment Policies in Glasgow 1890–1905' in PAT THANE (ed.) *Origins of British Social Policy, op. cit.*
37. J. HARRIS, *Unemployment and Politics, op. cit.*, p. 380.
38. E. GAULDIE, *Cruel Habitations*, Allen & Unwin, London (1974); W. ASHWORTH, *The Genesis of Modern British Town Planning*, Routledge & Kegan Paul, London (1954) Chs. VI and VII.

Most states whose economies had developed past the level of pre-
dominant dependence upon subsistence agriculture, provided by
the 1870s some residual publicly-financed relief for the destitute.
Nowhere was this provision as comprehensive or relatively as uniform as that provided by the British Poor Law. In most countries,
notably in such partially decentralized confederations of states as
Germany and the USA, poor relief policy varied considerably from
one district to another, though it was normally, as in Britain,
minimal. In the immigrant society of Australia charity flourished
and the extent of poverty was relatively small; there was no official
system of poor relief, except in South Australia, although the governments of the Australian States (they were federated into the
Commonwealth of Australia only in 1901) subsidized charitable institutions for the destitute.[1] In general internationally, publicly-
funded 'poor laws' existed where there was no other generally
available provision for the destitute, i.e. where there were large
numbers of landless poor (as was the case in Britain at an earlier
period than elsewhere) unable to provide for their own basic subsistence by production of food, by wage labour, family or community support, or resort to charity.

The growth and variety of charity was evident in all countries
with significant numbers of inhabitants able to afford donations;
everywhere the influence of religion upon philanthropy was considerable. There were close links and considerable cross-
fertilization among charitable activities in different countries. The
'case-work' practices of the COS in Britain had been adopted from
a model established in the mid-nineteenth century in the German
textile town of Elberfeld and imitated and adapted by other German communities. Notably, however, the Elberfeld system was

organized and financed by the municipality. Flourishing Charity Organization Societies, operating on similar principles to the English model, were established in Australia in 1887 and in all major cities of the USA from 1877. In both countries they were powerful forces against state action. Labour colonies supported by voluntary funds were established also from the mid-century in Germany, Belgium, Holland and Switzerland. The settlement movement spread from Britain to the larger American cities, notably Chicago and New York, and also to Australia. Both charity and 'poor laws' gave least to the landless poor when they were marginal or despised groups in their society, such as blacks in the southern USA or Australian aborigines.

In all economically developing countries, as in Britain, from the 1870s a variety of pressures emerged demanding more comprehensive government action for the amelioration of social problems, a demand for something qualitatively new. Most developing economies, whether the leading growth sector was agricultural (as in New Zealand or Denmark) or industrial, experienced similar problems of unemployment, underemployment, low pay, disease and poor housing. These problems were least in immigrant countries such as Australia, New Zealand and in the Western USA, where a high proportion of the population were relatively young immigrants and there was land to spare, and in such an exceptionally prosperous economy as that of Denmark.[2] But they existed to some degree everywhere in the developing world, and, of course, in the much larger areas of the world which lay outside this definition. Although in this peak period of imperialism between 1870 and 1914 more of Asia, Africa and Latin America was drawn into formal and informal dependence upon richer countries, few efforts, other than sporadic distress funds in times of acute famine or other hardship, were made or proposed to alleviate their normal situation of mass poverty. By contrast the 'white' colonies composed largely of immigrants from Europe, such as the British colonies of Australia, New Zealand, Canada and South Africa, were allowed a high degree of self-government – unlike for example, India – and pursued their own social policies.

Of the imperialist countries, Germany was the first to make significant provision of a new kind for her own citizens. In 1884 Bismarck, Chancellor of Germany, introduced the first system in the world of compulsory national insurance against sickness. All regularly employed German workers thereafter paid weekly contributions, graduated according to income, into a national fund, and received weekly benefits and health care when needed. In 1889 the insurance scheme was extended to include old-age pensions, payable at age sixty-five, and financed by further contributions.[3]

State-supported old-age pensions were indeed among the first state measures to be introduced in many countries. Denmark in 1891 introduced non-contributory old-age pensions for those over sixty-five who could prove destitution, through a means test. Similar schemes were introduced by each of the Australian states from 1900, and by New Zealand in 1898. France introduced pensions for miners and railwaymen in the 1890s. The timing of pensions legislation was not clearly related to changes in the proportions of old people in each population.[4]

No country before 1900 followed Germany's lead in introducing contributory insurance, although it was widely discussed in Britain, Scandinavia, Austria, Belgium and Holland, France, Australasia and the USA, and limited schemes were introduced in Austria and in Italy in the 1900s.

Germany, or rather Prussia, its dominant state after unification in 1870, had still earlier taken the lead in the provision of state education. By 1833 80 per cent of Prussian children were attending schools. After 1870 the German state encouraged and financed, throughout Germany, schooling, higher technical education, and part-time education of young people in employment.[5] Free publicly-financed, although not everywhere compulsory, education was also widely available in the USA. The federal government had been committed to the principle of free education since 1787 and thereafter each township was expected to provide a local school. By the end of the nineteenth century most of the population of the USA had access to free education, although least provision and least encouragement to attend school was given to blacks, especially in the south.[6]

Indeed in every developing economy of the period education was the first of the major social services to which governments devoted attention and finance on a large scale. It was one of the priorities of the Japanese government during the great push towards economic modernization following the Meiji restoration of 1868. Progress in Japanese education was slow since it started from a base of much more widespread illiteracy than in societies whose economic transformation was less sudden, i.e. most developing economies of the time. However, between 1868 and 1910 the literacy rate rose from around 30 per cent to around 70 per cent of the population; it was larger among males than among females.[7]

In France it became obligatory in 1833 for every commune to establish and finance an elementary school. These schools were inspected, as in Britain, by central government, which from 1867 also subsidized communal schools. Elementary education became free in 1881 and compulsory to the age of fourteen in 1882. By 1911 85 per cent of children were attending school and, as in all countries, the attendance rate among boys was higher than for girls. In France, as in Germany, the USA and Japan (rather less in Britain), the state throughout the century and especially from the 1860s encouraged advanced technical and scientific education.[8]

In all of these countries the state played a much smaller role in the provision of working-class housing, although all experienced similar problems of severe urban overcrowding as a result of population growth (spectacular in every country except France), the decline of rural occupations and the growth of urban employment. In most countries employers and philanthropists met a small part of the housing need. Employers, however, were most likely to build housing when their businesses were situated in relatively remote districts where new housing was required in order to attract labour, as did the mine owners of the Ruhr from the 1850s,[9] of the Tarn in southern France, and large employers in various industries in the United States.

As in Britain, belief in the inviolability of private property and the high potential cost of public housing provision compared with, for example, the relatively low cost of state education, held back publicly-financed action. In most countries greater efforts were made to improve urban sewerage, sanitation and water supplies, due to the dangerous levels of public ill-health in most large towns and cities. Death rates in the larger town and cities of Europe and the USA in the later nineteenth century were generally even higher than in Britain.[10] Attempts by private enterprise, generally supported by local or central legislation, particularly in Germany and the USA, to plan the growth of towns, providing 'garden' suburbs and cities at low density with provision for public and private open space, rarely benefited the poor. In both countries the rapid growth of towns occurred later than in Britain at a time when planning was physically and organizationally more feasible. Town planners in Britain in the 1900s looked with envy at the housing and planning legislation of Prussia, Hesse, and Saxony, and at the municipalities of Dusseldorf, Ulm, Stuttgart, Magdeburg, Frankfurt-am-Main, Cologne and Mannheim. Land was purchased in anticipation of urban growth and building plans developed. The new developments had wide streets, often planted with trees. Suburban Chicago was planned on similar lines.

Earlier still, the impressive rebuilding of central Paris under the Second Empire (1851–70) eradicated some of the teeming streets from which had poured the revolutionaries of 1848. They were replaced by wide boulevards, department stores, offices and public buildings, echoing on a larger and more elegant scale the rebuilding of English provincial city centres. The chief beneficiaries were the property developers and owners of Paris; the slum-dwellers were crowded into new habitations on the fringes of the centre. There had also been town extension Acts in 1865 in Italy, in 1873 in Sweden, and in 1875 in Austria-Hungary, where the expansion of Vienna was carefully planned.[11]

By 1914, most governments often under trade union pressure, made some provision for improved working conditions, accident compensation, and shorter hours, although these were generally confined to the larger industries and firms. The Australian states were especially notable for effectively establishing a minimum wage from the late 1890s, by means of wages boards with powers to fix wage rates (the first being established in Victoria in 1896) and by the establishment of law courts to arbitrate and conciliate in labour disputes concerning wages and other matters.[12]

There were, then, interesting similarities in social policy concerns and provision in a number of countries in this period, and also important differences in the pace and emphasis of public and private action. Both require explanation.

It is clearly inadequate to interpret the growth of social provision, public or private, as a simple response to awareness of the social costs of industrialization. Some of the countries which made notable advances in some areas of provision were not industrial. Both Denmark and New Zealand were among the leaders, for example, in the provision of publicly-funded old-age pensions; both were among the wealthiest countries in the world in the 1900s, in terms of *per capita* income. In both, the leading growth sector of the economy was agriculture rather than industry. Neither, however, can usefully be categorized as 'pre-industrial', nor were they 'traditional' societies of subsistence cultivators. In both countries agriculture was highly capitalized and concentrated, with high rates of productivity, worked largely by wage labour. In terms of the structure of ownership and finance of the means of production, distribution and exchange, they were very similar to contemporary industrial societies.

On the other hand, in industrializing Japan, local and central government, then as now, in every sphere other than education, regarded social provision as primarily the responsibility of the family and the employer rather than of the state. Central government action in the industrial United States was also very limited, although some states of the union under Progressive control did take action, notably in Wisconsin in the 1900s. Nevertheless by 1913 public welfare expenditure in the USA at all levels totalled only 1 per cent of all public expenditure, compared with 9 per cent in Britain.[13]

Among the developing capitalist economies of the half century before 1914 there was no clear correspondence between stages of economic development and of public interest and action concerning social problems. British industrialization started earlier than that of most other countries and was well established by the 1870s, when Germany, the USA and, less spectacularly, France, became major industrial powers. In the last decades of the nineteenth century Japan, Australia, Norway, Sweden, Italy and Russia were just beginning, at varying paces, the large-scale expansion of their industrial sectors.

Why then did societies at such differing stages of economic development, some primarily industrial, others primarily agricultural, begin at around the same time to take similar types of action on certain similar social problems? And how do we account for the differences in their priorities? Although altruistic concern about social problems was a real force in all of these societies, it was nowhere a new development in the 1870s and cannot alone explain why concern began so widely to be translated into political and social pressure, and more gradually into political and voluntary action, at this time. More important was the fact that despite their different forms and levels of economic growth most developing economies were facing similar pressures from the 1870s. Most notable was the intensification of world competition, as more countries competed to sell their goods and all suffered a degree of economic instability in the later nineteenth century. All, including the agricultural economies, were under pressure to maximize productivity and efficiency. Britain, which had been able to industrialize at a relatively leisurely pace while she was indeed the 'workship of the world' in the mid-nineteenth century, faced this pressure in a severe form for the first time. Other countries, such as Germany, the USA and Japan, had to come to terms with it almost from the beginning of their large-scale expansion.[14]

Responses to these pressures took a variety of forms, most obviously that of increased capital investment and mechanization, but also of intensified demands upon labour. Workers in key industries came under pressure to work more intensively, even when working hours were reduced. Also employers became increasingly concerned about the need to keep their workforce at maximum efficiency, especially their most highly skilled key workers. Employers, as Rimlinger has pointed out, became increasingly aware of the 'significance of investment in human capital'.[15] One response to this was the growth of labour movements in all of these countries.

Another result was the gradual removal from the labour market of its least efficient members. Children, who had less to contribute to the more sophisticated industries of 'high' industrialization than to the early industries, were removed into lengthening periods of education. Older and slower workers found themselves laid off, having previously expected to work for as long as they were physically able. The historically new notion of a fixed retirement age spread through European, American and Australasian business. Provision of occupational pensions and pressure for the provision of publicly-funded pensions enabled employers to make this change with clear consciences. The disabled also found employment harder to obtain.[16] Employers became more concerned about the health of key employees, since ill-health diminished efficiency. Some larger employers provided medical care through the firm. Owners of smaller businesses who could not afford such provision either dismissed chronically sick employees or advocated state and charitable health care. The relative roles of employers and of the state in such provision varied from country to country, but these changes are noticeable everywhere. There was also variation in the priorities given to various forms of welfare. These differences were profoundly influenced by differences in political structure, ideology, and social and economic structure.

Germany

For example, in Germany, in contrast to Britain, liberalism had flourished briefly in the mid-nineteenth century, but by the 1880s had by no means the hegemonic role evident in Britain. Rather Germany was a highly autocratic and bureaucratic state with exiguous national democratic institutions and few effective parliamentary or other sources of liberal opposition to the actions of the

Chancellor Bismarck. The chief opposition faced by Bismarck was the largest socialist party in the world in the 1880s, the Social Democratic Party (SPD). The SPD grew rapidly and began at the end of the 1870s to win seats in the, as yet, politically almost powerless Reichstag. Bismarck in the 1880s strove both to suppress the SPD – it was outlawed from 1876 to 1890 – and to cajole its working-class supporters into allegiance to conventional politics. Seriously afraid of the threat of socialism and of outbreaks in Germany to match the Paris Commune of 1871, Bismarck quite explicitly saw the insurance legislation as a means of winning working-class allegiance and of destroying socialism.

Bismarck's actions stood in a tradition long established in Prussia. Since the late eighteenth century, Prussia had provided certain benefits for some of its population, for example social insurance for miners, while vigorously and reciprocally repressing signs of labour dissidence among the same groups. After 1870 Bismarck extended a similar approach to the whole of the new Germany, under pressure from the growth of socialism, from the need to maintain social harmony and state control in the newly unified nation; from social reformers horrified by the conditions of the labouring poor as industrialization expanded, local authorities who objected to paying through poor funds for sick and aged workers; and from some influential employers, especially in the heavy industries, who were prepared to support social reform in return for state protection of their industries, state aid in compensating victims of industrial accidents among their employees, and destruction of the socialist threat. The national government possessed the bureaucratic resources necessary to carry out wide-ranging schemes.

The SPD itself did not favour Bismarck's measures. Apart from an understandable dislike of Bismarck's openly expressed desire for their own annihilation, it shared with other socialist parties affiliated to the Marxist Second International a deep suspicion of government sponsored 'welfare'. This was, its members argued, designed not just to improve the material circumstances of the labouring poor, but to prevent their organizing the struggle for greater and permanent improvement and elimination of their material and political repression. The workers needed not welfare from the state, but full employment, high wages, a share of the national product commensurate with the labour they contributed to it, and a full share of political decision-making, which could be achieved only by rejecting the blandishments of the state and fighting for maximum change. Once such changes had been achieved, many causes of poverty, such as low pay, would be eliminated and for others, such as periods of sickness or old-age, working people would have the wherewithal to save and to be self-helping.

The SPD had not the power, however, to prevent Bismarck from putting social insurance proposals into action. The schemes covered most regularly employed manual workers but excluded the lowest-paid irregularly employed workers from whom, due to their frequent changes of employment, it was difficult to obtain contributions. The great majority of women were also excluded because they did not work regularly. Even for those who benefited, the sums received were low and accident compensation was notably difficult to obtain. The insurance legislation which emerged was much amended in the Reichstag and was less far-reaching than Bismarck had intended. In Germany, as elsewhere, this social legislation did least for the poorest.

Although Germany, like most comparable countries, experienced dramatic revelations about poverty and subsequent discussion of alleviating measures, attempts at further legislation by Bismarck's successors in the 1890s were frustrated, partially by strong lower-middle-class opposition to further taxation for the benefit of the working class. The size and level of political organization of German small farmers, businessmen, shopkeepers and white collar workers, greater in the 1890s than in any comparable country, made their opposition highly effective. One of the few major changes in legislation, the Social Insurance Act of 1911, was chiefly designed to extend social insurance to cover white collar workers. Larger employers, also, now preferred to restrict the 'welfare' role of the state, retaining it in their own hands. They were aware of the benefits to their own businesses of providing extensive occupational welfare benefits, including leisure facilities. By this means, they believed, they could maintain a stable, hard-working and peaceable labour force. Under Bismarck's scheme their own contributions had been higher and their control less than they had anticipated. Large employers, both in Germany and the USA, who provided welfare benefits on the largest scale, tended to be most passionately opposed to trade unionism. By providing welfare facilities, they removed one of the incentives for workers to join unions. The failure of Bismarck's measures to stem the growth of socialism (both SPD and trade unions continued to flourish) convinced many of them that they could check the growth of labour organization more effectively than could the state.

Hence, further action by central government in Germany was

very limited before 1914.[17] Some towns and states provided a limited amount of housing from public funds and were in advance of the central government in pioneering other reforms. Problems of unemployment, for example, were as vigorously discussed in Germany from the 1880s as in England, and for similar reasons. The numbers of unemployed began to be counted by the German state from the 1890s and the causes analysed: they were similar to those in Britain, as was the pattern of trade depression. Towns throughout Germany began to establish labour exchanges from 1894 and pioneered relief works, mainly stone-breaking and snow-clearing. Trade unions also offered unemployment insurance; 3.2 million workers were covered by 1913. Sixteen municipalities had introduced unemployment insurance schemes by 1914, mainly those in which unemployment was periodically most acute, the labour movement strongest, and where employers were not opposed to such measures. So also had Ghent in Belgium from 1901, and St. Gall in Switzerland, following the international depression of 1894–96.

However, the central government in Germany made no unemployment provision until 1914. Implementation of the legislation of that year was prevented by the war. Social and political divisions in Germany kept publicly-financed unemployment provision a little behind that of Britain. The very strength of the German labour movement, since it aroused and was opposed by equal strength, for a long period prevented rather than encouraged further developments. However, given the limited nature of British provision and the extent of local, trade-union and employer provision in Germany, and the neglect of the problems of the chronically unemployed, of women, rural workers and peasants in both countries, it is difficult to argue that Britain was far in advance of Germany in real provision for the unemployed by 1914.[18]

Germany shared Britain's concern about a declining birth rate and high infant mortality rate, and for similar reasons. Similar debates were conducted in both countries, the military imperative being especially strong in Germany. Eugenic arguments were rather more influential in Germany and potentially more dangerous given the depth of German anti-semitism. The divorce law was liberalized on the grounds that 'it hinders population increase if one compels people to live together when they could create even more children for the state in better assorted partnerships'. The education system devoted much time to educating girls in the skills of motherhood. Otherwise activity to support poor mothers, to provide medical care, milk, etc., was voluntarily organized, sometimes with municipal subsidies, often initiated by middle-class women. The active feminist movement before 1914 proposed birth control and even abortion, but with little response.[19]

Hence, features of German ideology, constitution and social structure have to be taken into account if we are to explain the specific nature of developments in social policy. Differences in these features explain the different nature of developments elsewhere.

Japan

In Japan, with a similarly authoritarian government structure, in the early stages of industrialization it was assumed that the sick, old or unemployed urban worker would return to his peasant family and community with whom he retained close links, and many did so. The same was true in European Russia. As urbanization spread in Japan and links with the countryside diminished, the business firms, unlike those of Russia, took on the historic role of the family and provided most social benefits. In Japan the modern system of employer paternalism began to take shape with state encouragement. In this early phase of Japanese industrialization this should not be romanticized. The problem common to all societies, of creating a stable labour force from a rural population unaccustomed to factory discipline, was solved in the largest new industry, textiles, by the creation of dormitories for male and (a much larger number) female workers. The distinction between these institutions and prisons was not always obvious. Or rather, as a Japanese historian has put it, they were 'store-houses for the human factor of production'. The workers were strictly disciplined, worked long hours and had high mortality rates. Trade unionism was weak, although where unions existed, as among metal workers, they provided welfare benefits.

However, the Meiji government, which lasted until 1912, was increasingly aware that such labour conditions harmed both Japan's productive capacity and its 'image' abroad. Under the slogans 'civilization and enlightenment' and 'a rich country and a strong army' they both financed education and sought to encourage employers to provide conditions which would improve the health and efficiency of the labour force. As in Britain, it was found that young men who had been over-worked, under-fed and provided with minimal or non-existent medical care were unfit for military service, and that similarly maltreated females made wretched mothers unable to rear good workers and soldiers. Employers at first rejected attempts to persuade them of the virtues of paternalism but, faced with firmness from the government and the gradual recognition that healthy workers were more productive, they gave way. Government and employers were stimulated to these actions also by the publication of studies of the shocking conditions of the Japanese poor, notably *The Lower-Class Society of Japan* by Gennosuke Yokoyama, published in 1898, which received considerable publicity. The government itself contributed to such revelations. In 1903 the Ministry of Agriculture and Commerce published *The Conditions of Factory Labour*, which had a similar effect. Yokoyama in particular emphasized the inhumanity of the emerging industrial society. His royalties were used for the promotion of the labour movement and of social work among textile workers.

Other research demonstrated the physical hazards of industrial work, and many industrial disputes among ununionized workers, derived from workers' demands for safe working conditions. The emergence of a new generation of employers educated abroad, or with closer foreign contacts than their predecessors, also contributed to the new approach. As capital became increasingly international there was a notable cross-fertilization of ideas concerning, among other things, labour management.

With government encouragement, larger employers began to improve their dormitories, providing educational and recreational facilities and shortening working hours in order to improve both the health of their workers and their willingness to stay with the firm. Medical facilities, first introduced into some firms for the purpose of checking on the feigned illness of reluctant workers, began to have a positive role of prevention and cure of actual sickness. In the Nagasaki shipyard in the 1900s technical education was provided for employees and relief or assistance schemes were introduced for injury, sickness, disablement, death, unemployment and retirement.

From the 1880s the government tried to embody in legislation the responsibilities they wished to place upon employers. After much opposition, in 1911 it introduced a Factory Law. This established maximum hours and minimum working conditions, especially for younger and female workers. It was concerned only with industrial workers; for peasants (the mass of the population) nothing was done.[20]

Australia and New Zealand

In New Zealand, by contrast, the state had played a major role in developing the new country and there were fewer sources of opposition in principle to state action than, for example, in Britain. The first reform measures both in New Zealand and Australia came from their first Lib-Lab governments, voted into power in the 1890s. These were the first countries in the world in which acknowledged representatives of working-class interests played a substantial role in government. The social basis of this labour support was the migrant population of largely British working-class origin, voting for protection against the ill-effects of severe depression and unemployment in the 1890s. Although socialist and labour movements everywhere tended to be suspicious of public welfare provided by bourgeois and aristocratic parties, once in power they were prepared to promote welfare measures. The general justification was that their actions were not designed to undermine their own movements; in better intentioned hands than those of capitalist governments, state welfare could achieve real redistribution of wealth and power.

In Australia and New Zealand there was considerable discussion of the problem of unemployment but no publicly-financed action, despite the well publicized investigation of unemployment in Australia in the 1900s by the English trade unionist Tom Mann. New South Wales led the world in introducing a non-contributory invalidity pension in 1907, although it was confined to the severely disabled. This was extended to the whole of Australia when the Commonwealth was formed in 1901.

A more important change came not from the state and federal governments but from a decision in the Commonwealth Court of Conciliation and Arbitration in 1907. Mr Justice Higgins ruled that every unskilled Australian adult male worker should be paid a wage 'appropriate to the normal needs of an average employee, regarded as a human being living in a civilized country'. The 'normal needs' standard was to be one 'sufficient to ensure the workman food, shelter, clothing, frugal comforts, provision for evil days, etc.' The court placed it at a minimum of 7*s.* per day, which contemporary surveys showed to be adequate to provide subsistence.

Higgins was a scholarly radical, long concerned about the problem of the poorest workers, influenced by the Webbs' notion of a 'national minimum'. His action was quite deliberate. It distressed Australian employers, but left them little alternative but to comply or to risk prosecution. They tried, unsuccessfully, to challenge the ruling in the courts. Higgins' decision was a product of a highly developed arbitration system in Australian labour relations and suggests that, by 1907, the influential Australian labour movement had gone further than those of other countries towards the first half of the universal labour demand for adequate wages and 'the right to work'. In this context the failure to tackle unemployment is the more difficult to explain. Casual underemployment was a problem in the big cities and periodic unemployment was a severe as elsewhere. The failure to introduce labour exchanges, unemployment insurance or other benefits can perhaps be explained by the survival of the belief that in an expanding colony such as Australia, or New Zealand where the problem was also neglected, there was always work to be found on the land. Such measures would have appeared inconsistent with the continuing policies of governments of attracting migrants from abroad to expand the workforce. They might indeed have deterred migrants. Certainly Australia did not suffer from the European problem of an overall oversupply of labour, rather it sought to attract the European surplus. It did, however, suffer the problem of mismatch between un- or under-employed urban labour and high demand for rural labour.

In addition, secure Australian workers were as contemptuous as their European counterparts of the feckless 'residuum' of chronically under-employed, more so perhaps in view of the greater availability of work on the land. The capacity of the secure sections of the Australian working class for saving and self-help appears also to have been greater than in Europe. They held more life assurance per head of population than was held in the UK, the USA or Canada. A higher proportion than in the UK were savings-bank depositors and members of Friendly Societies, although here also these rarely provided for women.

Hence Australian labour and Australian public policy tended more than elsewhere to concentrate upon the 'deserving' who manifestly could not be self-helping: the aged poor, children, the employed but low-paid; and to provide the machinery for the remainder, through industrial negotiation, to help themselves. It became increasingly evident, however, that self-help or mutual aid was more difficult in some respects than others. Individuals could not buy health care when this was patchily available and too costly. The problems of supplying health care were especially acute in a society in which a high proportion of the population lived in remote rural districts. Hence when Labour narrowly took control of the government of New South Wales in 1910, it embarked on an active policy of subsidizing hospitals and dispensaries in order ultimately to provide a universal health service. As in Britain, it faced the hostility of doctors to state control and had to remain content by 1914 with financing new and existing institutions, including nursing services for remote bush districts. Friendly Societies were also subsidized and membership encouraged. Thus, improved medical services at low cost were made widely available in New South Wales.

The division of labour between the federal and state governments in Australia after 1901 left health, education and personal social services to the states' initiatives. However, federal legislation supplemented the activities of the states. From 1912 it provided free medical inspection and treatment for children in state schools, establishing its own salaried service of doctors and nurses to carry out this task often in the remote districts with few medical services.

Australia, also without benefit of any especial stimulus from war, was as active as Britain in providing medical care for children. It shared the international concern with population growth. Not only was there pressure to increase immigration but worry about the low birth rate and high infant mortality rate. To counter the latter, maternity benefits were introduced in 1912, followed in New South Wales by measures to improve the training and increase the supply of midwives to provide skilled attendance at all births. Clinics and health visitors were introduced in New South Wales to provide support for mothers. In most states, notably in South Australia, the needs of poor women and children were met by 'boarding out' schemes, including the payment of mothers to 'board' their own children in their own homes.

As elsewhere also the encouragement of population growth and of immigration was selective. The 'White Australia' policy was the first major Commonwealth enactment excluding black, or more probably yellow, immigrants: Pacific Islanders were repatriated from Queensland; the aborigines were explicitly excluded from Australian social legislation as were the Maoris from that of New Zealand. No alternative provision was made for them.

The introduction of national health insurance, and its extension to include old-age pensions, was widely discussed in Australia before 1914. It was not implemented, perhaps due to the strength of 'self-help' institutions and the continuing importance of voluntary agencies. By 1914 Australia, like Britain and indeed most Western European nations, had made selective forays into the morass of social problems they experienced in common. Large gaps remained, including the much needed provision of housing which in Australia, as everywhere, was the last and potentially the most costly major social problem to receive public attention or finance.

Australia, however, could justifiably claim to 'lead the world' in some fields of social policy.[21] This was in notable contrast to another large white British colony, Canada. Canada had one of the fastest expanding economies in the world in this period. It was notably deficient in social provision either at national, state or municipal level. A Government Annuities Act of 1908 enabled individuals to buy old-age annuities at favourable rates of interest. A Juvenile Delinquents Act of 1908 provided, like the British Childrens Act of the same year, a separate judicial system for young people under sixteen. Other needs were provided for if at all by charity and by local relief funds.

Canada and the USA

Canada's rapid development started rather later than that of Australia. The relatively greater strength of the independent pioneering ethic, the assumption with some, if imperfect, basis in truth that opportunities were there for all in an expanding country, may account for the absence of attention to social problems by more than a small minority of town-dwellers. They were also difficult to implement for a scattered population in often inhospitable territory. Nor was there, as in Australia, a strong labour movement to press such issues.

The example to Canada from across the border in the USA was ambiguous, although there, too, the still pioneering states of the West made less social provision than the long settled Eastern states. There was as much detailed information available concerning social conditions in the United States as in any other country, enabling the US Commission on Industrial Relations to comment in 1915: 'Have workers received a fair share of the enormous increase in wealth which has taken place in this country . . . as a result largely of their labour . . . The answer is emphatically – No!'[22] This Commission found 50–60 per cent of working families to be poor, despite the earnings of wives and children, and 30 per cent of the population to be living in 'abject poverty'. This confirmed the findings of successive surveys since 1900. Poverty was as severe in rural as in urban areas; worst among blacks, for whom the 'Progressive Era' (as the period of American history from the mid-1900s is conventionally known) spelled little progress. Their segregation made it possible for social reformers to ignore them and the tradition of land ownership in the rural south bred no tradition of paternal philanthropy towards freed slaves. There had been no need to woo slave labour by kindness. Nor was any help extended to American Indians who were as effectively excluded from the 'legal nation' as the native inhabitants of Australia, New Zealand and South Africa.

'Progressive' reforms under Roosevelt's presidency took the form chiefly of attacks upon monopoly and corruption and measures to facilitate self-advancement and to remove obvious exploitation, rather than to make provision for the needy. Hence the Food and Drug Act 1906 penalized both adulteration and undue profit from the manufacture of these products. This was, however, the period in which socialism and trade unionism flourished in the United States as never before or since, on the West Coast where syndicalist unions were strong, in the East and in the white rural South West. It had some influence upon the federal government under Roosevelt and in some 'Progressive' states, but faced powerful employer hostility.

In 1909 a federal income tax was introduced, for the first time offering a potential new source of revenue for federal action. There was little such action. Successive attempts to regulate child labour were frustrated by employer opposition. There was considerable discussion of provision for the unemployed, the aged, sick and children, of insurance and redistribution. In 1906 a Federal Employee's Liability Act was passed; and during 1911 ten states enacted workmen's compensation laws. By 1919 all states but three had introduced separate courts and treatment for juveniles. In 1912 the publicly-financed National Children's Bureau was established to collect and disseminate information concerning the welfare of children, following a public campaign similar to that in Britain concerning infant and child care. As elsewhere, this was motivated by the response to the high infant mortality and falling birth rates. The USA, like Australia, was simultaneously anxious to attract white migrants. However, the considerable Chinese migrant population in the West was treated with as little enthusiasm as were the blacks. Chinese immigration was indeed restricted from 1882. Legislation thereafter progressively limited migration of those of unacceptable colour, political views or physical efficiency.

In 1911 Illinois began to provide public funds for the care of children in their own homes. This was seen as a victory for

'Mothers Aid' – the equivalent of the British 'Endowment of Motherhood' campaign. The many voluntary agencies active in the field of child care and support to mothers were hostile to such public action but increasingly co-operated in its administration. By 1913 twenty states had emulated Illinois. In all of them the support was given primarily to widows; hence much of the USA was in advance of most other countries in providing non-punitive support for widowed mothers, in response chiefly to the plight of numerous widowed homesteaders in isolated and rural areas. The central concern, however, was for the health and welfare of the children rather than of their mothers. The demand for efficient 'human capital' was as great in the United States as elsewhere.

By contrast very little provision was made for the unemployed, other than local relief programmes in some states and municipalities. Health remained the concern of the individual, the employer, or of charity, as did care in old age and housing. The contributions of employers and philanthropy were considerable, as was the importance of mutual aid organizations of all kinds. After the family, they provided the main source of support for the American poor.[23] They emerged among those for whom there was no official or unofficial alternative, such as the southern blacks or among the small white farming communities of the mid-west. These developed, perforce in view of their isolation, a powerful tradition of independence, democracy and equality in which mutual aid played a part and which was also to be found among the many immigrant groups, urban and rural – Russian and Polish Jews and Italians in New York and elsewhere, Poles in Chicago, Germans everywhere – who partially carried on old traditions but were also driven by necessity and by the desire to retain their identity in the new society. The Poles in particular regarded it as a matter of personal and communal shame to appeal for support to the host community, and in particular to submit to investigation of their affairs by outside authorities. By such means large groups in American society provided for their own needs when sick, aged, unemployed, orphaned etc., both formally and informally. The extent of public provision at the local level in America has not, however, been systematically examined.[24]

Europe

In Europe, France also experienced widespread debate about social problems with, outside the field of education, limited results. Such provision as was made at central and local level, such as the old-age pensions provided for miners and railwaymen in the 1890s, was directed at key sectors of the industrial workforce. The large French peasantry was assumed as elsewhere to be capable of surviving, as it always had, by means of family and community support. French industry was based to a greater extent than in Germany, the USA or Britain upon relatively small family firms which made little provision for their workforce; trade unions as elsewhere provided some social security for members, but the level of unionization in France was low. The numerous small businessmen provided effective opposition to increased redistributive taxation for welfare benefits; and at least until the years immediately before the war, French socialists were too divided on the issue of public welfare, as on much else, to provide effective countervailing pressures.

In France, however, the population problem was especially acute. France had had the slowest rate of population growth in Europe in the second half of the nineteenth century. Growth continued to be slow thereafter and the infant mortality rate was, as ever, high. As a result of economic and, even more importantly, military concern about the demographic picture, following the defeat by Germany in 1871, France had by the 1900s the most extensive network of child welfare clinics and free or subsidized milk supplies in the world. Most were run by voluntary agencies, some by municipalities or with substantial municipal subsidy. Infant mortality declined sharply in the 1900s, as did general mortality, the latter assisted by the availability of free medical care for those in need from 1893, and by a law of 1902 which made anti-smallpox vaccination compulsory. The concern about infant mortality and population growth produced a considerable amount of literature on child rearing and the relative influences of hereditary and environment, from the late 1890s.[25] Changes in the law relating to the employment of children (from 1840), to their education (compulsory from 1882), the taking into care of child victims of family cruelty or neglect (from 1889), the provision of a separate more rehabilitative system of juvenile courts and penal or 'reformatory' institutions (in 1912) synchronized remarkably with similar changes in Britain.[26]

Due to the low birth rate the proportion of old people in the French population remained high at about 10 per cent compared with about 3 per cent aged over sixty-five in Britain. In 1911 a parliamentary commission proposed compulsory old-age and disability insurance for the employees of industry, trade and farming. Employees, chambers of commerce and employers all strongly objected to the proposal that they should contribute. Socialists and trade unionists again, as everywhere, preferred the 'right to work' and fully redistributive welfare. Only in 1910 was compulsory sickness and old-age insurance introduced for eight million urban and rural workers. However, a law court decision in 1912 questioning the legality of compulsion enabled a high proportion of employers and workers to evade the law.[27]

The Netherlands in 1913 introduced state non-contributory pensions for those over seventy, similar to those in Britain. In Italy (where Giolitti nationalized a life insurance company) and Austria, and in Russia, after the unsuccessful revolution of 1905, there were mild moves towards provision for the old, the very young and the sick.

Russia

In Russia poverty, even famine, and illiteracy remained severe alongside growing industrialization. This was as true of the peasants who made up 80 per cent of the population as in the industrial centres. Many urban workers were recent and often temporary migrants from the countryside, housed in overcrowded barracks. After the limited provision of health care and education through the *zemstvos* in the 1860s, the only gestures by the Russian state towards the impoverished mass of peasants were land reforms, introduced after the revolution of 1905, which mainly benefited a small number of better off peasants. The introduction of free primary education and increased salaries for school teachers only slowly penetrated the vastness of Russia. In 1915 only 49 per cent of children aged 8–11 were attending school; in rural areas the percentage was less than half of that figure. By 1918 the most literate section of the labouring population was that of urban male workers, 79 per cent of whom possessed some degree of literacy; only 44 per cent of female factory workers were literate. Russian peasants in this period gained more from migration to the USA or to Siberia than from state action.

Other 'welfare' efforts by the Russian government were confined to the minority of industrial workers. In 1897 working hours were restricted. In 1903 provision was introduced against industrial accidents. In 1912 two laws provided accident and sickness insurance, restricted to about 20 per cent of workers (those in the large firms which appeared to be central to the industrial advance sponsored by the absolutist government). They were financed from workers contributions and by a grant from employers, and were administered by boards composed of workers, five elected and four appointed (by employers).[28]

Between 1912 and 1914 the Bolsheviks, operating under considerable harassment, through their newspaper *Pravda*, worked to ensure that workers extracted the maximum benefit from these limited measures, since they recognized that the workers' committees established under the legislation were the only near autonomous workers' organizations in Russia, which the government could not easily suppress, having itself established them. Between 1912 and 1917 the Bolsheviks strove with some success to use these bodies with their worker-elected majorities not only to improve the welfare of workers, but, more importantly in their eyes, as respectable 'fronts' for political organization. In Russia insurance legislation contributed directly to the successful revolution.[29]

The education and insurance legislation excluded not only many peasants and urban females, but the many non-Russian minorities within the boundaries of the Russian Empire. Nationalism was pursued as vigorously as elsewhere, indeed considerably more brutally. Jews received the vote only in 1905, followed in 1906 by another in a long series of terrible pogroms. The non-Russian speaking inhabitants of the Baltic lands were not killed, but nor was their education or welfare encouraged.[30]

Scandinavia

In Scandinavia, Denmark, the wealthiest Northern country with the most developed labour movement, from 1907 provided for unemployment by means of government subsidy to, and supervision of, trade union unemployment funds. Norway underwent a period of accelerating economic growth and urbanization. From the 1880s to 1914 a debate continued among the Liberals who controlled the Norwegian government, the powerful Conservatives and the increasingly influential socialists and trade unionists concerning means of providing old-age and sickness benefits. This took a very similar path to that in Britain, with the labour movement deeply suspicious of 'capitalist welfare' and prepared to accept reforms only if they were redistributive. Hence they opposed social insurance, which was supported by Liberals and Conservatives, as being insufficiently redistributive. They attacked proposals for sickness insurance as 'a class insurance through which the ruling classes try to obtain a new guarantee against the poorest classes and thus a new injustice'. The socialists demanded free medical care, education, progressive taxation, and, in general, universality of benefits. In all three political groups, as in Britain, there was strong suspicion of the growth of central control. The chief legislative results in Norway were in extension in 1908 of national accident insurance to fishermen and in 1911 to seamen, both important groups in the Norwegian economy. In 1909 health insurance became compulsory for all wage-earners below a certain income level. It provided both benefits and treatment, the level of which was left to the discretion of local authorities. Broadly similar changes occurred in Sweden.[31]

In Finland, where the economy began to expand though at a rather slow rate, based primarily upon the timber industry, from the 1890s, discussion of social problems focused upon industrial problems, despite the fact that industry contributed only about 15 per cent of GNP up to 1914. The most serious problems of poverty were among small farmers and rural labourers, described in two studies in 1898 and 1901; while legislation concentrated upon industrial workers. In 1889 workmen's compensation was introduced, and in 1897 statutory poor relief funds. During the 1900s there was considerable discussion of social insurance, accompanied by the introduction of universal suffrage, and the foundation in 1907 both of a trade union federation and an employers' federation. No social legislation followed.

Conclusion

A wide range of societies with 'developing' economies between the 1870s and 1914 experienced an historically new upsurge of public and private interest in 'the social question'. The legislative outcome was everywhere meagre by 1900, and only a little better by 1914. Such new publicly-funded provision as emerged tended to help the rather more secure urban male worker, rather than the urban 'residuum', the rural labourer or peasant, or females. The aims of such provision were mixed, combining the desire for social improvement with those for social stability, national cohesion and economic efficiency. The growth of organized labour in all of these countries resulted from increased concentration of industry and increased pressure upon working people from unemployment and from management within the workplace. This growth of labour and socialist movements stimulated the expansion of public and private welfare. This was not simply, as is sometimes assumed, because workers demanded it, for they were often divided on the issue or actively hostile to state welfare. It derived partly from the desire of employers and politicians to check the very growth of labour. Working-class movements tended most to favour state welfare when they were closest to controlling its administration through close participation in government.

Even so, the nature and timing of the response varied according to the prevailing ideologies, economic and social structures of each society. As Richard Titmuss pointed out: 'When we study welfare systems, we see that they reflect the dominant cultural and political characteristics of their societies.' He might have added economic characteristics.[32]

REFERENCES

1. J. ROE, *Social Policy in Australia*, Cassell Australia Ltd (1976) Ch. 1.
2. K.-G. HILDEBRAND, 'Labour and Capital in the Scandinavian countries in the 19th and 20th Centuries', Ch. XI of *The Cambridge Economic History of Europe*, eds. P. MATHIAS AND M. M. POSTAN, Pt. 1, Vol. VII, Cambridge University Press (1978).
3. G. A. CRAIG, *Germany, 1866–1945*, Oxford University Press (1978) pp. 150–3.
4. W. A. ACHENBAUM, *Old Age in the New Land. The American Experience since 1790*, Johns Hopkins University Press, London and Baltimore (1978). P. STEARNS, *Old Age in European Society*, Croom Helm, London (1977).
5. G. A. CRAIG, *op. cit.*
6. L. E. DAVIS AND R. E. GALLMAN, 'Capital Formation in the United States in the 19th century', Ch. I of MATHIAS AND POSTAN, *op. cit.*, Vol. 2.
7. K. TAIRA, 'Factory Labour and the Industrial Revolution in Japan', Ch. IV of MATHIAS AND POSTAN, *op. cit.*, Vol. 2.
8. Y. LEQUIN, 'Labour in the French Economy since the Revolution', Ch. VI of MATHIAS AND POSTAN, *op. cit.*, Pt. 1, Vol. 1.

9. J. J. LEE, 'Labour in German Industrialization', Ch. IX of MATHIAS AND POSTAN, *op. cit.*, Pt. 1, Vol. 1.
10. E. E. LAMPARD, 'The Urbanizing World', Ch. 1 of *The Victorian City*, eds. DYOS AND WOLFF, 2 vols., Routledge & Kegan Paul, London (1973).
11. W. ASHWORTH, *The Genesis of Modern British Town Planning*, Routledge & Kegan Paul, London (1954) pp. 177–8; 185.
12. J. ROE, *op. cit.*
13. J. AXINN AND H. LEVIN, *Social Welfare. A History of the American Response to Need*, Harper & Row, New York (1975) Ch. 5.
14. P. MATHIAS AND M. M. POSTAN (eds.) *op. cit.*
15. G. RIMLINGER, *Welfare Policy and Industrialization in Europe, America and Russia*, John Wiley & Sons, New York (1971) p. 103.
16. P. THANE, 'The history of retirement at 60 and 65', *New Society*, (Aug. 1978); W. A. ACHENBAUM, *op. cit.*, pp. 48–51; P. STEARNS, *op. cit.*
17. G. A. CRAIG, *op. cit.*, Chs. III and VII; A. J. P. TAYLOR, *Bismarck*, Hamish Hamilton, London (1955); G. RIMLINGER, *op. cit.*
18. J. HARRIS, *Unemployment and Politics 1886–1914*, Oxford University Press (1972).
19. R. J. EVANS, *The Feminist Movement in Germany 1894–1933*. Sage Publications, London and Beverly Hills (1976).
20. K. TAIRA, *op. cit.*
21. J. ROE, *op. cit.*
22. J. AXINN AND H. LEVIN, *op. cit.*, p. 118.
23. J. AXINN AND H. LEVIN, *op. cit.*, Chs. 4 and 5.
24. W. I. THOMAS AND F. ZNANIECKI, *The Polish Peasant in Europe and America*, Dover Publications, New York (1958); R. PINKER, *The Idea of Welfare*, Heinemann, London (1979) Ch. 9.
25. T. ZELDIN, *France 1848–1945*, Vol. 1, Oxford University Press (1973) pp. 315–25.
26. J. DONZELOT, *The Policing of Families*, Hutchinson, London (1979).
27. P. STEARNS, *op. cit.*, p. 59.
28. O. CRISP, 'Labour and Industrialization in Russia', in Ch. VI of MATHIAS AND POSTAN, *op. cit.*, Vol. II.
29. S. MILLIGAN, 'The Petrograd Bolsheviks and Social Insurance. 1914–17', *Soviet Studies* (1969).

30. H. SETON-WATSON, *The Russian Empire 1801–1917*, Oxford University Press (1967).
31. H. HECLO, *Modern Social Politics in Britain and Sweden*, Yale University Press, New Haven and London (1974).
32. J. ROE, *op. cit.*, p. 7.

Chapter five

THE FIRST WORLD WAR AND AFTER

THE IMPACT OF WAR

The 'Great' war brought, for the first time in modern history, almost full employment in Britain, partly because millions of men were employed, and many of them destroyed, in the armed services. War at last provided the long sought device for syphoning off surplus labour. At first men were recruited into the services as volunteers, though under powerful pressure to enlist, not least from the insecurities of pre-war employment; then from 1916 as conscripts. The growth in industrial sectors essential for war production further increased job supply for both men and women. Women were employed in large numbers in the highly dangerous process of making explosives and increasingly, and in the face of much male opposition, in manual occupations previously exclusively male, such as engineering, as they were vacated by men entering the services. Not only working- but middle-class women entered newly opened occupations, many working women transferring from lower-paid traditionally female occupations such as domestic service. Middle-class girls (relatively few married middle-class women except in voluntary service) entered the workforce in large numbers, mainly in white-collar secretarial, teaching and clerical jobs, escaping for the first time from their chaperones and from boredom to freer lives away from home. Such women benefited decisively from the war. Wartime changes in the occupational structure enabled them to retain their jobs and independence after the war, when working-class women were thrust back into the home as mothers or as servants, or into other traditional occupations.

Paid work was no novel experience for working-class women. What was new was the wider range of occupations available and higher rates of pay, often at the insistence of trade unions. The latter, as much fearful that employers would take the opportunity about equality for women, demanded equal rates of pay for women with men in equivalent jobs. The average pay of women, however, remained below that of men.

Most importantly, during the war many men and women had *regular* employment for the first time, and considerable opportunities for working overtime, as important a gain for many of them as higher rates of pay. Where such employment was available, individual and family incomes rose as wives and daughters worked and as, also, younger and older people were drawn back into the labour force. A number of old-age pensioners eagerly forsook their meagre pensions when labour shortages offered them an opportunity to work. A shortage of teachers, as the men enlisted, led some local authorities tacitly to suspend compulsory education for older children.

Demand for employment was high in armaments-producing districts (parts of London, Carlisle, Birmingham, Glasgow, among others), shipbuilding towns on the Tyne, Mersey, Clyde and Thames, and in the countryside, as pressure mounted to be self-sufficient in food in the face of German blockades; textile districts benefited from the need to clothe the army; factories and ships required large quantities of home-produced coal.

It took time, however, for the economy to adjust to the changed demands of wartime. The initial impact of the war was to increase hardship as men went off to war leaving families unprovided for and as demand temporarily fell off, especially for export-based industries such as textiles. The numbers of malnourished children reported in the large towns rose.[1] Women in the 'sweated' branches of the clothing industry suffered acutely in the first months. Sylvia Pankhurst was horrified by the conditions she found among mothers and children in East London.[2] [doc 9] The numbers of applicants for poor relief increased in 1914–15.

Later, as industry was reorganized on a war footing, unemployment diminished. Unemployment statistics (covering only trade unions making returns to the Board of Trade) remain unsatisfactory for this period but give an indication of the trend: in 1914 3.3 per cent of trade unionists were reported as unemployed; in 1915 1.1 per cent; for the remainder of the war between 0.4 and 0.8 per cent p.a.[3]

From October 1914 the government began for the first time to pay allowances to the families of members of the armed services: these had previously been provided only from charitable funds. Now 12s. 6d. was paid to a dependent wife; 2s. to each child.

These allowances were extended even to the numerous unmarried cohabitees of servicemen, after some hesitation and only 'where there was evidence that a real home has been maintained'. From November 1915 pensions were paid to the widows and orphans of the war dead. The sums were small and often paid only after outrageous delays, but they at least removed such families from poor relief. Such measures and, still more important, rising employment and wages, led to a reduction from the end of 1914 in the intensified poverty of certain groups in the early months of the war.[4]

The beneficial effects of regular employment, longer hours (a financial if by no means a social gain) and rising wages in certain industries were offset by rapidly rising prices of essential goods. In June 1915 food prices were 32 per cent up on those of July 1914. Prices of sugar, meat, eggs and fish rose especially fast. Over the whole period of the war the retail price index rose 110 per cent. The cost of living for an unskilled workman's family rose by 81 per cent, for a skilled workman's family by 67 per cent. Rents rose fast in many large towns in the first year of the war.

Due to deficient information as to actual individual or family earnings, as distinct from official wage rates, it is difficult to estimate whether earnings rose faster than prices. The problem of assessing the impact of war upon living standards is complicated by the very different experiences of different occupational groups. The large numbers employed in occupations essential to war production almost certainly gained, at least in the latter part of the war. In these industries there was considerable labour militancy and willingness on the part of employers to appease workers in order to maintain high production and profits (as in munitions and engineering). The problem is further complicated by the rise of new industries, such as aircraft production, and technological change in old ones as employers strove through mechanization to overcome labour shortage. A major effect of the latter was to increase the supply and regularity of semi-skilled employment at the expense of skilled. This became a permanent feature of the post-war economy.[5] Other groups, such as clerical workers, experienced relatively fixed hours and wages, and it was in this sector that women most notably replaced men. Experiences varied considerably according to occupation. A government investigation in the northeast in 1917 reported:

The high price of staple commodities has undoubtedly laid a severe strain upon the majority of the working classes, and in some instances has resulted in hardship and actual privation. It is no doubt true that in some industries wages have risen to such an extent as largely to compensate for the increased cost of living, but there are workers whose wages have been raised very slightly, if at all, and some whose earnings have actually diminished and on these the high food prices have borne heavily.[6]

Families with a number of adult members obviously fared better than those with a number of young children.

A. L. Bowley concluded from a survey of wartime living standards that wage-earners in general benefited during the war, and that unskilled and semi-skilled workers gained relatively more than the skilled.[7] Wage-rate differentials between these strata narrowed and a general improvement in working-class living standards is also suggested by the decline in mortality among adult males who did not enter the services. For this it is difficult to construct any explanation other than improved diet despite rising food prices. Medical services for adults did not improve during the war, indeed they deteriorated due to the absence of 13,000 of the 24,000 pre-war doctors at war. Infant mortality continued its pre-war trend of decline.[8]

An official committee on the wartime working-class cost of living reported in 1918:

Fuller employment and more profitable employment do result in improvements in the workers' position under war conditions which, in turn, ensue largely to the collective benefit of the family, of which the worker forms part . . . we have found, on the evidence of the budgets of working class expenditure, that in June 1918, the working class as a whole, were in a position to purchase food of substantially the same nutritive value as in June 1914. Indeed our figures indicate that the families of unskilled workmen were slightly better fed at the later date, in spite of the rise in the cost of food.[9]

The evidence seems strong that by the latter stages of the war many poorer families were experiencing higher standards than before the war. Partly this was the result of the government's gradual and often reluctant introduction of rent controls (in 1915), price controls (from 1917) and (in 1917) effective rationing and food supply. The latter ensured adequate diets for all who could afford them, often of better standard than the very low levels of nutrition of many families before the war.

By the end of the war it had become conventional to comment upon the improved behaviour of the masses. Apart from a distressing tendency to strike, they appeared more regular in their habits, less prone to drunkenness and fighting; they looked less barbaric to refined eyes. The 'residuum' appeared almost to have disappeared. This was widely attributed to the success of restrictions upon sales of alcohol introduced during the war – the beginning of modern licensing restrictions – to prevent drunkenness disrupting the war effort.[10] More plausibly, it was the result of regular work and higher incomes.

If it is reasonable to suppose that very many working people benefited from the war, at least in respect of wages and nutrition, there is also evidence of a growing gap between this majority and a minority who were unable to take advantage of the new opportunities. Death rates rose among those over sixty-five, from 64.7 per 1,000 among males aged 65–74 in 1914, to 70.7 in the bad year of 1915, to 67.5 in 1917; among women of the same age they were 51.4 in 1914, 56.2 in 1915, and 52.2 in 1916, both reversing the pre-war trend of decline. In the first year of war there was pressure from trade unions and MPs to increase the 5s. pension to take account of price rises. In April 1915 the government responded minimally by allowing earnings and family support of up to 30s. per week, without loss of pension rights, for the duration of the war. Further pressure and demonstrations supported by churches, trade unions and Friendly Societies persuaded the government in 1916 to increase the pension by 2s. 6d. per week for pensioners suffering hardship due to price rises; and in 1917 to extend this to all pensioners for the duration of the war. Many pensioners who were unable to work must have benefited from the increased capacity of their families to support them; the difficulties of those who did not (and surveys preceding the introduction of old-age pensions in 1908 had demonstrated how many old people did not have families) were perhaps reflected in the rising death rate among the aged.

Similar problems befell all on fixed incomes, including the dependents of live and dead service men. War disablement and widows' pensions rose in 1917 to a maximum of 27s. 6d., plus allowances for children. They did not rise in line with inflation. The government persistently denied the existence of severe need by pointing to the declining numbers receiving poor relief. This, however, evaded the probability that although the numbers in severe poverty were lower than before the war their standard of living had absolutely deteriorated.[11] Charity made some provision for them, notably the Citizens' Committees of middle-class women formed in many towns which were especially concerned with child welfare. Charitable effort, however, tended to be concentrated upon war refugees, and the families of dead and wounded servicemen.[12]

The gap between those workers who benefited from the war and the mass of the middle class may have narrowed slightly, though all of them fell far behind the small group of employers who profited from war production, especially before 1916, after which the government mildly restrained business profits by restricting them to 20 per cent above the high levels of 1914. Taxation was raised a little in Lloyd George's rather timid budgets of 1914 and 1915. His successors McKenna and Bonar Law were bolder. Over the war period income tax was raised from 1*s*. 2*d*. to 6*s*. in the pound. It became more redistributive, ranging by the end of the war from 13 per cent on earned incomes of £500 p.a. to 43 per cent on earned incomes of £10,000 and over. Up to 80 per cent could be levied on excess profits after 1916. Changes in indirect taxes were slight. As a result the better off paid relatively more tax by the end of the war than did manual workers. Since most of the revenue went into the war effort the direct redistributive effects were slight. A minority of landed families were hard hit by death duties due to the premature deaths of one or more heirs. A number of landed estates were broken up as a result, slightly hastening a process discernible before the war. The war had, however, little lasting effect upon the distribution of wealth or income.[13]

Some of those of the working-class who experienced improved employment opportunities and diets suffered deteriorating living standards in other respects. This was especially true of housing. Construction, unless directly related to the war effort, almost ceased during the war. Building workers entered the services; factory building absorbed available labour, the war economy much investment. This alone would have worsened the already serious pre-war shortage of working-class housing. The problem was further worsened by the movement of large numbers of workers to the centres of war production, mainly cities such as London, Glasgow and Birmingham where the housing problem was already acute. The housing stock for the working-class was increased a little by the removal of the servantless middle classes into smaller houses, leaving their previous dwellings for multi-occupation. Nevertheless, the housing shortage remained acute in most larger towns and cities; severe rent rises resulted.

Munitions manufacturers, shipbuilders and other employers in acute need of labour partially met the problem by building for their own workers. Vickers Armaments Combine built half of the new housing in Barrow during the war. Clyde shipbuilders restricted rents on their housing in order to retain and attract labour. Such action, however, could meet only a tiny part of the need, which resulted in an unprecedented number of rent strikes and demonstrations for lower rents and better housing. Not only the poorer working-class were affected: the first of a series of Glasgow rent strikes began in May 1915 in a district of the city inhabited mainly by clerical, supervisory and skilled workers. Shopkeepers and tradesmen also suffered from rent rises and supported the militancy. Indeed, the fact that better off members of the working and lower-middle classes were more seriously affected by the housing crisis than before the war was one likely reason for the strength of the opposition to rent rises. Another was that the main objectives of the pre-war labour movement – full employment and higher wages – were achieving some success in 1915; many of the unofficial strikes of the war period were successful. This concentrated anger against housing as the remaining major problem affecting the everyday lives of many working people. Rent strikes and demonstrations in Glasgow, the London suburbs, Coventry and elsewhere were notable for a rare unity of skilled, unskilled and lower-middle-class men and non-working women.

As Willie Gallagher described a strike in the Govan district of Glasgow:

Mrs Barbour, a typical working-class housewife became the leader of a movement such as had never been seen before . . . Street meetings, back-court meetings, drums, bells, trumpets – every method was used to bring the women out and organize them for the struggle. Notices were printed by the thousand and put up in the windows: wherever you went you would see them. In street after street, scarcely a window without one: WE ARE NOT PAYING INCREASED RENT.[14]

The rent strikes in Glasgow and elsewhere led directly to the Rent and Mortgage Interest (Rent Restriction) Act 1915, which placed statutory restrictions upon rent and mortgage interest rises. Rent controls have never since been entirely removed. Thereafter housing conditions remained appalling due to the continuing low level of housebuilding, but this was not a problem which protest could solve in a war economy. Evictions for non-payment of rent continued, indeed rose substantially in Glasgow. This problem, which presumably most afflicted the poorest, caused little public protest. Working-class protest concentrated rather upon price rises and wages, often successfully, but there was never the same local unanimity on a single issue. Unity over rent controls did not develop into a more extended class struggle, partly because tenants did not face a capitalist class united against them. The main employers on Clydeside had actively supported rent controls, because high rents caused discontent at work and deterred labour from moving to the Clyde. They played an important part in persuading the government to control rents. Controls were opposed mainly by property-owners and financiers who were anxious to protect investment in housing.[15]

Medical care also deteriorated during the war, but not being for most people a day-to-day preoccupation, in view of the previous inadequacy of such care, this caused fewer crises than housing. By 1918 the number of school children examined by the school medical service had fallen by 28 per cent. The reason above all was the diversion of medical resources, personnel and equipment, to the war effort. This diversion took place, as did many things during the war, amid some chaos, as public and voluntary organizations (including the Red Cross) vied for control. For the first time the government subsidized voluntary hospitals to enable them to meet the needs of war casualties, thus enabling them to improve their facilities. On the other hand, doctors who in peacetime worked in voluntary hospitals had to face and to recognize the poor conditions and equipment of Poor Law infirmaries converted to war use. Their previous inmates were ejected or removed to hurriedly converted alternative institutions. Many voluntary hospitals closed their outpatient departments and civilian wards, or civilians were turned away after treatment with insufficient time for convalescence. All these problems worsened as the war progressed and casualties increased.

Although increasing numbers of nurses were trained, they remained insufficient to meet war and civilian need. In the struggle to keep nursing or medical staff for civilian care, Poor Law and voluntary hospitals were forced to increase pay in line with military pay. The TB sanatoria developed before the war were crippled; deaths from TB rose.

Deficiencies in civilian medical care may have contributed to the increased death rate of old people during the war and to the very high death rate in the exceptionally virulent influenza epidemic of 1918–19. However, the removal into military service of almost half of all doctors appears to have had no otherwise detectable effect upon the death rates of less vulnerable groups of young adults and children, except from TB. The impact of influenza (151,446 died) was so remarkably uniform throughout Europe, in belligerent and neutral, rich and poor, countries, and in all social classes, that it is difficult to ascribe the high death rate to any cause but the strength of the virus.[16]

One aspect of civilian medical care which did continue to improve throughout the war was that of infants. Infant mortality continued its downward trend during the war though at a faster rate except, again, in the bad year of 1915; the birth rate fell more sharply than before. The proportion of illegitimate births rose to 6.26 per cent of all births and the death rate was rather higher among illegitimate babies. One result was the formation in 1918 of the National Council for the Unmarried Mother and her Child.

The improvement in the medical care of mothers and infants continued to be encouraged by the LGB. Just before the outbreak of war a circular to local authorities had proposed that they undertake comprehensive ante- and post-natal care. The LGB offered to meet 50 per cent of the cost of clinics, health visitors for expectant and new mothers, increased hospital space and provision of skilled midwives. By 1916 this provision had progressed sufficiently for the LGB to offer to pay the salaries and expenses of inspectors of midwives, for nurses and health visitors, for the provision of doctors and midwives for the poor and for understaffed regions such as the north of England, for the full expenses of ante-natal clinics and for hospital treatment of infants. In this aspect of medical care there was no sign of pressure to reduce public expenditure in wartime.

Similarly, from 1915 the Board of Education financed child care classes for mothers, and the 1907 Notification of Births Act was extended to permit the appointment of local committees empowered to provide in any way they saw fit for the care of expectant mothers. The Midwives Act was amended in 1916 to make midwifery training more rigorous: midwives had now to take six months' training, to attend at twenty cases and to pass a written examination before qualifying. Nearly half of the 12,000 midwives who gave notice to practice in 1915 were untrained; between 50 and 75 per cent of all deliveries were attended by midwives. Most of these measures derived from concern about infant mortality and sickness, rather than with the health of mothers. The Milk and Dairies Consolidation Act of 1915 enabled local authorities to establish milk depots for the sale of milk for infants at cost price. In 1918 a Maternity and Child Welfare Act further enabled local authorities to establish grant-aided ante-natal and child welfare clinics.

The number of full-time health visitors in England and Wales rose from 600 in 1914 to 1,355 in 1918, many of them employed by grant-aided voluntary societies. The number of qualified midwives rose from 37,000 in 1914 to 43,000 in 1918, whilst the birth rate fell.

The absence of doctors hardly affected the mass of poorer women who had never experienced the attendance of a doctor at childbirth. For those who had, the absence may have been beneficial: unlike doctors, midwives rarely practised instrumental deliveries and the decline in the use of forceps may have led to a decline in the number of babies damaged by them. The continuation and expansion of infant welfare in wartime whilst other forms of welfare provision declined was partly due to its being concentrated in the hands of women. The pressure upon all women to participate in paid or voluntary work for the war effort drew large numbers into these activities. It was seen as 'a form of war work'. But the chief reason for such extensive official support and finance was fear for national survival. The Bishop of Fulham told an audience: 'while nine soldiers died every hour in 1915, twelve babies died every hour, so that it was more dangerous to be a baby than a soldier.' A *Daily Telegraph* leader proclaimed: 'If we had been more careful for the last fifty years to prevent the unheeded wastage of infant life, we should now have had at least half a million more men available for the defence of the country.'[17]

An Infant Welfare Propaganda Fund was established and paid travelling organizers to stimulate interest in the subject: two hundred health centres were said to have resulted from these efforts. Money poured in to this and other charitable funds for the same purpose; 'National Baby Week' was held in early July 1917: a week of propaganda on the infant welfare theme. As during the Boer War, such sentiments were encouraged by revelations of the large numbers of men deemed physically unfit for the armed services. Of every nine men conscripted for the armed services in the year 1917–18, three were reported as 'perfectly fit and healthy; two were upon a definitely infirm plane of health and strength . . . three could almost (in view of their age) be described with justice as physical wrecks; and the remaining man as a chronic invalid with a precarious hold on life'.

Better care in and before childbirth, mostly at home, accounted for part of the wartime drop in deaths in the first month of life. However, since only 60,000 of the 700,000 babies born in each year were under the care of health centres by 1918, the fall in mortality in the later months of infant life probably owed more to rising family living standards. It was further helped by the fixing of the price of milk in October 1917. Very little attention was given to the continuing high rate of maternal mortality which did not fall during or before the war, despite increasing expressions of concern on this issue from organizations of working-class women. They supported the lobby for improved free health services; they demanded maternity benefits for all women with incomes below the income tax limit, and of increased amount; maternity centres staffed by female doctors, cheap food for mothers and 'home-helps' for mothers of newborn babies. The heartrending *Maternity: Letters from Working Women* recounting women's experiences of repeated childbearing and child loss in poverty, published in 1915 by the Womens' Co-operative Guild, made their case widely known but as yet little heeded.[18] The improvements in infant health gave, as we shall see, further impetus to the movement for an integrated national health service.

Demands for 'national efficiency' were strengthened by the war in other respects also. The pre-war trend towards rationalization, i.e. merger and monopoly of businesses, progressed, as did the introduction of mass production techniques and 'scientific' methods of labour management. One aspect of the latter was increased provision of factory welfare facilities. These had been growing before the war and their expansion was encouraged by the government through the new Special Welfare Department of the Ministry of Munitions. Factory canteens providing cheap hot meals (by October 1917, 710 of these had been set up in works employing 920,000 munitions workers, half of all the munitions labour force), health centres, better sanitary and washing facilities, were a response above all to labour shortages and to the imperative of increasing productivity.[19]

The government took much closer control of economic and social life, including running essential industries, communications and distribution. With trade union agreement it 'intervened' increasingly in the organization of labour, banning strikes from 1915, conciliating in many of the unofficial strikes and regulating factory conditions. Food was rationed later in the war. As a natural result of this growing range of government activity the civil service grew in size.

Intervention was, however, reluctant and haphazard rather than planned, taken up slowly in response to crises, such as the shortage of munitions in 1915 and of food in 1917. Inside and outside government, the belief that government should not take on these responsibilities permanently remained strong. They were seen by many politicians and civil servants as temporary measures, to cease with the war. The resistance to grasping the wartime opportunity to achieve necessary long-term social changes was especially obvious in the failure to plan the transition from war to peace.

'RECONSTRUCTION AND REACTION', 1917–21

Lloyd George claimed in his speeches towards the end of the war that Britain faced a choice between 'reaction and reconstruction'; he implied that he preferred the latter. However, throughout the war the forces favouring 'reaction' were at least as strong as those for progress.

'Reconstruction' was a term in political vogue as early as 1915. It emerged early in the war because the war was expected to be short. Its meaning was different for different people and clear to few. There was much in British society in need of 'reconstruction', and a widespread but not universal feeling that society was being so changed by the war that exceptional conditions existed to facilitate further change. But there was no consensus concerning the degree or pattern of desirable change, and considerable influential opposition to change. Asquith, as Prime Minister until December 1916, established a small Reconstruction Committee which accomplished little. When Lloyd George ousted him he established a Ministry of Reconstruction headed by his supporter Christopher Addison, a doctor and a radical Liberal. Its purpose according to the War Cabinet was 'not so much a question of rebuilding society as it was before the war, but of moulding a better world out of the social and economic conditions which have come into being during the war'. Addison's Ministry established a number of subcommittees to investigate and recommend changes in aspects of social and economic policy.

Health

The recommendations of most of these committees were contentious and the resulting conflicts outlasted the war. Most fraught of all, due to the number of conflicting interests involved, was that dealing with health. Morant and Newman remained strongly committed to the establishment of a co-ordinated national health service. Addison shared their aim and all three believed that this could best be fulfilled by the establishment of a Ministry of Health whose very existence would emphasize the importance of their cause. This Ministry, Addison hoped, would remove health care from the Poor Law and take over the health responsibilities of the Board of Education and the National Insurance Commission. In particular he hoped to provide free services for 'the crucially important needs of women and children'.

These aspirations were broadly supported by Lord Rhondda, the President of the LGB from the end of 1916. However, when Rhondda's inclinations became public, the opposition began to mass. The LGB feared for its existence; the Health Insurance Commission objected to any association with the old LGB lest health insurance should be tainted by any link with the Poor Law; Poor Law Guardians feared to lose their health powers. Lloyd George's chief concern appeared to be to avoid a revival of the controversies of 1911 at a time when the Cabinet faced more serious concerns. His response was to move Rhondda to the Food Ministry. Rhondda complied only after extracting a promise from Lloyd George to establish a Ministry of Health – a promise that Lloyd George made and broke. Without Cabinet support Addison could do little to reconcile the warring interests. Rhondda's successor at the LGB, W. Hayes Fisher, was determined, along with his civil servants, that no new ministry would dismantle the existing powers of the Board.

A Ministry of Health was finally established in 1919, after Hayes Fisher had left the LGB, with Addison as its first Minister. Essentially it was the old Local Government Board with the National Insurance Commission attached. Its establishment was a compromise between the opposing factions. Its existence did not guarantee the improvements in national health care which Addison and his friends had sought, nor did it immediately produce any. Effectively the opponents of a national health service had won.[20]

The Poor Law

A major obstacle to the creation of a national health service under a Ministry of Health was the continued existence of the Poor Law. It had extensive health powers, yet while it continued to exercise them the administrators of other forms of health provision would not be associated with its stigma. Partisans of the Poor Law saw the campaign for a Ministry of Health as part of a renewed attack upon it and they had some reason to do so: the campaign against the Poor Law was mounting once more.

The evasion of Poor Law reform by the pre-war Liberal government, and their preference for dismantling it from without, had led
to the scattering of responsibilities for social administration around
some rather surprising corners of Whitehall. The Board of Education had wide responsibility for the health and education of
mothers and schoolchildren: the Privy Council was responsible for
the Midwives' Acts; the Ministry of Pensions (established in 1917)
administered service dependents' allowances and war pensions; the
National Insurance Commission was an independent body; the
Board of Trade supervised unemployment insurance; the Treasury
supervised old-age pensions, the LGB still controlled the Poor
Law, housing and infant welfare. As a result, individuals and families were served by different administrative bodies for similar and
often overlapping needs.

Efficient co-ordination was the keynote of much wartime
change. Those who favoured similar rationalization of the social
services did not believe that this was possible under the Local Government Board. It was felt to be too set in old habits and too much
dominated by Poor Law principles. This was largely true, although
some responsibility for its conservatism lay with the Treasury
which had long kept it understaffed and underfinanced. Over-
worked civil servants had little time to contemplate new approaches;
nor for a long time had they received imaginative leadership from
ministers or senior civil servants. Such experiences intensified at
the LGB the tendency towards inflexibility and preoccupation with
administrative minutiae to which any large bureaucracy is prone;
hence Addison's belief that effective co-ordination of social provision was only possible within a new Ministry of Health. Co-
ordination and improvement of health services also necessitated
dismantling the Poor Law.

Mrs Webb quickly realized that war conditions offered an
opportunity at last to bring this about. She was seized with a be-
lated desire to heal the breach, largely created by herself, between
the Majority and Minority Reports of 1909. When she was invited
by Asquith's Reconstruction Committee to prepare a memorandum
on Poor Law reform, she offered instead 'to get some sort of agreement between the majority and minority of the late Poor Law Commission and the Local Government Board'.

The result was the appointment by the Ministry of Reconstruction in July 1917 of a sub-committee chaired by Sir Donald Maclean, deputy speaker of the House of Commons. He was, as Lord
George Hamilton put it, 'a capable Chairman, especially since he

knew little about the subject'. The committee consisted of Mrs Webb and Lord George Hamilton (the leaders of the opposing groups of 1909), Morant, Sir Samuel Provis of the LGB and J. H. Thomas, the Labour MP.

The committee took no evidence, feeling that there was little need to add to the many volumes produced by the Royal Commission. They did however, for the first time, review the services which had developed since 1906. Their report, issued in January 1918, described the overlapping of services at the local level: administrative districts rarely coincided; seven different local authorities gave money in the home; six provided various forms of medical care, all operated different forms of assessment; relations among the services were poor if not openly belligerent. This 'complex evil', the committee mildly concluded, caused 'occasional failure to detect cases of need'.

The Report recommended that: the Board of Guardians and Unions should be abolished and their functions merged with those of county and municipal councils, who ultimately should take local control of all social services; the general mixed workhouse should cease to exist and be replaced by separate institutions for the separate categories of need; a new body, a Prevention of Unemployment and Training Committee of local authorities, should be created. Its function should be to provide public works and work-training to assist migration and to create and administer 'any specialized provision of the kind required by the unemployed'. It would also have 'new powers . . . for dealing with recalcitrant persons'. These were to include compulsory detention in labour colonies for those of the unemployed who refused re-training. The committee assumed that the further extension of unemployment insurance would reduce the numbers in need of local provision when, as they assumed, chronic un- and underemployment returned after the war. Perhaps in the interests of harmony, Mrs Webb did not insist upon her pre-war proposals for counter-cyclical public expenditure, although elsewhere she and Sidney Webb continued to support them. A committee of the local council to be called the 'home assistance committee' should supervise, on case-work principles, all social service activities. They should have supervisory powers over all families of which any member received benefits. Thus, it was hoped, needs would not go undetected.

The committee aimed for the destruction of 'less eligibility'. The new structure would be 'free from any suspicion of using the "workhouse test" and the policy of deterrence'. It should be implemented as quickly as possible in view of the likelihood, as the members believed, 'that the effect of the war will be to stimulate a demand for the improvement of social conditions'.

The Maclean Report embodied the main elements which the Majority and Minority Reports had had in common: the dismantling of the Poor Law and of the principle of deterrence, except for the recalcitrant 'residuum', and the establishment of specialized services for all categories of need within a nationally uniform structure. The proposed structure of specialized services co-ordinated by the 'home assistance' committee reconciled the minority's over-emphasis upon specialization with the majority preference for co-ordination of services and the treatment of the family as a whole. In their desire to present acceptable recommendations the committee neglected the difficult and controversial issue of local government finance.

With this exception, the Maclean committee offered a coherent and plausible alternative to the Poor Law. The Cabinet was persuaded by Addison to accept the Report, which was immediately opposed by Poor Law Guardians and the Poor Law division of the LGB. Even when he became Minister of Health, Addison was unable to overcome this opposition. After the war, discussion of Poor Law reforms again diminished.

The Poor Law's unscathed survival of the war suggests the strength of forces against change, as had the fate of health reform. Opposition to change could be especially effective when the leadership of the government was understandably more concerned with the war and the post-war settlement than with social policies. Lloyd George repeatedly evaded major conflicts by doing nothing. The supporters of the Poor Law, chiefly its administrators, were strong enough during the war to avoid reform and amid the industrial conflicts in the two years following the war they succeeded remarkably in presenting themselves as a major bastion against the near revolution which had afflicted post-war Germany, Italy, Austria and Hungary. By providing a 'safety net', they argued, they had protected the nation from political excesses resulting from starvation. They had little reason for such self-congratulation; severe poverty was considerably less in post-war Britain than in many continental countries. A more important reason for the survival of the Poor Law was the absence of any powerful political will or pressure to destroy it. As severe economic depression hit Britain from the autumn of 1920, after two years of unforeseen prolongation of prosperity, the difficulty of reforming the Poor Law mounted;

substantial claims for relief were renewed. The longest established official provision for welfare proved astonishingly resilient.[21]

Old-age pensions

One of the functions acquired by the new Ministry of Health from the defunct LGB was control over the local administration of old-age pensions (the pensions committees). At the end of the war the government was committed to the automatic withdrawal of the temporary wartime increase in pensions. Since prices remained high, a return to the pre-war 5s. pension seemed likely to cause considerable hardship and protest, so the government announced the continuation of the wartime concession pending the report of a Committee established in February 1919 under the chairmanship of Sir Ryland Adkins.

The most remarkable finding of this committee was the strength of opposition to almost every aspect of the 1908 pension scheme. All witnesses including civil servants believed that the pension should be increased, to amounts varying from 10s. to £1 per week, and the means limit substantially raised if not abolished. Only the Treasury defended the age limit of seventy; most witnesses advocated sixty-five. A group of Labour women's organizations, in one of the most comprehensive blueprints for reform presented to the committee, recommended a pensionable age of sixty for men and women. They pointed out that in many districts labour exchanges regarded women over sixty as unemployable, and that in general women found difficulty in obtaining work when they were past that age. Critics and no defenders were found for all of the disqualification clauses.

Surveys carried out by Labour women's groups demonstrated that almost half of all pensioners (450,000) had total incomes of under 10s. per week; many of them survived, somehow, on the pension alone, despite the fact that they would have been better off on poor relief: relief rates were rarely below 10s. per week by 1918 and sometimes as high as 15s. Others supplemented their pension by part-time work as cleaners or dressmakers, caretakers or night-watchmen. About one-third had some support from family or friends. Others lived in squalid rented rooms, or in common lodging houses for 4d. per night. One pensioner interviewed, a Mrs Thompson, had a total income of 9s. 6d. per week, 2s. being supplied by a charity. When rent, fuel and funeral insurance were paid for she had 2s. 10d. per week for food. The only meat she consumed was 4 oz. of bacon each week. She drank no fresh milk and a single tin lasted a fortnight. 4 oz. of butter, one loaf of bread, 2 oz. of tea and a little coffee formed the bulk of her weekly diet. Such testimony was supplemented by a sample of pensioners' budgets collected by Mrs Pember Reeves [doc 10]. These demonstrated that one of the greatest difficulties for pensioners was footwear: second-hand boots were rare in poor communities and new ones impossibly expensive.

It was clear that poverty in old age had been only slightly alleviated by the introduction of pensions. The difficulty of finding a better scheme acceptable to the Treasury had changed hardly at all. Treasury representatives informed the committee that they did not expect the economy to be better able to finance increased pensions after than before the war; hence they could not agree to anything more than the supplementation of the pensions of the most needy by poor relief. They would only countenance an increase if pensions were shifted onto an insurance basis [doc 11].

The committee considered the latter proposal but concluded that it would be politically unacceptable since people had become accustomed to non-contributory pensions. Also the difficulty remained of including the low-paid and women in an insurance scheme. They recommended a doubling of the pension to 10s. per week, and its supplementation by poor relief for those in need. A majority of the committee proposed the removal of the means test, due to the hardship experienced by those just above income limit. They also recommended further investigation of a contributory scheme for pensions to be payable between the ages of sixty-five and seventy and the abolition of the imprisonment and 'failure to work' disqualifications, the former because it imposed a double punishment, the latter because it had proved inoperable. Aliens and their wives were to receive pensions after ten years residence in Britain. Most members of the committee emerged from their investigations convinced that the pensionable age was too high and the pension too low, but that the Treasury would accept only minimal changes.

The Cabinet accepted all of these recommendations except the abolition of the means test. Instead, the means limit was raised by about two-thirds. The changes were rushed through Parliament in a single day in December 1919.

Housing

Addison had one more major preoccupation during the transition from war to peace: housing. Asquith's Reconstruction Committee had surveyed housing needs. It had offered no proposals but had concluded, in June 1916, what had been obvious to many before the war: that private enterprise could not meet national housing needs and that local authorities must be induced, possibly by government grants, to enter the field more vigorously. But, despite repeated pleas by Addison, neither Cabinet nor Treasury would commit themselves to a promise of post-war housing subsidies. As Minister of Reconstruction, Addison established the Salisbury Committee to estimate post-war housing needs and means of meeting them. It reported in August 1917 that 300,000 houses would be needed immediately after the war (certainly an under-estimate) and that local authorities should begin to plan housebuilding and to buy suitable sites with Treasury assistance. The Report urged that provision of sufficient housing should become a duty of local authorities and that they should have priority in the likely post-war scramble for building materials. In the same year the Committee of Enquiry into Industrial Unrest pointed out that poor housing conditions continued to contribute to this unrest, and that it could be dispersed only by a state commitment to solving a housing problem 'which appears to have grown too great for private enterprise to meet'.

Addison next established the Carmichael Committee to plan supplies of labour and materials for a post-war housebuilding programme. By the summer of 1918 it had drawn up proposals. The Tudor-Walters Committee meanwhile made recommendations about the construction and layout of working-class housing. Much influenced by the pre-war town planning movement, this committee recommended the building of low density 'cottage estates'. At the same time the thirteen female members (plus two female secretaries) of a Women's Housing sub-committee of the Ministry of Reconstruction surveyed the housing 'wishes and requirements' of working women in England and Wales. They recommended 'only such improvements as are demanded by working women themselves'. These included: larger houses of a higher standard of construction, with adjacent gardens; playgrounds and social centres; a separate bathroom; hot and cold water; cheap electricity supplies. They also usefully surveyed the most convenient and economical facilities for cooking and the possibility of communal laundries, cafes and holiday homes.[22]

Hence by the end of the war the government had to hand analyses of housing need and detailed recommendations for meeting it.

In spite of this no firm plans were accepted by the Cabinet before the end of the war. The immense potential boost to post-war employment that could have resulted from a planned building boom was ignored, despite government fears of post-war unemployment and the urging of the labour movement on just these lines. The LGB, as the Ministry responsible for housing, opposed the proposals of the Reconstruction Committee and had none of their own. Housing looked like another victory for chaos rather than for reconstruction, despite Lloyd George's public rhetoric in the last year of war about the need for 'Homes fit for Heroes'.

Only early in 1919, when Addison became President of the LGB and Lloyd George began to turn his mind from war and diplomacy to domestic issues, did his action begin to echo his rhetoric. Lloyd George urged the Cabinet that housing for the working classes must be pursued seriously if the masses were to be expected to retain any faith in their traditional leaders and to reject the spectre of Bolshevism which was haunting Europe in the wake of the Russian Revolution. Intelligence reports from working-class districts informed the government of marked unrest on the housing issue. Many strikers in the year following the war took up social and political as well as industrial issues. They dismissed, with reason enough, the wartime reconstruction promises as 'nebulous talk'. The grant of the vote in 1918 to all men over twenty-one, enfranchising the poorest, and to most women over thirty, added to the political urgency of the question. Housing remained an issue more central to working-class politics than health or the Poor Law. As a result there was strong pressure upon the government, from employers also, to act on this issue rather than upon other aspects of social policy.

With Lloyd George's support at last, Addison introduced the Housing and Town Planning Act 1919. This laid upon local authorities the duty of surveying local housing need and of providing for it at rents that workers could afford. They were to finance building by borrowing on the capital market, the loans being guaranteed by the Treasury. In effect this introduced the first large-scale government subsidy to local authority housebuilding. From the summer of 1919 until the end of 1922, 170,000 new dwellings were built under the Act. Under a second Housing Act, initiated by Addison in 1919, 30,000 houses were built by private enterprise with government subsidy. This was an especially remarkable achievement in view of the post-war dislocation, the notorious inefficiency of the building industry, and the inexperience of most local authorities in this field. Rent control was continued after the war. When in 1920 the government allowed 'some relief to the houseowner', with a 15 per cent rise in rents, there were renewed rent strikes on Clydeside, mainly among skilled workers. Strikes erupted again in 1922, though in neither year had they the solid support of 1915.

The cost to the Treasury was considerable, as, under pressure of demand, building costs and interest rates rose. The refusal of the building unions to accept 'dilution' of labour by taking on unemployed ex-servicemen to fill the shortage of skilled building workers slowed the building programme. All of these problems mounted during 1920. Most important in the end, however, was pressure from the City of London for a reduction in public borrowing. The City was disturbed by the dislocation of the capital market and the pressure on interest rates brought about by large-scale local authority borrowing for housebuilding. In January 1921 the Cabinet responded by cutting the housing programme and dismissing Addison from the Ministry of Health. Addison had little support in the Conservative-dominated coalition government elected in December 1918, in which there was considerable opposition to the principle of state intervention in the property market, as there was also in many local authorities. In June 1921 the Cabinet agreed to end housing subsidies. This had the full support of Lloyd George who remained Prime Minister. Amidst mounting unemployment, strikes had fallen off. It was now more important for Lloyd George to hold the support of Conservatives in Parliament than that of workers outside.

The gains from the Addison housing legislation were real, though small in relation to the need and locally various. Leeds built more houses than any other city: 3,329 in 1922. It was estimated that about 1,074,000 houses were needed nationally between 1919 and 1923; 252,000 were built.

For the first time, decisive state action had been taken on the major problem of housing. The initial post-war impetus died, due not only to the gathering depression but to the gathering strength of those who had always opposed it. It was the most costly social problem to solve. The amount of capital required aroused the powerful opposition of financiers whose political might by 1921 was greater than that of those in need of housing. Housing subsidies were seen to be becoming necessary before 1914; war conditions and labour reaction to them caused in 1919–21 a short-lived leap ahead into reconstruction which was speedily overtaken by reaction. However, as we shall see, the reaction was not total. The housing problem was never again as severe as before 1914.[23]

Unemployment

The reluctance of the war and post-war governments to plan post-war reconstruction was clearest on issues relating to the labour market: un- or under-employment and low pay. William Beveridge, who remained at the Board of Trade until 1916, saw the war as the perfect opportunity for a necessary restructuring of the labour market. In the early days of the war he was responsible for measures to relieve the widespread unemployment due to industrial dislocation. From 1915 he urged the checking of the unregulated rush of essential skilled workers into the services and, with Llewellyn Smith, the direction of labour into essential industries and the upgrading and training of semi-skilled male and female workers. In the longer term, Beveridge aimed to decasualize labour, especially on the docks, and to extend the coverage of unemployment insurance. By the end of the war Beveridge, together with Llewellyn Smith, had achieved legislation whereby 25 per cent of the workforce was included in the insurance scheme. They faced, however, considerable employer and worker opposition to its further extension. This was also true of decasualization. Employers were prepared to accept it during wartime but determined to retain flexibility in the labour market after the war; the workers feared that the alternative was regular work but for fewer people.

Beveridge also faced opposition from civil servants and politicians due both to hostility in principle to planned restructuring of the labour market and to fear that attempts at planning would increase labour militancy. The Cabinet, the Treasury and other Ministries also rejected proposals from Beveridge for planned demobilization after the war to prevent hardship amid the dislocation of the transition from war to peacetime production. Similarly rejected were Labour Party and TUC proposals for planned post-war investment in construction and other industries to counter the threatened unemployment.

As a result, when the war ended unexpectedly in November 1918, the government had made no plans for the impact of peace on the labour market. The Cabinet hastily introduced a non-contributory 'out-of-work donation' for ex-servicemen and civilians. In addition, servicemen were to be demobilized gradually to assist their absorption into the labour market. This caused considerable dissatisfaction and even mutiny among men kept idle for months in French camps.

The rates of 'out-of-work donation' were high in comparison with other cash benefits: 29s. per week for men, 24s. for women, plus dependents' allowances of 6s. for the first child and 3s. for other children. It was available to all ex-servicemen for twenty-six weeks in the first year after demobilization, and to any civilians who had paid health insurance contributions for thirteen weeks between December 1918 and May 1919. It cost £62 m. by May 1921 when the last payments were made.

Its high cost at last convinced the Treasury of the virtues of wider unemployment insurance cover. The donation was regarded as a strictly temporary measure, but it did much to raise popular expectations of the desirable level and coverage of benefit. In mid-1919 the Treasury established a committee, including Beveridge, to propose new insurance legislation. The result was the Unemployment Insurance Act 1920. This extended the 1911 scheme to all manual workers and to non-manual workers earning less than £250 p.a., with the exception of agricultural workers, domestic servants and certain groups among whom unemployment was rare, mainly civil servants and teachers. The rates of benefit were 15s. for men, 12s. for women, with half-rates for those under eighteen, i.e. lower than the rates of 'out-of-work donation'. No more than fifteen weeks' benefit could be claimed in any one year. The Act passed with little comment during a period when unemployment was lower than had been anticipated.[24]

Low Pay

Pre-war surveys had consistently shown low pay to be a more serious cause of poverty than unemployment. There was no obvious reason to expect it to be less so after the war. The Fabians had long advocated a national minimum wage. In 1916 Beveridge gave this partial support by proposing a minimum wage for the largest low-paid group – women. Like so many of his other proposals, this was ignored. Also in 1916 a minimum wage was established for munitions workers, and for agricultural workers in 1917. During the war, Trade Boards were extended to a wider range of non-unionized industries and by 1921 they covered sixty-three occupations and three million workers, many of them rather better paid than in the 'sweated' industries for which the Boards had been established in 1909. Also, following a 1917 recommendation of a government sub-committee under J. H. Whitley MP, 'Whitley Councils' were established in certain industries to represent both employers and trade unionists, to discuss not only wages and conditions, but participation, job security, technical education and improvements in management.

The Ministry of Labour, as the Board of Trade Labour Department became in 1917, placed much hope in these councils. They would, they hoped, pave the way towards an effective minimum wage, greater worker participation in industry and closer co-operation between workers and employers, regulated by the participants rather than by government – 'home rule for industry' as this dream was known to the Ministry. The Whitley Councils, however, were greeted without enthusiasm by the largest trade unions, who regarded them as a stratagem to circumvent collective bargaining. But they had something to offer non-unionized workers, and by 1921 they covered 3.5 million workers. They gained little from them, however, due to the unwillingness of either the post-war governments or employers to give genuinely equal weight to the needs and opinions of workers. They were most successful among white-collar and municipal employees.

Many trade unionists were unenthusiastic about actions which they interpreted as increasing state control. 'Servile state' arguments remained influential during and after the war. Many activists preferred to progress via free collective bargaining to improved wages, conditions and participation in industry, on terms established by themselves rather than by government. As before, there was tension within the labour movement between this suspicion of the growth of the bureaucratic 'enslaving' state and the belief, strong in the political movement, that wartime controls and planning should be retained and extended, since such controls on the free market could pave the way towards a socialist planned society.

At the end of the war the Wages (Temporary Regulation) Act empowered the government to maintain the wartime wage level for eighteen months, to prevent too catastrophic a wage decline when industry changed onto a peace footing and the labour market was flooded with demobilized servicemen. The Cabinet and some prominent employers flirted with the notion of establishing a minimum wage. There were, however, considerable difficulties in its path: a minimum wage would increase demand and could therefore be inflationary; it might also lead to pay demands from higher paid workers anxious to preserve pay differentials relating to skill and custom. If the now largely unionized skilled workers could effectively preserve these differentials, the relative position of lower paid workers would not improve. It might also lead to unemployment, as employers sought technological and other means of reducing a rising wage bill.

Few of these implications were recognized in 1919 except partially by the Webbs, whose influence upon government policy was minimal. The minimum wage was powerfully opposed for other reasons. The new Ministry of Labour felt that fixing of wage levels on a national scale was inconsistent with the policy of 'home rule for industry' and would arouse the considerable latent opposition to bureaucratic intervention. Trade Boards and Whitley Councils, the Ministry believed, could, through local negotiation, achieve wages closer to the actual variable needs of workers than a nationally fixed minimum.

There was a further problem as to whether the wage should be based on the needs of the worker (which varied according to size of family) or upon the ability of the industry to pay. The former consideration was to be a major focus of debate throughout the interwar years. One solution to it, increasingly advocated by women's organizations during the war, was family allowances. These, it was argued, would solve the problem by supplementing incomes according to family size. They were not yet seriously considered by the government. The Ministry of Labour's approach came under increasing attack. As prices fell and unemployment rose from the end of 1920, employers in affected industries complained that Trade Boards were fixing artificially high wages. Unions pressed for preservation and extension of the scheme; their suspicions of state intervention diminished when it appeared to be their only bastion against gathering depression. More importantly, the Treasury had disliked the extension of Trade Boards beyond the 'sweated' industries, in which the Treasury recognized the need for improved wages. They regarded the extension of the system as intruding to an unacceptable degree into the free market. From early 1920 the Treasury frustrated the proliferation of Trade Boards by restricting the number of officials who could be appointed. This was an aspect of a general increase in Treasury control over the civil service after the war. In the post-war reconstruction of the Civil Service the Treasury was established as the premier department.

The combined attack by the employers and the Treasury, part of a general attack upon public expenditure in 1921, brought the expansion of the Trade Boards to an end in 1921. With them went any hope of establishing a minimum wage. It had no powerful political support. Lloyd George's enthusiasm for this, as for other things, had been high in 1919 but was extinguished two years later. As with housing, a brave attempt to tackle a major social problem was almost destroyed by 1921.[25]

Education

Education experienced a similar fate. Post-war changes in the education system were more effectively planned than other social policies. By 1916 the Board of Education was proposing an improved post-war future for a system then in some disarray. In December 1916 H. A. L. Fisher, an historian and vice-chancellor of Sheffield University, became the first professional educator to be appointed President of the Board of Education. In March 1917 a Committee on Juvenile Education criticized the trend to premature withdrawal of children from school into work and recommended their improved education.

Early in 1917 Fisher appealed to the Cabinet for a large state subsidy for education. In August 1917 he placed a major Education Bill before the Commons, hoping that a new structure could be established for immediate implementation when the war ended. Optimistically, he referred to the 'increased feeling of social solidarity which has been created by the war', which he believed would increase public willingness to finance mass education.

The Bill proposed, among other things, raising the compulsory leaving age to fourteen, the abolition of half-time education, and the introduction of compulsory part-time education for young people over fourteen who were in employment. 'Social solidarity', however, had its limits. Local authorities and employers opposed the Bill; Fisher was accused of encroaching too much upon the rights of parents. The Bill was withdrawn.

It was reintroduced in a modified form in 1918 and passed in July 1918. This major Education Act instructed all local authorities to submit plans covering all levels of education in their districts. The school-leaving age became fourteen; compulsory day continuation schools were introduced for those in employment between the ages of fourteen and eighteen; all fees in elementary schools were abolished. Schools were to be provided for handicapped children; nursery schools were to be established. For the first time elementary schools were to provide advanced courses for their older and more able pupils, beyond the very basic curricula previously provided. Fisher hoped to pave the way for raising the compulsory leaving age to fifteen. He intended to improve standards of education for children over the age of eleven who remained in the higher forms of elementary schools, having failed, due either to poverty or inability to pass the examinations, to transfer to local authority or voluntary secondary schools. Technical training for children over the age of eleven was also encouraged. The earnings of elementary school teachers were to be doubled and their pensions trebled. The financial rewards of teaching became sufficient for it to rank thereafter as a middle-class rather than a working-class occupation, at least for women, whose professional opportunities were otherwise still limited. The Board of Education maintained however that 'in material prospects the teaching profession can never hope to compete with other professions'.

These reforms were intended both to improve opportunities for working-class children and to assist the economy, the former taking priority in Fisher's eyes. A major problem concerning the latter was a shortage of graduates caused by war enlistment, since most undergraduates were male. Fisher aimed to repair this by increased government subsidies to universities. The University Grants Committee was established in 1919 as an autonomous agency for channelling state funds to universities, with minimum state interference in their activities. In 1920, 200 state scholarships were instituted. More finance was also given to teacher training colleges.

The post-war education system provided more and better education for working-class boys and girls. It also provided greater, though still limited, avenues for upward mobility for those who could pass the examination at age eleven to enter a grammar school and then attain one of the 200 free university places – provided also that their parents could afford both to forego their incomes from the age of fourteen and to provide the uniforms and other unsubsidized costs of entry to essentially middle-class schools. Since many could not, secondary education remained acutely socially stratified. Entry to the élite stratum, the unsubsidized public schools, remained closed to poor children.

The system was able to expand to educate all to the age of fourteen and increasing numbers thereafter, largely due to the availability of sufficient numbers of educated middle-class girls to staff the system. This was due to a combination of the pre-war expansion of girls' education and the continuing restrictions on their occupational opportunities. Even the legislation of 1918, which opened the civil service, the legal and other professions to women, in practice provided only limited new opportunities for unmarried women.

Despite the availability of teachers, many of Fisher's hopes were dashed by severe expenditure cuts in 1921.[26]

Expenditure cuts

Demands for economies in all aspects of public expenditure mounted in the early months of 1921. It was argued that such expenditure, by necessitating high taxation, restricted necessary industrial investment and that industrial expansion was further hampered by the limitations on the free market entailed by certain of the wartime and post-war measures. The *Daily Mail* and other papers launched a furious 'anti-waste' campaign, pillorying 'squandermania'; MPs and the City demanded economies. All of this fitted perfectly with the existing long-held Treasury view of the correct government approach. With powerful Treasury support, growth of government expenditure stopped in most areas. The next step was to cut it. In August 1921 the government appointed a Committee under Sir Eric Geddes (a businessman and wartime Minister of Transport) to examine the following year's estimates and to recommend economies. Its first Reports were issued in February 1922 and recommended severe cuts in all social expenditure.

The belief that the economy could only be revived as a result of expenditure cuts did not go entirely unchallenged. At least one civil servant in the Ministry of Labour, John Hilton, argued that: 'The present slump is due not to high prices but to the falling off in demand.' Anticipating the later arguments of Keynes he argued that unemployment could be reduced not by cutting wages but by raising them, to increase demand and hence production. He made no impact upon the prevailing preference for cutting expenditure. As we shall see, the 'Geddes axe' cut sharply into the limited post-war advances in social policy.[27]

Conclusion

The dismantling of such wartime and post-war policy changes as were introduced is often attributed simply to the Depression and the prevailing Treasury view as to how it should be reversed. Rather, the Depression appears to have strengthened the already very powerful forces which had always preferred 'reaction' to a situation closely approximating that before the war, to 'reconstruction'. We have seen that many, though not all, politicians and civil servants had always regarded the growth of government intervention in wartime as a regrettable temporary necessity. They blocked many attempts at planned 'reconstruction', with the result that many of the measures taken at the end of the war were hasty and their implications ill-considered. As soon as the war ended, Members of Parliament, the newly formed Federation of British Industries and other employer organizations successfully insisted upon the dismantling of wartime controls on industry; of the mines and railways, food supplies and price controls. They were not strongly opposed within the civil service. Against those, such as Beveridge, who remembered the poverty of the pre-war years and were anxious to grasp the wartime opportunity for planned reconstruction, were many who saw no need for permanent change. Many influential individuals looked back to a nostalgic vision of the Edwardian period from which gross poverty, industrial, feminist and Irish unrest had been removed. The war had not fundamentally changed their views. Their characteristic cry after the war was for a return to 'business as usual'.

In so far as there was progress in social policy during and after the war, it was due less to an increasing sense of social solidarity in the face of total war, as is sometimes argued, than to social and industrial conflict (as with rent controls) and to the desire for 'national efficiency' (as with infant care).

Employers were divided in their attitudes to social policies. Many of them had discovered before the war the gains to productivity which might derive from social welfare. Also labour had grown in strength, organization and political influence during the war and both politicians and employers feared the effects of withdrawing benefits and promises too hastily, especially amid the revolutionary fever which had infected much of Europe since the Russian Revolution. However, once, by 1921, labour was weakened by unemployment, the balance of power shifted back to those employers, civil servants and politicians who had always felt that post-war social policies had given the workers too much. Like labour, employers had become better organized and had acquired new lines of communication with politicians and civil servants during the war; some of them at least used this influence to destroy the new social policies, often in the sincere belief that expenditure cuts were essential to save the economy in the long run.

Hence few of the lasting changes resulting from the war, for good or ill, had their origins in conscious governmental social and economic policies. The reorganization of industry, stimulated by the demands of the war economy and shortages of skilled labour, permanently changed the structure of the labour market. The civil service had grown in size and had acquired habits and experience of intervention which did not disappear after the war. The future of many 'human factors of production' was also determined by Britain's permanent loss of overseas markets whilst she was absorbed in war, to countries such as Japan and America which were not, a loss partly facilitated by the decline in the role of the City of London as the centre of world finance. The electorate trebled after 1918. Labour was a more effective political party as a result of its participation in wartime government and its increased numbers of potential voters. The wartime experience had increased the confidence of organized labour and the belief that it could carry equal or greater political weight than that of employers, but employers also were more organized and influential than before. The effective political world in Britain was larger and organized on different lines after the war. The experience of almost full employment, higher incomes and strong signs that the government could be forced to provide better housing at controlled rents, profoundly influenced attitudes and expectations in the coming years.[28]

OTHER COUNTRIES 1914–20

Discussion in Britain of the relationship between war and social policy has been extensive but somewhat insular. If any useful generalizations can be made they must be applicable at least to some other societies. We have seen that the war did not bring to Britain, at least in the short term, any spectacular, lasting, planned social gains, rather a number of unplanned changes whose implications were ambiguous.

Both 'reconstruction' and 'reaction' took more dramatic forms in a number of other European countries. Most profoundly affected was Russia, where the revolution of October 1917 brought to power the first socialist government in the world. For the first time a government was theoretically committed to the planned achievement of social and economic equality. The problems of advancing this in Russia were considerable, with its vast poverty deepened by war and with an acute shortage of experienced administrators, teachers and doctors. The difficulties were further exacerbated by the hostility of other governments and of owners of capital, especially in view of the extreme dependence of pre-revolutionary Russian industry upon overseas investment. Hence despite efforts to increase and equalize incomes and to improve social security and other services it was not until the early 1920s that the USSR was able to begin to build a new society rather than to ward off crisis.[29]

Lenin expected Russia's problems and her isolation to be diminished by successful revolutions elsewhere, above all in Germany. In the later part of the war Germans suffered from food and fuel shortages far more severe than in Britain. In November 1918 the autocratic monarchical state founded by Bismarck was replaced by the parliamentary republic of Weimar, elected by direct universal suffrage. The majority party in control of the new government was the now distinctly non-revolutionary SPD. Like the British Labour Party, the SPD had participated more closely than before in government during the war and had gained in respectability as a result, although it had experienced a split between left and right. Militant trade unionism had also gained strength during the war. This, combined with the failure of the government both in military and civilian organization, brought about the post-war change in the structure of government. It did not, however, break the considerable power and influence of the army and of the bureaucracy, nor did the new government succeed in doing so.

The SPD had achieved their dream of controlling a German republic, but in the worst of circumstances. Even the minimal planning for the transition to peace demonstrated in Britain was impossible in a defeated country in disarray. Hunger and unemployment were widespread; bands of leaderless troops wandered the country. Left-wing socialists in Bavaria, opposed to the moderation of the new government, declared a socialist republican Bavaria, inspired by the Russian example. In January 1919 the Spartacists, led by Rosa Luxemburg and Karl Liebknecht, made a similar attempt in Berlin. Soldiers' and sailors' councils were formed at major bases and workers' councils in large industrial towns. Socialists took over local government in many localities. Much of this activity was not consciously designed to bring about a Russian-style revolution, so much as to achieve short-term economic and social security and, in the longer term, greater social justice by peaceful means. However, after 1917 fear of any possibly revolutionary manifestation was strong among non-socialists and the moderate socialists of the SPD feared that a premature revolution would strengthen the right; the potential revolution was crushed by the SPD government allied with the army.

Thereafter the government tried to plan for peaceful social and economic transformation, for example, they retained and strengthened the rent controls introduced in 1917, but faced strong opposition, especially in the civil service.[30] Germany's treatment by the victors in the war strengthened the forces which argued that German self-respect demanded reassertion of traditional values. The views of conservative nationalists outweighed those of social reformers. For example, the Weimar Constitution specified a uniform type of elementary school for all children and that entry to secondary school should be determined by talent rather than by income. It urged local authorities to give financial assistance to poor children, with very few results. The Constitution in this as in other respects was little more than a declaration of intent. One of the few changes in education was the admission of women to the universities. Previously this had been forbidden in some states, including Prussia, and rare in most.

Women had made an important contribution to the German war effort: caring for the families of servicemen, directing women to jobs made vacant by mobilization, and maintaining the supply of foodstuffs. They established soup kitchens, worked in hospitals and with orphaned children. A feminist was placed in charge of the war office department concerned with female labour. The demand for the vote revived at the end of the war, the women appealing to their contribution to the war effort. It was supported and ultimately conceded by the SPD. As in other countries, it was less the female war effort than changing political alignments which ensured that women got the vote at around this time. They received it in Denmark in 1915, Norway in 1913, Finland in 1907, Holland in 1917 and in Russia after the revolution.[31] The Weimar Constitution piously guaranteed equal rights for women. Their employment opportunities, however, remained extremely limited.

The German political right was strengthened in the elections of June 1920; the forces both of reaction and of socialist reconstruction were more aggressive than in Britain and there too the former ultimately won. However, the strength of the movement for reconstruction was strong enough to lead to continuing conflict in the coming years.

The whole of central Europe suffered starvation, influenza and political upheaval at the end of the war – it was in disarray due to the breakup of the Austro-Hungarian Empire. In this situation of economic and political crisis a short-lived socialist republic was established in Hungary and was almost emulated in Vienna. Shortly after the armistice Beveridge was sent to Berne as British delegate of an inter-allied mission on the relief of German Austria. He found Vienna 'literally starving', with women and children suffering especially severely. In Hungary and Czechoslovakia conditions were almost as bad. The relief mission was able to organize some supplies. Beveridge tried to persuade the British representatives at Versailles to urge the victors to organize food supplies and the speedy economic recovery of the defeated nations, lest distress should lead to further conflict. Again he failed. A year later he found Vienna still starving. Whatever slight social solidarity the war had engendered did not cross national boundaries.[32]

Italy, the one allied power to have been defeated by the Germans, also experienced severe poverty during and after the war. She found difficulty, after the war, in establishing a stable government. In the major industrial towns, notably Turin, workers' committees occupied the factories, part of the international movement of the post-war years for shorter hours, higher pay and greater participation in the running of industry and of politics. Peasants marched, struck and occupied land, wringing from reluctant landlords more favourable shares of their produce. The size and effectiveness of these movements of labouring people combined with the international fear of Bolshevism led directly to a re-grouping of the forces of reaction, the growth of fascism and Mussolini's seizure of power in 1922.

Among the countries which had suffered most during and after the war, political and social formations were decisively changed by the war. Set against these cataclysmic changes, social policies were of minor significance, although the context of their later development was decisively changed. They could only be implemented effectively in stable and reasonably prosperous societies and compared with most of her European allies, these conditions of stability existed in Britain. The same was largely true of France. Parts of Northern France had suffered seriously during the fighting, as had Belgium – from 1915 the German-occupied areas suffered near starvation and the destruction of industry during the fighting. In France, as in Britain, the state assumed new responsibilities for the organization of the economy including the allocation of food and labour. There also this role was taken up hesistantly, and on the assumption that it would be temporary. Controls were rapidly dismantled after the war. During the war, however, adequate food supplies were maintained. Women made an unprecedented contribution to the economy, although they were not rewarded with the vote until 1941. The demands of war production led to the restructuring of industry and improved living standards for many industrial workers and peasants. As in Britain, significant numbers of businessmen entered the government.

After the war the French government faced the urgent need for the physical reconstruction of much of northern France, far greater than any equivalent need in Britain. A compulsory national town planning law of 1919 required every damaged community to make improvement plans. A law of November 1918 allowed the public expropriation of whole zones in need of reconstruction. Every new building had to conform to new standards of construction and sanitation and the reconstruction was heavily subsidized by the state in the form of full compensation for wartime losses. This led to considerable profiteering and a public expenditure crisis. There were continuous and largely successful strikes in France during the war, followed in 1919–20 by an even bigger strike wave which fed fear of Bolshevism, but had few long-term successes.[33]

The world outside Europe was relatively untouched by the war, except in so far as non-European economies gained from Europe's absorption in warfare. Japan experienced a period of rapid growth in opportunities and investment accompanied by the further development of new-style management and state guided social provision. The Factory Law of 1911 was finally implemented in 1916, with further elaboration: it specified the frequency and method of wage payment, although the amount of wages was left to private agreement; the continued schooling of employed school-age youths had to be guaranteed by the employer; young workers and women discharged due to no fault of their own were entitled to travel expenses to their homes; employers could be fined for non-compliance; compensation for injury at work was introduced, also disability and death benefits and a funeral allowance; employers might, but were not forced to, pay redundancy allowances. In 1921 state employment exchanges were established. Health and old-age pensions insurance schemes were introduced but were not to be implemented until 1927. In Japan as elsewhere the trade union movement grew rapidly, providing welfare as well as industrial benefits. As unemployment grew, so did strikes.[34]

The US economy also gained from the war, which it entered in 1916. The pre-war growth of the labour movement came to an end with a sharp employer reaction from 1916. 'Progressive' policies at federal and state level continued their slow uneven pace.

In Australia, however, the pre-war social initiatives came almost to a halt after 1914. Apart from expensive repatriation and rehabilitation services for ex-servicemen, Australia no longer 'led the world' in what had previously been seen as an uninterrupted march towards what was later known as a 'welfare state'. The Australian economy benefited vigorously from the war. Labour split over the issue of military conscription and after the war lost ground to nationalist conservative parties in Commonwealth politics. However, Labour continued to dominate some state legislatures. Ex-servicemen and their dependents were favourably treated for fear that should they return to face unemployment, seeds of Bolshevism planted in their minds in Europe might grow. The war was followed, however, by no trace of breakdown in public order.

The pre-war establishment of a minimum wage was eroded, firstly by price rises then by government action leading to Higgin's indignant resignation from the Arbitration Court. A Commonwealth Department of Health was established in 1921 but like its counterparts elsewhere it made little progress towards a national co-ordinated health service. In some states there were continuing developments in infant and maternal care.

Trends discernible before the war contributed to this near stasis in Australian social policy during and after the war. In an expanding colonial economy in which the most prominent and least obviously culpable groups had been cared for, 'self-help' was thought preferable for the rest and its pursuit an essential element in growing national pride. The counter pressures were weak in a largely unchanged social structure.[35]

The 'war to end wars', then, changed much in the societies most fundamentally disrupted by it, though not necessarily, especially in the defeated nations, in the direction of greater social solidarity and progress. In these countries the reverse was rather more evident. Elsewhere the beneficial outcomes of planned change were few and short-lived. More important were the structural social, economic and political changes in all countries closely involved in the war, and the re-orientation of the international economy, the implications of which, intensified by depression, were soon to become evident.

REFERENCES

1. A. MARWICK, *The Deluge*, Penguin, Harmondsworth (1965) p. 133.
2. S. PANKHURST, *The Home Front*, Hutchinson, London (1932).

3. B. R. MITCHELL AND P. DEANE, *Abstract of British Historical Statistics*, Cambridge University Press (1962) p. 65.
4. A. MARWICK, *op. cit.*, p. 43.
5. A. MILWARD, *The Economic Effects of the World Wars on Britain*, Macmillan, London (1970) (Studies in Economic and Social History) pp. 24–44.
6. A. MARWICK, *op. cit.*, p. 222.
7. A. L. BOWLEY, *Prices and Wages in the UK 1914–20*. Oxford University Press (1921).
8. J. M. WINTER, 'The Impact of the First World War on Civilian Health in Britain', *Economic History Review* (Aug. 1977).
9. *Ibid.*, pp. 500–501.
10. A. MARWICK, *op. cit.*, p. 329.
11. *Ibid.*, pp. 133, 144.
12. R. G. WALTON, *Women in Social Work*, Routledge & Kegan Paul, London (1975) pp. 91–101.
13. A. MILWARD, *op. cit.*, pp. 24–44.
14. S. DAMER, 'State Class and Housing: Glasgow 1875–1919', in JOSEPH MELLING (ed.) *Housing, Social Policy and the State*, Croom Helm, London (1980) p. 93.
15. J. MELLING, 'Clydeside Housing and the Evolution of State Rent Control' in MELLING (ed.) *op. cit.*
16. J. M. WINTER, *op. cit.*, B. ABEL-SMITH, *The Hospitals*, Heinemann, London (1964) Chs. 16 and 17.
17. WINTER, *op. cit.*, p. 498.
18. M. LLEWELLYN SMITH, (ed.), *Maternity – Letters From Working Women*, reprint, Virago, London (1977); J. M. WINTER, *op. cit.*; J. LEWIS, *The Politics of Motherhood*, Croom Helm, London (1980).
19. A. MARWICK, *op. cit.*, pp. 121–3.
20. B. B. GILBERT, *British Social Policy 1914–1939*, Batsford, London (1970) Ch. 3; F. HONIGSBAUM, *The Struggle for the Ministry of Health*, George Bell & Sons, London (1972).
21. S. & B. WEBB, *English Poor Law History*, Pt. II, Vol. II, Longman, London (1929) Ch. VIII.
22. W. ASHWORTH, *The Genesis of Modern British Town Planning*, Routledge & Kegan Paul, London (1954) pp. 195–6; B. B. GILBERT, *op. cit.*, pp. 137–61.
23. B. B. GILBERT, *op. cit.*, pp. 137–61; J. MELLING, (ed.) *op. cit.*, Introduction and pp. 139–67.
24. J. HARRIS, *William Beveridge*, Oxford University Press (1977) Ch. 9; B. B. GILBERT, *op. cit.*, Ch. 2.

25. R. LOWE, 'The Erosion of State Intervention in Britain 1917–24', *Economic History Review* (May 1978); K. MIDDLEMAS, *Politics in Industrial Society*, London, Andre Deutsch, 1979, pp. 137–8.
26. A. MARWICK, *op. cit.*, pp. 297, 306.
27. C. L. MOWAT, *Britain Between the Wars*, Methuen, London (1955) p. 130.
28. A. MILWARD, *op. cit.*, pp. 44–52; K. MIDDLEMAS, *op. cit.*, pp. 68–151; P. ABRAMS, 'The Failure of Social Reform 1918–1920', *Past and Present* (1963).
29. E. H. CARR, *The Russian Revolution from Lenin to Stalin 1917–1929*, Macmillan, London (1979).
30. G. CRAIG, *Germany 1866–1945*, Oxford University Press (1978) Ch. XI.
31. R. EVANS, *The Feminist movement in Germany 1894–1933*, Sage Publications, London, Beverly Hills (1976) Ch. 7; R. EVANS, *The Feminists*, Croom Helm, London (1977).
32. J. HARRIS, *op. cit.*, pp. 245–7.
33. T. ZELDIN, *France 1848–1945*, Vol. II, Oxford University Press (1977) pp. 1086–92.
34. K. TAIRA, 'Factory Labour and the Industrial Revolution in Japan', Ch. IV of P. MATHIAS AND M. M. POSTAN, (eds.) *The Cambridge Economic History of Europe*, Vol. VII, Pt. 2, Cambridge University Press (1978).
35. J. ROE, *Social Policy in Australia*, Cassell, Australia (1976) Ch. 2.

CONDITIONS

The inter-war years are popularly remembered as a time of depression. There are good reasons for this. Unemployment mounted from the end of 1920 and during the two following decades significant numbers of people suffered long-term unemployment. Statistics of unemployment, though still imperfect, were available and regularly published. The staple industries of the pre-war years – coal, engineering, shipbuilding, textiles – declined, bringing mass unemployment to industrial towns in South Wales and the North and hunger marches of unemployed men to the South.

But this was not the whole picture. From the mid-1920s new industries began to develop and old ones to diversify and to introduce new methods of production; electricity, domestic appliances, motorcars, cycles, aircraft were produced. New iron and steel products and new textiles, such as rayon, were made by old industries. The service sector also grew fast. However, many of the expanding industries were lighter than those in decline, employing a higher proportion of women and concentrated in the Midlands and South of England. To these regions they brought reasonable though not uniform prosperity; a boom in housebuilding covered them with semi-detached suburbs; the number of chain stores and smaller shops, and of services such as hairdressing and cinemas, multiplied. Many of the employed for the first time took holidays with pay: eleven million after the Holidays with Pay Act of 1938. The new occupations on the whole provided fairly regular employment, though seasonality persisted in the building trades, electricity and even in motor-car manufacture. Indeed, too rosy a picture of the new occupations and life in the 'boom' areas would be misleading. Work on a production line paid at piece-rates, under close

supervision, according to the increasingly fashionable tenets of sci-
management, could be dreary, frustrating and insecure for those
unenthusiastic about submitting to discipline. New semi-detached
houses were too often 'jerry-built' and cramped. Areas of poverty
persisted even within 'boom' areas.

Nevertheless, by the late 1930s Britain was split by a new kind
of social, economic and geographical division. The majority of
those who were in work experienced rising real incomes and living
standards; those who were unemployed experienced poverty,
though a poverty with different causes and often among different
people from that of the pre-war years. All, however, gained from a
fall in food prices.[1]

Responses to poverty were also different. The Depression rather
than the equal, possibly greater, prosperity of the period has lived
in popular memory because it was concentrated geographically and
because it was difficult for the relatively prosperous of the time to
ignore it. They also feared that if the familiar world could once
change so thoroughly, it could change again and for the worse. The
unemployed made their distress felt by the tragic marches of gaunt
men through the southern towns. They provided endless grim
copy for newly flourishing mass communications. When most
households possessed a radio and took a daily newspaper, and the
cinema with its newsreels was at a peak of popularity, more was
known, if imperfectly, about the world outside the individual's
immediate community.

Also it was difficult to blame the unemployed for their condition. They, in turn, were not all the helpless 'residuum' of the
pre-war years, growing up with no experience but poverty. Many
of the unemployed belonged to trades and communities which had,
with reason, long prided themselves on their hard work and respectability. Skilled engineers and shipbuilders, and many miners, had
not grown up expecting months or years of unemployment and dependence. They experienced it not as the normal way of things but
as an affront, though not one that they could easily challenge. They
were affronted too by the investigations of their circumstances, the
means and character tests, which stood in the way of unemployment relief. They had learned to regard these, wrongly but profoundly, as society's just means of dealing with the feckless voluntarily destitute. They were reluctant to forsake the skills that in the
past had been the passport to respectability if not to prosperity; but
even when they were willing to retrain and move to new jobs they
found that new industries had little need of middle-aged miners or

engineers when younger or female labour could be had at lower cost and with no tradition of trade union organization or industrial conflict.

Workers in traditional industrial occupations who kept their jobs also posed new problems for employers and for the government. Better organized and more confident than before the war, they were less willing to accept reduced wages. But militancy among the employed, as among the unemployed, was constrained by a certain hopelessness about the prospects for labour, especially after the failure of the 1926 General Strike. This contrasted with the optimism of the pre-war years, deepened with the Depression and was relieved only a little by the coming to power of Labour governments in 1924 and in 1929–31, since both were minority governments constrained by the difficulty of obtaining a parliamentary majority and by uncertainty about the solution to economic depression.

However, the fact that Labour could come to power at all suggested the degree of change from pre-war political configurations. The Liberal party was divided and diminishing as an effective political force from 1916. The leading theorists of social reform of the period – notably R. H. Tawney, G. D. H. Cole and, still, the Webbs – were closely associated with the Labour party, although the pre-eminent economic theorist J. M. Keynes supported the Liberals.

The response of the increasingly powerful Treasury and of the City of London to the Depression had, however, changed little since before the war. As we have seen, their first response was to demand and to achieve cuts in government expenditure (the 'Geddes axe'). This was a manifestation of a comprehensive view of correct procedure which prevailed in financial circles, including the Treasury. This was that the Budget should be balanced by contraction of government expenditure rather than by increasing revenue through increased taxation (which was held to increase business costs and to reduce demand); by controlling inflation through limiting the printing of paper money (as had been done during the war) and ceasing public borrowing for 'unproductive purposes' (such as social services). A central role in the achievement of these aims was played by the controversial return to the gold standard in 1925. This restored the pre-war automatic link between the supply of money and the supply of gold in the country. Hence if Britain imported more than was exported this deficit would have to be financed in gold, the gold supply would fall and less money would be available for investment and for public and private expenditure.

This was expected to lead to unemployment, falling wages and lower prices which would, it was assumed, boost exports further, creating economic recovery.[2]

This model remained influential throughout the 1920s, until it became clear, at least to some, that it was not having the desired effect. The central problem was that, the labour movement being more organized than before the war, wages and hence costs did not fall as the model required; rather the attempts to reduce business costs further increased unemployment. Also world trade was at such a low level that exports could not recover as quickly as was assumed. Arguably also the parity between gold and paper money fixed in 1925 was too high, thus raising the cost of exports, although it is not certain that this contributed as much to the rise in unemployment as the other two factors. In general, Treasury policy in the 1920s had the intentional effect of increasing unemployment, on the assumption that this was a necessity in the short term in order to achieve long-term prosperity. Throughout the 1920s and with diminishing force in the 30s the Treasury and the Bank of England defended this orthodoxy against the increasingly influential alternative theories of Keynes.[3]

The nature and causes of deprivation varied between declining and expanding areas and over time. Unemployment itself was a major cause of poverty, palliated to some degree by unemployment benefits, yet it became clear from contemporary social surveys that unemployment was not the only, and probably still not the major, cause of poverty. Evaluation of real changes in living standards for the employed was no easier after the war than before. More women, many of them transferred from the declining domestic service sector, were employed in manufacturing and new service industries from the later 1920s onwards, a factor which had some influence upon family incomes. Many of them were unmarried and it is possible that the opportunities for poorer mothers to supplement family incomes by casual and part-time employment diminished, as, for example, commercial laundries took the place of the washerwoman, and tenants of the growing numbers of new council houses were forbidden to take lodgers.

At the same time, family size and hence family costs declined sharply. The birth rate reached its lowest level in 1933, continuing the pre-war trend and spreading it further among the working classes, due partly to the spread of knowledge about contraception. At the same time infant mortality continued to fall, to 80 per 1000 in 1920–22, 64 in 1930–32 and 55 in 1940–42 in England and Wales.

The Scottish figures remained higher. Maternal mortality rates did not fall until the later 1930s, being 4.03 per 1000 live births in 1911–25, 3.90 in 1921–25, 4.30 in 1931–35, 3.26 in 1937. Again the rates were higher in Scotland.[4]

Wage rates, regularity of employment and the incidence of over-time of course varied among occupations. Few wage-rates rose in the period and many fell, especially after the crisis of 1929. The average weekly wage was about £3 per week throughout, but coal-miners were more likely to earn nearer to £2 and agricultural work-ers less. Women still rarely earned more than half the pay of men. Real incomes, however, rose, due to falling prices of food, domes-tic goods and clothing, though not of housing. This benefited all, including those on fixed incomes such as pensioners – fortunately, since the 10s. pension did not rise during the period.

Social surveys found fewer in severe poverty compared with the pre-war surveys. Bowley and Hogg repeated in 1924 their five towns survey of 1913, calling the published conclusions *Has Poverty Diminished?* They adopted the same stringent poverty line used in 1913 with slight adjustments for changing habits of life (2 lbs. of 'butcher's meat' per adult per week was now included in the diet). They remained aware of its deficiencies. They assumed that the minimum wage now required by a family of five was 37s. 6d. per week and they found 6.5 per cent of the working class still in poverty in the five towns (Reading, Northampton, Warrington, Bolton, and Stanley, Co. Durham). The survey was taken before the Depression made its major impact, for example in the Bolton cotton industry or in Durham mining. Only 2 per cent were found to be in poverty in Bolton (a textile town) in 1924; this compared with 12.6 per cent in 1913. They found 11.3 per cent of children under fourteen to be living in poverty overall, compared with 12.6 per cent in 1913. In Reading as many as 46 per cent of children had been in poverty in 1913; there were 14 per cent in 1924. However, the continued extent of child poverty was the most alarming finding of the survey. This and other forms of poverty resulted mainly from insufficient wages or the absence, death or disability of a male head of household. Fewer families were dependent on poor relief and charity than before the war. Bowley concluded that the lowest wages had risen during and since the war, leaving only those with large families or lacking a regular male income vulnerable to severe poverty.

The *Social Survey of Merseyside* of 1928, carried out by Liverpool University, reported 16 per cent in poverty, only 2 per cent of whom received any public assistance. This survey used a rather more stringent poverty line than others of the period, influenced by the Merseyside tradition of survival amid severe poverty and low pay. The *New Survey of London Life and Labour* headed by Llewellyn-Smith, published in 1934 but carried out in 1929–30, partly repeated Booth's great London survey and applied his definition of poverty. They found, after forty years, that around 14 per cent of the population of 'Booth's East London' were 'subject to conditions of privation which, if long continued, would deny them all but the barest necessities and cut them off from access to many of the incidental and cultural benefits of modern progress'. The percentage for the whole county of London was 9.6. In Poplar 24 per cent were in poverty, compared with 44.6 per cent in the 1880s; in Bethnal Green 17.8 per cent, compared with 44.6 per cent. The survey found that almost half of East London poverty was caused by unemployment and under-employment. Improvement there had been, but the authors saw no room for complacency, especially as regards unemployment and poor housing.

In 1936 Rowntree repeated his study of York using a slightly more generous poverty line than in 1899, which allowed for a higher level of food expenditure and a very small margin above bare necessity for such items as newspapers and a wireless. He, like the other investigators, was aware that the sum fixed as the poverty line still cut clothing 'down to an unsatisfactory minimum'. He found 18 per cent of the York population to be in poverty, half of these in 'primary' poverty. Those beneath the poverty line included half of all working-class children over the age of one. Again there was improvement since the war, but not, in Rowntree's view, enough. He found low pay to have diminished as a cause of poverty, unemployment to have risen.[5]

A 1931 study in Southampton, a relatively prosperous town, found that 34 per cent of working-class families with dependent children were in danger of falling into poverty.[6] These conclusions were reinforced by Tout's survey of Bristol at the end of the 1930s. Bristol experienced little unemployment, and had shared more than most in the growth of new industries – indeed, it was one of the most prosperous manufacturing centres in the country – yet 10 per cent of a sample of wage-earning families were in poverty. Worst off, again, were those with large families and no adult male in regular work.[7]

All the surveys showed old-age, sickness and widowhood still to be significant causes of poverty. Rowntree's 'cycle of poverty' still operated. All the surveys defined poverty stringently and were carried out over short periods of time. The numbers very close to poverty and experiencing it at some point in their lives were considerably larger. Professor John Hilton estimated in 1938 that 17 per cent of all families had no margin whatever for saving; hence any crisis could plunge them into poverty. A survey by Sir John Boyd Orr in 1936 for the Ministry of Agriculture found 10 per cent of the population (and 20 per cent of children) to be very badly fed, and up to 50 per cent 'ill-fed'. His findings were open to criticism: the national sample was small and the standards of nutrition used not generally accepted in a field in which knowledge remained far from complete. A later more careful survey by Colin Clark showed the position to be less bad in smaller towns but severe in London, and among children even worse than Orr had suggested.[8]

Other investigations suggested that cleanliness and general health increased with improved housing and water supplies. In London in 1912, 39.5 per cent of children were found to be verminous, in 1937 7.9 per cent. In Northampton the average height of a boy of 12½ rose from 55.4 inches in 1910–13 to 57.3 inches in 1933; his weight from 74.3 lb. to 79.9 lb. However, Boyd Orr found the average heights of boys of fourteen at a public school, at Christ's Hospital (a charitable foundation) and at a council school to be 63.7 inches, 61.1 inches and 58 inches respectively. The relative class differences in height had not changed since 1883.[9]

It was clear that, as a result of wartime changes in the labour market, by the early 1920s the quantity of severe poverty had diminished. The size of the underemployed 'residuum' had contracted, unskilled jobs were rather more regular and better paid, although casual employment continued to be normal in certain occupations such as building and dock labour. Another important influence upon living standards was the decline in family size. The incomes of the increasing numbers with small families did not buy prosperity but enabled most to avoid poverty. The narrowness of the margin is suggested, however, by the numbers in poverty who had more than two dependent children. This was as true in the growth areas of new industry as in the depressed areas – indeed possibly more so, since unemployment benefit included children's allowances, whereas wages did not.

In 1938 the German *emigre* economist Jurgen Kuczynski demonstrated the extent of the continuing problem of low wages. He compared Ministry of Labour wage statistics for 1935 with Rowntree's 'human needs' standard of 53s. per week for a man, wife and three children. He showed that about two-thirds of cotton weavers needed a rise in weekly full-time earnings of 33 per cent or more in order to reach Rowntree's minimum. The proportion of workers in various industries who earned wages below this level was: in coal mining 80 per cent; in railways 25 per cent; in building 50 per cent; in textiles 40 per cent of men and 50 per cent of women; in clothing 12 per cent of men and 35 per cent of women. In all, four million adult male workers and two million adult female workers earned less than the minimum. This, including dependents, affected ten million people. Kuczynski pointed out that between 1931 and 1938 real wages had risen by only 5 per cent and industrial production per employed worker by 20 per cent.[10]

As Kuczynski's figures suggest, there were few signs of change in the distribution of wealth and income during the period. In 1911 wages took 38.1 per cent of national income; in 1924 42.1 per cent; salaries 13.6 per cent and 25.4 per cent respectively. The growth of service occupations had increased the number of salary earners, although many of these salaries were low. The share of profits decreased from 33.8 to 25.1 per cent in the same period. The proportion of national income going to super-tax payers was 8 per cent in 1911 and 5.5 per cent in 1924. It rose thereafter. Bowley estimated that in 1910 1.1 per cent of income receivers took 30 per cent of national income; in 1929, according to Colin Clark, 1.5 per cent took 23 per cent.

In 1919 2.5 per cent of the population over the age of twenty owned two-thirds of all wealth; by 1930 there had been little change. The very wealthy made slight gains during the 1930s. In 1913 the working class paid in taxes more than it received in social services. In 1925 it still paid 85 per cent of the cost of social services, including national insurance, but received £55 m. more than it contributed. By 1937 it received between £200 m. and £250 m. more: the effect was to raise working-class income by between 8 and 14 per cent. Some redistribution was at last taking place but it was slight. Death duties and super tax in particular had some effect in reducing the largest incomes – though it, too, was slight.[11]

PROVISION

The poor, as ever, helped themselves and one another, assisted by pawn-shops and credit, including the new and increasingly flourishing system of hire-purchase. State social provision and commercial insurance, however, continued to replace Friendly Societies as sources of support. Charity increasingly operated in close co-operation with, and often subsidized and directed by, statutory authorities.

This continued the pre-war trend. It is unclear how much, if at all, the numbers and amounts of money devoted to voluntary effort declined. The much criticized indiscriminate alms-giving so commonplace in the later nineteenth century almost disappeared after the war. Female charitable activity increasingly took the form of unpaid service, for example as health visitors, and of membership of children's care committees and pensions' committees, responsible to public officials such as Medical Officers of Health. Many of the advances in policy in the pre-war years had depended upon this voluntary service. By 1918 most provincial COS branches had been replaced by less ideologically militant Guilds of Help and Councils of Social Service, which achieved the degree of co-operation with public social services for which the COS had unsuccessfully aimed. Voluntary organizations, however, retained an important innovative role in providing and agitating for groups neglected by public policy, such as unmarried mothers and their children. Much voluntary effort was co-ordinated by the influential National Council of Social Service. Increasingly, by the 1930s, voluntary donations and effort were directed towards relief for the unemployed in the depressed areas.

Despite, and to some degree because of, the economic crisis the growth of action concerning social and economic problems by central and local government was more striking than in the previous generation. This change was accompanied by increased control by central and local government.

Unemployment and economic policy

The problem of unemployment was central to the politics of the inter-war years, a major influence upon political and economic practice and theory. In the 1920s and 30s, as never before, the state provided for the unemployed. The story of this provision is a complex one of constant detailed shifts of policy. Its theme was the desire of successive governments to provide enough to prevent unrest without giving so generously as to offend the City of London or to raise the spectre that, as the economist Barbara Wootton put it, 'the working classes would belie their name'.[12]

The slump in trade in 1921–22 was followed by a fall in manual earnings due partly to diminishing availability of overtime which was not fully compensated by price reductions. The *Economist* estimated that working men had lost three-quarters of their wartime wage increases by 1922.

The numbers of unemployed persons covered by unemployment insurance rose from 691,103 (5.8%) in December 1920 to 1.3 m. in March 1921, to 1.9 m. in December 1921 (16.2%) and 1.4 m. in December 1922. In shipbuilding 36.1 per cent of insured workers were unemployed in December 1921, as in the same month were 36.7 per cent in iron and steel, 27.2 per cent in building. Twenty-five per cent of the insured in Northern Ireland were unemployed, 21 per cent in Scotland, 18 per cent each in the Midlands and North-East. Hartlepool had 60 per cent unemployed in August 1922, parts of Glasgow 59 per cent.[13]

These percentages of *insured* unemployed underestimate total unemployment, as do all unemployment figures for the period. Those above omit those not covered by insurance. The number officially recorded as unemployed was not to fall below a million for nearly twenty years, fluctuating between 8.7 per cent of insured workers in May 1927 and 22.4 per cent in September 1931. The trough was reached during the world-wide decline in trade and industry following the Wall Street Crash of 1929.

Such large-scale unemployment destroyed the foundations of the unemployment insurance system, which had never been designed for such a crisis. Immediately the government effectively abandoned the insurance principle. Under the Unemployment Insurance Act of March 1921, those in occupations covered by the insurance scheme could receive benefits for up to forty-seven weeks in any year, although contributions were calculated to cover only fifteen weeks. This concession was named 'extended benefit'. Contributions were raised, but not sufficiently to cover the benefits paid. As a result the unemployment insurance fund went increasingly into deficit. 'Extended benefit' was intended to be temporary because the length of the Depression was not anticipated – it was not yet recognized that industry faced major problems. Lloyd George, however, as Prime Minister, renewed his pre-war advocacy of a national development fund through which the government would lend on capital schemes designed to expand industry and exports. The Trade Facilities Act 1921, provided a fund of £25 m. (more limited than Lloyd George had hoped, due to opposition from the Bank of England) which made loans to industry, without discernible effect, until its abolition in 1927.

'Extended benefit' remained in force for five years; after further amendments in April 1922, benefit could be drawn almost continuously. This situation arose because the employment insurance scheme had been intended to cover only short-term unemployment. No other official provision existed for the long-term unemployed apart from the Poor Law.

Long-term 'insurance' benefits were expensive. The government responded so generously, despite continuing calls to slash public expenditure and actual cuts in other areas of public policy, largely due to fear that unemployment and poverty in Britain would lead to revolutionary upheavals such as had shaken post-war Europe. Realistic or not, these fears were fed by widespread strikes in 1920 and 1921, notably a bitter coal strike, by demonstrations of the unemployed and the formation in 1921 of the National Unemployed Workers Movement (NUWM) by the Communist Wal Hannington. The Communist Party of Great Britain was formed in 1920. These fears were further encouraged by alarming weekly reports to the Cabinet from the Home Office Directorate of Intelligence, of disturbances among the unemployed.

The rate of unemployment insurance benefit was 15s. per week for males, 12s. for women. Pressure to equalize male and female benefits foundered on the problem that this would raise female unemployment benefits above those for female health benefits (12s.) and provide an incentive for women to claim unemployment benefit when actually sick. Fifteen shillings was in any case an insufficient sum on which to support a family even with falling prices. Under strong trade union pressure, and still fearing unrest, in the autumn of 1921 the government introduced dependents' benefits into the unemployment insurance scheme, 5s. for a dependent wife or husband, 1s. per child. Having previously conceded such bennefits for the post-war 'out-of-work donation', the government was in a weak position to refuse their reintroduction as unemployment mounted.

Falling prices increased the real value of unemployment insurance benefits throughout the 1920s. The rates of benefit were also increased in 1924, 1928 and 1930. In real terms benefit for a family of four rose by 240 per cent between 1920 and 1931. Although contributions rose, by 1931 the scheme was costing the state £37 m. p.a., 23.3 per cent of all social service expenditure (compared with 3.4% in 1920).

Even this sum did not provide for all of the unemployed. Many workers, including all agricultural labourers and domestic servants, were excluded from the unemployment insurance scheme. The government also continuously sought ways further to restrict the coverage and cost. This was considerably assisted by a clause in the Unemployment Insurance Act of 1922 whereby 'extended' benefit was payable only to those 'genuinely seeking whole-time employment but unable to obtain such employment'. By the end of 1923 one in twenty of all claimants were failing this test.

The test was justified as a means of preventing abuse by malingerers but was difficult to implement due to imperfect knowledge in many areas of the amount of work available 'genuinely' to be sought. The labour exchanges administered the scheme, but received notification only of one-fifth of all vacancies. The discretionary criteria by which extended benefit might be granted or refused were never published. Effectively the test was an investigation of character, whereby officials assessed, on little evidence, the propensity of the claimant to malinger.

The chief effect of the 'genuinely seeking work' test was to exclude married women from benefit. They were assumed to have less need for a full income than a man and they were less likely to protest at its withdrawal. The debate about women's unemployment in the 1920s was dominated by upper-class conviction that women would use any means to avoid redressing the shortage of domestic servants. Often, however, they had no choice – it was the only work available for women in many districts, and from the end of the war the Ministry made it clear that if a woman had ever done service it was still suitable work for her; if domestic vacancies existed, she could not receive benefit. As in the case of pre-war health insurance, fear of the propensity of women to 'scrounge' vastly outdistanced the extent of the problem, whose very existence was never established.

In February 1922 a means test was introduced for extended benefit as a further cost-cutting measure. It was applied to single persons resident with relatives (unless they could demonstrate that the relatives were unable to support them), married persons whose partners were in work, short-time workers and aliens. Effectively it removed from benefit those with incomes above 13s. per week. The numbers receiving the benefit immediately fell, although the test was administered more stringently in some districts than others. Overall, however in the 1920s fewer of the unemployed were disallowed benefit as a result of the means test than under the 'genuinely seeking work' clause. How many were deterred from applying by the existence of both tests is of course unknown.

The means test was, not surprisingly, vastly unpopular. The first

Labour government removed it in 1924, despite opposition from employers. Labour was much less critical of the 'genuinely seeking work' test, indeed the 1924 government tightened its administration. Respectable working people had always disliked 'scroungers' as heartily as any employer, and Labour was slow to recognize that it was being used also against respectable applicants. The Labour government also raised unemployment insurance benefit to 27s. for a family of four.

Baldwin's Conservative government of 1925–29 not only reimposed the means test but sought new ways to cut the costs of benefit. To this end they established, in 1925, the Blanesburgh Committee, to investigate the administration of unemployment insurance. This Committee, chaired by a former judge, found no significant evidence of 'scrounging'. Their Report, published in January 1927, was chiefly remarkable for its assumption, derived from signs of a revival of the economy, that high levels of unemployment could not last much longer. The Committee assumed a rate of only 6 per cent p.a. unemployment, to follow a transitional period of about eighteen months before trade was expected to revive. They recommended a return after this transitional period to a fixed ratio between contributions and benefits, abolition of 'exended benefit', and retention of the means test and 'genuinely seeking work' clause but with its regulations clearly spelled out in legislation.

The Ministry of Labour disliked the latter request and it was dropped from the subsequent legislation. The remainder was substantially embodied in the Unemployment Insurance Act 1927. The 1927 Act was widely interpreted as an aspect of the Conservative backlash against the working class, following the General Strike of the previous year. Under the Act, for the eighteen-month transitional period until trade was expected to recover, the unemployed who had exhausted their entitlement to insurance benefit were still to receive 'extended benefit', now optimistically renamed 'transitional benefit'. It remained in existence for seven years.

Many of the unemployed continued to be disallowed benefit under the 'genuinely seeking work' test, though appeal was possible to often unsympathetic courts of referees. The fate of the disallowed was unclear until 1931, when a survey was carried out by a group of academics for the Royal Commission on Unemployment Insurance. This found that of 2,354 disallowed persons in eight areas, 31.8 per cent of the men secured some work during the 6–13 weeks following rejection of their appeals, as did 43.8 per cent of the single women and 18 per cent of married women. Much of the work, however, was of short duration and often merely pushed others out of work. The inescapable conclusion was that there was insufficient work for everyone who needed it.

Twenty-nine per cent of the men and 40 per cent of the women covered by the survey drew poor relief, the proportion being highest (60%) among men with dependents. During the enquiry 82.5 per cent were supported at some time by means other than employment relief; in Sheffield over half for the whole period of the survey. Men were supported by their wives and children, whole families by relatives, friends or neighbours:

In this way the burden was not removed; it was only spread. Nor were the financial sacrifices by any means confined to the family circle. Even landladies were reported as having come to the rescue; for example, in Glasgow twelve persons were being fed and housed free in this manner. It seems indeed that the reluctance to be associated with the Poor Law affects more than those who are legally liable for his support. It is felt by the whole circle of which he is a member. Undoubtedly it was this vicarious sense of pride and self-respect which induced many relatives and friends to give support to disallowed persons in their time of need.[14]

When Labour returned to office in June 1929 it was more widely recognized that the economy appeared to be in long-term desperate trouble. The 'Treasury view' came under increasing attack as the nature of the crisis was more clearly analysed and alternative proposals were developed for ending it. From 1925 the Liberal Party had engaged in an exhaustive analysis of *Britain's Industrial Future*, as its first product was called. This advocated central planning including a large programme of government investment and public works. Thereafter a committee, including Lloyd George and Seebohm Rowntree, with the advice of Keynes, worked out a detailed scheme of national development, published in 1929 as *We Can Conquer Unemployment*, the cornerstone of the Liberal election campaign of that year. It argued that free enterprise could not solve the current emergency and that planned restructuring of the economy with government assistance and a short-term programme of public works were necessary. A hundred businessmen produced a manifesto in favour of the Liberal proposals. The Treasury, however, feared the effects upon the City of extensive government borrowing and failed to be persuaded.

The actions of Labour's two years in office were constrained by the conflicting pressures of the orthodox Treasury response and of the very different views of the trade union movement and of Labour and Liberal intellectuals. Nevertheless, Margaret

Bondfield, the first female Cabinet Minister, introduced the Unemployment Insurance Act 1930 which laid down that benefit would be refused only if the claimant had refused an offer of suitable employment. The costs of unemployment benefit soared, due more to worsening recession than to the new legislation. Nevertheless 'scroungermania' revived and the government came under strong City and Treasury pressure to cut benefits. This was opposed by the unions and by many Cabinet members, notably Oswald Mosley who, with advice from Keynes, argued for the planned restructuring of the economy with capital raised by the government. Rather the government established in 1930 a Royal Commission to investigate, again, unemployment insurance, and Mosley resigned in May 1930 in protest at the rejection by Treasury and Cabinet of his proposals.

In June 1931 the government recommenced severe cuts in benefits. The Cabinet had rejected any change in the levels of benefits or contributions but agreed to the means-testing of transitional benefits for married women and short-time workers. Still, however, the expenditure battle continued amid deepening international crisis. On 31 July, the Committee on National Expenditure under George May, Secretary of the Prudential Assurance Company, estimated a huge budget deficit and recommended drastic economies. The resulting loss of confidence by foreign financial centres and panic in the City intensified pressure on the government further to reduce unemployment benefits. This broke the Labour government. A majority of the Cabinet led by Arthur Henderson refused to accept reduced benefits and the government was forced to resign.

A government beset by the entirely conflicting pressures from trade unions and from the City of London and by conflicting advice as to economic strategy could not easily have taken a different course. It was quite unclear to contemporaries whether the recommendations of Keynes or Mosley would indeed have had the beneficial effects they claimed. Their proposals that the government shift investment into production for the domestic market would have required major new interventionist institutions (for example to prevent the flight of capital abroad) and would have aroused opposition from industry and from the City which could in itself have destroyed the government. The British economy was in crisis but the crisis was not so severe from the point of view of capital as to force them to see the necessity for such controls; it was less severe in 1929–31 than in many other countries. The trade unions, on the other hand, were strong enough to prevent effective implementation of the alternative orthodox deflationary policy proposed by the City and the Treasury.[15]

The Labour government was replaced by a 'National government', announced whilst Parliament was conveniently in recess, headed by MacDonald. Snowden remained Chancellor of the Exchequer, but it was otherwise largely composed of Conservatives. Apart from this defection of a few of its leaders, the Labour party held solidly together. Free to act as he, and the Treasury, wished, Snowden's next Budget of September 1931 raised income tax from 4s. 6d. to 5s. in the pound, increased surtax and reduced exemptions and children's allowances. The salaries of Ministers, judges, MPs, police and the armed services were reduced by an average of 10 per cent, those of teachers by 15 per cent. Unemployment benefit was cut by 10 per cent, contributions raised, the benefit period reduced and a means test reintroduced for transitional payments. This was the fifth major reconstruction of the unemployment insurance system since 1911. A strident, unpleasant election campaign followed, with Labour, also freed from constraints, declaring that capitalism had broken down and that socialism was the only solution, entailing planning of industry, import controls and the nationalization of banking and credit. Snowden and the Conservatives denounced this 'Bolshevism run mad'. Labour was heavily defeated. In the re-elected 'National government' MacDonald remained Prime Minister but Neville Chamberlain became Chancellor of the Exchequer, symbolizing the effective Conservative victory. He remained so until May 1937 when he became Prime Minister, after MacDonald had been succeeded by Baldwin in June 1935. George Lansbury became leader of the Labour party, with Clement Attlee, late of Toynbee Hall, as his deputy.

The new government at last partially abandoned free trade. Under pressure of the continuing economic crisis, the 'Treasury view' began slowly to retreat. From November 1931 duties and later import quotas were introduced on certain manufactured imports. Britain began to manage her currency exchange rates. Food production was subsidized and Marketing Boards established to regulate the prices of agricultural products. Interest rates were kept low. The influence of Keynes, though still small, was greater than the government admitted.

The economy, indeed, began to recover quite rapidly from the crisis of 1929–31. In 1933 unemployment was falling and Britain's share of world trade rising slightly. This owed less, however, to government policy than to international recovery and the impact of the new industries on an expanding home consumer market, as the cost of living fell due to falling world commodity prices. To some extent Britain gained at the expense of producers in other countries, with some assistance from import tariffs. The heavy industries also showed uneven signs of revival. As a result of this recovery the Budget of 1933 reduced income tax once more to 4s. 6d. in the pound, the cuts in unemployment benefits were removed and half of the reduction in public salaries restored. They were fully restored in 1935. Cautiously, and without openly admitting that they were following policies they had always opposed, the government assisted economic recovery by guaranteeing interest on loans required for such enterprises as railway, ship and London transport construction. These developments were not, however, concentrated in the areas of greatest need for new employment.

In 1933 the government felt able to attempt a major reconstruction, a new beginning, for unemployment insurance. The Unemployment Act, passed in 1934, created two bodies, the first, the Unemployment Insurance Statutory Committee was to take charge of the supervision of unemployment insurance. Insurance benefit was now to be payable only in strict ratio to contributions; the scheme was to return to an orthodox insurance basis, as employers had long advocated. Insurance was also now available from the age of fourteen, in place of the previous age of sixteen. The second board, the Unemployment Assistance Board, was to administer non-contributory benefits for the uninsured unemployed. It was to be separate both from the insurance scheme, replacing transitional benefits, and from Public Assistance which had replaced the Poor Law in 1929. This new system was to be introduced in 1934.

Such measures, however, were designed to palliate rather than to cure unemployment. Debate still raged as to how to solve the long-term problems of the economy. Economic planning became fashionable from the early 1930s, even in circles which previously had shunned it. Political and Economic Planning (PEP) was founded in 1931 as an anonymous group of civil servants, businessmen, academics and professional people devoted to the impartial study of economic and social issues. They published throughout the 30s and beyond a succession of thoughtful and influential studies. Harold Macmillan, a young Conservative MP with a constituency in the depressed North-East, published in 1933 *Reconstruction: a plan for a National policy*, and in 1938 *The Middle Way*. The latter argued the need to abolish poverty if freedom was to be preserved, and the responsibility of all for planned social reconstruction. In 1934 Barbara Wootton published, from the Labour side, *Plan or No Plan*, advocating a planned economy and contrasting the Russian economy (which almost alone and isolated from the world economy escaped the Depression of 1929–31) favourably with unplanned systems.

There was surprisingly little discussion of the principle of state planning, in view of the extent of previous hostility. F. A. Hayek at the London School of Economics was almost alone in attacking the assumption that the state was competent to plan. He argued that no organization had sufficient understanding of the complexities and contingencies of economic and social life to plan successfully; big plans could lead to big mistakes. In the current state of knowledge, he argued, reliance on the free market, 'the apparent haphazard interplay of free individuals' was more likely to produce a satisfactory outcome.[16]

Employers were predictably divided on the issue of planning, according to the degree of their perceived need for state support. But many more of them and of their organizations came during the 1930s to accept the principle that at least an overall national economic strategy was desirable. Since, however, even such expressions of intent did not sweep aside the general preference for free enterprise in influential circles, and far reaching planning was not attempted, they were never tested as to how far this goodwill could stretch.

Apart from Hayek's unfashionable dissension, public and academic debate centred rather upon the desirable extent and implications of government planning, in particular (for Labour democrats such as Wootton, Cole, Tawney and Harold Laski) on the difficult problem of the degree of democratic participation possible in the formulation of increasingly technical policy decisions. They stressed the need for an informed and educated electorate but recognized the inevitability of delegation to those with the required technical expertise, a conflict which they did not succeed in resolving.

Beveridge underwent post-war disillusionment with government control as the solution to economic and social problems. He believed this to be neither 'politically acceptable nor pragmatically desirable' in time of peace, sharing some of the doubts about planning of Hayek, his colleague at the London School of Economics (LSE), of which he was director from 1919 to 1937.

However, as the crisis lengthened he began to fear that the free market approach was unsuited to periods of prolonged crisis. He returned in the 30s to hopes for thorough-going planning, partially influenced by the Webbs' enthusiasm for Soviet planning, though he was intensely unenthusiastic about Communism. Indeed, like many of his contemporaries, he went through a period of vacillation between competing approaches. Unwilling to accept Keynes' *via media*, which he found politically appealing but theoretically rather difficult to understand, and fearing that planning was incompatible with democracy, he shared the general uncertainty as to the way forward from an unprecedented crisis.

Beveridge was not involved in unemployment policy making after 1920, being little liked in the Ministry of Labour. He felt strongly that the unemployment insurance scheme should be kept separate from the long-term benefits it had never been intended to provide and that it palliated but did nothing to solve the underlying economic problems. In 1934, however, he became chairman of the Unemployment Insurance Statutory Committee established under the Act of 1934, a post which he held for the next ten years. On his advice, improvements were introduced into the scheme, such as the inclusion of agricultural labourers in 1936. Touring the country in this role, meeting the unemployed, Beveridge was impressed by the extent of popular enthusiasm for unemployment insurance. It was now widely seen to be preferable to any means- or character-tested scheme. He also became aware of pressure from white-collar workers and from the self-employed for inclusion in the scheme – further evidence of feelings of insecurity even among those benefiting from economic growth. His experiences of these years had a profound influence upon his wartime Report of 1942.

The other body instituted by the Unemployment Act 1934, the Unemployment Assistance Board, had a more troubled beginning. Nationally uniform scales of relief and a family means test were established. The proposed benefits were to be lower than those paid by Public Assistance Committees in many districts. This proposal was made with little apparent forethought and despite Labour warnings. The Treasury, as was Chamberlain's habit, had thought more about tidying up the administration than about rates of benefit. Their implementation in January 1935 met with uproar: large demonstrations, and protests from town councils, trade unions and Members of Parliament of all parties. Alarmed, the government gave way and authorized the UAB to pay PAC scales in areas, covering more than half of the country, where these were higher than the new scale. This did not entirely remove opposition, because the new means test was hedged around with such complex regulations, and allowed such a large area of official discretion, that considerable numbers of claims were rejected. New higher scales of UAB relief were introduced at the end of 1936; 24s. per week for a husband and wife, 26s. (the insurance rate) if they had no other means, plus allowances for children. For most recipients this was an increase in rates of relief; for 60,000 a slight reduction. Equally important, officials were instructed to use their discretion more flexibly. Nevertheless, the means test continued to be bitterly opposed, with good reason – for many people it still operated harshly.[17]

The scales of unemployment relief paid both by the UAB and the Unemployment Insurance Committee remained, however, below Rowntree's stringent 'human needs' minimum. This was due partly to financial constraints but also to the determination of the administrators concerned, including Beveridge, to keep benefits below the level of wage rates lest they should provide a disincentive to work. The 'less eligibility' principle in social policy was not dead, although it became somewhat refined during the inter-war years, due to the assumed need to pay higher levels of contributory benefit than of non-contributory; on the grounds that contributions conferred a right to preferential treatment. Hence benefits were kept low by the low level of wages and lower still by the effect of dependents' allowances. During the later 1930s officials were increasingly concerned that an unemployed person with a large family could receive more in benefit than in wages, and would as a result be disinclined to take advantage of increasing employment opportunities.

These fears outlived the discovery by an official investigation in 1937 that average insurance benefit rates for men, including dependents' allowances, were only two-fifths of the median wage: 24s. 6d. against 55s. 6d. There was considerable inequality in wage rates but only 2.3 per cent of men and 5.2 per cent of women received more from UAB than they had earned when last employed. Nevertheless, both the UAB and the Insurance Committee insisted, up to 1939, upon the disincentive danger and refused on these grounds to raise benefit rates. The result, as we shall see, was to focus attention on the separate but related problems of low wages and of child poverty.[18]

In the later 1930s unemployment eased, assisted considerably by armaments production. Meanwhile, however, the hunger marches reached their peak. The contrast between the grim areas of long-term unemployment and the trim new suburbs of the South was at its most stark. In Crook, Co. Durham in 1936, 7 per cent of the unemployed had been so for five years or longer. Some young people had never had work. In Jarrow in 1934, 67.8 per cent of insured workers were unemployed. There were a number of official and unofficial enquiries into the effects as well as the causes of long-term unemployment which stressed the Depression and the sense of hopelessness which it bred. In 1936 43 per cent of the unemployed were drawing insurance benefits; 37 per cent received payments from UAB: about 334,000 were still maintained by the PAC.[19]

Already in 1934 the problem of whole areas suffering long-term unemployment had led the government to introduce the Depressed Areas (Development and Improvement) Bill. During its progress through Parliament it was renamed, euphemistically, the Special Areas Bill. Once passed it established commissioners to initiate and aid measures for the 'economic development and social improvement' of 'depressed' or 'special' areas, assisted by a grant of £2 m. The sum was small in proportion to the need and the results were not spectacular: grants were given for water supply and sewerage schemes, hospital building, parks, swimming pools, social centres. The first Commissioner for Special Areas, Sir Malcolm Stewart, reiterated, with mounting intensity as his experience grew, the importance of improved health, sanitary and social services in the 'special areas' both to improve the condition and morale of their inhabitants and to attract industry, including management. He encouraged and subsidized voluntary social services. A little subsidy went to housing schemes; much, with little result, to help transfer unemployed families to the land. More were transferred to more prosperous industrial areas. The failure to achieve more had much to do with the government's continuing reluctance to intervene sufficiently in free enterprise to give real incentives for the establishment of new firms in the areas of highest unemployment. This failure led to Campbell's resignation after three years. He was convinced that the preference of businessmen for establishing firms in the Midlands and South had little rational economic motivation, rather success attracted success; businessmen were concerned with profit rather than with social responsibility and also were repelled by the history of industrial and unemployed turbulence in the depressed areas. In particular Campbell criticized the huge unplanned growth of London in this period, predicting, correctly, the problems that the size of the city would cause in the future. He argued that although industry could not and should not be told where to develop, it could be restrained from adding to the congestion of overpopulated and fully employed areas; further development in London should be forbidden and tax incentives and loans given to business to place 'a magnet in the Special Areas'. Such proposals were supported by the TUC, but not by business. [doc 12]

Stewart's resignation, combined with the march of the men of Jarrow to London in 1937, induced the government to offer, in the Special Areas (Amendment) Act 1937, remission of rents, rates and income tax for five years to firms which would establish themselves in the 'special' areas. As a result trading estates were established in South Wales, Scotland and the North-East but they chiefly attracted light industries producing such things as neon signs, clothes and ice-cream and employed mainly women. The government did nothing to prevent larger numbers of businesses being established in the more prosperous areas.

To keep the unemployed in condition for work should it ever become available and to re-train them for new jobs, the Ministry of Labour established training centres and instructional centres. In the latter men cleared forests, dug ditches, made roads, levelled land or broke stones. For women there were Domestic Training Centres which did not prove popular. Attendance was voluntary although sometimes 'encouraged', especially for single men seeking unemployment assistance. As fears grew of the long-term effects of unemployment on young people who had never known employment, attendance at training centres effectively became compulsory for many of them as a condition of benefit. Since training was rarely followed by regular employment they were not greeted with enthusiasm by the unemployed.

A great deal of voluntary effort was directed towards the unemployed in the 1930s. Settlement Houses, the NCSS, the YMCA, Salvation Army, Quaker organizations and, on a small scale, the NUWM, established clubs for the unemployed, eventually assisted by small government grants. Wealthier areas 'adopted' poor ones: Surrey adopted Jarrow; Bath, Redruth in depressed Cornwall. To the more militant of those unemployed, in the NUWM, such charity stank of patronage; certainly it could do little to solve the fundamental problems of unemployment.

These were indeed only solved by the coming of war in 1939. The needs of the armed services and war production absorbed those who had not benefited from the economic revival of the 30s. Throughout the inter-war years successive governments had succeeded, rather remarkably, by means of often ill-thought-out panic measures, in avoiding serious social unrest amid unprecedented long term unemployment. The economic crisis had forced them into a degree of social and economic intervention which, although still limited, would have been politically impossible before or immediately after the war of 1914–18.

The 'break-up' of the Poor Law

Unemployment dominated the history of the Poor Law in this period as it dominated all else; it led at last to its abolition. The recommendations in 1922 of a civil service committee, the Betterton Committee, for closer co-ordination of local authority social services, were ignored amid the crisis forced on the Poor Law by unemployment. The flood of uninsured unemployed men and women onto poor relief after 1920 presented problems. Too numerous to be placed in the workhouses, most received out-door relief, sometimes in kind only, sometimes on performance of test labour. Guardians received little guidance from the Ministry of Health as to how to provide for them. As a result, as the Webbs put it: 'The complicated and disordered dispensation of outdoor relief... is hard to describe in a way that will leave on the reader's mind any other impression than a senseless confusion of methods and aims.'[20] The Ministry of Health reminded local Guardians in 1921 that even in the 'exceptional circumstances' of mass unemployment, relief 'should of necessity be calculated on a lower scale than the earnings of the independent labourer who is maintaining himself by his labour'.

The problem of the able-bodied unemployed was increased by the strikes of 1918–21 and the General Strike of 1926. Conflict as to whether strikers should be supported from public funds did not begin or end in the 1920s. A Court of Appeal judgment of 1900 (the Merthyr Tydfil judgment) had established that relief might not be paid to able-bodied men who refrained from work when employment was available to them. Relief might be paid to their families and to the men (and, though it was not considered, women) when destitution reduced them to a physical state which could no longer be deemed able-bodied. As always, the judgment was observed with varying degrees of punctilliousness. Guardians sympathetic to strikers evaded it by paying sufficient sums to wives to cover the entire family. It was widely evaded during the coal strike of 1921 and the 1923 dock strike. The Ministry of Health greeted the General Strike by reminding Guardians to observe the strict letter of the law and laying down scales of relief lower than those currently paid in many unions. The miners' unions had largely exhausted their strike funds before the General Strike. The total number of paupers in England and Wales rose from 1.2 m. before the strike began to 2.1 m. at its peak; in the month after the strike they totalled 2.4 m. due to the cumulative effects of the coal dispute which had precipitated the General Strike and outlasted it by many months. In most unions in which mining was a significant industry more than 50 per cent of mining families were on relief. Again Guardians responded variously, influenced less by the political inclinations of their members than by local conditions. In general Guardians in areas of high unemployment, whatever their political views, treated strikers more generously than those elsewhere, although in parts of the Midlands the miners were almost literally starved back to work by intransigent Guardians. The Ministry approved of such policies so long as they remained within the letter of the law: when the Guardians of Lichfield proposed to withdraw all relief, indoor and out-door, to miners' dependents, on the grounds that 'the miners had work to go to and it was the Guardians' duty to see that they went back', they went too far. The Ministry reminded them of their duty to relieve destitution, whatever the cause; they could not defensibly insist upon adherence to the law if they also countenanced its flagrant abuse.

The Ministry tried increasingly to control excessively generous Boards, primarily by refusing to sanction loans to supplement rate income. This power was strengthened by the Board of Guardians (Default) Act of July 1926 which enabled the Ministry to suspend, and replace by an appointed Board, any Board of Guardians which persistently raised loans above the permissible limit. This forced most Guardians to behave with circumspection, although the Boards of West Ham and Chester-le-Street were suspended in August 1926 and that of Bedwellty in January 1927.[21]

This increased use of the Ministry's power to restrict local spending, which was predictably used most vigorously against unions with low rate incomes, intensified the debate about rate equalization. This had been highlighted in 1921 when thirty Poplar borough councillors went to prison for refusing to pay their contribution to general LCC expenditure. They argued that, rather than paying this precept, poorer boroughs and unions such as Poplar should be subsidized by richer districts. This forced the Ministry to introduce a system of equalization for London only – elsewhere the problem remained.[22]

The General Strike brought starkly to the fore a problem which growing unemployment was gradually revealing: the government's difficulty in establishing a national policy for unemployment when local Guardians pursued, and jealously defended, their autonomy. The urgency of the problem for the government was increased, first, by the apparently greater willingness of strikers and the unemployed to apply for relief. They were encouraged by strike committees and by political organizations to assert the right to relief of the labouring poor and put pressure upon Guardians to increase relief rates. Second, the government faced an increased number of Labour-controlled Boards, part of the general increase in Labour's political representation in the 1920s which had been stimulated by the removal of pauper disfranchisement in 1918; paupers were now debarred only from standing for local office.

Some officials felt that they faced a conspiracy to subvert the Poor Law. They felt justified in pursuing stringent policies on the grounds that the 'deserving' unemployed were provided for by unemployment insurance. To encourage generous poor relief was to aid the malingerer and to increase the already substantial public cost of unemployment relief.

Many Guardians in the mid-1920s were trapped in their recognition of the extent of poverty by the conflicting pressures from the poor to increase relief and from the central government to reduce it. The cost of relief to the unemployed and to the strikers prevented Unions in the depressed areas from significantly improving their services for other categories of the poor. Some were removed from their care, including many widows and orphans and those aged between sixty-five and seventy, when pensions were provided for them in 1925. Children in Poor Law care were increasingly boarded out on the advice of the Ministry of Health. Institutions for the sick and aged continued to improve in Unions able and prepared so to spend from their rates. They did so, however, under the constraint of persistent Ministry of Health discouragement of capital expenditure for institutional improvement. The numbers in Poor Law institutions never returned to their pre-war totals; in particular, the able-bodied did not return to them. Very few, even of the strictest Boards of Guardians, now used workhouses to deter the unemployed. Workhouses now became receptacles for those in need for whom no other arrangements had been made, locally or nationally, in particular for the mentally handicapped, as distinct from the seriously mentally ill. The latter were generally in specialized hospitals, often of low standard. For the 'feeble-minded' few other institutions existed.[23]

The government won the battle to control out-door relief. Between 1926 and 1929 this control took the form not only of financial sanctions but of increasing intervention by inspectors in the day-to-day work of suspect Guardians: attending and intervening in meetings and discussions of relief applications, even visiting the homes of paupers and of those refused relief, urging the use of the workhouse test or the labour test for those suspected of reluctance to seek work, harassing Guardians with criticisms of slackness in record-keeping and accounting. These, however, were temporary measures whilst Chamberlain formulated a permanent scheme to restrict local Poor Law autonomy. This was embodied in the Local Government Act 1929, which disbanded Poor Law Unions and Boards of Guardians. The aim was formally to separate the troublesome dual responsibilities of the Poor Law for the able-bodied, primarily the unemployed, and for the non-able-bodied, mainly those in institutions. Care of the latter was gradually to be dispersed to the health, education and other specialist committees of local authorities, with the aim of improving provision. The able-bodied were to be provided for by newly established Public Assistance Committees appointed by the local authorities. They were to be financed dually, from rates and from the Exchequer, a measure designed both to solve equalization problems and to increase Treasury control.

The Guardians rose as always in their own defence, though as a result of the acute variations in their principles of operation they were not united. More surprisingly, for the first time in its history, the Poor Law received its strongest defence from the left. Activists such as Lansbury suspected, rightly, that this 'break-up' of the Poor Law was based on no desire to provide adequately or sympathetically for the deserving poor, rather the reverse. The experience of the 1920s had shown that local needs were more vividly appreciated at the local level than by central government, and that at last, despite the constraints imposed by the Ministry, the unemployed had in many areas won the sympathy of Poor Law administrators who had gone as far as they were able to help them. The Act was precisely designed, in the eyes of Labour, to put an end to this hopeful tendency. Such arguments, of course, won little support. They probably contributed to the Act's easy passage through Parliament.

Administrative arrangements were left to be worked out after the Act was passed. Almost immediately Chamberlain issued circulars to local authorities urging imaginative use of their new powers, particularly as regards the takeover from the Poor Law of health and other institutional responsibilities for the 'deserving'. However, the Ministry of Health gave little financial encouragement to such improvements. Rather there was until 1939 a continuation of the previous 'rudderless drifting towards specialized institutions'.[24] The PACs, generally using Poor Law personnel, operated more stringently than many Boards of Guardians had done. They retained some autonomy and some continued to overstep the limits imposed by the Ministry, but their opportunities for doing so were severely constrained.

Hardly surprisingly, given the circumstances in which it occurred, the 'break-up of the Poor Law' did not occur with the drama for which the Webbs had hoped. In 1939 local authorities still supported one million paupers.

Health

Chamberlain devoted rather less of his considerable energy to the health responsibilities of his Ministry. More people had access to better medical care after 1918 than before, but high levels of ill-health remained and became an especial focus of concern in the 1930s. This was one aspect of the general search for means of reconstructing the British economy for the achievement of maximum efficiency. Once again, as Stewart repeatedly stressed in his Reports as Commissioner for Special Areas, the poor quality of 'human capital' was seen to be hindering economic development. Also, as PEP pointed out in 1937, extensive ill-health caused the diversion of capital investment from industry into health care. PEP calculated that the cost of ill-health to the nation was £300 m. p.a.: £120 m. of this was due to working days lost through illness, the remainder being the costs of treatment and prevention. Furthermore, the latter were both, PEP argued, quite inadequate to meet the real need.[25] [doc 13]

Once again, as another war approached, the poor physical condition of military recruits was invoked as evidence of low general physical standards. Of volunteers for the services in 1935, 6,210

were reported to be 'below the comparatively low standard of phy-
sique required by the army'.[26] This suggested that at best there
had been little improvement in male health since the war. The central cause of ill-health was, as Rowntree pointed out, poverty,
which caused poor diet and living conditions. The problem was
compounded by major deficiencies in the system of treatment and
prevention. There was still in the mid-1930s too little co-
ordination among statutory services and between statutory and
voluntary services, and each of them had serious independent deficiencies. Unemployment may have contributed to low standards
of health, although it must be remembered that the heavy industries in which unemployment was greatest had long been responsible for high rates of industrial injury, sickness and death.

As soon as he became Minister of Health, Addison had appointed
a Council on Medical and Administrative Services, chaired by a
doctor, Sir Bernard Dawson. In 1920 this Council recommended
the 'close co-ordination' of preventive and curative services and
spoke of 'the increasing conviction that the best means of maintaining health and curing disease should be made available to all
citizens'. It recommended a network of health centres in which
services would be concentrated. It did not recommend a free health
service, as an advisory committee of the Labour party, (strongly
influenced by Beatrice Webb) had proposed in 1918. This committee had also envisaged that all doctors would work exclusively in
health centres. A free health service remained Labour policy between the wars, although the wo Labour governments had little
opportunity to implement it.[27]

After Addison left the Ministry of Health, demands for a unified
service diminished. The National Health Insurance Act 1920 had
raised insurance benefits and increased doctors' fees, but there
were no other significant changes in health administration after the
war. In 1918 the right to enter the health insurance scheme had
actually been withdrawn from the self-employed.

Those covered by national health insurance had access everywhere to a limited choice of GP. These 'panel' doctors, however,
were maldistributed. In Manchester each might have more than a
thousand patients, in Gloucestershire less than seven hundred.
'Panel' patients complained that they were treated more hurriedly
and less courteously by doctors than were private patients. The dependents of insurance contributors still, by 1939, had no certain
access to free doctoring outside the Poor Law (later the PAC)
although in many areas GPs, encouraged by the BMA and Friendly

Societies, had established voluntary contributory schemes for dependents of insured persons, at least 650,000 of whom were so covered by 1939. Lower-middle-class families with incomes above the £250 p.a. limit for the national insurance scheme also increasingly joined such organizations.

But the insurance scheme itself was far from uniform. Approved societies which accumulated a surplus from contributions due to low levels of sickness among their members (especially agricultural workers and better off urban workers) were allowed to pay higher levels of benefit and for such 'additional benefits' as dentistry, eye care, convalescence and nursing. The maternity benefit, raised in 1920 to £2, was low and, being paid in cash rather than (as in other countries) in the form of care, there was an obvious temptation for poorer families to spend it on domestic necessities. Insured women, especially married women, still made larger numbers of claims for benefit than did men, thus enhancing their reputation for malingering. Administrators remained uncertain as to whether women were 'scrounging' or whether, as was more likely, the national insurance system was bearing the burden of the inferior diet and medical care of women especially during and after pregnancy. Women's sickness claims had declined during the war and rose immediately with the onset of unemployment; they were highest where unemployment was most severe.

The national health insurance system was investigated by a Royal Commission in 1926. It was appointed in 1924 amid growing criticism of the system of approved society administration. Neither the Labour government which appointed it nor their Conservative opponents had much enthusiasm for change in the system, amidst the more pressing and expensive problems of unemployment. The Commission was so constituted as to make an irresistible unified demand for change unlikely; it produced two Reports. Both recommended dependents' allowances, as for unemployment insurance, and also certain further benefits, including medical care in childbirth, dental and ophthalmic treatment. Neither majority nor minority Report commented upon the question of women's claims. Both Reports criticized the lack of co-ordination among health services and the local variations in standards of provision through the approved societies. They differed as to remedies: the minority recommended the abolition of approved societies, their functions to be taken over by local authorities to ensure uniformity and coordination; the majority preferred the less radical and rather more politically acceptable solution of pooling and redistributing the surpluses of the societies to bring about 'pooling of risks', i.e. redistribution from those whose members had a low to those with a high propensity for sickness.

No changes resulted from these Reports, largely because in 1926 the government was more concerned with cutting social service expenditure than with costly innovations. The Reports of the Royal Commission were followed by the Economy (Miscellaneous Provisions) Act, the work of Chamberlain and Churchill, whichs incorporated a wide range of cuts, including the government contribution to the health insurance scheme. Further cuts followed the crisis of 1931. In 1932 the National government reduced health benefits to the unemployed; sickness benefit for married women was also reduced from 12s. to 10s., their disability benefit from 7s. 6d. to 5s. It would have been cut further but for an unusual parliamentary alliance of Labour and female MPs, the latter led by Lady Astor.

The only further change in the scheme was the inclusion in 1937 of juveniles between the ages of fourteen and sixteen. Despite much criticism no change was made in the discrepancy between unemployment and sickness benefit; the latter by 1939 was 17s. per week for an insured man, 10s. for his wife and 3s. per child. The health insurance scheme still, except for the most prosperous approved societies, offered contributors no right to hospital treatment. In 1939, still less than half of the population was covered by national health insurance.[28]

The hospital services were maldistributed and especially poor in rural areas. The voluntary hospitals provided 25 per cent of all beds and had increasing financial problems. As early as 1921, a Committee headed by Viscount Cave on the finances of voluntary hospitals pointed out that they were suffering from rising costs and recommended a £1 m. subvention from the state to assist them. The government provided half of this and refused any permanent commitment to support the voluntary hospitals. The steadily improving capacity of medicine to cure created demand for better equipped hospitals. This, combined with the increasing salaries of medical staff, outstripped the growth in income from voluntary sources. Increasingly they became dependent upon means-tested payment by patients, upon payment from local authorities for treatment undertaken on their behalf, and upon local authority subsidy, this being cheaper for some authorities than establishing their own public hospitals. Most voluntary hospitals established contributory schemes for low earners which entitled contributors to care when in need. These, however, were expensive to operate. Hospital Saturday and Sunday funds continued to supplement hospital incomes and were widely popular.

Voluntary hospitals had been established to care for the sick poor in an age when the better off were attended at home or in private clinics. This continued to be their chief function and largely accounted for their financial difficulties. The general wards were restricted to those with incomes of under £6 per week. However, increasing numbers of the lower middle classes could not afford private care, even when they were privately insured. Also they and the better off justly suspected that individual doctors and small nursing homes could not match the standard of medical knowledge and treatment now available in the major voluntary hospitals. To meet the resulting increased demand and to ease their financial positions these hospitals began to provide wards for fee-paying patients. Nevertheless, by the end of the 1930s many such hospitals were in financial difficulties.

The public hospitals remained under the control either of the local authority or of the PAC up to 1939. Many authorities were notably slow to take over the Poor Law hospitals after 1929. In 1937, 466 public hospitals remained under the control of PACs, compared with 111 under local councils. Both types of hospital were financed jointly from local rates and from the Treasury grant. Poorer patients sometimes preferred public hospitals where they felt less patronized and free to complain of poor treatment to their local representatives. However, they were likely to have more to complain about: standards of medical and nursing care were often lower in the low status public hospitals. The buildings were often old and ill-equipped. They carried the burden of much chronic sickness, whilst the voluntary hospitals specialized in acute cases. The public hospitals were worst, despite expenditure by the Special Areas Commission, in the depressed areas. Richer counties such as Surrey, Staffordshire and Essex were by 1939 planning comprehensive hospital services and new hospitals. A few health centres were established on the model recommended by the Labour party. An alternative experiment in Peckham in 1935, on the initiative of medical men, was not followed up.[28a] In general, hospital care improved in the 1920s and 30s. Numbers and standards of nurses improved. But by the later 30s it was plain that neither the private nor the public sectors could provide adequately for need or demand.[29]

The maternity and child welfare and school medical services continued to function separately from the national insurance and hospital services and from one another. By 1937 the overwhelming majority of infants under one year were seen by health visitors, a smaller majority (382 in every 611 live births) was taken to infant welfare centres; a rather smaller proportion of expectant mothers (338 in 629 births) attended ante-natal clinics: fewer still (217 in 629 births) were seen by health visitors. Infant mortality remained low, although in the depressed areas it did not decline below the pre-war levels. Concern that it was still too high mounted, due to the rapidly falling birth rate which was at the lowest previously recorded rate in 1933. Fears that the population was not replacing itself grew as war came closer.

A new focus of concern in the inter-war years, however, was the maternal mortality rate. This declined slightly before the war, rose sharply (from 5 to 7.60 per 1000 live births) between 1914 and 1918, fell in the early 1920s to its pre-war level and then rose slowly and persistently until 1934. Thereafter it fell rapidly. Maternal mortality was unusual in being highest on average among the better off. This was attributed to the higher proportion of first births due to the smaller families of the higher social classes and to the higher average age of the mothers.

But maternal mortality was also a severe, and, it was hoped, more readily soluble problem among poorer women. It was increasingly suspected that the chief cause was malnutrition. Awareness of the relationship between diet and health and of the extent of malnourishment grew in the 1930s. An experiment in the Rhondda Valley in 1934 showed that improvement of ante-natal services effected no reduction in maternal mortality although when food was distributed to some expectant mothers the reduction was remarkable. In the mid-30s most local authorities in England and Wales began to supply free or subsidized milk to expectant and nursing mothers. This helped to account for the decline in maternal mortality after 1934, although this was chiefly due to the discovery of antibiotics able to counteract sepsis, the major cause of maternal deaths.

Other changes were also important: the Midwives Act 1936 created a full-time salaried midwifery service in place of the previous jumble of public and voluntary arrangements and enabled the Ministry of Health to declare it an offence for an unqualified midwife or nurse to attend a delivery. At the same time the number of maternity beds in hospitals increased, although most confinements still took place at home. Doctors increasingly insisted upon the need for medical care in childbirth, although it is unclear whether this was as vital to maternal survival as improved availability of skilled midwifery and insistence upon basic hygiene during a delivery.[30] A number of local authorities appointed home helps for the post-natal period.

The incidence of abortion as a cause of maternal mortality is unknown. It was certainly an element in the drive among some women for the dissemination of birth control information, although a less important one than the desire to relieve women of the burden of continual unwanted childbearing. The spread of the practice of family limitation, without official assistance, indeed in the face of strong male opposition, contributed to the improved, though still poor, general health of working-class women and hence to lower risks of maternal mortality.

The Ministry of Health and the Board of Education recognized in 1929 that children between the ages of two and five between the infant welfare clinics and the school medical service, were neglected by existing services. Nevertheless, the Board of Education continued its policy of extending nursery schools only in areas of greatest poverty and overcrowding, and then rarely. The school medical service continued in many areas to be deficient in the provision of treatment.

The 1930s saw a revived concern with 'national efficiency', even though the term itself had now disappeared from political debate, one of whose manifestations was a new concern with occupational health. Workmen's compensation was costing industry £12.5 m. in 1936. In 1938 a new Factories Act increased the staff of factory inspectors to include eleven medical inspectors, with the aim of reducing accidents at work and the conditions which promoted the onset and spread of disease.

Eugenic arguments achieved prominence, as they had in the previous period of alarm about national inefficiency, though once more they were a shadow of their more virulent counterparts elsewhere in Europe, notably in Nazi Germany. There was a fairly general assumption that even though inherited disabilities might afflict a considerable section of the population, the only solution was by all means possible to maximize their remaining abilities. Still, however, it was suspected that this was least possible in the case of mental deficiency (still imperfectly defined). A Departmental Committee on Voluntary Sterilization recommended in 1934 that voluntary sterilization should be more readily available in such cases. The recommendation was not officially followed, although sterilization of 'defectives', not always voluntary, occurred.[31]

Concern with national efficiency and national fitness was reflected rather in the Government's National Fitness Campaign, launched in the late 30s, and in the flourishing Women's League for Health and Beauty. It also intensified criticism of the inadequacy and inefficiency of health services, and may have helped to raise the previously low popular expectations of a 'normal' state of health. Doctors recognized that they had much to gain from improvements in services to a level at which they approached meeting the need for health care, and also that such services (as demonstrated by the plight of the voluntary hospitals) required public finance. Just as it had become clear by 1914 that the free market could meet neither the need nor, by 1918, the demand for housing, so in the 1930s it was becoming evident that it could meet neither the need nor the demand for health care. Hence in 1939 the BMA voted narrowly in favour of the extension of national insurance to dependents and the subsidized co-ordination of services; however, the details of such arrangements remained a source of dissension within the profession. In particular many doctors remained opposed to a salaried service. Nothing was done before the outbreak of war. During the inter-war years central government devoted little attention or energy to health problems compared with most other social issues; rather local authorities were the major source of initiative and of increased expenditure.[32]

Old-age and widows' pensions

Chamberlain's desire to reconstruct social administration and the wider desire to cut expenditure led to changes in the system and coverage of pensions. Pressure for increased old-age pensions continued in the early 1920s, accompanied by a campaign from the 'anti-waste' lobby for the closer and more efficient administrative integration of the income support services, for 'all-in' insurance as it was called. Despite the attraction of the savings which might have resulted successive governments shied away, chiefly for fear of pressure to equalize health and old-age benefits with those paid to the unemployed. The already high cost of old-age pensions disturbed cost-conscious governments. By 1922 they were costing £25.3 m., more than the cost to the Treasury at that date of all forms of unemployment benefit. Ninety-three per cent of pensioners were receiving the maximum rate; 70 per cent of them were women. The number of pensioners had been increased by about 10,000 p.a. by the Blind Persons Act 1920 which granted pensions under the terms of the Old-Age Pensions Acts to blind persons over the age of 50 (a product of pressure on behalf of the war blind). Geddes had been unable to discover any possible cuts in the administration of pensions.

Pensioners themselves gained from falling prices in the 1920s: by 1921 the pension was closer to a subsistence payment than at any time since its institution. Nevertheless, in 1923 Bowley and Hogg estimated that the average married couple on maximum pension still had 2s. 2d. less than was needed to buy the 'necessities of life'. The Conservative government had, however, more inclination to cut the cost of pensions than to increase the amount paid. The most feasible means of effecting cuts appeared to be their transference to an insurance basis. Since the beginning of the century Conservatives had supported the notion of contributory old-age pensions as strenuously as Labour had opposed it. The Conservatives included pensions in the brief to a Committee established in 1923, chaired by Sir John Anderson, to investigate all aspect of national insurance. Its first Report, in January 1924, rejected the suggestion that the existing pension should become contributory and pointed out that the problem still remained of obtaining contributions from the irregularly paid and from non-working women. They were as critical of the existing scheme as the Ryland Adkins committee had been, but could also find no way acceptable to the Treasury of improving it, though they recommended raising the means limit.

The Report was shortly followed by the entry of the first Labour government. Snowden, the Chancellor, had long advocated universal pensions. After a short time at the Treasury he became convinced that 'its cost is in present circumstances, prohibitive'. However, his first budget earmarked £38 m. for the lowering of the pensionable age to sixty-five, the reduction of food taxes and the introduction of widows' pensions. For the latter there had always been some Labour pressure, increased by the large numbers of women who flooded into the Labour party after they obtained the vote in 1918. It was a popular proposal in view of the numbers of deserving women it could remove from the Poor Law.

Snowden's next step was to introduce an Old-Age Pensions Act which gave full pension (still 10s. per week) to all with incomes, other than from employment, of up to 15s. per week. It was available at a reduced rate on incomes up to 34s. per week. The innovatory exclusion of earned income was intended to encourage the elderly to leave the labour force in order to provide jobs for the young. Such a proposal had been surprisingly absent from Labour policy before 1914, but they emphasized it increasingly as unemployment mounted. The Act raised the number of pensioners by 50,000 to about 70 per cent of the over-seventy population. It now covered all of the aged in need.

The short-lived Labour government had no time to take Snowden's proposals further. The Anderson Committee delivered a second Report before they left office. This stated that the only practicable means of extending pensions was to introduce a contributory pension payable between sixty-five and seventy for those covered by national health insurance.

Chamberlain spent his eleven months of enforced leisure in developing detailed plans for the social legislation he hoped to implement on his return to office. This included Poor Law reform, the gradual shifting of the entire pensions scheme onto the cheaper contributory basis, and the lowering of the pensionable age to sixty-five. He was persuaded by the second Anderson Report to take a more modest step, and introduced in 1925 the Old Age and Widows and Orphans Contributory Pensions Act. Those covered by national health insurance were thereafter to pay additional contributions which would entitle them and their wives to a pension of 10*s*. per week between the ages of sixty-five and seventy, to the non-contributory pension at seventy, without means test, to pensions of 10*s*. per week for the widows of men dying otherwise than as a result of accident or industrial disease, and a weekly pension of 5*s*. for their orphans to the age of fourteen. Contributions were gradually to be increased until all pensions were financed on a contributory basis. The first contributory pensions were to be payable after two years' contributions.

The timing of the Act was determined by Chancellor Churchill's eagerness to announce it in his 1925 Budget. As Chamberlain noted, 'he was anxious to reduce taxation in order to relieve industry . . . but he would have to balance the benefits by doing something for the working class . . .'. The Exchequer's contribution to the scheme was calculated to be slightly below the estimated annual fall in the cost of war pensions, hence additional Exchequer expenditure would be nil and the future savings considerable. Predictably Labour attacked the scheme for its contributory nature but it passed easily through Parliament.

The pension rate did not change before 1939. In 1930 the *New Survey of London Life and Labour* described London pensioners as generally adequately nourished in summer but not in winter when fuel took a higher proportion of their incomes. Their clothes and household goods were in poor condition and they could not afford replacements. They estimated that a minimum of 12s. per week was required to live in East London, exclusive of rent which averaged 4s. to 6s. per week for a single room. The survey found that 'none of the pensioners was grateful for the old-age pension, all of them thinking it was due to them and all of them complained about the smallness of it'. The commonest complaint was that 'we can't live on it, we only exist'.

In 1929 the Labour government extended widows' pensions to the wives of insured men who had died before the scheme came into operation, and to women previously disqualified because their husbands had been over the age of seventy when the legislation came into force. In 1937 contributory old-age and widows' pensions became available to lower-middle-class men earning £400 p.a. or less, and to women earning £250 p.a. or less, as voluntary contributors. Here, as elsewhere, it was recognized that the growing lower middle class were posing a new problem: many of them were ill-paid and they could not afford to pay for adequate provision in times of dependency. State welfare measures had been directed towards manual workers, whilst they had received only increased demands from direct taxation. By the 1930s they too were increasingly demanding and receiving state support.

By 1933 302,000 widows and 340,000 orphans were receiving pensions; 446,000 women and 264,000 men were receiving pensions between the ages of sixty-five and seventy. After 1925 three types of old-age pension existed, all payable at the same rate of 10s. per week; the contributory pension paid between sixty-five and seventy to those eligible for national health insurance; the partially contributory over-seventy pension, paid without means test at the standard rate of 10s., to the same people at the age of seventy; and the non-contributory means-tested over-seventy pension, paid on a sliding scale for those who had not been, or been married to, NHI contributors. By 1938 96.4 per cent of the latter were receiving the maximum 10s. pension. The numbers receiving the non-contributory pension, as established in 1908, fell steadily from one million in 1926 to 597,147 in 1938. It was expected eventually to disappear.

Those of the aged who required institutional care received little public attention during the period. Poor Law institutions continued, slowly, to improve and after 1930 gradually to be separated from the control of the PACs, although generally still housed in old workhouse building.[33]

Children

Belief in the desirability of caring for children within a family rather than an institutional environment became more firmly established in the inter-war years. Poor Law authorities and voluntary organizations, often under local authority pressure, as they became increasingly dependent upon public subsidies, 'boarded-out' children with foster parents where possible and provided smaller scale 'family homes' when it was not. Such provision, however, developed faster than that of trained workers for such institutions; too often the homes were depressing and over-disciplined.

Adoption of children became legally possible under the Adoption Act 1926. Although this had occurred previously it had had no legal sanction. Legal change came about largely due to the effects of the wartime rise in illegitimacy. For the same reason, also in 1926, the Legitimacy Act allowed the legitimation of children after the marriage of their parents – an important move in a society in which illegitimacy still carried immense social stigma. These measures were associated with the growing influence of psychologists upon the theory and practice of child care, and the emphasis they placed upon defects in early home environment and social experiences as causes of delinquency. It was also accepted that the treatment of the 'young offender' might determine whether or not he or she grew up to a life of crime. Fines and probation, enabling the child to remain under supervision at home, replaced commitment of young people to penal institutions in an increasing number of cases.

Changes in child care culminated in the Children and Young Persons Act of 1933. The Juvenile Courts were now to deal with all offenders up to the age of seventeen. Members of this age group could now be judged to be 'in need of care and protection' in a wider range of instances than before, including 'falling into bad associations or exposed to moral danger or beyond control or (being) ill-treated or neglected in a manner likely to cause unnecessary suffering or injury to health'. Remand homes were removed from police or Poor Law control and placed under that of the education authority. If the court deemed a child to be in need of care he or she could be sent to newly designated 'approved schools' under Home Office control but local education authority administration; these replaced the previous reformatory and industrial schools. Voluntary homes were for the first time to be inspected, approved and registered and, where necessary, financed by the Home Office.

The purpose of the system, including that of the Juvenile Courts, was now formally said to be the promotion of the 'welfare of the child' rather than punishment. Education authorities were to provide the courts with information about the family and school background of any child brought before them. On the basis of such reports, the court had powers 'to remove him from undesirable surroundings and for securing that proper provision is made for his education and housing'. The local authority was enjoined wherever possible to board the child out in a foster home; it was given no duty or encouragement to return the child to a rehabilitated home. This was despite the fact that the children's branch of the Home Office persistently pressed for co-operation with and rehabilitation of the families of children in care. Nor was there any suggestion that a 'child' or even a 'young person' should be consulted as to his or her views on the form of care. Effectively, however, the Act of 1933 removed children from the care of the remnants of the Poor Law.[34]

Education

Of more significance for the majority of children, the more imaginative of the 1919 Fisher provisions for the extension of state education were destroyed by the Geddes Axe. In 1923–24 only 12.6 per cent of all children remained in education beyond the age of fourteen. However, one aspect of the renewed drive for 'national efficiency' in the 20s was increased recognition of the amount of national talent wasted due to the deficient education of the mass of children, especially beyond the age of eleven. In theory, since 1907, the 'free place' system at grammar schools ensured that no child of suitable ability was debarred from furthering his or her education. The number of grant-aided schools continued to rise. However, in 1926 Kenneth Lindsey's *Social Progress and Educational Waste* pointed out that a very high proportion of working-class children selected for grammar schools refused the places offered. It was not enough to abolish fees. Parents could not afford the obligatory uniform of such schools, nor could they afford to forego the child's earnings to the age of sixteen (the age of taking school certificate) to which pupils were expected to remain at selective schools, still less to the age of eighteen which was essential if they were to go to university. In Bradford, one of the few places under a Labour council to investigate the situation thoroughly, it was found that more working-class children refused places than accepted them. Children who refused or did not obtain grammar school places remained until the compulsory leaving age of fourteen in the higher forms of elementary schools.[35]

By the mid-1930s only 0.4 per cent of elementary schoolleavers in England went on to university. The Labour movement had long been committed to improved free education to university level, with maintenance grants to compensate for loss of earnings. In the 1920s they pressed, as a first step, for 'secondary education for all', the title of a party pamphlet written by R. H. Tawney, the most distinguished Labour advocate of educational improvement. Tawney pointed out that although the state education system had been transformed since the beginning of the century, it still undervalued the intellects of most children and was inferior in this as in other respects to that of most other countries. Education, Tawney believed, should be 'an inspiration not a machine', seen as a humane good not as a process of engineering factors of production for the labour market. Since local traditions and individual needs and abilities varied, secondary schools should not be of a single type; they should be of varied type but of equal esteem.[36]

The 1924 Labour government referred to the standing consultative committee of the Board of Education (chaired by Sir Henry Hadow) the question of the most suitable courses of study for children at secondary school. This committee, of which Tawney was a member, in 1926 recommended raising the school leaving age to fifteen (already Labour policy), and the re-organization of schooling for children after the age of eleven. Children were to be divided into one of three groups according to aptitude. The academically able should be sent to an expanded and more evenly distributed network of selective schools; those with a technical bent to technical schools; the remainder to a new type of school, to be called a 'modern school'. In these schools 'the courses of instruction though not merely vocational or utilitarian should be used to connect the school work with interests arising from the social and industrial environment of the pupils'. Elementary schools would take no children over the age of eleven.

The Hadow Committee had been convinced by Tawney and by the National Union of Teachers, among others, that educational experience had demonstrated that most children were capable of and willing to benefit from improved educational opportunities. They were convinced that the economy required a more educated workforce and that improved schooling could help to solve the problem of juvenile delinquency. They were convinced also that the three types of secondary school proposed should and could carry equal social esteem.[37]

The break at eleven had already been advocated in a Board of Education Circular in 1925 and was already practiced by some local authorities. Despite the intensified economy drive of the Conservative government of 1925–29, by 1931 one-third of all children over eleven were being educated under the system recommended by Hadow and encouraged by the Board of Education.

An attempt by the Labour government of 1929–31 to raise the school leaving age to fifteen was defeated by the opposition of the churches. Roman Catholics in particular pleaded that they could not afford the increased burden of costs the change would place upon them. The legacy of church domination of early developments in education now hindered further advance.

It became increasingly plain, however, that the Hadow Committee's hope of establishing real 'equality of opportunity' for children of differing talents and levels of ability ran against the grain of the enduring status consciousness of the English, as institutionalized in the severely socially-stratified educational system and reflected in the failure to put equal resources into each sector. Tawney pointed out in *Equality*, published in 1931, that 'modern' schools were already being regarded as repositories for 'failures', worse staffed and equipped than the grammar schools of the 'successful'. These in turn were regarded as socially inferior to the 'comically misnamed' public schools. He now argued that the latter should effectively be abolished.[38] There was indeed wider, legitimate, concern about standards in many private schools. Five per cent of all children attended such schools of various quality, from the élite institutions such as Eton, Winchester and Roedean, to small and often educationally poor suburban day schools. In 1932 the Chuter Ede Committee on Private Schools recommended Board of Education inspection and registration of all private schools, those failing to reach minimum standards to be closed. This was not implemented until 1944.[39]

The improvement of state secondary education, then as now, was constrained by conflicting views as to its goals. One view emphasized the need to select out and to encourage the full resources of talent among working-class children and was less concerned with the less obviously talented. It was argued that the poverty of education for the poor from the earliest ages prevented talent from emerging. A second view was that expressed by Tawney that *all* children should be educated to the highest possible standard, as under the existing system plainly they were not. A third was that talents were genetically determined and present most frequently in the higher social classes and hence there was no justification for large-scale expenditure to discover among the working classes qualities which few of them were likely to possess.

Proponents of all three views were increasingly confident that it was possible to define and to assess the different aptitudes even of the most deprived children. This conviction derived from the work of psychologists, notably that of Cyril Burt, psychologist to the LCC from 1913. Burt asserted that it was possible to devise tests to measure scientifically innate 'general intelligence'. Such tests were as attractive to Labour educationalists as to others since they appeared to offer a neutral means of assessing the aptitudes of children from deprived backgrounds and of allocating them to appropriate schools. Burt's work also, however, served to counter excessive dissatisfaction with the existing social distribution of educational opportunity. He and his colleagues asserted, on the basis of 'evidence' which has since been found to have been largely fabricated, that high intelligence was largely genetically determined and that it existed in proportionately larger quantities in the higher social classes.

Education suffered especially severely from the expenditure cuts of the early 1930s, second only to unemployment 'benefit'. Teachers' salaries were cut by 15 per cent and the Exchequer subsidies to local education authorities were reduced. Hence any local authority disposed to improve its education service or even to maintain existing standards was forced to finance it from already overburdened local rates. Building improvements suffered especially. In 1933 'free places' were abolished and replaced by means-tested 'special places'. This hit lower-middle-class families harder than those of the working class, largely because they had been the chief beneficiaries of the free place system, being able to support their children until later ages but unable to afford fees. Progressive local authorities fixed means tests high enough to protect the free places of working-class children. The chief effect of the cuts was to halt the expansion of free and improved secondary education in such areas as parts of County Durham, Wales and in Manchester where there had been determined efforts at improvement.[40]

Also in 1933, the consultative committee on education, now chaired by Sir William Spens, was asked to report on the current state of secondary education. It reported in 1938 and recommended continuation of the Hadow system. It rejected the TUC's proposal for 'multilateral' secondary schools, designed to provide for all children of secondary school age, to diminish the social distinctions emerging from the Hadow system and ideally offering real 'equality of opportunity'. This view, supported by the National Union of Teachers, became strong, though not universal, in the Labour movement during the 1930s.[41]

The Spens Committee supported IQ testing as the best and most socially neutral means of selecting children at eleven. More strongly than the Hadow Committee, the Spens Report insisted upon the need for 'parity of esteem' between the different types of secondary school, and that all places should be free.[42]

The Labour movement was sceptical. At the very least, parity of esteem could not be achieved until there was parity of expenditure on different types of school. The percentage of national income spent by central government on education was 2.4 in 1922, 2.6 in 1932 and 2.2 in 1939, which left little slack for the increased expenditure required for the improvement of poorer schools. Local authority expenditure in education rose by 25 per cent between 1921 and 1939, but improved provision was unevenly spread among authorities.[43] During the inter-war years, central government encouraged the expansion of state secondary education whilst keeping its own expenditure to a minimum.

By 1939 most teachers in state schools had received formal training. In 1936 Parliament at last enacted that the school-leaving age would be raised to fifteen, on 1 September 1939. Voluntary, mainly church, schools were to be given the necessary building grants, thus removing church opposition. However, the proposal faced opposition from other sources: it would be costly and certain employers feared the loss of cheap juvenile labour. The Duchess of Atholl, MP for Kinross and Perth, for ten years in the chair of the Juvenile Advisory Committee of the Board of Education, asserted the need of the textile industry for 'small hands' to work their machines.[44]

Largely due to such pressures, the 1936 Education Act exempted children from staying at school after fourteen if they could secure 'beneficial' employment. To whom the benefit would accrue was not made clear; nor did the Act provide for maintenance allowances. Implementation was delayed for three years to allow for the provision of the necessary buildings and teachers. The date of Hitler's invasion of Poland was 1 September 1939; two days later Britain entered the war. The raising of the leaving age was once more delayed.

Secondary education undeniably improved during the inter-war years. In 1938 46.9 per cent of pupils in secondary schools paid no fees; however, in 1937 only 19.2 per cent of the fourteen to seventeen age group were in school. Most was gained by the lower middle classes, who could afford to forego their childrens' incomes. Local authority initiative, especially in Labour and progressive Liberal controlled authorities, such as Bradford and Manchester, effected the most striking improvements.

Poorer children gained least, due both to family poverty and to the poor quality of primary education in low income districts. The expansion of secondary education dominated the educational debate between the wars. State 'primary' education, as it came to be called after the Hadow Report, suffered from expenditure cuts. It remained almost exclusively working-class, with large class sizes and poor equipment.

After 1926 education in primary schools was increasingly dominated by the demands of the selective examination at the age of eleven. Too often this did not ensure, as it might have done, high general standards, but rather that in large classes at best children seen to be bright were selectively encouraged and others neglected. By 1939 still over 2,000 children were in classes of over 50, two million in classes of over 40, many of them in old, ill-equipped and even insanitary buildings. Nursery education expanded hardly at all.[45]

Housing

As with education, inter-war state housing policy first helped the lower-middle and better off working-class and only belatedly poorer manual workers; also, although there was closer government involvement with housing than ever before, much of the initiative lay with the local authorities. As we have seen, the Addison Housing Act of 1919 led to the building for the first time of substantial numbers of council houses. This had, however, only a small impact upon the housing shortage, partly because building and rents were subject to close central control which demanded both high standards and high rents. High rents were the result of the Treasury desire to keep down expenditure and to prevent the disincentive to the growth of the privately rented sector which low public sector rents would provide. The orthodox view was, and remained, that the privately rented market should continue to provide, as it had always done, the bulk of housing. Council housing was seen only as a short-term supplement to the private sector.

Most of the new council houses were built in low density suburbs at some distance from central work places, thus raising their residents' travelling costs. This, combined with rents of 13s. to 20s. per week made them inaccessible to the poorer working class who remained overwhelmingly in privately rented accommodation, much of it of poor quality. The rent controls which had favoured this kind of accommodation came effectively to trap them therein. The relaxation of controls in 1920 and 1923, in particular the measure of 1923 which removed control on a change of tenancy, was a disincentive to movement even when families grew in size. Hence controls, due to such changes introduced in response to landlord pressure and the official preference for maximizing freedom in the market, contributed directly to increased overcrowding in the 1920s, helping to prevent the 'filtering up' of the poor to better private accommodation left vacant by council house tenants which had been the justification for the high rents of council housing.

The 1919 Act benefited the better off, skilled or white-collar worker, whose need for better housing was real and whose capacity to demand it was more effective than that of the very poor. It also helped considerably to sustain the private building industry, which did most of the building under contract to local authorities. This stimulus to the building industry led to a gradual revival of private housebuilding for rent and for sale.

Building under the 1919 Act diminished as soon as Sir Alfred Mond replaced Addison at the Ministry of Health in 1921. In 1922 grants under the 1919 Act were stopped. The resulting outcry led to the Housing Act of 1923, introduced by Chamberlain on his arrival at the Ministry of Health. This provided a flat rate subsidy of £6 p.a. for twenty years for each house built both by local authorities and by private enterprise, provided that they met approved standards. These standards were, however, lower than those laid down by the 1919 Act.

Chamberlain still saw the private sector as the chief potential supplier of new homes and felt that, with state encouragement, it was now in a position to do so. The subsidy was to be given to local authorities only where the Minister could be convinced that private enterprise could not meet the need. The 1923 Act also gave local authorities new powers to advance loans to those who wished to become owner-occupiers but who could not afford the initial deposit. The result was a high level of private building, mostly for owner-occupation. Many fewer houses were built for private renting than Chamberlain had hoped. Housing for rent had become since the war a less attractive form of investment than before. Also important in bringing about the trend towards building for owner-occupation was the considerable demand for small new housing among white-collar and skilled manual workers. Both were anxious for the security of ownership and to escape the shared bathrooms and relative lack of privacy of much privately rented accommodation. The privately rented sector had entered a long-term decline but this was not yet evident to the government or to the Treasury, which long continued to try to encourage it.

Labour saw subsidized local authority housing as the long-term solution to the housing problem. It was believed that the free market could not provide adequate housing at a cost many working people could afford: it had plainly failed to do so in the past and there was no reason to hope for better in the future. Purpose-built housing was also seen as more desirable than the multi-occupied, formerly middle-class housing to which the Conservatives expected the poor to 'filter up'.

The most substantial achievement of the 1924 Labour government was its Housing Act. The Minister of Health, John Wheatley, had been a leader of militancy on the housing issue on Clydeside and was the most radical member of the Labour Cabinet. His Housing Act increased the state subsidy, to local authority housing only, to £9 p.a. for forty years for houses built to rent at controlled rents.

Equally important, Wheatley negotiated with the building unions to increase the building labour force by increasing the number of apprenticeships and shortening their duration. He also won the support of the building employers by assuring them that new building under the Act would be provided by private building firms under contract to local authorities.

The Act abolished the clause in the 1923 Act which allowed local authority building only to fill gaps in the private market. It was the most determined attempt of the period to expand local authority housing. Local authority housebuilding increased as a result, especially under Labour and progressive Liberal controlled authorities such as those of Manchester or Sheffield; but the problem remained that, even at controlled rents, the mass of the poorer working class could neither afford the rents nor the costs of travel from the suburbs. [doc 14]

Chamberlain, on his return to the Ministry of Health at the end of 1924, attempted no further changes in housing policy. Building for private sale was expanding and builders had reason to be satisfied with their gains also from providing local authority housing. Local authority housing was expanding fastest in the larger cities, where it was unlikely that private enterprise could meet both the needs of the working class and the demands of the better off.

By the time of Labour's return to office in 1929 the more tractable end of the housing problem – the poor accommodation of skilled and white-collar workers – had largely been solved by a combination of local authority housing and increased building for sale of small houses for owner-occupation, which became cheaper as the costs of labour and materials fell in the later 1920s. The glaring remaining problem was that of the 'slums', overcrowded, often insanitary and bug-ridden privately rented accommodation in town and country. Labour policy shifted from house building to 'slum clearance' and building. 'Slum clearance', it was hoped, would physically remove the worst privately rented housing, which could be replaced by council housing. Furthermore, city centre clearances would release land for rebuilding close to workplaces. The Housing Act of 1930 subsidized local authorities on the basis of the number of families re-housed from cleared slums and the cost of rehousing. Each authority was instructed to survey their housing stock and to produce a five year plan for clearance. The 1930 Act at last provided the means for a direct assault upon the housing problems of the poorest.

However, the clearance drive had hardly begun when the economy drive of 1931–33 put an end to building under the Wheatley Act. This meant the effective end to substantial additions to the total stock of working-class housing from local authority building. Subsidized building was possible only for the replacement of cleared housing and additional building had to be financed from local rates which were already bearing the additional cost of education, health and unemployment relief expenditure. Those who were ill-housed, but not ill-housed enough to qualify as 'slum dwellers', lost any reasonable chance of obtaining a council house. This remained broadly true for the remainder of the 1930s. The fall in council housebuilding after 1932 was accompanied by a boom in private building, mainly for owner-occupation, assisted by falling interest rates, reduced costs due both to falling wages and new pre-fabricated methods of construction, and an increased flow of investment into building as the crash of 1929–31 temporarily reduced the confidence of investors in other forms of business investment. Mortgages became easier to obtain. Large building firms, such as Taylor Woodrow, had grown fast on the secure basis of local authority contracts under the Wheatley Act and were well placed to take advantage of increased opportunities for private building. The private houses built were of variable quality; some were well built for the changed needs of the relatively wealthy, in a decade in which servants became harder to find and a compact, well-equiped, easily managed house seemed desirable. Others were so poorly built at low cost that the end of the 30s saw a wave of 'mortgage strikes' by 'owners' unwilling to pay for new houses with leaking roofs or warped window-frames until they were repaired.

Owner-occupation was attractive to Conservatives in view of their preference for encouraging private enterprise rather than state action. Some also recognized potential political advantages from its growth. The leader of the Leeds Conservative party told his Labour opponents in 1926 'It's a good thing for the people to buy their houses. They turn Tory directly. We shall go on making Tories and you will be wiped out.'[46]

But owner-occupation was inaccessible to the poorest. Housing conditions at the lower end of the privately rented market were deplorable and there were growing signs that they were once more becoming the focus of militancy, especially on Clydeside and in East London.

The first action of the National government in the housing field was the Rent Act of 1933 which decontrolled half a million larger or more expensive houses. By this time the rent control system had become so confused that it was difficult to know which tenancies were controlled and which were not, a situation which some landlords were quick to exploit. As a result, local Labour parties and tenants' associations, notably in Glasgow, began to form unofficial rent advice bureaux to establish whether or not tenancies were controlled and to aid tenants in challenging deceitful landlords.

In the face of the size and potential explosiveness of such action the National government appears to have judged it better to encourage the removal of the worst privately rented property, which was the source of most disputes concerning rent controls and whose tenants could least afford a market rent. If the poorest could be shifted from private 'slums' into council housing, the problem of obtaining rent from them would become the responsibility of local authorities, which increasingly in the mid-1930s became controlled by the party which was supporting tenants' interests, Labour. (The LCC became Labour controlled in 1934, Glasgow in 1931, Leeds briefly in 1933, the other big cities followed.)

The National government under a new Minister of Health, Sir Hilton Young, revived 'slum clearance' in 1935 with enthusiasm: the Prince of Wales was mobilized to make powerful speeches against the slums and to make well-publicized visits to a selected few. The Church of England issued a national 'slum clearance' appeal; the BBC and leading newspapers made special investigations and published horrifying revelations about slums.[47] The Housing Act 1935, again, requested local authorities to survey their slums and to submit clearance plans. It also specified that council rents should not fall below the market price for similar property in the locality. This was explicitly designed to support the private sector, meeting the demands of the building industry by ensuring that council houses did not attract those capable of renting or buying in the private market. In effect it attempted to ensure, once more, that council housing merely supplemented the private market in localities and for social groups where the latter could not meet the demand.

This policy, of course, conflicted with the aim of rehousing the poorest who could not afford market rents. This problem was left to the local authorities, who were forced to create the means of solving it: differential rent schemes. Leeds had introduced such a scheme in 1933 when the beginning of their effective slum clearance drive raised the problem of rehousing those least able to pay rent regularly. On the initiative of the country's first Director of Housing, appointed by the Labour council in 1933, Leeds introduced a system whereby tenants rather than houses were subsidized and paid a rent determined by their income rather than by the size and cost of the house; below a certain level of income the tenant paid no rent. This system overcame the previous problem of overcrowding in council houses. Since tenancies had been allocated on the basis of capacity to pay a certain level of rent, rather than on the basis of housing need, tenants had not always acquired the most suitable housing. The desire to solve this problem was a major reason for the active support of the growing numbers of professional housing administrators for differential rents. Such schemes, however, met Labour opposition on the grounds that they might encourage the payment of low wages, that they redistributed within the working class rather than from rich to poor and that they were necessarily means tested. Leeds Conservatives exploited the resentment which arose among tenants who paid different amounts of rent for the same housing; they accused Labour of establishing a 'socialist city state', and returned to power in Leeds in 1934 largely on this issue. After their election Conservatives modified the rent scheme so that all tenants paid some rent but, significantly, they did not abolish it. It was clear even to those, like the Leeds Conservatives, with a strong preference for the private housing market that some such scheme was essential if the poorest were to be rehoused.[48]

Similar schemes were operated by 110 local authorities of every political colour by 1939. They conveniently solved the contradictions within a national housing policy designed both to encourage private building and to eliminate the lower end of the privately rented sector, which on the one hand encouraged high council rents but, on the other, pushed into the council sector tenants least able to pay them.

'Slum clearance' was persistently and predictably opposed by slum landlords. Their pressure, however, had little effect, other than a further relaxation of rent controls on higher rented properties in 1938. They were outweighed politically by the combined concern of the National government, the labour movement, housing administrators and of employers, all for different motives, that the slum clearance programme proceed. Its importance for the maintenance of social order appeared all the greater as tenants' organizations grew further in the late 1930s and organized increasingly effective rent strikes, for example in Stepney in 1939. Employers were concerned that their workers should be well housed, secure and peaceful. Housing administrators were anxious to extend and rationalize the public sector. Labour favoured the removal of the worst housing and its replacement by local authority housing which, they argued, progressed too slowly in the 1930s.

The 1935 Act defined 'slums' for the first time by the administratively simple but inadequate yardstick of overcrowding. All local authorities were instructed to assess the degree of overcrowding within their district. A rather relaxed standard of overcrowding was adopted, of two persons per room, including all living- and bedrooms, allowing for segregation of the sexes. On this standard, 3.3 per cent of all housing in England and Wales was found to be overcrowded. Actual overcrowding was certainly greater. In Leeds, for example, on a more stringent definition, which included only rooms used for sleeping, 21.1 per cent of households were found to be overcrowded. The difficulty of taking overcrowding as the chief index of slum living was that it took no account of other housing deficiencies, such as bad sanitation, poor construction or the back-to-back dwellings of parts of the North. On this basis, though with some local authorities adopting a more ambitious definition of a slum, by March 1939 472,000 slums had been scheduled for closure and 272,000 had been cleared.

Between 1931 and 1939, 2.5 million new homes were built in Great Britain, under 600,000 of them by local authorities, aided not at all by a further cut in subsidies in 1938. Three-quarters of newly built private housing was in the South and Midlands, where economic growth created a buoyant market. Most council houses were built in London (where East London did not share the boom affecting other parts of the metropolis) Scotland and the North. By 1939 the nature of the transformed national housing stock physically embodied the different conditions of the 'two nations'.

Little was done about the poor state of much rural housing. City centre rebuilding increasingly took the form of high density flats, as in central London and the model Quarry Hill development in Leeds. However, both council and owner-occupied housing was built more characteristically in low-rise, low-density 'garden' estates, partially realizing the dream of a generation of town planners, partially only because their spread contributed also to further urban sprawl, especially to the elephantiasis of London, and relatively little building took place in new 'garden cities'. This trend was persistently attacked by planners. Many of them felt that the suburbs were consuming too much of the countryside and, also, that current trends were destroying the potential of the cities themselves to provide a civilized environment; many European cities demonstrated that well-planned and comfortable high-density building was both possible and desirable and did not lead inevitably to slums. Such pleas foundered on the antipathy of the English to flat-dwelling and, in the 1930s, on that of their rulers to whole-hearted planning. The British notion of town planning remained throughout the inter-war years severely limited. The Ministry of Health, dedicated to maximization of free enterprise wherever possible and opposed to controls on development, did little to encourage it. The Act of 1919 obliged all urban authorities to prepare town planning schemes and a new planning department of the Ministry was established. However, the obligation was never enforced and in 1932 the obligation was removed, though some planning did occur on local initiative.

In 1920 a Ministry of Health committee had recommended the building of garden cities to relieve London's overcrowding. The suggestion was not adopted. Welwyn Garden City was founded privately soon after the war on land bought for the purpose by Ebenezer Howard. Some attempts to build planned satellite communities with factories were made by Manchester Council in their Wythenshawe estate and by Liverpool at Speke, both built in the 1930s. There were no serious attempts at large-scale regional planning.

The proliferation of suburbs increased the spread of and demand for public transport, and for roads, as the number of private cars multiplied. The history of urban development demonstrates with especial clarity the limitations of the public commitment to planning in the 30s and the priority still given to unplanned free enterprise, to the detriment of the environment, in respects that have become fully recognized only much later.[49]

Low pay and family allowances

As we have seen, low pay remained a major cause of poverty in the inter-war years, and it was increasingly recognized that its effects were especially acute when associated with above-average family size. There were no further legislative attempts to raise wages, indeed the Treasury preference was for wage cutting where possible. After 1920 cuts occurred in many occupations and were a major cause of the continuing crisis of industrial relations in the coal industry.

The poverty surveys, especially in view of their revelations of child poverty, led to persistent criticism of low pay and its effects. Rowntree concluded his survey of York in 1936 with the suggestion that a statutory minimum wage was the only solution. He recognized the possible objections to such a proposal but argued that it could be implemented without increasing the costs of industry and therefore prices, if it was associated with the reorganization of industry to achieve more efficient and economical methods of production and distribution.

This did not, as Harold Macmillan pointed out in *The Middle Way* a year later, meet the difficulty that reorganization of the kind envisaged by Rowntree was not equally possible in all industries, that where it was possible it might create unemployment, and that the attachment of a strong craft-based trade union movement to pay differentials might obstruct any attempt to improve the relative position of lower paid workers.

Macmillan, however, felt that it was essential, ideally on a higher level than the stringent minimum advocated by Rowntree, both in order to establish a high level of demand in the economy and as a necessary measure of social justice. He believed that it could be achieved, without serious ill-effects, only within the framework of a planned economy. Macmillan recognized that planning did not have wide influential support by the late 1930s because the economy had appeared to revive without the aid of drastic reorganization. He argued, however, as did Keynes in 1937, that the economic recovery of the 1930s was temporary, limited and 'artificial', and that a new slump was imminent which would demonstrate the necessity for wholesale economic reconstruction.

The central problem, Macmillan argued, was that Britain in the 1930s had neither a free competitive economy nor a planned economy. He believed that an entirely free market was neither feasible nor desirable. The alternative was planning, to preserve the best features of the existing economy and to eliminate the worst. Hence he proposed that private enterprise should be left free to innovate, with capital supplied by a National Investment Board where necessary. This Board would direct capital to where it could be most productively used but such established industry as could be made profitable should be encouraged to avoid wasteful competition and duplication and to operate with maximum efficiency. By agreement with a majority of employers, and force applied if necessary to recalcitrant minorities, each industry should be encouraged, with state financial assistance where necessary, into co-operation, merger and technological improvement to attain maximum efficiency, without state interference in their day-to-day management. Industries which could not be made profitable by these means should be discouraged unless they were essential 'to national well-being or safety' (e.g. transport or coal), in which case they should be run as national enterprises, their losses to be made good by the profits of successful industries.

Macmillan proposed controls upon the money supply and interest rates, and price controls and restrictions upon profits to avoid the ill-effects of monopoly which might result, and to reduce the vulnerability of industry to irresponsible speculation. Wages would also be controlled and a minimum wage could then be established. To avoid trade union opposition to such proposals Macmillan insisted that it was essential to preserve the roles and freedom of trade unions including the right to strike, essential indeed that trade union membership should become compulsory. The role of trade unions would be to negotiate 'fair' wages and conditions of employment; the role of the state would be merely to intervene, preferably by persuasion rather than by force, where wages fell too low to be compatible with social justice or the need to maintain demand, or too high to promote efficiency. If the system was seen to be just, Macmillan believed that unions would co-operate. He recognized that the necessary restructuring of industry would cause some unemployment, but he believed that re-training and long-term economic growth would solve this problem. [doc. 15]

Macmillan's humane, intelligent, if somewhat idealistic 'middle way' did not attract immediate or widespread influential support. Industry was not widely regarded as being in such crisis that politicians and employers felt forced to contemplate such drastic and politically difficult measures. The Treasury and many employers remained wedded to the belief that a low-wage economy was essential to economic recovery,[50] hence many of those concerned about the problem of low pay felt forced to seek more limited and more immediately politically plausible solutions. Increasingly the answer appeared to be the introduction of family allowances to supplement the incomes of larger families. These had been advocated before the war by Eleanor Rathbone and others. In 1917 Rathbone was a leading figure in the foundation of the Family Endowment Society which was dedicated to the achievement of family allowances in order, primarily, to enhance the status of women both as mothers and as workers, because 'it would strike at one of the main popular objections to "equal pay for equal work", i.e. the plea that a man requires a family wage whereas a woman requires only an individual subsistence wage'.[51] Equally important, they wished to achieve some redistribution of income in favour of families, especially poor families.

The Society pressed actively during the 1920s and 1930s for the principle of 'family endowment' to be accepted in as many areas of government policy as possible; for example, differential rents proportional to family size. The revelations of child poverty from the Bowley and Hogg survey onwards increased support for measures to diminish it and led to the formation of the Children's Minimum Council, again initiated by Rathbone, with the support of such organizations of the reforming centre as the Fabian Society, radical Conservatives such as Harold Macmillan, and Liberals such as Beveridge. The Council took up the general cause of the welfare of mothers and children.

The specific issue of family allowances became more urgent in the 1930s due, on the one hand, to fear of population decline and to suggestions that cash incentives might reverse this process, and on the other to recognition that low wages were leading to still lower welfare benefits and indeed were in danger of preventing any general improvement in welfare services. The continuing adherence to the principle of 'less eligibility' in the formulation of social policies ensured that their general standard was kept low by the fear of providing disincentives to work. Employers, also, were coming to recognize that a system of family allowances, paid preferably by the state, would diminish pressure for a general increase in wage rates and hence might facilitate the twin objectives of reinvigorating the economy and of maintaining political and social stability. Some employers themselves introduced family allowances for employees, largely as an alternative to raising wages.

Hence by the end of the 1930s family allowances appeared as a politically feasible solution to a different kind of problem from that envisaged by the Family Endowment Society at its foundation. Equality for women was no longer a leading motive of its supporters. They were opposed, however, by the labour movement which, with some reason, feared the employers' enthusiasm for this cheap substitute for higher wages. Although there was support in the trade unions and in the Labour party for measures of child support, such as school feeding and maintenance grants for schoolchildren, there was general opposition to wage subsidies. Family allowances, however, were incapable of solving the fundamental problems whose identification provided them with so much support, rather their very limited nature highlighted the gravity of these problems.[52]

CONCLUSION

The leading imperative behind government policy-making in all fields in the 1930s was the desire to stimulate economic growth on a free enterprise basis whilst maintaining social order. This implied for social policy not only the need to make provision, as in the fields of housing and unemployment benefits, to prevent disorder, but so to improve the social infrastructure in the areas of education, working class housing and health that impediments to 'national efficiency' were minimized. Achievement of these aims necessitated closer central government control over social policy and administration, and official economic policies demanded minimum public expenditure.

These perceived necessities were partly compatible and complementary but embodied one major contradiction: that improvements in social provision were in all fields constrained by the danger that, at a certain point, they would conflict with the needs of a free economy for both investment capital and cheap labour, which was available and eager for work and was not immobilized by the counter-attractions of a higher income from welfare. Hence the infrastructure could not be improved sufficiently to assist economic growth without conflicting with the means chosen by employers and by the state to achieve that growth. This problem arose more acutely in the provision of cash benefits than of services such as education and housing. Hence increasing central control was exercised over cash payments, as for unemployment relief and the Poor Law, and their cost was minimized where possible, as with pensions. The extent and social importance of unemployment made increased expenditure unavoidable although all possible means were taken to restrain it. Housing and education expenditure were less severely constrained but the increase was borne by local rather than central government. For example, central government expenditure on education was £59.3 m. in 1921; £65.3 m. in 1939. That of local government £73.9 m. in 1921, £100.4 m. in 1939. There was a comparable disparity in the burden of housing expenditure, and also disparities in the willingness and ability of local authorities to spend on such services.

The conflict at the heart of social policy was perceived by Harold Macmillan, from another perspective by Keynes, and pressure of events forced it also upon Beveridge. Macmillan argued that in a planned economy 'less eligibility' could at last be abandoned and a high level of social services established. A prosperous economy would be able to afford improved services and they were essential to its achievement and growth. In a more socially just society there would be no need to drive men to work. Macmillan argued that

the overwhelming majority of workers are particularly anxious to obtain employment and would not be deterred from seeking it, however high the rate of benefit might be. This is not because of any excessive virtue, but because most men actually prefer useful work to meaningless idleness. Their sense of duty makes them prefer to be useful creative citizens occupying their place in the social scheme of things on an equal footing with other men, rather than become unproductive dependents living a life devoid of constructive purpose. Very often the incidents that give rise to the view that men prefer benefit to wages arise not because benefit is too high but because the wages offered are too low.[53]

He accepted that 'laziness exists and that society has to protect itself against it'. However, he argued that 'it would be rather an excess of caution to penalize the great majority of workers in order to guard against a few'.

Macmillan expressed especially cogently the dilemma facing the British economy and society at the end of the 1930s and offered one solution to it. It was a dilemma of which many in the labour movement had long been aware but had lacked the power to solve. Not all in the labour movement accepted the substantial support for free enterprise explicit in Macmillan's proposals, but his broad framework contained much that appealed to them. Many others who were daily at the forefront of this dilemma as administrators of social services or of industry were also being forced into recognition of its existence and of the need for a drastic solution, for a changed direction in government policies. Among civil servants and within the Federation of British Industry (FBI) there were by 1939 signs that ideas put forward by Macmillan and other advocates of planning (such as PEP and the representative collection of 'Establishment' figures who signed the demand for planning published in 1935 as *The Next Five Years*) were beginning to be taken seriously.[54] At the same time, the different and ultimately more influential solution offered by Keynes, which advocated management of the economy by fiscal and monetary means rather than by strict physical planning and controls, was slowly gaining influence in similar circles.[55]

An historically novel broad consensus of opposition to the failures and incompatible goals of the existing system was beginning to emerge. Whether this could take the difficult next step of developing into a consensus as to the way forward was not put to the test in peacetime. No economic crisis occurred which was sufficiently severe to enforce a marked change of direction in public policy; rather the state continued to move in the direction of increased intervention and controls at the slow pace made possible by the partial recovery of the economy in the 1930s. Instead, the next step was taken under the influence not of economic crisis but of war.

REFERENCES

1. C. L. MOWAT, *Britain Between the Wars*, Methuen, London (1955); J. STEVENSON AND C. COOK, *The Slump: Society and Politics during the Depression*, Cape, London (1977); J. SAVILLE

AND A. HOWKINS, 'The Nineteen Thirties: A Revisionist History', *The Socialist Register*, Merlin Press, London (1979).

2. R. SKIDELSKY, *Politicians and The Slump*, Penguin, Harmondsworth (1967) Ch. 1.

3. R. SKIDELSKY, 'Keynes and The Treasury View 1920–1939' in W. MOMMSEN (ed.), *The Emergence of the Welfare State in Britain and Germany*, Croom Helm, London (1981).

4. R. MITCHISON, *British Population Change since 1860*, (Studies in Economic and Social History) Macmillan, London (1977).

5. B. S. ROWNTREE, *Poverty and Progress*, Longman, London (1941).

6. P. FORD, *Work and Wealth in a Modern Port*, Allen & Unwin, London (1934).

7. H. TOUT, *The Standard of Living in Bristol*, Bristol University Press (1938).

8. C. L. MOWAT *op. cit.*, 461.

9. *Ibid.*, p. 506.

10. J. MACNICOL, 'Family Allowances and Less Eligibility' in PAT THANE (ed.) *The Origins of British Social Policy*, Croom Helm, London (1978) p. 192.

11. A. L. BOWLEY (ed.), *Studies in the National Income 1924–1938*, Cambridge University Press (1944); C. L. MOWAT, *op. cit.*, pp. 490–94.

12. B. WOOTTON, *Social Science and Social Pathology*, George Allen & Unwin, London (1959) p. 41.

13. C. L. MOWAT, *op. cit.*, pp. 125–27.

14. A. DEACON, *In Search of the Scrounger, The Administration of Unemployment Insurance in Britain 1920–1931*, G. Bell & Sons Ltd, London (1976) pp. 65–6.

15. R. SKIDELSKY, *Politicians and The Slump*, *op. cit.*; R. MCKIBBEN, 'The Economic Policy of the Second Labour Government 1929–1931', *Past and Present*, (1975).

16. R. BARKER, *Political Ideas in Modern Britain*, Methuen, London (1978) pp. 134–41.

17. J. HARRIS, *William Beveridge*, Oxford University Press (1977) Chs. 12, 13, and 14.

18. J. MACNICOL, *op. cit.*, p. 191.

19. C. L. MOWAT, *op. cit.*, pp. 470–72, 483; B. B. GILBERT, *British Social Policy 1914–1939*, Batsford, London (1970) pp. 162 –93; 214–15.

21. P. RYAN, 'The Poor Law in 1926' in MARGARET MORRIS (ed.) *The General Strike*, Penguin, Harmondsworth (1976).
22. N. BRANSON, *Poplarism*, Lawrence & Wishart, London (1979).
23. M. A. CROWTHER, 'The Later Years of the Workhouse' in PAT THANE (ed.) *The Origins of British Social Policy, op. cit.*
24. S. AND B. WEBB, *op. cit.*, p. 821 ff.; B. B. GILBERT, *op. cit.*, pp. 203–34.
25. S. M. HERBERT, *Britain's Health*, Penguin, Harmondsworth (1939) p. 19.
26. C. L. MOWAT, *op. cit.*, pp. 512–13.
27. P. HALL et al., *Change, Choice and Conflict in Social Policy*, Heinemann, London (1975) Ch. 11.
28. B. B. GILBERT, *op. cit.*, pp. 255–308; S. M. HERBERT, *op. cit.*, Ch. 7.
28a J. LEWIS, 'The Peckham Health Centre: An Inquiry into the Nature of Living', *Bulletin of the Society for the Social History of Medicine*, No. 30–1, (June and December 1982).
29. B. ABEL-SMITH, *op. cit.*, Chs. 18–25; HERBERT, *op. cit.*, Ch. 8, M. SPRING RICE, *Working Class Wives* (1939) Virago, London (reprint) (1981).
30. J. LEWIS, *The Politics of Motherhood*, Croom Helm, London (1980) Chs. 4 and 5; M. SPRING RICE, *op. cit.*
31. S. M. HERBERT, *op. cit.*, pp. 161–2; M. FREEDEN, 'Eugenics and Progressive Thought', *Historical Journal* (1979).
32. B. ABEL-SMITH, *op. cit.*, pp. 417–23.
33. B. B. GILBERT, *op. cit.*, pp. 235–54; SIR ARNOLD WILSON AND G. S. MACKAY, *Old Age Pensions. An Historical and Critical Study*, Oxford University Press (1941) Part II.
34. J. HEYWOOD, *Children in Care*, Routledge & Kegan Paul, London (1959) pp. 114–32.
35. H. SILVER, *Equal Opportunity in Education*, Methuen, London (1973).
36. *Ibid.*, pp. 8–17; W. VAN DER EYKEN, (ed.) *Education, The Child and Society*, Penguin, Harmondsworth (1973) pp. 264–67.
37. H. SILVER, *op. cit.*; W. VAN DER EYKEN, *op. cit.*, pp. 306–7.
38. R. H. TAWNEY, *Equality*, George Allen & Unwin, London (*reprint*) (*1964*).
39. H. SILVER, *op. cit.*, pp. L18–27.
40. D. RUBINSTEIN AND B. SIMON, *The Evolution of the*

    Comprehensive School 1926–1966. Routledge & Kegan Paul, London (1969) pp. 7–20.
41. *Ibid.*
42. *Ibid.*, pp. 15–18.
43. B. MITCHELL AND P. DEANE, *Abstract of British Historical Statistics*, Cambridge University Press (1962) p. 399.
44. N. BRANSON AND M. HEINEMANN, *Britain in the Nineteen Thirties*, Weidenfeld & Nicolson, London (1971) p. 177.
45. VAN DER EYKEN, *op. cit.*, p. 320.
46. J. MELLING (ed.) *Housing, Social Policy and the State*, Croom Helm, London (1980) p. 116.
47. J. STEVENSON, *Social Conditions in Britain between the Wars*, Penguin, Harmondsworth (1977) Ch. 3.
48. J. MELLING, *op. cit.*, pp. 127–33.
49. J. MELLING, *op. cit., passim.*; B. B. GILBERT, *op. cit.*, pp. 137–161; 197–202; N. BRANSON AND M. HEINEMANN, *op. cit.*, Ch. 13; W. ASHWORTH, *The Genesis of Modern British Town Planning*, Routledge & Kegan Paul, London (1954) Ch. VIII.
50. H. MACMILLAN, *The Middle Way*, Macmillan, London (1938); A. MARWICK, 'Middle opinion in the Thirties: Planning, Progress and Political "Agreement"', *English Historical Review* (1964).
51. P. HALL *et al.*, *op. cit.*, p. 164.
52. *Ibid.*, pp. 157–79; J. MACNICOL, *op. cit.*, pp. 173–202.
53. H. MACMILLAN, *op. cit.*, p. 332.
54. A. MARWICK, *op. cit.*
55. D. E. MOGGRIDGE, *Keynes*, Fontana Modern Masters, London (1976).

Chapter seven

THE SECOND WORLD WAR AND AFTER

Discussion of the influence of the experience of the war of 1939–45 upon social policy has long been influenced by Richard Titmuss' assumption that the war period bred decisively new attitudes to social policy. Titmuss argued that 'the circumstances of the war created an unprecedented sense of social solidarity among the British people, which made them willing to accept a great increase of egalitarian policies and collective state intervention'.[1] He claimed that the impact of bombing and evacuation had dramatically exposed certain chronic social evils that had hitherto lain concealed from the public eye – (for example) child poverty, malnutrition and the gross geographical imbalance of health and medical services that prevailed at the start of the war; and he thought that the war for the first time made central government fully aware not merely of the moral desirability but of the sheer strategic necessity for having a civilian population that was contented, efficient, well nourished and physically fit. All these pressures, Titmuss concluded, came to the fore at the time of the retreat from Dunkirk in June 1940: they meant that 'for five years of war the pressures for a higher standard of welfare and a deeper comprehension of social justice steadily gained in strength ... the mood of the people changed and, in sympathetic response, values changed as well ... (they) summoned forth a note of self-criticism, of national introspection, and set in motion ideas and talk of principles and plans'.[2]

These ideas, principles and plans, it is argued, led to far-reaching official proposals for post-war social and economic reconstruction emerging during the war, to the victory of the Labour party in the election of 1945, and to the wide range of social legislation introduced by that government.

Was Titmuss correct? How much change in attitudes to and legislation for social welfare was brought about specifically by the war?

If there was change, did he correctly analyse the causes? We have already seen that before 1939 public and official attention had already been drawn repeatedly to such problems as child poverty, malnutrition and the weaknesses of health, education and housing provision. All of these had been discussed within the context of the wider-ranging problems of the British and international economies. Titmuss did not attempt a comprehensive history of wartime social policy but concentrated exclusively on areas of policy designed to meet the war emergency: provision for evacuation and medical services for civilian and military casualties. Were conclusions derived from this limited investigation valid also for other areas of policy?

During the period of the 'phoney war' (from September 1939 to the spring of 1940) when a speedy allied victory was expected, Chamberlain's government was concerned primarily with those aspects of social and economic policy which appeared essential to the conduct of the war. These included arrangements for the control of essential industries and communications, for increased taxation to finance the war, for the evacuation of cities before the anticipated bombing and for the reorganization of health services for military and bombing casualties. All of these actions had been planned before the war. Their implementation necessitated considerable extensions of government action and control. All in practice posed unforeseen problems and hence stimulated pressures for new kinds of change.

But the government faced constant criticism that their preparations did not go far enough. Underlying the growing opposition were justified doubts of the capacity to lead a war government of the group of appeasers who had failed to appreciate the necessity for the war. The result was the fall of Chamberlain in early May 1940 and his replacement as Prime Minister by Churchill. A coalition government was formed which included prominent Labour Ministers and was controlled by a small War Cabinet. The political parties agreed to suspend party differences for the war period.[3]

The near defeat of Dunkirk followed almost immediately. It was then clear that the war was serious and likely to be long. The effect of Dunkirk upon civilian attitudes, according to Ministry of Information surveys, was to make most people more concerned about their personal and family safety and about winning the war than with issues of social justice or post-war reconstruction.[4] Most of the War Cabinet, notably Churchill, were understandably more immediately concerned with problems relating to the conduct of war than with wider, long-term social questions. An exception to this was Ernest

Bevin, who was determined to use his role as Minister of Labour to fulfil many of the pre-war aims of the trade union movement.

On 18 June 1940, the day after the fall of France, the Director-General of the Ministry of Information asked members of the War Cabinet whether the government should immediately make promises about social reform after the war, to boost civilian morale. The response was the establishment of the War Aims Committee in August 1940. Until the end of the war this was responsible for discussing post-war reconstruction, but it did little for some time. Little conscious central planning of post-war economic and social policy was discernible in mid-1940; indeed, the appointment of Arthur Greenwood, whose career was plainly past its peak, to control of the committee in January 1941 was taken as an indication of the low priority given by the War Cabinet to social issues. There was little planning for post-war reconstruction as a matter of Cabinet policy until Greenwood's dismissal in February 1942.[5]

Below the level of the War Cabinet, however, proposals for social and economic change came from individuals, such as Keynes, who was an economic advisor to the War Cabinet from the summer of 1940, and Beveridge, who was for some time outside government circles. Also, within certain Ministries consideration of policy development continued in ways initially little affected by the war.

EDUCATION

This was most obvious at the Board of Education, a department in which certain sections were relatively unaffected by war demands, although others faced the considerable problems of teacher shortages and of relocating schools from bomb-threatened cities. Evacuation severely disrupted the education of many children. Discussion of the future of education was active in the Board during 1941 and received some stimulation from the low levels of literacy discovered among young military recruits, but seems largely to have continued on the trajectory established before the war.

In 1941 a memorandum, *Education after the War*, was issued and circulated privately to many organizations as a basis for discussion. Over the following two years comments on the memorandum flowed into the Board; there were meetings, conferences and pamphlets on a variety of educational matters. These discussions were already well advanced, initiated by the civil servants, when R. A. Butler became President of the Board of Education in June 1941. As Chairman of the Conservative party committee on post-war problems he was already interested in education and sympathetic to the policies being developed within the Board.

Discussion of educational reforms continued with Butler's support, despite efforts by Churchill to stop it. Churchill was anxious to avoid political controversy during the war and was especially worried about the revival of religious controversy. More generally, Churchill regarded social issues as secondary to military ones during the war and was unwilling to devote too much government time to them. However his, and the War Cabinet's, preoccupation with the conduct of war diminished central control and observation of the activities of individual ministries.

Education after the War accepted the Spens tripartite system and the notion of 'parity of esteem' , arguing that 'equality of opportunity' did not mean 'that all children should receive the same form of education . . . at the secondary stage there must be ample variety of educational opportunity'.[6] Many of the responses to the memorandum were critical of this approach. The TUC, the Labour Party, with the support of its annual conference, the Society of Friends, the LCC and some Welsh county councils continued to support multilateral schools. Other minorities advocated the continued pre-eminence of grammar schools for the preservation and encouragement of academic excellence. However, there was more general concern to raise standards of education for all children, whatever the chosen system. This was the aim of the Council for Educational Advance which was established in 1942 by the TUC, the Co-operative Union Education Committee, the National Union of Teachers (NUT) and the Workers' Educational Association (WEA), and of most other organizations concerned with teaching or educational administration. Most of these organizations supported the tripartite system whilst insisting upon the need for genuine 'parity' of esteem and of standards.

From the middle of 1942 an allied victory in the war seemed more or less assured. The resulting more relaxed climate of opinion led to a revival of overt if peaceable social conflict and a more widespread interest in the shape of the post-war world. Party political conflict re-emerged. The number of strikes, few in 1940–42, rose sharply in 1943 and 1944.[7] Thereafter, to maintain civilian support for the war in this new climate and with an eye to maximizing post-war social stability, the government gave more attention to social reconstruction, though this was still sometimes equivocal in view of the internal political conflicts of a coalition government. The main division was between the Labour and progressive Conservative members who favoured concrete social and economic planning and legislation for reconstruction, and those Conservatives who argued that planning and action should be delayed until it was clear whether or not the post-war economy could yield the resources to finance new measures. Some argued this from conviction, others tactically, being opposed in principle to extensive change.

In this political climate the Board of Education continued on its established path. In July 1943 it published a White Paper, *Educational Reconstruction*, one of many White Papers issued in 1943–44. This reflected many criticisms of the existing system in commenting that: 'There is nothing to be said in favour of a system which subjects children at the age of eleven to the strain of a competitive examination on which not only their future schooling, but their future careers may depend.' It went on to advocate the tripartite system which necessarily involved selection, or 'allocation', at the age of eleven but emphasised that there should be full interchange between different types of school and perhaps, in certain circumstances, a combination of all three on one site or in a single building.[8]

Almost immediately followed a report on *Curriculum and Examination in Secondary Schools* from a special committee of the Secondary Schools Examination Council, under the chairmanship of Sir Cyril Norwood, former headmaster of Harrow School. This committee, on the basis of no specialized advice, announced that there existed three 'rough groupings' of children with different 'types of mind'. These were: 'the pupil who is interested in learning for its own sake, who can grasp an argument or follow a piece of connected reasoning'; 'the pupil whose interests and abilities lie markedly in the field of applied science and applied art'; and the pupil 'who deals more easily with concrete things than with ideas . . . abstractions mean little to him . . . his horizon is near and within a limited area his movement is generally slow'. Different types of school should be provided for these three different types of mind.

The Norwood Report was much criticized by educationalists and by psychologists for the unscientific basis of its assertions. It introduced a new pejorative note into the definitions of suitability, in particular for 'modern' schools. The LCC described it as a 'clever piece of rationalization' for a system which had emerged not out of real differences in human aptitude but out of social and economic divisions. The tripartite system, it argued, would perpetuate these divisions, 'modern' schools becoming no more than receptacles for those who failed to enter grammar or technical schools. Cyril Burt challenged the existence of such differences of aptitude.[9]

The Norwood Report, however, provided influential support for the official policy. The 1943 Education White Paper was unusual among the many reconstruction White Papers of that year in being translated into legislation before the end of the war, in 1944. This was largely due to the determination of R. A. Butler, with the support of his civil servants. Butler was partly motivated by the revival of party conflict as the war reached its end. He recognized the potential political gains to the Conservatives from his piloting through such a measure, but also feared that party politics might lead to modification or changes in policy if legislation was delayed until after the war, in particular to Labour moves to abolish or restrict the private sector and moves on the right of the Conservative party to restrict expenditure on poorer children.

On the former issue Butler had established the Fleming Committee, chaired by a Scottish judge, to consider the future of public schools. This reported in 1944, recommending that the schools should both receive local authority subsidies and make a quarter of their places available to pupils from the state sector. This satisfied neither the supporters nor the opponents of private education but sufficiently confused the issue to make action avoidable.[10]

As yet, however, in 1944, party differences on education were limited. There was indeed a large measure of agreement between progressive Conservatives such as Butler and much of the Labour party on educational issues. Butler worked harmoniously with J. Chuter Ede, the Labour junior Minister at the Board (a former school teacher), and although Butler made it clear in Parliament that he had the tripartite system in mind as the best available system) he made compromises in the 1944 Act to accommodate one significant area of party difference: the Act of 1944 made no explicit reference to the tripartite system. However, the Act did not prevent the establishment of 'multilateral schools'. No concessions were made, however, on the issue of private schools.

Butler was one of very few wartime ministers in a social policy department determined to effect change and one of the few wartime proponents of effective post-war reconstruction in a position to put into effect the changes he supported. He was able to use the temporary muting of normal political processes and conflicts effectively, though admittedly in an area of policy in which potential conflicts were not very great.

From 1944 the Board put most of its influence behind the establishment of grammar, modern and to a lesser extent the expensive 'technical' schools, arguing that multilateral schools were suited best to sparsely populated districts, such as those of Wales, although it was conceded that there might be 'judicious experiments elsewhere'.

Under the Act, the school leaving age was raised to fifteen (this was implemented in 1947) and provision was made for a further rise to sixteen 'as soon as the minister is satisfied that it has become practicable'. The Board was re-named the Ministry of Education. All education authorities were to submit within a year plans for the development of education within their areas. This was a new step, strengthening Ministry control over local education authorities. The LCC immediately proposed the reorganization of London schools – many of them destroyed by bombing – on a 'multilateral' or 'comprehensive' basis. Most education authorities planned a tri- or bi-partite structure which most easily suited their existing buildings, effectively carrying on the incomplete pre-war reorganization.

Fees in state secondary education were abolished and grants to universities and for those attending them increased. The post-1945 Labour government brought no obvious change in the direction of education policy despite pressure from the National Association of Labour Teachers, among others, to promote multilateral schools. The belief that working-class children had much to gain from the expected greater equality of opportunity to enter grammar schools and universities remained strong. The religious lobby was appeased by increased grants to their schools, over which the chuches retained considerable control, and by the insertion in the Act of an obligation upon all schools to provide daily religious instruction.

The Education Act of 1944 increased educational opportunities for some bright working-class children, for whom access to grammar and university education was improved. Since, however, grants to children remaining at school beyond the compulsory learning age were not introduced, although this was still Labour policy, such increased opportunities owed as much to post-war full employment and higher working-class incomes as to changes in the structure of education. Still, by the 1950s most working-class children still did not remain at school beyond the compulsory leaving age. In general, however, however, standards in education rose from their pre-war level.

It is hard to see that the Education Act of 1944 owed much to wartime conditions so much was it a continuation and completion of the considerable inter-war changes. If the war led to improvement in standards in state education, it was due in part to the national and international economic changes which created for many children living standards in which they could better profit from education.[11]

HEALTH

Similarly, discussion of reform of the health services followed its pre-war path with civil service encouragement. Civil servants in the Ministry of Health were already discussing reorganization of the health services in 1941, on the lines widely discussed in the 1930s; so also were leading members of the medical profession. In February 1941 the Ministry received a TUC delegation requesting improved health benefits and hospital care for the insured and their dependents, equalization of approved society benefits, and the overhaul and integration of hospital services.

Ministry consideration of the organization of health services was further stimulated by the immediate impact of war needs. With the outbreak of war an Emergency Medical Service (EMS) was established, as planned before the war. It was a centralized state agency originally designed to provide treatment for victims of air-raids, whose numbers were expected to be larger than resulted during even the most severe air-raids. Its doctors and nurses were directly employed and paid by the government, often at higher rates than they had experienced before.[12]

As in the previous war, access to civilian medical care was severely curtailed due to recruitment of doctors into government service. Once more, however, standards of health improved in wartime, largely as a result of improved living standards, especially standards of diet. The system of food rationing introduced early in the war maintained adequate food supplies and, whilst restricting the diet of the better off, certainly improved that of the poor.

By taking over both voluntary and public hospitals, as well as establishing new ones in a variety of buildings, EMS both brought about some unification of the two hospital systems and demonstrated the advantages of centralized planning. It also strengthened Ministry awareness of the deficiencies of existing hospitals. Wartime reorganization led to the ejection from hospitals of large numbers of patients whose beds mostly remained empty until some were used for service casualties. The system of subsidy for war casualty beds only deterred financially pressed hospitals from readmitting the unsubsidized civilian sick. In desperation, the Ministry agreed to continue the subsidy for a fixed proportion of beds, even when used other than for war casualties. Voluntary hospitals, however, continued to be even more selective of cases than before the war and as a result some public hospitals became seriously overcrowded. The Ministry, throughout the war, took great care not to intervene in the autonomy of the voluntary hospitals. The deficiencies of the system were, however, plain.

By February 1941 Ministry civil servants were agreed on the need for a comprehensive health service for the whole community, wherein GPs would be grouped into health centres linked to local hospitals. In October 1941 the Minister, Ernest Brown, a Liberal, announced that although immediate hospital reorganization was impossible a 'comprehensive hospital service' for all would be introduced after the war. Patients 'would be called on to make a reasonable payment towards the cost whether through contributory schemes or otherwise'. A survey of hospital provision was set under way.

The voluntary hospitals, well aware that their financial problems would return after the war, began to campaign for co-operation between the two hospital systems. Already in August 1940 the BMA, the MOHs and the Royal Colleges had set up a commission to plan post-war medical services. Enforced short-term reconstruction made it plain to them also that the system could not return to its unsatisfactory pre-war condition. They also recognized, as the secretary to the commission, Charles Hill, a future Conservative Minister, recorded, that 'those who planned first would be more likely to influence the final form'. Senior consultants had been responsible for planning EMS. This experience, and that of working in the service, had made many of them newly aware of the poor state of many provincial hospitals and other services. Similarly, working for EMS as voluntary workers brought many middle- and upper-class people into fresh contact with the reality of the medical experience of the masses. The discovery that mothers evacuated with their children and the wives of servicemen often had difficulty in paying for GP services increased the pressure for extension of insurance benefits to dependents. The Ministry meanwhile insisted that their needs should be met by the PACs. Underemployed EMS doctors had time to contemplate the state of the medical services. Reform was constantly discussed in the letter pages of *The Lancet* and the *British Medical Journal*. In 1940–41, on the initiative of the voluntary hospitals, voluntary regional cooperation between voluntary and public hospitals was organized.

In May 1942, the doctors' commission proposed a national health service available to all, with no upper income limits; health centres; the payment of GPs in part by salary, and the unification of hospitals under regional administration. This was a notably more radical programme than that of the BMA in 1938. The BMA itself was still opposed to payment of GPs by salary rather than by fees and launched an active publicity campaign in support of its views.

Also active in pressing the idea of the free national health service, including salaried GPs, upon the Ministry were the small but very active Socialist Medical Association and G.D.H. Cole's Nuffield College Reconstruction survey. This was established in 1941 with Treasury finance and spent the war period investigating and pressing for comprehensive post-war social and economic reconstruction. The Ministry itself published in March 1942 a paper contemplating a salaried GP service, but was slow to produce more comprehensive proposals: Ernest Brown and the Conservative Henry Willink, who became Minister in November 1943, were more responsive than Butler to Churchill's preference for avoiding controversy in wartime.[13]

The strongest stimulus to the Ministry of Health to produce comprehensive proposals for the post-war reconstruction of the health services came from the publication of Beveridge's famous Report of 1942 on *Social Insurance and Allied Services*. The Board of Education had not required similar stimulus, due both to Butler's determination and the less controversial nature of its proposals among those professionally and politically concerned; fewer conflicting vested interests were concerned in the reconstruction of education, largely due to the smaller size of the private educational sector. Beveridge's report will be discussed in detail later. Its importance for health was Beveridge's assumption that a free national health service would be introduced after the war. He did not discuss this in detail since this lay outside his brief. He also assumed the continuation of private practice, though he believed that this would contract when most needs were covered by a free service.

Still, however, the Ministry made no pronouncement, although discussions continued. In 1943, perhaps to assess the extent of potential controversy, the Ministry of Information commissioned Mass Observation to survey public attitudes towards a national health service. This revealed widespread enthusiasm for the principle, but some fears that a salaried service based on health centres would lead to more bureaucratized and impersonal treatment and perpetuation of the unpopular aspects of panel practice, especially the limited choice of doctor.

In February 1943 the government announced its acceptance of the principle. The Reconstruction Priorities Committee, set up to examine Beveridge's recommendations, invited the Labour Secretary of State for Scotland, Tom Johnston, and Ernest Brown to submit their ideas about a National Health Service. These coalition Ministers proved unwilling to nationalize the voluntary hospitals but they assumed that doctors would be salaried and would, at least in towns, no longer work in individual private practice but in health centres. They also assumed that both health centres and hospitals would be regionally directed. They regarded the system of payment by fees as unjust since it did not necessarily give most reward to the best doctors, and illogical in a health centre system in which GPs would not be in competition for patients.

The government then embarked upon negotiations with the medical profession. It became clear that practicable health service proposals might be hindered less by party political or popular resistance than by professional opposition. At its annual meeting in September 1943 the BMA began to retreat from the profession's bold plans of the previous year. It opposed local authority control and reverted to its pre-war preference for extension of national insurance. The medical profession had always been divided as to the extent of desirable change, the MOHs being most committed to a universal free, largely nationalized service. Those GPs who were in closest contact with the health problems of the poor and with least access to profitable private practice were more enthusiastic about a national health service, from which they had much to gain, than were some hospital consultants and GPs with prosperous practices. There were significant differences in the interests of these two groups. The *BMJ* began to express fears of interference from bureaucrats 'entirely ignorant of medical matters'.

In February 1944 a White Paper was published in which, on Labour insistence, health centres and a salaried service had a prominent part. However, due to the objections of Conservatives such as Butler to too high a proportion of salaried staff, lest it should lead to deterioration of services, and a short-lived attempt by Churchill to prevent its publiction, the White Paper was equivocal. Separate general practice could continue alongside health centres. GPs in health centres would not be salaried local employees, but under contract to the central health authority. A number of health centres were to be provided on an experimental basis, with a view to more widespread development should they prove successful. This cautious approach was stated to be the consequence of the variety of current conceptions of the size and role of health centres. It was true that, although these were widely supported in principle, specific proposals differed widely. Also the medical profession and the local authorities differed as to which of them should control the centres.[14]

The White Paper stressed the need to rationalize the distribution of medical services, to make adequate health care available to all, and to encourage early treatment. It emphasized that it was not intended to construct an entirely new structure but to build upon the old: the machinery of local government and of health insurance. The voluntary hospitals would retain their independence but would be encouraged to co-operate with public hospitals in their locality and to perform certain functions for the national service for which they would be remunerated. All medical services would be regularly inspected to ensure maintenance of standards. Medical education would be expanded.

The White Paper was strongly supported by PEP. The BMA continued its retreat, still opposing full-time salaried service, despite Willink's assurance that he had no such intention, now also opposing a universal service and claiming that the voluntary hospitals had an insufficiently prominent role in the proposed system.

The BMA still, however, tended to speak for the consultant elite. A poll of the whole profession conducted by the Association later in 1944 found 60 per cent of doctors in favour of a universal free service; 68 per cent favoured health centres in principle, (24% opposed them), 62 per cent a totally or partially salaried service, 29 per cent opposing. Doctors in the services, accustomed by 1944 to working in a bureaucratic framework, were especially willing to continue therein, favouring by a large majority both health centres and a salaried service. Many of them, however, were willing to work under central but not local authority control.[15]

After negotiations with the BMA, by July 1945 the Minister conceded that private practice would be allowed in health centres and that they would be rented from local authorities by GPs who would control their running. Local authority control would be diminished, overall control to be in the hands of regional planning bodies containing representatives of voluntary hospitals alongside local authority representatives.

The general election of that month brought a new Labour Minister of Health, Aneurin Bevan, by reputation a left-winger. He made it clear that he did not feel himself bound by any decisions of the previous government. He did not, however, overturn them. The views of the leaders of the profession were clear when he took office. His central aim was for a universal free service, and for this he was prepared to pay a certain price; such were the limits of political authority against a determined interest group. When the health service Bill was presented to the Commons in May 1946 it proposed nationalization of all hospitals, voluntary and public, placing them under the control of regional boards consisting of representatives of local authorities and of voluntary hospitals. Hospital endowments were to be removed and redistributed; however, the influential teaching hospitals (almost entirely voluntary) were to be allowed considerable independence, retaining their own endowments and with their own governing boards. Doctors were to be free to pursue private practice within the hospital – a desirable alternative, Bevan believed, to the threatened development of inadequate private nursing homes. GP, dental and other services would also be regionally directed by 'executive councils' consisting half of professional and half of lay representatives. Health centres were to be the main feature of GP services provided and maintained by local authorities, the doctors to be paid partly by salary, partly by capitation fees. There was no further mention of their experimental nature, although differences of opinion as to their role remained. Many GPs made plain their opposition to compulsory health centre practice and to local authority ownership. Other health services, including maternity, child care, health visiting and ambulance services, in which doctors played little part, would remain under local authority control. They were to be expanded and many of them made mandatory for the first time.[16]

The National Health Service Act of 1946 did not achieve the integrated service long before envisaged by Morant, Newman and their associates. Rather it established three nationally directed and financed systems: the hospital, GP and local authority services. Bevan intended the health centres to be the kingpin of their coordination and a duty was laid upon local authorities to provide them. They were to combine GP, dental, ophthalmic and local authority services and to work in close co-ordination with local hospitals. The problem of equalizing the socially and geographically uneven distribution of all health services was left to be solved after the establishment of the new structure.

GPs were not entirely happy with the new system although the more influential consultants had been appeased by the arrangements for private practice and for voluntary hospitals. The new service came into operation in July 1948. Under BMA pressure Bevan shortly introduced an amending Act abandoning salaried payment for GPs in favour of capitation fees. A circular of December 1947 cancelled the requirement in the Act for the submission of proposals for health centres, though the Ministry continued to emphasize their importance as 'a key feature in the general reconstitution of the country's health service'. On 5 July 1948 twenty-seven dispensaries and clinics were taken over from voluntary organizations to be used by local authorities as health centres. However, the Ministry of Health's Annual Report for 1949 announced that newly built centres would be given priority only 'in those areas where there is an immediate need for accommodation for doctors, dentists and for clinics'. Although many doctors supported health centres in principle, the Labour government was constrained from developing them further (few had been sanctioned by the time of the Conservative election victory of 1951) partly by post-war constraints on finance and upon building resources, by continuing uncertainty as to the best design and role for health centres, and by the unresolved conflict as to the relationship between local authorities and GPs in their control. The failure to build health centres diminished the possibility of close co-ordination of the three health services.[17]

The financial constraints also prevented a real equalization of health services throughout the country. After 1948 the state of health care was an immense improvement on the pre-war situation. In particular, working-class wives received access to medical care as never before. Female health benefited decisively from the new service.[18] However, regional and social class disparities remained. The medical profession had gained considerably from the injection of state finance into medical services and from the reorganization many had realized was necessary before 1939. Even a Labour Minister committed to change had been able to push the medical profession little further than they wished to go.

Local authority health services received less discussion and caused less controversy than hospitals or GP services, since fewer conflicting interests were involved. The chief professional interest involved, that of medical officers of health, was in favour of mandatory status for the range of permissive local services developed from the early part of the century. As during the previous war, local infant, child and maternity services had expanded in wartime. Evacuation of children, mothers and pregnant women in the summer of 1939 put unprecedented pressures on such services as existed in rural areas and small towns. Provision for them was restricted until late in 1940 – one year after the major evacuation, but at the beginning of serious air-raids – due to the unwillingness of the Treasury to sanction exceptional local government expenditure. Voluntary effort carried much of the burden. Late in 1940, many of the restrictions were removed and a wide range of emergency services were encouraged. By mid-1941 660 nurseries and hostels had been established in England and Wales accommodating around 10,000 children, mostly cases too difficult for foster parents and local authorities to handle. Also established were clubs and canteens for evacuated mothers, emergency maternity homes and residential nurseries mainly for war orphans. They were largely staffed by voluntary labour, notably from the Women's Voluntary Service.[19]

The evacuation of women and children generally from the poorest districts of big cities (all who could afford it made their own arrangements), some of them to respectable middle-class rural homes, demonstrated sharply and personally to some better off individuals the reality of the poverty, malnutrition, inadequacy of health care and of access to running water and adequate sanitation which the social surveys had repeatedly revealed before the war.

Titmuss emphasized the degree to which these revelations increased the pressure of the 'haves' to improve conditions for the 'have nots'. To what extent this was true is unclear. Some were stimulated to demand better social services; others to blame feckless mothers for the condition of their families. They may have done as much to increase antagonism as social solidarity, as mothers and children resented advice and criticism of their way of life and reception households were shocked by bed-wetting children and mothers escaping to the pubs. Many families returned home as rapidly as they could, when the bombs did not fall immediately.[20]

More certainly, those already committed to reform used the moment to publicize proposals they had long made. The combination of these pressures and the discovery, once more, of the poor physical condition of recruits to the services, increased the desire to improve maternal and child survival rates. Hence the official Food Policy Committee, chaired by Attlee, in June 1940 approved grants of fuel and subsidized milk to mothers and to children under five. This the Treasury had rejected in August 1939 as financially impracticable. In July the Board of Education decided that free school meals should become generally available. In July 1940 130,000 children each day were receiving either free or paid meals. By February 1945, 1,650,000 received school meals, 14 per cent of them free, the remainder paying between 4*d*. and 6*d*. per meal. In July 1940 50 per cent of children received milk at school, in February 1945, 73 per cent.[21] Free vaccination against diphtheria was also provided for children, thus removing a major pre-war child-killer; the blitz intensified fear of the spread of epidemics. Many of these developments, however, had at least as much to do with the change of government in May 1940, the need to encourage mothers to work, fears about levels of mortality and ill-health, the antagonism of the new Cabinet, including Churchill, towards the Treasury, as to Dunkirk or feelings of social solidarity. The diminution of Treasury authority after May 1940 – the Chancellor of the Exchequer, Kingsley Wood, was most unusually not a member of the War Cabinet – diminished its power to stop certain measures and gave their supporters a long awaited chance.[22] As before, some local authorities took more advantage than others of official encouragement to expand services.

The experiences of war almost certainly speeded up the integration and improvement of health services in directions which increasing numbers of reformers and medical professionals had advocated during the war. The reorganization of services to meet war needs demonstrated more starkly than before the deficiencies of the services and increased medical support for reform. Similar changes would surely have proceeded far more slowly and amid still greater conflict in peacetime.

Much the same can be said of wartime innovations in provision for the disabled. The Disabled Persons Employment Act 1944, was another of the few pieces of wartime social legislation. Its passing owed much to Bevin's initiative. Little had been done by 1939 specifically to assist those disabled from any cause. Before the war there was growing trade union pressure to extend workmen's compensation and to include rehabilitation services for those disabled due to accidents at work. The medical profession also expressed concern at the absence of assistance for the disabled to lead lives as independent as possible.

Bevin had been active, as a trade unionist, on this issue. He recognized that the wartime need to maximize manpower resources and the increased awareness of the problems of the disabled, due to the numbers of war casualties, combined to provide a unique opportunity to legislate for the disabled. In 1941 he introduced an interim re-training scheme, followed in December 1941 by the interdepartmental Tomlinson Committee on the Rehabilitation and Resettlement of the Disabled. The Committee was intended to be, and was, a mouthpiece for Bevin's own aspirations. Its proposals provided the framework for the 1944 Act.

Hence the legislation was profoundly influenced by the important but limited concerns of the trade unions, centrally by their desires that disabled workers should be enabled to return to work but not in such a way as to compete unfairly with other workers. The Act established rehabilitation centres and vocational training for the disabled. Industry was to reserve a quota of jobs for the disabled, to be paid at normal rates, such jobs to be filled from a voluntary national register. Candidates for the register were to be sufficiently fit to carry out a job as 'effectively' as a non-disabled person, not subject to treatment under the lunacy or Mental Health Act, in prison or of 'habitual bad character'. Those demonstrating insufficient enthusiasm for work deemed suitable would be removed from the register. Sheltered workshops were provided for those who did not meet these criteria.

Another important influence limiting the scope of the Act was the unwillingness of employers to hire at full pay workers who were not fully 'effective', unless they received compensation, which the government was unwilling to give.

The Act was passed, like much else in this period, amid a rhetoric of equalizing opportunities and protection from stigma to the disabled. In practice, it did much for a minority of the disabled whilst doing less than was possible to assist many others to achieve independence. The war made its passage possible, but the influence of the limited interests of unions and employers much limited its schope.[23]

FAMILY ALLOWANCES

Another major pre-war social issue was that of child poverty and the closely related issues of low pay and maldistribution of income. Discussions of these issues in wartime were much affected by the diminution of Treasury influence and by Keynes' role as unpaid economic advisor to the government, responsible to the War Cabinet rather than to the Treasury.

Keynes was determined to avoid the inflation which had arisen during the 1914–18 war. His proposals for doing so were outlined in his book *How to Pay for the War*, published in 1940. They included progressive taxation and strict controls over prices, wages and other allowances, and the supply of essential goods, all to be closely linked. This unavoidably raised, more acutely than before, the problem of the incomes of large families. It was difficult to control wages at a level which covered their needs but was not inflationary. Keynes favoured establishing an effective 'national minimum' by introducing high and progressive levels of direct taxation with an exempt minimum. This could not itself solve the problem of child poverty and from 1940 Keynes proposed family allowance as a means of escaping this difficulty. The pre-war supporters of family allowances, including Beveridge, kept up their pressure during the war and attracted increasing support.[24]

This aspect of Keynes' proposals was, however, slow to be accepted. Others had more immediate, if incomplete, success. The Budget of 1941 substantially increased direct taxation and reduced allowances, including the child allowance. The standard rate of income tax was increased from 8s. 6d. to 10s., purchase tax and 100 per cent excess profits tax, both introduced at the outset of war, were continued. Prices were controlled, food prices subsidized and rationing extended with the introduction of the 'points system' for food and clothing purchase. Tax rates did not change again during the war. This single change brought many more manual workers into the tax-paying class. In October 1938 the average adult male wage was £175 p.a.; a married man did not pay tax until he earned £225 p.a., if he had one child until he earned £300 p.a. After 1941 a married man with one child paid tax at earnings of £161. 20s.; with two children at £265 20s. Average male employed earnings were £288 p.a.[25]

At lower levels of income the tax structure was regressive; from middle income levels upwards it was more progressive than before. The regressive effects at lower levels were enhanced by increased national insurance contributions. Family allowances were, Keynes recognised, capable of offsetting some of these regressive effects.

The aim of the 1941 Budget was to finance the war as far as possible from domestic sources and to stabilize the internal war economy. It had not, however, touched on the aspect of that stabilization which both Keynes and the Treasury regarded as essential – wage controls. These were opposed by the trade union movement who had a powerful advocate in the War Cabinet in Ernest Bevin.

The unions opposed such controls as 'class legislation' if no comparable controls were placed on the incomes of employers. Bevin and the TUC also argued that wage controls would be unnecessary if prices and supplies were controlled, since workers would not be pressed by cost-of-living increases into demanding higher pay. The trade union movement preferred voluntary to compulsory controls. To avoid the industrial conflicts of the previous war the government avoided wage controls, relying on voluntary restraint, despite constant press and parliamentary criticism. Largely due to Bevin's efforts, the policy was successful.

However, the system of voluntary restraint did not remove the problem of the inadequacy of the lowest wages to meet the needs of large families. As a result, by 1941 the Labour party and the unions began to support family allowances. They recognized that in wartime general wage increases were out of the question, and hence that this could no longer be held to be the solution for low-paid workers with large families. They believed, although it was difficult to prove, that real wage rates had declined in wartime for many such workers, due to price rises, and that this had not been fully compensated by longer hours and overtime working, nor by increased household earnings – the latter were likely to be least in large families with young children. Nevertheless, family allowances continued to be opposed by unions containing large numbers of low-paid workers, chiefly the T&GWU and NUGMW. They still regarded family allowances as a cheap substitute for higher wages.[26]

Support for family allowances was further increased by the fact that by 1941 the position of the low-paid civilian worker was anomalous, as one of the few forms of income which included no allowance for children. Apart from income tax allowances, unemployment insurance, workmen's compensation, dependents' allowances and orphans' pensions, which had existed before the war, allowances were paid for children of servicemen and for unaccompanied evacuated children.

In June 1941 an all-party deputation of MPs headed by Leo Amery took a memorandum to the Chancellor of the Exchequer, asking for investigation of a scheme of family allowances:

  (i) to prevent an increase in malnutrition due to poverty aggravated by high prices;
 (ii) to prevent the spread of discontent between:
    (a) the richer and poorer classes and
    (b) those who get allowances – evacuees, the servicemen and the unemployed – and those who do not.
(iii) to prevent a fall in the birth rate;
(iv) to fulfil (i)–(iii) without inflation and
 (v) to prevent an overlap between unemployment benefit and wages because family allowances are paid to one and not to the other.[27]

Kingsley Wood promised to investigate. The result was a government White Paper, *Family Allowances*, published in May 1942 amid increasing pressure from MPs and from the Labour movement. The White Paper set out the main arguments for family allowances, as already outlined.

Against these, the White Paper suggested that family allowances might prejudice wage negotiations and divert money from other forms of social expenditure. The Chancellor personally favoured a universal flat rate system, although the White Paper did not commit the government to a specific scheme. The Labour party announced that it would support only a non-contributory scheme which included every child, as did the TUC in 1942, although not unanimously. Otherwise, opinion was divided between supporters of universal or of selective allowances for those in greatest need. The Conservative party favoured a contributory scheme, but their proposal to Kingsley Wood was turned down. The Chancellor had also considered but rejected both the abolition of child tax allowances and a complementary relationship between tax allowances and family allowances. Due to wartime increases in earnings, by 1942 tax allowances were worth about 6s. per child per week to the average earner with three children, rising to 10s. for higher earners. The abolition of tax allowances would have brought no net gain to better off families from the introduction of family allowances. Although this outcome might have been socially equitable, the government was anxious about the political results of what was effectively a further increase in taxation. Outright opposition to family allowances came only from small numbers on the left and from unions of low-paid workers, and from the right who opposed it as one more blow against *laissez-faire*. Apart from Eleanor Rathbone and Edith Summerskill and others in the Labour Party, few supported them with feminist arguments.

In December 1942 the Beveridge Report also insisted upon the need for family allowances, which were to be non-contributory, graduated by age and to grant an average of 8s. per week per child. Beveridge pointed out that this was a means of avoiding the danger of allowing 'benefit during unemployment and disability to equal or exceed earnings during work'. Beveridge's proposals were discussed with and supported by Keynes. Using Rowntree's pre-war measure of subsistence, Beveridge estimated that 9s. per week was the average needed to cover the needs of a child. However, he estimated that increased school meals and milk provision already provided a portion of this, hence 8s. per week would be sufficient.

However, Keynes made clear to Beveridge that his proposals exceeded the limit placed by the Treasury on the amount they were prepared to spend on family allowances. Beveridge proposed, therefore, to meet the Treasury limit by not making payments for the first child in the family, on the grounds that poverty was greater in large families. Beveridge's proposed allowances were slightly higher on average than those paid to servicemen's children in 1942, lower by 6*d*. per week than the average payment for evacuated children, but higher than the 3*s*.–4*s*. paid to children of the unemployed, the 7*s*. 6*d*. orphans' pension, the 3*s*.–4*s*. paid under workmen's compensation and the average of 6*s*. per week paid by PACs.

Despite, or perhaps because of, the government's reluctance to commit itself to implementing Beveridge's full proposals for the reform of social insurance, the Chancellor in February 1943 announced the government's intention to introduce family allowances. The allowances, however, would be of only 5*s*. per week for the second and subsequent children. Wood denied that this was an attempt to save money, rather, he argued, the value of benefits would be made up by provision of services. He emphasized that adequate provision was necessary to encourage population growth. Family allowances in this form became law in 1945, a partial solution to a major pre-war social problem.

It is difficult to assess the contribution of the war experience to their introduction. The size of the problem of child poverty, and the unlikelihood of its being solved in any other way, was clear by 1939. The war created conditions which diminished the opposition of Labour and of the Treasury. The revival of party rivalry in 1943 and in particular the growth of wage demands and of industrial strife encouraged Conservative members of the coalition both to seek electoral popularity and to increase working-class incomes by this means. As a relatively cheap solution to a pressing problem of poverty and an alternative to the problem of establishing a minimum wage they might have proved equally attractive to a peacetime Conservative government.[28]

BEVERIDGE AND SOCIAL SECURITY

The role of the Beveridge Report of December 1942 in stimulating government action upon health and family allowances was considerable. Neither issue, however, was central to the recommendations of the Report. As we have seen, Beveridge's enthusiasm for state welfare revived in the 1930s. As war approached he became more strongly committed to far-reaching state planning to achieve efficiency and equality, partly due to the influence of G.D.H. Cole. By 1936 Beveridge believed that war was probable and until the outbreak of war he urged official preparation for the organization of civilian welfare and of the economy in wartime, including planning of food controls, mass evacuation and the appointment of an 'Economic General Staff'. Planning, he argued, was no longer an ideological question but one vital to national survival, as the experience of the previous war had demonstrated. Before the war and in its early months he denounced civil service reluctance to make such plans, both publicly, in newspaper articles, and in letters to civil servants. His proposals included limited control of the labour market, food subsidies, progressive taxation and advance planning of post-war reconstruction both to avert post-war catastrophe and to maintain civilian morale.

Keynes shared many of Beveridge's ideas and frustrations. Both were convinced that the 'old gang' in charge of the government could win neither the short-term military nor the long-term economic struggle. In the winter of 1939–40 they and other veterans of the 1914–18 administration met to share their frustrations and to plan an alternative strategy. From these discussions emerged Keynes' *How to Pay for the War* in 1940 [docs. 16]

Beveridge had leisure for consideration of such matters largely due to the failure of Chamberlain's government to offer him a post. He wished to control civilian manpower, his chief interest at this stage. His continuing unpopularity within the civil service and among politicians (not diminished by his constant criticisms of official handling of the war) helped to prevent such an appointment. However, in July 1940, after the government reorganization, he was appointed by Bevin as chairman of the Manpower Requirements Committee of the Production Council. This, to Beveridge's disappointment, was an advisory rather than an executive position. Beveridge bombarded Bevin, whom he severely underestimated, with proposals, for example for the direction of labour, and with criticisms of Bevin's failure to implement them. He behaved indeed much as during the previous war: clear-sighted in his proposals but lacking the political and diplomatic skill to persuade rather than to instruct. Bevin did possess these skills, wisely using Beveridge to formulate rather than to implement policy. He became, however, increasingly impatient with his advisor. In June 1941, to escape this irritation, he offered Beveridge the chairmanship of a new interdepartmental Committee on the Co-ordination of Social Insurance. Beveridge was bitterly disappointed. He had hoped for a more prominent executive post but now recognized that this was unlikely.

Gradually, he realized that the Committee (otherwise composed of civil servants) had some potential importance, a view which the War Cabinet did not share. Its appointment arose from trade-union pressure for revision of workmen's compensation and pressure upon the Ministry of Health to raise NHI benefits. It was not intended to make major policy statements but to review these and related questions. The Treasury was anxious that it should sit secretly, for fear that its recommendations might be publicly regarded as statements of policy. Only with difficulty did MPs extract information as to the existence of this and other wartime Committees.

The numerous, uncoordinated and overlapping systems of social insurance and non-contributory income support had changed little in the first eighteen months of war. In January 1940 the pensionable age for insured women and wives of national insurance contributions had been reduced to sixty. This followed a campaign by women's organizations protesting, correctly, that independent women found difficulty in obtaining work by the age of sixty, i.e. at an earlier age than men, and also that wives tended to be younger than their husbands. Hence household incomes suffered during the period between the husband's retirement from work and the wife's attaining pensionable age; alternatively, husbands were deterred from retirement until their wives qualified for the pension. The lowering of the age for women passed easily through Parliament. At the same time a supplementary pension of 5s. per week was introduced for pensioners 'who are in straitened circumstances', based on a household means test to be administered by a newly appointed board. Insurance contributions were raised to meet the cost of these changes. Over 100,000 pensioners applied for their supplement within eight months of its introduction, more than double the anticipated number.[29]

In other respects the patchwork of pensions, health and unemployment insurance, UAB benefit, workmen's compensation, war pensions and PACs remained as the succession of official and unofficial enquiries of the inter-war years had described. A large body of well-formed ideas for their reform existed to be drawn upon when the committee began its work. The very fact that responsibility for these services was divided among a number of official departments meant that, unlike health and education, no one body had responsibility for considering improvements in the whole income support system. Rather such activities were subordinate functions of Ministries with wider and often more pressing responsibilities, although proposals for change existed within all the Ministries concerned. Beveridge quickly grasped that his Committee had an opportunity to fill this gap.

The Committee's terms of reference were vague. Its members other than Beveridge were busy civil servants unable to devote much time to the inquiry and with differing expectations of its purpose. The Treasury representative expected just a tidying-up exercise; the Ministry of Health and Home Office representatives something more far-reaching, but less than resulted. Beveridge rarely allowed them to influence him on fundamental questions. He used them for advice and information and was determined to use his report to lay down long-term social policy goals and as a means of forcing the government to commit itself to them. It became a one-man enterprise, dedicated to rethinking income support policy. Its almost messianic nature was encouraged by Beveridge's future wife Jessy Mair, who urged him: 'How I hope you are going to be able to preach against all *gangsters* who for their mutual gain support one another in upholding all the rest. For that is really what is happening still in England . . . the whole object of their spider-web of interlocked big banks and big businessmen [is] a frantic effort to maintain their own caste.'[30]

Beveridge began quickly to formulate the principles which were to underlie his final Report. In general he less initiated new principles and proposals than took the opportunity to channel and publicize proposals already worked out and strongly supported within the Ministries and elsewhere. These included the Home Office desire to reform workmen's compensation to compel employers to insure, to enable injured workmen to pursue their claims free of legal charges, and to receive both compensation and treatment, and Ministry of Health advocacy of integrated local hospital and personal social services and either medical benefits for dependents or a publicly financed health service. Both of these sets of proposals Beveridge immediately adopted. He performed the valuable role of co-ordinating the different aspirations of reformers in individual Ministries, within a coherent framework. The framework which he envisaged from the beginning of the investigation was that of a reform of all social services designed to provide a minimum of subsistence and care for the whole population. Since, he argued, all ran the risk of unforeseen poverty, provision should be universal.

He believed that such a minimum was impossible unless unemployment was abolished, a national health service and family allowances established, and adequate housing provided for all. The details of such provision lay outside his brief, but he insisted that such complementary reforms, ensuring reasonable human standards in normal times, were as vital as the reform of social insurance to the eradication of poverty, since the latter was designed only to provide for periods of crisis.

He believed that a national minimum was now attainable. He based his belief on the survey evidence of the considerable decline in poverty in the inter-war years, in particular of the decline of low wages as its major cause. He believed that severe poverty had been reduced to manageable proportions and to causes eradicable by provision of benefits and services. His proposals embodied a number of enduring themes in his career; dislike of means tests, of 'police supervision' and of the 'Santa Claus' state, concern to do justice to women's needs, belief in the psychological value of contributory insurance, the desire to encourage voluntary action and thrift and to prevent commercial bodies profiting from the needs of individuals for social security. He expected the proposed minimum subsistence provision to be supplemented by private and voluntary means and decisively rejected the notion of a 'national minimum' provided through redistributive taxation.

On this basis, Beveridge proceeded to examine means of establishing a unified universal social insurance system, designed to cover all groups in actual or potential need. He defined seven such groups: employees, the self-employed, housewives, those below and above working age, the 'blind and other incapables' and 'others of working age fit to work'. For these he believed seven different kinds of cash benefit should be provided: unemployment and sickness benefits, 'loss-grants' for the self-employed who suffered theft or bankruptcy; 'special provision' for the 'marriage needs of women', disability benefit (also to cover industrial injury); funeral benefits, family allowances and old-age pensions (to be paid on condition of retirement, to encourage the elderly to remain productive members of the labour force rather than costly dependents). The benefits wouuld all be flat-rate, all calculated on the same subsistence basis, and all financed through single weekly contributions from employer and employee, plus an Exchequer contribution. The whole system would be underpinned by a scheme of means-tested Exchequer-financed public assistance of deterrent character but much reduced in scope, much of the work of the PACs being taken over by the comprehensive insurance scheme. Approved societies were to be abolished, although Friendly Societies and other voluntary organizations would continue to carry out administrative functions on behalf of the state. The whole system would be administered by a single new Ministry of Social Security.

The necessary subsistence level for all weekly benefits, including family allowances, Beveridge concluded, should be calculated according to Rowntree's 1937 'human needs' scale, plus rent, which Beveridge believed was adequate, if stringent.

Beveridge developed these principles and proposals in the winter of 1941–42, before consulting outside opinion or members of his Committee. The administrative and financial details remained to be established by specialist sub-committees, which received advice and submissions from 127 experts, including Rowntree (a member of the subsistence sub-committee), G.D.H. Cole, the Fabian Society, local authorities, the TUC, employers and women's groups and other interested organizations. A strikingly high proportion of these bodies concurred with or had already formulated proposals similar to those of Beveridge. Dissent was generally on points of detail rather than of substance, even when agreement entailed criticism of the witnesses' own roles, as in the case of Friendly Societies and public assistance officials. The latter group vigorously condemned the inadequacy and inefficiency of existing public assistance arrangements.

Such considered responses came mainly from organizations closely involved with social welfare issues. Others, such as the FBI, while not dissenting, wanted all action to be delayed until after the war. The business community was, however, divided. The official view of the FBI was that Beveridge's proposals would increase the post-war costs of industry and hence keep exports low. However, in November 1942, 120 industrialists set out a 'National Policy for Industry'. This endorsed the improved welfare provision since 1940 and envisaged its expansion, but partly in the form of corporate paternalism. Industrialists should be responsible for the housing of their employees and for supplementation of state pensions and subsidies to prevent unemployment. The state meanwhile would provide family allowances and raise the school leaving age to sixteen, both of which actions they believed would benefit industry. Some businessmen recognized the gains to industry from increased social security provided by the state to the workforce. The trade union and labour movements now almost unanimously supported Beveridge's proposals for contributory insurance and bureaucratic collectivism, as necessary means to improve social conditions.[31]

On many points, however, Beveridge's proposals were vague or posed difficult administrative and political problems. In particular the sub-committee on subsistence payments failed to resolve Beveridge's paradoxical proposals for both flat-rate and subsistence benefits. After much discussion his proposal stood. It was clear that actual living costs varied individually and regionally but it proved difficult to build the desirable adjustments into a scheme based on the insurance principle, the more so in view of the opposition both of the Treasury and of Beveridge to income-related benefits or contributions, such as existed in many other countries.

Another source of difficulty arose because, unusual among male reformers, Beveridge had long been concerned to give recognition to the particular problems of women and to give women an equal footing in social provision. He proposed to give single employed women equivalent insurance status to men and married women a wide range of benefits based on the husband's insurance. Married working women were to be given the choice of these options, though they were to receive lower benefits than employed men in return for lower contributions. Beveridge argued that wives were less likely than husbands to be responsible for paying rent among other unavoidable household expenses. This was opposed by women's organizations but won civil service support.

Beveridge was especially concerned that justice should be done to non-working housewives. He proposed that, in return for their husbands' contributions, they should receive maternity benefits and benefits not only in widowhood but on divorce and separation; dependents' allowances during the husband's unemployment and sickness, and an allowance for domestic help during their own sickness. He argued that the work of housewives was as important, socially and economically, as waged work and should be given equal recognition in the social security system. He described separation allowances as equivalent to allowances made to victims of industrial hazards.

Women's groups showed no great interest in deserted or divorced wives' allowances. These faced wider opposition on the grounds of 'subsidizing sin' and were reluctantly abandoned by Beveridge due to the difficulty of distinguishing 'innocent' from 'guilty' wives, thus leaving a major social problem unsolved and such women to the uncertain mercies of the law courts for obtaining separation allowances. His other proposed benefits for housewives, in particular the domestic benefit for sick housewives, was dismissed by the Treasury on grounds of cost and of administrative difficulty. An alternative proposal by the National Council of Women for a regular allowance for housewives, equivalent to a wage, was opposed by Beveridge, with the support of Eleanor Rathbone, as being politically impracticable. Another significant female problem, that of 'domestic spinsters' who remained at home to care for elderly parents, was also reluctantly abandoned by Beveridge due to the difficulty of fitting them into a contributory scheme. Hence most of Beveridge's brave plans for women were unsuccessful.[32]

A central difficulty facing Beveridge's fellow Committee members was financial; especially the cost of subsistence level old-age pensions, the most expensive item in his proposals. The total cost of the proposals, including family allowances and a universal health service, was estimated as £535 m. in the first year, of which £302 m. would fall on the Exchequer – almost three times the level of Exchequer expenditure on equivalent services in 1941. Beveridge sought advice from Keynes, who pronounced himself 'in a state of wild enthusiasm' about the proposals and who did his best to win Treasury support for them. Keynes suggested, however, first, that benefits be fixed at a level which took account of wartime inflation and that pensions be paid out of the current contributions in each year, rather than on the insurance basis of accumulation of contributions over a working life. This was rejected by Beveridge, who felt strongly that people preferred to believe that they were paying for their individual pensions and that such a sentiment reinforced a desirable preference for self-help. Keynes later substituted a proposal for a gradual transition to subsistence-level pensions. Beveridge was persuaded to agree to a transitional period of twenty years, for fear that the cost of immediate subsistence pensions would destroy the chances of acceptance for other aspects of the scheme. It was also at this point that he agreed to remove family allowances from the first child.

With these concessions, the final Report was prepared and published in December 1942, signed only by Beveridge. The Cabinet had decided that signature by the civil service members would appear to give the proposals official sanction. The proposed system was marked, Beveridge claimed, by 'economy in administration, adequacy in benefits and universality in scope'.

Beveridge himself drafted the Report. It set out clearly the principles and assumptions upon which his proposals were based. Written with a rhetoric designed to attract public notice, it aimed, Beveridge asserted, to give a new purpose to democracy: 'A revolutionary moment in the world's history is a time for revolution, not for patching.' He emphasized the need for these measures not only to meet needs but to promote social solidarity based upon a common freedom from and opposition to 'the demoralizing pressures of poverty'. It received immense publicity and popularity, encouraged initially by the Minister of Information as a means of boosting wartime morale, on groundwork carefully prepared by Beveridge himself.

He had lost no opportunity in the months preceding the Report to make the public aware that dramatic proposals were on their way. Public opinion surveys after publication found it to be popular even with upper income groups, although they also discovered widespread criticisms that the proposed pension rates were too low, and still stronger fears that the government would water down or ignore the Report. Amid all the discussion the Report received, including newspapers of all political colours, it was nowhere seriously suggested that the social and economic problems discussed by Beveridge would be better solved through the operation of the free market which had previously created rather than solved such problems.[33]

The draft Report may have expressed the views of a wide cross-section of influential opinion, but this did not include leading members of the government. Its proposals were opposed by the Chancellor, on grounds of cost, and by Churchill who believed that it should be considered in the context of the doubtful prospects for the post-war economy and of the danger of raising popular hopes beyond a level which a post-war government could satisfy.

Beveridge had, characteristically, aroused antagonism among politicians and civil servants by the high-handed manner in which he presented his proposals to the public, overlooking possible difficulties in their implementation, and, in particular, for the optimism of his assumption that the post-war economy could provide the resources to finance them. There were good reasons for doubt on these grounds. Beveridge assumed a willingness and capability on the part of the government to reorganize the post-war economy of which there were few unequivocal signs. The danger was real that after the war the economy would return to its pre-war difficulties. Much of the opposition expressed was less to the principles outlined by Beveridge than to the possibility of their implementation.

As was normal, the Report was submitted to the scrutiny of a civil service committee, chaired by Sir Thomas Phillips of the

Ministry of Labour, long an opponent of Beveridge. Early in 1943, this committee reported its doubts about the possibility of achieving the historically unprecedented level of full employment assumed by Beveridge. It queried the need for family allowances and suggested that if unavoidable they should be paid in kind rather than in cash. It argued that there was an irreducible feckless class for whom a deterrent Poor Law would always be needed; and it rejected the principle of subsistence, on the grounds that universal flat-rate benefits which it endorsed could never provide subsistence for everyone in need. They accepted, however, the principles of universality and of a comprehensive health service.

The Treasury expressed serious doubts about the possible effects of Beveridge's plans on the post-war fiscal situation. They feared that it would require a high level of taxation which would discourage saving and hinder post-war expansion. A fierce debate was conducted among government economic advisors between those who argued that need could be met more effectively and cheaply by benefits means-tested on the same basis as the newly introduced annual tax returns and adjusted to local cost-of-living variations, and Keynes, who admitted the logic of this view but argued that this was impossible without a reform of the system of direct taxation, which was not immediately practicable, and that contributory insurance was a useful means of making employers share the costs of welfare. Keynes was convinced that the Beveridge plan was 'the cheapest alternative open to us' and that the feared financial difficulties could be avoided by careful Treasury management.

The Report received backbench support in all parties, but the opposition of a group of Conservative businessmen and of Beatrice Webb who now opposed 'reform within the context of capitalism'.[34] Churchill and other Conservative leaders refused to commit themselves to firm plans for reconstruction until after the war. Under pressure from this source, the Ministry of Information retreated from its initial enthusiasm for Beveridge. The Labour leaders Attlee and Hugh Dalton welcomed the plan but not pressure for its immediate implementation, for fear that this would cause Churchill, as he threatened, to call, and win, a general election. Bevin strongly opposed the plan, convinced that it was contrary to the interests of the trade unions, which were best met by higher wages. This was in the tradition of his own union, the T&GWU, but the TUC voiced its support.

The Report had vast sales and Beveridge was in demand as a

public speaker. Amid such popular enthusiasm, Cabinet hopes that the action on the proposals could be shelved until after the war retreated. In February 1943 backbenchers forced a debate on the Report in the Commons and won the greatest anti-government vote of the war, with a call for a commitment to implementation of the 'Beveridge plan'. As a result another Whitehall committee was established to draft government proposals arising from the Report. Beveridge was not a member of this committee and, to his profound disappointment, was not invited to take his official enquiries any further. Beveridge was convinced that his Report should be acted upon before the end of the war and equally convinced that the government was unlikely to do so except under strong external pressure. He set out to mobilize that pressure in association with G. D. H. Cole. He remembered the contrast between the promises and proposals of the previous war and the succeeding inaction. He was not alone in such fears. Again, in 1944, the Home Intelligence surveys of the Ministry of Information found that 'many people especially workers while approving the plan are sceptical as to its ever becoming law in anything like its present shape; a smaller number think that even if it is implemented this will not be for many years'. Fears were expressed that 'big vested interests' would ensure that the proposals were whittled away; others said that 'there will be a catch . . . they'll give us a family allowance for children and then take it away again by reducing the income tax allowance for children.'[35] Beveridge believed that wartime full employment and high wages offered an immediate opportunity to finance the new system.

More than any other wartime blueprint for post-war social reconstruction the Beveridge Report caught the popular imagination and came to symbolize the widespread hopes for a different, more just, world. These hopes were embodied in the term which, although not quite new, came into wide currency after the publication of the Report: the 'welfare state'. Its meaning was often unclear and it was disliked by Beveridge himself who, with characteristic purism, preferred the more precise 'social service state'. But the term 'welfare state' expressed for very many people something greater than a simple description of the activities of government in respect of one area of its activities. It expressed the desire for a more socially just, more materially equal, more truly democratic society, in short, everything that pre-war society had not been. The ideals bound up in the term went beyond Beveridge's own proposals but his Report was felt to approach them more closely than any other official pronouncement.

The government still responded sluggishly. The committee established in 1943 produced in 1944 the Social Insurance White Paper. This accepted the principle of universal insurance but not that of subsistence. But the government would not announce a date for implementation. Churchill publicly emphasized the need to delay this and other essential reforms until after the war. Although the Treasury began preparations for implementation, no action was taken until after the election of the Labour government in July 1945. It was then rapid, but with some important deviations from Beveridge's proposals.

The National Insurance Act of 1946 and the National Assistance Act of 1948 established a system of flat-rate universal pensions, sickness and unemployment benefits for insured women and men and their wives, and a means-tested national assistance scheme as a 'safety net' for those whom the system did not cover. Pensions, however, were not fixed at subsistence level, nor was there any costly commitment to make them so in future. The only new form of benefit proposed by Beveridge that was introduced was a funeral benefit payable on the death of an insurance contributor.

The new benefit levels were 26s. per week for sickness, unemployment and retirement, with 16s. for a wife and 7s. 6d. for a first child. This was an increase by 2s. per week in unemployment benefits, 8s. in sickness and 16s. in the pension. In addition the National Insurance (Industrial Injuries) Act 1946 revised workmen's compensation legislation on the lines developed in the Home Office early in the war and adopted by Beveridge. The outcome of Beveridge's great work was the necessary reorganization and rationalization of the social insurance system and its universalization, to the real advantage, especially, of many women and also of those of the lower middle classes who had previously been excluded from most social insurance benefits. The real value of pensions was significantly increased. The redistributive effects were small. The Labour legislation together with the wartime introduction of family allowances came closer to the introduction of a national minimum than any previous government action. The failure to go further was due largely to understandable doubts about the economic effects of increased social expenditure and in particular to doubts as to whether Beveridge's goal of full employment could indeed be achieved.[36] [doc 17]

FULL EMPLOYMENT

Beveridge's assumption in the Report that full employment was possible was a new facet of his thought and a surprising one; long-term full employment had never previously been known in peacetime. He, like Keynes, saw it as the crucial problem to be solved, without which real social improvement was impossible. Beveridge's conviction that it *could* be solved, derived from his conversion during wartime to the belief that the free market system had irretrievably broken down and that government planning and control of investment, the location of industry and of labour and public ownership of land and housing, even the gradual phasing out of all private ownership of the means of production, was essential for prosperity, indeed for national survival at an acceptable general standard of living. He pointed out in 1942 that unemployment had disappeared during the war in a period when state control of production had been enormously extended without, as he had previously feared, the destruction of democracy. Planning and individual and political freedom were, he now believed, compatible and could be practised in peacetime. These notions had little in common with Keynes' advocacy of management of the economy, which Beveridge still imperfectly understood, although they agreed on goals and on many means towards these goals.[37]

Beveridge expected, after the publication of his Report, to be invited to play a role in government planning of the post-war labour market. When no such invitation emerged, in 1943 he formed a private committee, financed by a group of progressive businessmen, to inquire in detail into means of achieving full employment. The committee consisted of young economists, mostly to the left of Beveridge, including Nicolas Kaldor, Barbara Wootton and Joan Robinson. This committee convinced Beveridge that Keynes' approach, of state regulation of demand, could achieve full employment as effectively and more practicably than his own previous preference for state ownership and direct control of the economy. The outcome, published in November 1944 as *Full Employment in a Free Society*, was a set of proposals including: state investment in certain essential industries notably transport and power; state spending on a range of 'non-marketable' goods and services, such as roads, hospitals, schools and defence; state subsidies to housing, medical services, food and fuel; and state regulation of private investment through control of interest rates, taxation policy and income redistribution.[38] [doc. 18]

The Treasury refused co-operation with this enterprise, but it appears to have precipitated publication of their own employment policy proposals which had been in preparation since 1941 – the government was anxious not to be pre-empted by Beveridge once more. Its plans emerged in the Employment Policy White Paper of June 1944. This much modified version of Keynes' ambitions proposed to maintain full employment after the war, particularly by the regulation of demand. The White Paper followed strong Treasury resistence to the ideas of Keynes. Treasury officials were still inclined to blame the structural problems of British industry for pre-war unemployment and to emphasize, as they had throughout the inter-war years, the need to restore Britain's export markets. The result was a compromise tilted towards Treasury orthodoxy: for the first few years after the war it would be necessary to retain controls to avoid unemployment resulting from the switch from a wartime to a peacetime economy. In the longer term, demand would be maintained by encouragement of exports, action (through control of interest and exchange rates) to influence the level of private investment, the careful timing of public investment and the regulation of consumption by varying the level of social insurance contributions. The White Paper implied more conscious management of the economy than had been previous practice, though less than Keynes envisaged, and little planning or physical controls. It specifically ruled out the use of a budgetary deficit to stimulate demand in a period of recession, as advocated by Keynes. The public response was the reverse of that to the Beveridge Report. The White Paper was welcomed by both front benches, criticized by Labour backbenchers for not going far enough and by Conservatives for going too far. It aroused little popular response.[39]

Full Employment in a Free Society, by contrast, contained wider ranging proposals, closer to those of Keynes, for a new kind of annual budget which would use taxation, borrowing and deficit-financing to determine levels of public expenditure, business investment and consumer demand. Its priority would be to adjust production to the total supply of labour. The location of industry would be planned and labour mobility encouraged. These processes would be managed by a new Ministry of National Finance, subordinating the Treasury to its traditional role of supervising departmental expenditure. Public and private investment would be supervised by a National Investment Board which would make available low-interest loans to private enterprise. Demand for labour would be adjusted so as always to exceed supply, leaving a margin of 3 per cent 'unemployment' to allow for labour mobility. Beveridge and his committee were not unduly worried by the possibly inflationary outcome of these proposals, believing that should this occur it could be restrained by voluntary or compulsory wage controls, assuming willing trade union co-operation in a socially just system.[40] Similarly, Keynes regarded inflation as a political problem, solvable by political rather than by economic means.[41] In common with Keynes, and indeed the Treasury, Beveridge and his associates saw unemployment as the chief problem to be solved after the war, as it had been the major international pre-war problem, and inflation as a less serious danger.

The post-war economic policies of the Labour government combined nationalization of essential but unprofitable industries – power and transport – to which there was little opposition, with the implementation of the moderate proposals of the employment policy White Paper. The Labour government talked the language of planning whilst practising a modified version of Keynesian management, approved by the Treasury. It did not develop the new institutions necessary for effective planning or diminish Treasury control. Rationing, controls on building, interest rates, exchange control and, to some degree, controls on labour mobility were retained to restrain consumer demand, as were price and voluntary wage controls to control inflation. Increasingly budgetary policy became an instrument of demand management through regulation of interest and taxation rates. The Labour leadership had never been profoundly committed to wholesale planning. Its introduction posed major political problems and as the economy recovered after the war it seemed unnecessary.[42]

The reasons for this recovery are complex and not entirely clear. They owed a great deal to large loans from the USA and to changes in the international economy, guided and unguided. The latter included the new international institutions established after the Bretton Woods conference of 1944, the International Monetary Fund and the World Bank, designed to prevent the protectionism which had harmed international recovery in the inter-war period, and to encourage international economic co-operation.

The Bretton Woods agreement owed much to the influence of Keynes, who had become increasingly convinced that if the pre-war crisis was not to recur, the solution lay in international rather than national action. He also, successfully, pressed upon the allied powers the importance of re-building rather than destroying the post-war German economy, to prevent the recurrence of one element in the inter-war crisis.[43]

The relative success of the post-war economy compared with what had gone before and what many had feared, in particular the achievement by 1950 of full employment without inflation, muted any lingering support for more far-reaching economic controls or more redistributive social legislation. The business community and the Treasury saw no reason for such changes and the Labour government showed little disposition to override them. The belief grew that growth in a revived economy would take care of remaining social problems. The transition from a wartime to a peacetime economy did, however, present the government with time-consuming problems. Resources for further social expenditure were limited in the short run. This held back plans for, among other things, housebuilding.

HOUSING

Housing problems created less crisis in this than in the previous war, despite the fact that Home Intelligence repeatedly discovered that housing was a major worry for many people.[44] Worry did not lead to unrest, partly due to inter-war improvements in provision and administration of housing and effective wartime rent controls. Bombing, of course, led to severe housing loss, although the Ministry of Works, under Lord Reith in 1940–42, deserved credit for its efficiency in repairing damaged housing and in replacing that lost with 'pre-fabs', despite their unpopularity.[45]

A major effect of the blitz and of the fear of bombing was to reduce the population of the big cities, largely by evacuation. The population of the East End of London, for example, fell by half; that of East Anglia increased. Broadly, also, the drift from the depressed areas continued, leaving them, in housing terms, relatively better off than other regions. Smaller towns such as Reading suffered increased overcrowding due to the location of war industries away from big cities and to evacuation, but not to the saturation level of, for example, Glasgow in the previous war. Housebuilding virtually ceased in wartime.[46]

The Report of the Barlow Commission on Distribution of the Industrial Population, appointed in 1937, appeared in January 1940, recommending more stringent, centrally controlled planning of the location of housing and of jobs and transport. Although the government was ill-disposed to consider such matters at this stage of the war, the objectives of the Report were supported by Reith and by his civil servants, who included the town and country planning department previously located in the Ministry of Health. They were also supported by continuously active pressure groups such as the Town and Country Planning Association.[47]

Like their colleagues in other Ministries, those officials responsible for planning spent the early period of the war peacefully pursuing lines of policy on which they had embarked before the war. This centrally concerned location, rather than, as during the previous war, numbers of houses. The major problem was seen to be the prevention of urban overcrowding and excessive growth of towns.

In 1941 Reith achieved the Cabinet's agreement in principle to the establishment of a national planning authority with wide powers, as proposed by Barlow. As first steps towards solving some of the major planning problems pinpointed by Barlow, Reith established the Scott Committee to consider the future of the countryside, the Uthwatt Committee on compensation and betterment and set Patrick Abercrombie and the LCC architect J. H. Forshaw to prepare a plan for post-war rebuilding over the whole area of the county of London. This reported in 1943 with a further report in 1944. It was one of a series of regional plans initiated by Reith, which ended with Reith's dismissal by Churchill in February 1942.

The Uthwatt Committee reported in September 1942 recommending, fruitlessly, that the state should nationalize the development rights in all land which had not yet been built up. This was too severe a blow to property rights for the Conservatives to accept, although the recommendation became Labour policy.[48]

. One of the chief aims of Reith and his civil servants was achieved in December 1942 with the establishment of a new Ministry of Town and Country Planning under W. S. Morrison. But it could do little when the major parties were unable to agree on the major problem of compensation and betterment. An interim Town and Country Planning Bill was introduced in June 1944 to empower local authorities to plan the redevelopment of blitzed or slum areas. An accompanying White Paper on control of land use proposed an 80 per cent levy on profits from development but it led to no action. With the end of the war it was necessary to face the problems of re-building bombed areas, of housing those whose homes had been lost, and of making up the backlog of new building and repairs neglected during the war. The Town and Country

Planning Act of 1947 made all development subject to compulsory planning permission for the first time and imposed a 100 per cent development levy on the value created by permission to develop land. This was repealed by the Conservatives in 1953; they had always opposed it.

Under this and other legislation, the Labour government inaugurated a New Towns policy to encourage the development of industry and housing in smaller units away from existing large centres of population. For the first time new town building was publicly financed. This implied considerable new housebuilding and much was needed. Churchill promised the electors in 1945 government control of the prices of building materials, a rapid increase in the labour force, continued rent control and, somewhat vaguely, 'planned use of land' – a policy little different from that of Labour. Gallup polls published in June 1945 indicated that four voters out of ten thought housing the major issue in the campaign whilst one in seven emphasized social security and one in fourteen full employment.[49] Bevin declared that Labour would build four or five million houses. By 1951 only one million had been built, due partly to a decision in 1947 to cut back the housing programme to aid the balance of payments.

In housing and planning policy, as in health, social security and education, the post-war legislation was to a large extent directed towards administrative reorganization, more centralised control, giving primacy to national over local needs, and more efficient deployment of resources along lines proposed before the war, a process which paralleled developments in private industry. In social policy, including housing, the pressures for more efficient deployment of resources were as powerful as more radical social aims. The need to rebuild following wartime housing losses precipitated the move towards more stringent planning controls, partly due to the determination with which the planning pressure groups urged their ideas upon the government.

CHILD CARE

Another area of social policy influenced by war experiences was that of child care. Certain problems were highlighted by the war. The increased numbers of illegitimate children led the Ministry of Health in 1943 to advise local authorities to appoint social workers specifically to supervise and to advise unmarried mothers, at last ending their association with the Poor Law. Shortly afterwards a shortened form of birth certificate was introduced to remove one source of stigma from the illegitimate.[50]

Increased and unprecedented numbers of residential nurseries were provided to encourage mothers to enter the workforce, a reversal of pre-war policy under pressure of the needs of the war economy. It was pressed by the Ministry of Labour, though never as successfully as Bevin wished, against Ministry of Health opposition. Many of the new nurseries were in temporary accommodation which facilitated their rapid closure after the war, when the Ministry of Health reverted to its pre-war policy of restricted provision for exceptionally deprived children. Mothers of young children, however, showed relatively little enthusiasm to work, except where the absence or death of a husband necessitated it. Unlike childless women they were not obliged by law to do so. Problems of shopping and running a home whilst working long hours also deterred many women from working. They received little official assistance in solving these problems which were rather increased by the consumer rationing system which necessitated registration at a specific shop.[51]

The problems of children evacuated or separated by war conditions from their parents increased knowledge and concern among psychologists and others about problems of child care. The need for improvements in this respect received further publicity as a result of the death in January 1945, due to neglect and ill-treatment, of a child in foster care, Denis O'Neill. The enquiries which followed this much publicized case, including the official Curtis Committee on the Care of Children of 1946, revealed once more the inadequacy of supervision due both to underfinancing and to the almost incomprehensively complex legal position concerning the roles of voluntary and statutory child care bodies.

The result was the Children Act 1948, which aimed to bring all child care under local authority control. Local authorities now had an inescapable duty to take into care, up to the age of seventeen, orphans and children whose parents were unfit and unable to care for them, and to register and supervise adoption societies (which had proliferated unsupervised since the legalization of adoption in 1926). Grants to local authorities were increased and they were given responsibility for giving grant aid to voluntary institutions, which were placed under stricter controls. Local authorities were given a primary duty to place children in foster care, and to support young people over the age of seventeen during the transition to work.[52]

In this area of policy also, the law was clarified and consolidated as well as extended, on lines advocated before the war, increasing local authority control over voluntary bodies and central direction of the whole process of child care. Again, necessary rationalization was the keynote of policy change.

STANDARDS OF LIVING

Perhaps the most significant effect of the war was that it led to a generation of unprecedented peacetime full employment. This was only partly due to wartime changes in the structure of industry. Wartime amalgamation of firms and more standardized methods of production were encouraged by labour shortages, by the government's planned placing of contracts with larger firms, and by the utility scheme which standardized essential products. As in the previous war there was pressure and need for efficient utilization of business resources.[53]

The war period chiefly affected living standards through, as in the war of 1914–18, the creation of full employment, the drawing into employment of previously marginal groups – some mothers of young children, aged and young people – which increased total incomes for a considerable number of households, though often in return for long hours of work. As during the previous war, it is impossible to say how many benefited in this war. However, the learning of the lessons of 1914–18 under the guidance of Keynes meant that such gains were less often counteracted by rising prices, rents and shortages of essential goods, due to the introduction of price and interest rate controls and rationing mechanisms. Few groups did so well as farmers as a result of the introduction of guaranteed farm prices as a highly successful incentive to produce. This gain was maintained by farmers after the war due to the maintenance of farm subsidies.

Limited redistribution of income resulted from the wartime tax changes. Indeed, it seems clear that the two wars were the only periods of significant redistribution of wealth and income in Britain before 1950; that redistribution was largely the result of taxation policies and was slight. The changes in taxation were a direct result of the needs of war finance rather than of any inherent pre-war tendency or of radical aspirations. Between 1938 and 1948 the real value of purchasing power in the hands of the top one-sixth of income earners fell by about 30 per cent, and that of the remainder increased by about 25 per cent. From 1947 real wage rates fell and the redistribution process decelerated, aided by the gradual reduction of food subsidies and rent controls. It must be said, however, that tax evasion grew to unprecedented heights during the war; the practice of rearranging financial affairs so as to pay as little as possible of the tax burden developed on a large scale – perhaps the most lasting gainers from the war were members of the accountancy profession. This was a response not only to the increased sums demanded in tax, but also the increased efficiency of its collection. From 1940 income tax became more widely payable at source: the beginnings of the present PAYE scheme. The redistributive effects of the social legislation of the post-war government were slight, due in part to the gains made by higher income groups from such free services as health and education.[54]

In the long run the greatest impact of the war upon Britain was upon her international position. Unlike the previous occasion, Britain entered the war with a deficit in her balance of payments. Despite Keynes' efforts to maximize internal finance for war needs, not all of which were accepted, Britain's indebtedness increased during the war, notably to Canada and the USA. This was offset partly by the sale of British investments abroad, notably in India and the United States, which further precipitated the long-run deterioration of Britain's position in the international economy and in international politics.[55]

CONCLUSION

To return to my initial question: was Titmuss' analysis of the processes involved in wartime policy change correct? Two things need to be borne in mind in the background to this discussion: first, there had been considerable official and unofficial investigation of and proposals for social policies in the inter-war years; second, there were more vigorous and frequent investigations of public attitudes to policy during the war than before. Hence we have no way of knowing whether public acceptance of more redistributive policies was actually heightened during the war; nor is it obvious that official awareness of social problems was greater in wartime. The virtual disappearance of unemployment in 1942 and the rising incomes of fully employed households diminished certain pre-war problems and concentrated attention upon the enduring problems of large families, old age, ill-health and poor education and housing. There is little evidence, from an examination of a wider range of social policies than Titmuss considered, that if 'a heightened government awareness' of social welfare existed, either as a tool of national efficiency or as a means of enhancing social solidarity, it drove the war government to enthusiasm for extensive social reconstruction. On the contrary, most ministers were fearful that an over-hasty commitment to long-term social reform would hamper the prosecution of the war and retard post-war economic revival.[56] The impetus to a reluctant and divided wartime government to introduce social policy proposals and, more rarely, legislation, came less from the impact of Dunkirk than from the revival of political and industrial conflict in the later part of the war and from the consequent need to contain it. Even then both Conservative and Labour ministers were reluctant to make binding commitments.

Few areas of social policy moved in a decisively new direction during and after the war; rather they followed the lines of proposals made before the war. The exception to this was the introduction of a more redistributive system of direct taxation. This, however, was temporary and the result of the needs of war finance rather than of more radical social objectives.

Arguably the experiences of war speeded up change in certain areas of policy, notably in the health services, social security, the treatment of the disabled, family allowances and town planning; the influence upon education is less obvious. To what extent this is so is unanswerable, since we cannot know what would have happened if the war had not. Nevertheless, the considerable impact of war needs upon the health services forced certain changes upon these services and influenced the attitude of members of the medical profession. Beveridge was given, and grasped to the full, an opportunity which was unlikely to have occurred in peacetime. War conditions spotlighted the problem of large poor families more clearly than before, and changed attitudes in the Labour movement; the blitz was an unforeseen gift to the town planning movement.

Yet those in a position of power who opposed social action during wartime largely had their way. During the war itself little was done other than to meet emergency needs. Butler's success with education owed much to his own determination and to the relatively uncontroversial nature of his proposals. The introduction of family allowances can, at least in part, be seen as an attempt to prevent demands for something still less attractive to the Treasury and to business: higher wages. The unexpectedly large post-war Labour victory ensured that leading wartime policy proposals were more fully translated into legislation than might have occurred under a Conservative government.

The great difference between the experience of the two wars of this century lies less in what happened during the war periods – both produced wide-ranging proposals for change and action more limited than those proposals – than in what happened before and after. The post-1945 Labour government faced some opposition from business, from Conservatives and from the Treasury, for its social policy and nationalization programmes, but this opposition was weaker than its equivalent in 1918–20. Both during and after the war the leading potential sources of opposition were prepared to accept actions to which they had been bitterly opposed during the previous war. This muting of opposition in the years immediately following 1945 cannot entirely be explained by the existence of the first ever Labour government with a decisive majority. It must also be seen in terms of the pre-war experience. The consensus among business leaders and politicians of the right in 1914, and still in 1918, was that pre-war society and economy had functioned satisfactorily enough, that there was little need for change and that the most desirable strategy was a return to 'business as usual'. Such people showed only limited interest in change before the war, and the war did not substantially change their attitudes. In fact the war and its consequences *had* changed Britain and the world, in particular it had changed Britain's internal and external economic position, but this lesson was only gradually learned.

By 1939 it had been partially learned, though the accompanying problems had not been solved. In 1945 only an intransigent few wished to return to 'business as usual', to the pre-war world of high unemployment, bankruptcy and low profits. Despite the partial recovery of the late 1930s, business had entered the war already aware of the need for change if that recovery was to be made permanent. Businessmen and progressive Conservatives, such as Macmillan, were already proposing planning for the more efficient use of resources and recognizing the potential contribution of an improved social infrastructure to a successful economy. The Treasury was moving towards some at least of Keynes' solutions.

The war experience did nothing to weaken such beliefs; indeed the practice of increased government control rather strengthened them. Hence those groups which had opposed change in 1918–20 emerged from the Second World War prepared in rather greater numbers to accept changes which removed the major pre-war problems: nationalization of industries which had proved incapable of profitability under free enterprise, yet were essential to the running of other private enterprises; measures which improved health and efficiency and removed major causes of working-class discontent. Similarly, more doctors were prepared to accept a high, but not total, degree of state responsibility for medical care in 1945 than in the early 1930s. The clear evidence that the leaders of Labour were far from revolutionary helped to sustain such support for their measures. Also of some probable importance was the decline of the threat of far-reaching central physical control of the economy as advocated by Macmillan, later by Beveridge and more radically by those further left. Keynes had demonstrated that economic recovery was possible by other means, with minimal long-run physical controls. Recognizing this, Beveridge's belief in the need for corporate planning retreated, as did Macmillan's. The Labour leadership showed no sign of resuscitating it. Even the dependence of that government upon American loans, which might in different circumstances have constrained reforms, proved to be an asset in view of the determination of the USA to encourage the reconstruction of the economies of Western Europe to prevent the recurrence of depression and of the socialist threat of the post-1918 period. British businessmen were less wary of change when they were aware that it was being experienced also by their peers in Europe.

Nor could any post-war government have ignored the popular demand for change which had grown so strong during the war, reaching a peak in the support for the Beveridge Report. This demand for a 'welfare state' comprised a wide range of hopes and ideals, some more easily accommodated within a pluralistic political system than others. One outcome of this new popular radicalism, the Labour party programme of 1945, proposing a degree of nationalization, a free National Health Service and implementation of the Beveridge recommendations, lay towards the extreme edge of a real consensus for change which had been born in the later 1930s and had come to maturity during the war. These proposals were potentially in conflict with the more conservative components of the consensus, which could, for example, accept nationalization of essential but unprofitable industries, but not of profitable ones, improved social services but not equality of their distribution nor more equal distribution of wealth and income. Labour, despite its majority, had to fight its path through these conflicting pressures. Where it used its majority to support the left of the uneasy consen-

---

sus, as in the nationalization of steel, its actions were reversed by the post 1951 Conservative government. In general. Labour used its majority to push the consensus further towards its limits than might have been expected of a Conservative government.

The social reforms of the Labour government were a profound improvement on what had gone before, but they were only a first step towards the establishment of more efficient administrative structures and minimum standards for universal services. It was the universality of provision of health care, social security and education, the real improvements in other services, such as housing, and in the new attempt to manage the economy, which constituted the claim of the post-war Labour governments to have established something qualitatively new, a new approach to the use of the power of the state consciously in the interests of social justice for the mass of the population, a 'welfare state'. The outcome was not the radical social and economic change for which many had hoped (how many, for how much change, remains unclear). Understandably the governments had underestimated the degree of institutional change necessary to achieve this outcome. Also, they were internally divided as to the desirable degree and direction of change, and they faced opposition from powerful sources to more fundamental change.

The success of the post-war economy compared with that of the inter-war years and with what had been feared during the war, muted pressure from any but the most deprived and their supporters for more far reaching measures. The number of the latter were relatively few in view of the euphoria resulting from the real improvements in the post- over the pre-war world. It was over a decade before a sense of unease began to spread that the post-war changes had not been radical enough.

REFERENCES

1. J. HARRIS, 'Social policy making in Britain during the second world war' in *The Emergence of the Welfare State in Britain & Germany* WOLFGANG MOMMSEN (ed.) Croom Helm, London (1981).
2. *Ibid.*
3. P. ADDISON, *The Road to 1945*, Jonathan Cape, London (1975) Ch. 3.
4. K. MIDDLEMAS, *Politics in Industrial Society*, André Deutsch, London (1979) pp. 274–5.

5. P. ADDISON, *op. cit.*, p. 167.
6. D. RUBINSTEIN AND B. SIMON, *The Evolution of the Comprehensive School 1926–1966*, Routledge & Kegan Paul, London (1969) p. 24.
7. K. MIDDLEMAS, *op. cit.*, pp. 280–6.
8. D. RUBINSTEIN AND B. SIMON, *op. cit.*, pp. 27–8.
9. *Ibid.*, pp. 28–30.
10. P. ADDISON, *op. cit.*, p. 239.
11. *Ibid.*, pp. 171–4; 237–9.
12. B. ABEL-SMITH, *The Hospitals*, Heinemann, London (1964) pp. 424ff.
13. P. ADDISON, *op. cit.*, pp. 178–81; 239–42; B. ABEL-SMITH, *op. cit.*, Chs. 27 and 28.
14. P. HALL *et al.*, *Change, Choice and Conflict in Social Policy* Heinemann, London (1975) pp. 277–8.
15. *Ibid.*, pp. 282–3.
16. B. ABEL-SMITH, *op. cit.*, pp. 480–81.
17. P. HALL, *op. cit.*, pp. 284–9.
18. M. SPRING RICE, *Working Class Wives*, Penguin (1939); reprinted Virago, London (1981).
19. R. M. TITMUSS, *Problems of Social Policy*, HMSO and Longmans Green & Co., London (1950); J. HEYWOOD, *Children in Care*, Routledge & Kegan Paul, London (1959) pp. 135–7.
20. A. CALDER, *The People's War*, Panther, London (1971).
21. P. HALL, *op. cit.*, p. 198, n. 155.
22. P. ADDISON, *op. cit.*, p. 116.
23. H. BOLDERSON, 'The origins of the Disabled Persons Employment Quota and its symbolic significance', *Journal of Social Policy* (1980).
24. P. HALL, *op. cit.*, pp. 179–95.
25. *Ibid.*, pp. 181–2.
26. *Ibid.*, pp. 184–6.
27. *Ibid.*, p. 191.
28. *Ibid.*, pp. 190–230; J. MACNICOL, *The Movement for Family Allowances 1918–45*, Heinemann, London (1980).
29. SIR ARNOLD WILSON AND G. S. MACKAY, *Old Age Pensions*, Oxford University Press (1941) pp. 207–27.
30. J. HARRIS, *William Beveridge*, Oxford University Press (1977) pp. 386–7.
31. *Ibid.*, pp. 401–02, 414–15.
32. *Ibid.*, pp. 402–06.
33. *Ibid.*, pp. 420ff.

34. *Ibid.*, p. 424.
35. P. ADDISON, *op. cit.*, p. 227.
36. J. HARRIS, *op. cit.*, pp. 424–48.
37. *Ibid.*, pp. 428ff.
38. *Ibid.*, pp. 438ff.
39. *Ibid.*, pp. 438–9; ADDISON, *op. cit.*, pp. 244–7.
40. J. HARRIS, *op. cit.*, pp. 438–41.
41. D. E. MOGGRIDGE, *Keynes*, Fontana, London (1976).
42. *Ibid.*, p. 147ff.; ALAN BUDD, *The Politics of Economic Planning*, Fontana, London (1978) Ch. 4.
43. D. E. MOGGRIDGE, *op. cit.*, Ch. 6.
44. P. ADDISON, *op. cit.*, p. 248.
45. *Ibid.*, p. 175.
46. A. CALDER, *op. cit.*, pp. 364–6.
47. P. ADDISON, *op. cit.*, pp. 174–5.
48. *Ibid.*, pp. 175–8.
49. W. H. ASHWORTH, *The Genesis of Modern British Town Planning*, Routledge & Kegan Paul, London (1954) pp. 224–37.
50. J. HEYWOOD, *op. cit.*, p.135.
51. D. RILEY, 'War in the Nursery', *Feminist Review* 2 (1979).
52. J. HEYWOOD, *op. cit.*, p. 140ff.
53. A. MILWARD, *The Economic Effects of the World Wars on Britain*, Macmillan, London (1970) pp. 35ff.
54. R. M. TITMUSS, *Income Distribution and Social Change*, George Allen & Unwin, London (1962).
55. A. MILWARD, *op. cit.*, pp. 44–52.
56. K. MIDDLEMAS, *op. cit.*, pp. 271ff.

Chapter eight

INTERNATIONAL COMPARISONS 1920 TO THE SECOND
WORLD WAR

Internationally, changes in social policy were closely affected by
the different impacts of the two World Wars and of the inter-war
economy upon individual countries. The economic crisis of the inter-war years and the associated political upheavals hit all countries
integrated into the international economy, although at different
times and to varying degrees.

Russia, being partially isolated from the networks of international investment and trade, largely escaped from the addition of exceptional new burdens to those she already suffered. From 1921
Russia was at last able to begin to restructure her society and economy, on the basis of the breathing space provided by Lenin's
'New Economic Policy' (NEP) which permitted a limited revival of
private trade in agricultural and consumer goods. This was only
possible, however, after a period of fluctuating prices and industrial employment and amid threats of a 'workers opposition', as
agriculture was favoured at the expense of heavy industry. However, NEP had always been seen as a temporary step backwards from
socialist ideals and, especially after Lenin's death in 1924,
Bolshevik leaders stressed the long-term danger to socialism from
excessive encouragement of free enterprise. The alternative was a
planned socialized economy, which was pursued with increasing
fervour from 1925. The aim of Soviet planning was, within a socialist
framework, to transform the USSR into a modern industrial
country matching those of the west and hence to make Russia
industrially as well as agriculturally self-sufficient, diminishing its
dependence upon imports from hostile countries and creating
a surplus for export, to increase national wealth.

The transition was painful. It was the more so since it was conducted by an administration increasingly under the control of a
man – Stalin – with fewer qualms than Lenin about the use of
force. In particular, controls upon peasant production and distribu-

tion were increased in order to supply the food needs of industrial workers. This was accompanied by a campaign to increase the efficiency of industrial workers; to curb drunkenness and absenteeism, and to improve vocational and political education. Hours of work for men and women were increased, to increase production; wages, like production, were planned and, despite the introduction of incentive bonuses, real wages fell for several years from 1928, due to the demands of investment and the difficulty of enforcing price controls upon small traders. Many goods were in short supply, including food. Trade unions lost their wage negotiating role. The first five-year plan, the final abandonment of NEP, was introduced in 1929. This and succeeding five-year plans covered social as well as economic provision, each being regarded as equally essential to the attainment of economic growth and social justice. By 1934 the private sector of the Russian economy was tiny, the result in part of the forced and deeply resented collectivization of agriculture.[1]

However, to whatever degree the form of socialism built in the USSR deviated from the ideals of Marx and Lenin, as it did above all in the suppression of democracy, its rulers aimed for and achieved, in the 1930s, improved living standards for workers and for many peasants. The losses which paid for this achievement were partially compensated by improved social services.

By the mid 1930s the USSR had developed a network of services which, though still imperfect, outstripped, at least in aspiration, those of many more prosperous societies. Their virtues were described, and rather exaggerated, by the Webbs and other British visitors to the USSR during the 1930s. Entranced, the Webbs saw in Russia the proposals of the minority report of 1909 brought to life: the skeleton of a universal network of specialist social services, administered by experts (many of them however far from 'unassuming'), designed to re-engineer society into greater equality, productivity and dedication, without sacrificing the obligation to work – a 'remaking of man' as they described it.

The Webbs emphasized the emancipation of women in the USSR, including their new equal rights to education and employment, maternity care and grants, crèches and leave of absence for mothers.[2] They were not alone in their admiration. Newsholme and a colleague also visited the USSR in 1933 and were 'filled with admiration...(by)...arrangements for the medical and hygienic care of mothers and their children'.[3]

Such visitors to Russia necessarily saw only part of that vast country. They recognized that services had improved only in major urban and industrial areas but the achievements of a still very poor country were nevertheless impressive. Between 1924 and 1934 the number of hospitals doubled and the number of hospital beds within rural areas expanded rapidly. In 1914 7 million Russians attended school; by 1929 14.3 m., in 1933 26.4 m. In the latter year all military recruits were claimed to be literate.[4]

Social insurance remained under the administration of trade unions, which effectively restricted its coverage to those in regular work and excluded the independent peasantry. It provided wage-related sickness, invalidity and old-age benefits, but none for unemployment. In place of the latter was compulsory re-training and compulsory movement of unemployed labour to available jobs. In an expanding planned economy under a highly authoritarian government, unemployment could not be allowed to exist.[5]

The progress of Soviet economic and social planning was halted by the vast demands made by the Second World War upon new and fragile social and economic structures. Planned reconstruction was a post-war necessity.

Most leading economies enjoyed reasonable stability from 1920 to 1929, with the USA, Australia and Japan in particular reaping the advantages of their gains in international trade during the war period. Exceptions were the UK, Scandinavia and Italy, all of which suffered severe recession in 1921, the UK most severely of all. The early arrival of Mussolini's fascism in Italy in 1922 soon provided another example of a planned economy under an authoritarian government. Mussolini aimed for planned restabilization, with heavy expenditure upon road and railway building and other works, followed by guided industrial investment, increasingly in heavy industry, much of it financed by American loans. Expenditure on education and other services also rose. Italian unemployment was less than that of comparable economies in the late 1920s and the 1930s, though this was due at least as much to arms expenditure in the 30s as to successful planning.

The Scandinavian pattern in the 1920s was similar to that of Britain (although unemployment levels were lower) with cuts in public expenditure and few developments in social policy. The decade saw in Sweden a succession of unstable minority governments. The severe effects of the slump of 1929–31 helped the Social Democrats to power in 1932 with a promise of social reform – a position which they retained for forty-four years. The new government's first measures were expenditure on unemployment benefits and public works to meet the immediate crisis. By 1939 a system of unemployment insurance had been established and the rate of old-age pensions raised.

In 1938 a Commission was established to investigate social insurance and related services but many of its recommendations were delayed until after the war. These included legislation in 1946 for family allowances, subsistence level contributory widows', orphans' and old-age pensions and extended, though not universal, health insurance. This was not effectively established until the late 1950s, after prolonged opposition by the medical profession, when the state also took closer control of medical services. In every field except health Sweden had made within a decade after the war minimum universal provision for most of the major causes of poverty.[6]

In Norway, also, the Depression of the 1920s and 1930s was followed by the election of a progressive government in the mid-1930s. In the short space until Norway was devastated by German occupation between 1940 and 1945, the government followed with some success a Keynesian-style policy of economic management, together with increased public expenditure. Health insurance was introduced for such economically important groups as seamen and fishermen; means-tested old-age and disablement pensions and comprehensive insurance were implemented.

After 1945 the acute need for reconstruction led to a coalition government determined upon comprehensive social and economic planning and a policy of full employment. The integration and expansion of old-age, health and unemployment insurance followed lines similar to the proposals of Beveridge, partially arising from the wartime exile in England of many government members. Housebuilding was subsidized. From 1946 the government embarked upon a policy of planned growth. A succession of four-year plans from 1949 laid down detailed social and economic policies leading to a stream of legislation in the early 1950s. Norway's economic recovery thereafter was remarkable.[7]

Another country to suffer German occupation, France, enjoyed relative stability in the 1920s but suffered relatively high unemployment from 1929. The left-wing Popular Front government, elected in 1936 in response to previous government failure to cope with the Depression, extended public works expenditure, social insurance and, in 1939, increased maternity grants and legislated for improvements in child and maternity welfare; France still experienced an unusually low rate of population growth. German occupation from 1941 prevented full implementation of the proposals and caused severe regression of living standards and services.

France, too, was faced with a major problem of post-war reconstruction, which was carried out with the aid of American loans. The post-war determination of the western victors in the war, led by America, to establish democratic structures proof against a resurgence of fascism or the spread of communism provided an additional incentive to avoid the recurrence of pre-war economic instability. This was seen as a contributor to the rise of fascism, and improved social benefits as one bulwark against communism.

Hence in France also, in 1945, the government aimed for a policy of full employment. Social insurance schemes were integrated and expanded, family allowances raised and maternity and child welfare services improved, as planned before the war. The training and organization of social workers was standardized and improved.[8] The other occupied Western European countries, Denmark, Austria, Holland and Belgium, had similar experiences.

The incentive for large-scale reconstruction was understandably less acute in countries whose physical involvement in the war was less total and less destructive. The effect of economic stability in Australia in the 1920s was to end her period as 'leader of the world' in social provision. There were few advances in social policy, despite the predominance of Labour in state legislatures. Queensland introduced a very limited unemployment insurance scheme in 1923, following extensive local unemployment. No other state followed this example. The Lang Labour government in New South Wales (1925–27), introduced widows' pensions and family allowances; the former was followed only in Victoria in the late 1930s; family allowances nowhere, despite their widespread discussion, mainly in relation to wage levels.

The authority of the Conservative Commonwealth government over the states was greatly increased by the first war. Capital was increasingly confident after the stimulus in the war period to vigorous economic development. The Labour movement remained divided as a result of a wartime split over conscription. Forces which before the war had only reluctantly accepted government intervention in the economy were strengthened by the war. The minimum wage was eroded and the arbitration court took so few counter-measures that Higgins resigned in indignation. The priority of the post-war government was national development, through the introduction of tariffs, and the encouragement of immigration. Strong measures were taken against strikers. Charity and self-help rather than legislation were offered as the solution to social problems.

The international slump of 1929–31 hit Australia hard. The resulting mass unemployment was met by special temporary state taxes to finance food rations and public works, rather than by establishing a permanent right to unemployment benefits. Australian governments remained reluctant to intervene in the free market, hoping that the slump would be temporary. Such measures as there were distinguished vigorously between 'deserving' and 'undeserving'. Since no breakdown in public order resulted, the stimulus to further measures was small. The slump did not, however, disappear quickly. Australia shared the international Depression of the 1930s. The Commonwealth governments struggled, as had the British government in the 1920s, to minimize taxation in order to stimulate industry. Immigration was restricted when Australia had few jobs to offer.

The failure of the Australian governments of the 1930s to solve the problems of the decade was one reason for a Labour government coming to power in 1941. It remained in office until 1949. Labour also controlled the majority of states in this period. The war period saw the implementation of a wide range of social policies, which Labour had long demanded. The Conservative government introduced child endowment in 1941 as a means of countering the effects of wartime inflation upon the lower-paid, including the families of servicemen. Labour introduced maternity allowances and funeral benefits in 1943, unemployment and sickness benefits and free medicine in 1944, free hospital treatment and an employment service in 1945. Also in 1945, the Commonwealth and the states co-operated in providing housing and financial assistance to hospitals. For the first time, aborigines were included in the benefits of wartime social legislation; they were required for the wartime labour force. Commonwealth expenditure on social provision increased tenfold between 1941 and 1949.

Unemployment had risen again in Australia in 1938–39 and, as in Britain, there were demands throughout the war for post-war reconstruction and a degree of planning or management of the economy, to prevent a post-war return to unemployment. During the war Labour was able to use its majority to implement policy changes which were seen as aiding this reconstruction, assisted by the need to stimulate popular enthusiasm for the war (low before the fears of Japanese invasion), the need to care for war casualties and to attract women, aborigines and the retired into the labour force.

There were, however, strict limits to the consensus for change.

The Commonwealth government failed in 1944 to acquire stronger permanent powers of economic intervention. They could not persuade the medical profession to accept a national health service and had to be content with insurance and subsidies to services. With the exception of family allowances, none of the new provisions were universal or provided as a right except on evidence of need. Widows' pensions were paid only 'if she is of good character'. Benefits, including unemployment benefits, remained low. The redistributive effects were slight. There was strong Conservative and business opposition to wartime commitments to expensive post-war government expenditure which by force of its majority the government was able partially to override. But Labour shared some of these doubts and was indeed not wholly committed to extensive redistribution; its own preference for self-help remained strong.

During and immediately after the war, Australia established minimum means-tested provision for most in need, on a lower level than emerged in Britain at the same time. In an economy about which there was reason for optimism, in which reluctance to provide for those capable of work had flourished throughout the twentieth century, the pressures against greater change were strong and Labour had neither the effective power nor a strong inclination to overturn them. The post-war success of the economy removed any pressure to go further. The Conservatives again controlled the Commonwealth government from 1949.[9]

In general, New Zealand's experience was similar to that of Australia. However, the Depression of the 1930s brought a Labour government to power a little earlier, in 1938. Between 1938 and 1946 it extended the limited system of family allowances, first introduced in 1926 as an alternative to a minimum wage. Earlier in the 1930s, however, the high unemployment following 1929 had led to the establishment of Labour Exchanges in 1930 and of an Unemployment Board to promote training and to give relief both to industry and the unemployed though, for the latter, means-tested at very low rates. Means-tested invalidity pensions were introduced in 1936.

In 1938 a Select Committee on social insurance recommended the introduction of a universal national health service and superannuation scheme. The former was not implemented due to professional opposition. In 1940 pensions were extended to all over sixty-five and gradually increased to subsistence level. In 1945 unemployment and other benefits were raised to the same level but remained means-tested.[10]

The US also experienced a cessation of social reform activity between 1918 and the slump of 1929. The 1920s, there also, were a period of prosperity, with high levels of employment and rising real wages, bringing a renewed belief that 'what was good for business was good for the nation'. Economic growth was seen as the solution to poverty. President Hoover's inaugural address in 1928 assured the nation that: 'We in America today are nearer to the final triumph over poverty then ever before in the history of any land.'

This confidence was accompanied by the determined suppression of the left and of trade unions, for fear of 'Bolshevism'. The flow of immigrants came under increasingly stringent controls in the 1920s; fewer of the desperately poor flowed in to America. The social reform pressure of the previous decade was dissipated by the apparent achievement of many of its goals. Much reform achieved by individual states was declared unconstitutional by the courts. Moral fervour was increasingly channelled into the demand for prohibition and against the supposedly debilitating effects of dependence upon welfare. Voluntary social work agencies concentrated upon 'constructive help' for the 'deserving' alone. As also in Australia, in the 1920s only the well-organized war veterans did not share the general diminution in social benefits. Yet, even in America's richest year of the period, 1928–29, 21 per cent of the population had incomes below the low level of $1,000 p.a.

The crash of 1929–31 had more serious effects upon the USA than elsewhere: unemployment was high throughout the 1930s. Throughout 1930 President Hoover campaigned on a theme of optimism, of recovery and of the need for balanced budgets. He was reluctant to sanction any intervention in the economy. Since, however, unemployment was clearly not the fault of the unemployed, temporary relief programmes, providing work and goods, were sanctioned by the Federal government. By 1932, when the economy clearly was not recovering of its own volition, Federal financial aid was given to business and to agriculture to attempt to aid their recovery. The government preferred to assist business rather than to give directly to the unemployed.

The inadequacy of this approach brought F. D. Roosevelt to the Presidency in 1932, promising a 'New Deal'. This was to include public works, unemployment and old-age insurance and, somewhat contradictorily, cuts in public expenditure. Throughout the 1930s the Federal government maintained an uneasy combination of policies designed both to stimulate demand and to protect the free market, and to maintain a balanced budget. Aid was given to banks

and financial institutions, interest rates and the currency were man-
ipulated to encourage investment and exports; house owners were
helped to refinance mortgages. Farmers were allowed credit on
easier terms and controls were placed on output to raise prices –
measures which drove smaller tenant farmers out of business, but
stimulated large-scale production.

Although the 'New Deal' policies were primarily designed to
stimulate business recovery, the high levels of unemployment (25%
in 1933, 14% in 1937 and higher still among blacks) could not be
ignored for fear of political unrest. The Federal government gave
first priority to provision of jobs, providing $400 m. in 1935 for
public works, supported by temporary cash relief for the unemployed, the relief to be financed by the Federal government. Federal aid was to be restricted to those normally in full employment;
'unemployables' remained the responsibility of the states, difficult
though this distinction became as the Depression lengthened.

Fearing to lose trade union support, Roosevelt legalized collective bargaining, established a forty-hour week (also designed to
reduce unemployment) and a minimum wage in certain industries.
Congress and the courts constrained further action: attempts further to regulate wages and prices were declared unconstitutional by
the courts on the appeal of employers. A committee on economic
security was established to review and recommend policy changes.
In 1935 it produced draft Bills aimed to secure adequate minimum
incomes and services for the unemployed and aged. Roosevelt recommended these proposals to Congress but with some caution. He
specified that Congress should not legislate for health insurance or
for Federal finance for old-age insurance. The result was the Social
Security Act of 1935 which established unemployment compensation, retirement insurance, aid to the blind and to dependent children, maternity and child health and child welfare services, all of
them restricted to lower income groups. Effectively this established
a tri-partite system: Federally-administered insurance, Federal aid
to state-administered assistance to 'deserving' groups, and state
provision for the 'undeserving'. It generalized and legitimated provision already established in most states. By 1935 aid to the blind
was provided in twenty-four states, to the aged in thirty-four and to
mothers in every state but Alabama, Georgia and South Carolina.
An appeals procedure was established for rejected claims under the
1935 Act. The Act provided essentially for the needs of those outside the labour market and was designed to encourage the old to
leave employment – aid to dependent children (which did help the

employed but low-paid) was markedly lower than that to the aged and blind. As in Australia, minimal services were provided for the deserving poor. Roosevelt was convinced, however, of the demoralizing effects of cash relief. Federal funds for this purpose ended in 1935 and were channelled instead into the provision of work. When production began to recover in 1937, all government spending was cut back. In the following year production fell once more.

The war, however, brought full employment and rising standards to much of the American population, although still, in 1947, 31 per cent of families had incomes below $2000. War prosperity created successful demands to phase out the remnants of the 'New Deal'. Wartime social policies concentrated upon the problems of families disrupted by the absence of fathers and the employment of mothers, and of communities affected by the relocation of war production and of army camps. For these purposes, day-care centres, schools and medical services were provided for the duration of the war.

At the end of the war, the need to maintain prosperity led to the Employment Act 1946, designed to 'maximize employment, production and purchasing power' by the use of fiscal and monetary controls and budgetary policy. A proposal by Truman in 1948 to nationalize health services was defeated by the American Medical Association. The late 1940s and early 1950s saw some Federal and state finance for housing and the extension of insurance to the disabled, but little more as prosperity continued and long-established hostility to state welfare regained full strength.[11]

Canada continued to be even slower than America to introduce national minimum standards. As in Australia, the wars of 1914–18 and 1939–45 strengthened the power of the Federal over the Provincial governments, as the needs of war forced it to take control of national taxation and war production. After prosperity in the 1920s, unemployment in the 1930s led first to Federal subsidies for the temporary unemployment relief administered by the provinces, then to the introduction of employment exchanges and unemployment insurance for low earners in 1940. An attempt to introduce these measures in 1935 had been declared unconstitutional.

From 1927 the Federal government subsidized provincial means-tested old-age benefits. These benefits were raised in 1935 when it appeared that the effects of the Depression had wiped out the savings of many old people. In 1939 compulsory contributions for pensions for low-income widows and orphans were introduced, but covered only the regularly employed. Depressed farmers were subsidized from 1939; family allowances were introduced in 1944 and from 1948 the Federal government subsidized medical services in the Provinces and, in 1941, contributory old-age pensions for those over seventy. As in Australia and the USA, well organized veterans received preference for these benefits after both wars; also, the Second World War saw the introduction of services for the newly economically important native Indians and Eskimos.

Canada, more insulated from the immediate impact of the war than either Europe or Australasia, with good reason for optimism about the underlying strength of her economy and with fewer problems of poverty than the USA, had less incentive than most countries to attempt extensive social and economic planning or reconstruction during or after the war of 1939–45.[12]

The crisis of the inter-war years forced all governments to rethink their economic and social policies. The immediacy of their response depended upon the seriousness of the crisis in each country and upon the extent of negotiation necessary to achieve change. In the 1930s all moved some way towards greater government intervention in a market which seemed incapable of regulating itself. Extensive regulations proved possible only under authoritarian governments as in the Soviet Union, Italy and in Germany after Hitler came to power in 1933.

Little information is available about the social policies of governments of the Weimar period in Germany. The rapid succession of governments made the development of coherent national policies difficult. The Social Democratic Party (SPD) government in 1918 established unemployment insurance benefits for all workers under local control. Unemployment policy was subject to six major revisions as unemployment worsened between 1920 and 1927, and amid mounting unemployment demonstrations, many of them Communist organized. However, in 1927, during a period of relative economic stability, the government attempted to standardize locally administered poor relief payments, which had previously varied considerably, by fixing them in line with the prices of essential goods. This met resistance from many local authorities and payments were generally reduced after the slump of 1929.

Also in 1927, since unemployment remained high, unemployment insurance was introduced, administered by national labour exchanges. Further increases in unemployment after 1929 were met partly by increased expenditure on public works.

The combination of economic crisis and government instability was one of the many reasons for Hitler's coming to power in 1933.

He possessed no clear economic policy, amid continuing high urban unemployment and rural poverty. He embarked in 1934 on a series of 2–4 year plans, designed to save agriculture and to cut unemployment. He retained and expanded the public works programmes of his predecessors; a major road-building programme was initiated with the support of big business, who had much to gain from improved communications; housebuilding was subsidized and work training established for school leavers and the unskilled. Tax incentives were given to aid the recovery of big business.

From 1933 the Hitler government campaigned to remove women from the workforce. Women were excluded from public service; given interest-free loans on marriage; family allowances and maternity benefits and child tax allowances were increased and maternity services improved. The imperatives of maximizing male employment, reversing the declining birth rate and building a Aryan super-race conveniently coincided. The curricula of girls' schools were modified to emphasize training in domestic skills; the Nazi party organized schools for mothers with the same object. Large families received cheap health care and railway tickets. Fewer women were admitted to universities.

Effective full employment was established by 1936. Wages were kept in line with the cost of living; health, accident and unemployment insurance were extended. Working conditions were regulated and improved; many more workers took paid holidays. However, the general economic improvement owed more to the sharp increase in arms expenditure and manufacture than to any other measure. The number of working women actually increased between 1936 and 1938 as employment opportunities increased, although the numbers remained low. In line with pre-war policies, however, the failure to conscript women during the war was one reason for Germany's low level of wartime production.

In the early years of the war little changed. Since extensive economic controls already existed few new ones were necessary. To maintain civilian morale, Hitler refused to allow any reduction in the production of consumer goods. Food supplies increased as a result of the occupation of other countries, which suffered accordingly. Initially the war was financed by such external, rather than by internal, means. As the war began to turn against Germany, Hitler refused initially to risk destroying morale by shifting from consumer to war production. Despite considerable reorganization in the later stages of the war, the suffering of the Germans in the war was severe. After 1945, however, in contrast to their fate after the previous war, the German economy was reconstructed with allied support and finance mainly from America. American determination to build democratic institutions in a stable Western Germany, as a bulwark against communism and a revival of fascism, led to allied encouragement of provision of extensive welfare measures including social insurance, health, welfare and education services.[13] Post-war policy was able to build on the basis of what had gone before, since the government of the Third Reich left intact the structures of local and national administration of most social services and benefits. Indeed, under the same stimulus, sometimes, indeed, as a condition of American loans, some variant of a 'welfare state' emerged everywhere in Western Europe. Similarly the reconstruction of post-war Japan was aided by American finance, building upon the structures of employer provision which had expanded in the inter-war years. With increased Soviet domination in the East after 1945, variants of the Soviet approach to social and economic planning were introduced.

Despite the very different economic and political experiences of so many countries between the wars and during the war of 1939–45, there were striking similarities in their approaches to social policy. In the 1920s all, with the exception of fascist Italy and the Soviet Union, made few advances in social policy, indeed made cuts whether in response to recession or relative economic success. The non-European growth economies saw little need for change except gradually to improve standards for deserving groups outside the labour market. The more troubled European economies cut public expenditure in the hope of emulating the success of their new rivals. One exception to this was British expenditure on unemployment benefits, necessitated by her exceptionally high unemployment levels.

The slump of 1929–31 was traumatic for all except Italy and the USSR and its effects were worsened by the extreme slowness with which the international economy recovered. This forced all states into degrees of economic and social intervention, both attracted by the relative success of the two planned economies, Russia and Italy, and repelled by the systems of government with which effective planning was associated.

Most non-totalitarian governments acted to unprecedented degrees to protect their internal economies from competition and to stimulate business, and introduced measures to protect the most deprived groups, especially the unemployed. The absence everywhere of serious political unrest among either the unemployed or the employed, opposition from business to further economic intervention and wider opposition to strong central government controls, constrained more extensive intervention. In general, Labour governments and their equivalents went rather further in this direction than others, although they also, in non-totalitarian systems, showed little enthusiasm for measures which would destroy viable free enterprise or threaten parliamentary democracy. Between 1929 and 1945 most countries severely affected by Depression and which escaped totalitarianism elected governments committed to this moderate degree of intervention.

The devastation of the war followed the unresolved economic crisis of the 1930s. The war was against a fascism which was seen as one result of the economic crisis. After the war, the desire that fascism should not recur, nor communism advance, were inextricably associated in Western Europe, North America, Japan and Australia with the need for economic, political and social security. The very term 'welfare state' had come into use with its modern resonance especially in Britain, from the late 1930s, signifying the antithesis to the 'power state' or the 'warfare state' of fascist or communist regimes. In principle, it meant a state in which measures to promote the economic and social well-being of the mass of the population were promoted within a democratic framework. Hence the great symbolic power of welfare measures in the postwar non-communist world.[14] Thus after the war most countries that had experienced the Depression saw the introduction of a degree of economic management, designed to establish full employment and to support essential industries which had provided incapable of thriving in the free market, and the implementation of extended social provision to provide a minimum for those incapable of helping themselves through the labour market. Provision was least extensive in countries where optimism for the future of free enterprise was greatest, i.e. in the most recently developed economies with obvious capacity for expansion: Australasia, USA, Canada.

In general, the minimum was given as a right to those, such as the aged, widowed mothers and children, who were normally out of the labour market and for recognized short-term hazards during working life, mainly sickness, accident and unemployment. Those of working age who faced longer term poverty had generally, and with difficulty, to overcome considerable administrative obstacles to establish their claim to a share of public resources. Everywhere cash benefits, whether or not given as a right, were below normal wage rates. Such actions were justified in terms of the need to preserve the incentive to work. The problem that normal wages might be inadequate for needs was generally met by the provision of family allowances. One exception to the general preference for minimum benefits and services was the establishment of the British National Health Service, which aimed in principle for universal access to an adequate standard of services. Why the medical profession in Britain was less effective in opposing this change than their colleagues elsewhere is an interesting and unexplored question. The answer may lie in the relative weakness of voluntary provision, including health insurance, in Britain.

Everywhere the experience of the war and of the pre-war Depression and its political results were inextricably interconnected, in the background to social policy change. In those countries for which the experience of war had been 'total' – in Europe and Japan – more wholesale post-war reconstruction was required than elsewhere, most of all in the defeated or occupied countries. The forms taken by that reconstruction were strongly influenced by the desires to avoid depression, fascism and communism.

REFERENCES

1. E. H. CARR, *The Russian Revolution from Lenin to Stalin 1917 – 1929*, Macmillan, London (1979) Chs. 11 – 16.
2. S. AND B. WEBB, *Soviet Communism: A New Civilization?*, Longman Green & Co., London (1935) Ch. X.
3. *Ibid.*, pp. 821 – 2.
4. *Ibid.*, pp. 805 – 78; 887 – 907.
5. *Ibid.*, pp. 664 – 71.
6. D. WILSON, *The Welfare State in Sweden*, Heinemann, London (1979) Ch. 1.
7. B. N. RODGERS, J. GREVE, J. S. MORGAN, *Comparative Social Administration*, Allen & Unwin, London (1968) pp. 83 – 104.
8. *Ibid.*, pp. 19 – 81.
9. J. ROE, *Social Policy in Australia*, Cassell, New South Wales (1976) Ch. 2; K. K. CROWLEY (ed.)*A New History of Australia*, Melbourne (1974).
10. P. R. KAIM-CAUDLE, *Comparative Social Policy*, Martin Robertson, London (1973) *passim*.
11. F. FOX PIVEN AND R. CLOWARD. *Regulating the Poor*, Tavistock, London (1972); J. AXINN AND H. LEVIN, *Social Welfare*: *A History of the American Response to Need*, Harper & Row, New York (1975) Chs. 6 and 7.

12. B. N. RODGERS *et al.*, *op. cit.*, pp. 157–222.
13. G. A. CRAIG, *Germany 1866–1945*, Oxford University Press (1978) pp. 448–55; 467–8; 603–630; 714–64.
14. M. BRUCE, *The Coming of the Welfare State*, Batsford, London (1968) p. 31.

The extent of social legislation in Britain has grown immensely in the past hundred years. Primary poverty has dramatically diminished. How, if at all, are these two phenomena related?

A recent study, headed by Peter Townsend, on *Poverty in the United Kingdom*, found that the proportion of the population in 'poverty' in the late 1960s, according to a variety of definitions, was between 6 and 9 per cent 'in poverty', with between 22 and 28 per cent 'on the margins of poverty'. These are strikingly, depressingly, similar proportions to those found by Booth, Rowntree and Bowley in the generation before 1914. The chief causes of poverty in the 1960s according to this survey were: pay too low adequately to support a family; the effects of widowhood and separation upon women; ill-health; unemployment and old age; again the main causes of poverty sixty years before.[1]

The condition of poverty discovered by Townsend and his colleagues was different from that of the past. The poor in the late 1960s usually, if not always, had more and better space in which to live, more furnishing, clothes, food, and better education for their children than their predecessors at the beginning of the century. Such improvements should not be exaggerated, but they were real. But if the poor have got better off over time, so has the remainder of society. Consequently there has been an increase in the resources required to fulfil 'the conditions of life which ordinarily define membership of society'.[2] The gaps in conditions of life separating the richest, those in the middle and those at the bottom have changed strikingly little over time, as have the proportions of the population in each group.

Whether or not we choose to define those at the bottom as living 'in poverty', this is a curious outcome from the great increase in public expenditure on welfare services in this country. Behind this lies generations of pressure from entirely well-meaning people for real redistribution of wealth, income and access to services; for, not absolute equality of condition, to which few have aspired, but for diminished inequality and, certainly, for all to enjoy a high if not precisely defined minimum standard which would provide for their children real 'equality of opportunity'.

This gap between the apparent aspirations behind the growth of government action and the outcome requires explanation. Part of of the explanation lies in what has occurred since 1950, which lies outside the scope of this book. However, the decisive change in the level of social provision came between 1939 and 1950 and was built on what had gone before. The framework and principles of post-war provision were established in this period and have not since been significantly changed – though such change is now, in 1981, beginning – and the outcome of such changes in policy and provision in the past seems to have been little real change in the distribution of resources and opportunities. Rather it seems, on the face of it, that the outcome of greatly increased government provision over time has been to keep the structure of this distribution more or less unchanged; to ensure, in effect, that the condition of those at the bottom rose only enough to keep them in a stable relationship to the rising standards of those above. How could this be the outcome of the hopes and demands of Booth, the early socialists, the new Liberals, of Rowntree, the Webbs, Morant, Addison, Tawney, Beveridge and many more? If we assume that the chief motivation behind the development of state social action has been the aspirations of the reformers, the removal or minimization of gross disparities in the distribution of material resources and of power over them, the results have been grossly disappointing. Perhaps, then, this assumption is wrong. That it may be wrong should be no cause for surprise. In no other area of policy does one expect governments to give primacy to the interests of the weak or to be motivated by single or simple pressures or principles. There is no obvious reason why the making of social policy should differ from other forms of political action.

It is however, the assumption which has lain behind many inter-pretations of the history of social policy. This history has often been interpreted as that of the growth of altruism, suggesting that, as Pinker puts it, 'men and women are by nature communally orientated and altruistically motivated and that the process of democratization makes manifest these natural and public virtues. From this assumption it becomes possible to argue that the welfare state is a staging post along a path which leads upwards from one form of collective enterprise to the next.'[3]

Pinker rightly questions this approach. To do so implies no rejection of the reality of altruism; rather it rejects the assumption that altruism has increased. The extent of nineteenth-century charitable giving testifies to its extensive existence in the past and suggests that, rather that increasing, altruism is now displayed in some different ways, through state agencies, alongside its older and still important manifestations such as voluntary action and family support. We may legitimately question the extent to which nineteenth-century charity was entirely altruistic in intent, but the same question may equally be raised about the role of the modern state. The question obviously arises as to why altruism and other motives for providing for the poor has come to operate through different channels than in the past.

One answer lies in the failure of voluntary action and of associated institutions of self and mutual aid – despite their considerable extent – to solve social problems as they were perceived by the end of the nineteenth century and the beginning of the twentieth. They appeared to have failed to solve, or be capable of solving satisfactorily in the future, problems whose solution appeared increasingly urgent economically, politically, socially and militarily.

This change from a primary emphasis on voluntary action to state action is sometimes explained in terms of the growth of 'citizenship'. This interpretation argues that the extension of formal democracy in this century and the associated increased recognition of the need for the state to win the active support of all of its members for the maintenance of social, economic and military success has led the state to provide, through its own agency, material benefits to all its members.[4] Underlying this interpretation is the assumption that the growth of organized labour – those who gained from the extension of democratic rights in the past century – led to the granting of social welfare benefits to manual workers in order to ensure their support for the state, and that the growth of democracy has made it more difficult to ignore their needs. We have seen that there is some truth in this but that the process has been a more complex one than that of the state giving benefits to the poor to secure the support of trade unions and working-class voters. The poor, those in greatest need, were usually not the most organized and politically influential section of the working class, and neither organized workers nor the state necessarily put their interests first. Organized workers, as we have seen in Britain and elsewhere, did

not necessarily even favour state welfare. Also, the state was frequently constrained from making too many concessions, even to
organized workers, by opposition from other influential groups.
However, reforms which benefited at least some workers and/or the
dependent poor sometimes at least partly escaped this opposition
since they were believed to be capable of providing benefits such as
economic and military efficiency or the maintenance of social order,
to a wider section of society. The economic importance of manual
workers was on occasion as significant as their political influence.
Even then, such reforms as resulted, for example from the Liberal
governments of 1906–14, were the product of compromise rather
than of simple concessions. Hence the 'growth of citizenship' argument must be adjusted to take account of such questions as
whether 'citizenship' has indeed been extended equally to all, or
whether certain groups exert more influence in the 'democratic'
system than others? Whether attainment of the vote is indeed an
adequate index of attainment of power? The least organized, notably the low paid and women, have gained relatively little from the
attainment of the vote.

The essentially political 'citizenship' argument rests upon one
perception of recent political history. The most popular models of
the history of social policy, the 'consensus' and 'conflict'
approaches, both derived from political theory, rest upon others.
The first of these argues that social policy initiatives emerge because a consensus develops around a particular proposition.[5] This
must be so. Under the modern British system of government no
policy can be implemented unless it has a reasonably broad basis of
support. But, as already suggested, this raises many questions.
How broad a base of support is needed? How is it constituted? Of
all citizens or only some, and if so, of whom? How does the consensus come about? What is it a consensus about? The implicit
assumption, again, is that it has been about benevolence, the redistribution of resources and life-chances from rich to poor. But it is
equally possible, in principle, that social policies, or some of them,
have rested upon consensus about the need to maintain social order
and economic stability. Consensus on either of these points may
lead to new social policies, but not necessarily to ones which are
extensively redistributive in intent or effect.

The consensuses on which policies have been based have often
been the outcome of conflict, notably during both World Wars.
Some interpretations stress the role of conflict, arguing that social
policies have been born of class struggle, of the deprived masses

forcing 'welfare' from their rulers rather than receiving the fruits of their benevolence. This interpretation has suffered in general from an acute shortage of empirical evidence. Some of the problems involved have already been discussed. If the approach is to be useful it must specify carefully the processes involved. Social policies may be the outcome of class conflict but were they the outcomes desired by working people, or compromises which gave equal or greater benefits to their opponents? We have seen the strong current of working-class opposition to state welfare as being an undesirable alternative to full employment, high wages and independence, and to 'police', to bureaucratic control, and the 'enslaving state' (fears not confined to workers) which ran, ineffectually, counter to the growth of centralized state welfare. The labour movement was often divided in its 'welfare' aspirations and this weakness may have limited its effectiveness even when, as after 1945, a majority Labour government was in power. Conflict over social policies has been real, but some conflict was internal to the labour movement and the working class (between for example, the needs of men and women, of the regularly employed and the 'residuum') and even where there was broad internal agreement on priorities they were not always successfully attained.

Considerable emphasis has been placed upon the role of one form of conflict, war, in germinating both consensus and social policy change. Yet even if we restrict this interpretation to the impact of the major wars upon Britain in this century, the role of war is by no means simple and easy to interpret. The war of 1914–18 produced many proposals for social action by government but few results. Such action as there was, such as housebuilding, was the result more of fear of social dissension than of social solidarity. Social division, the opposition of politically and economically powerful groups, prevented excessive change during and immediately after the war. The war of 1939–45 also produced proposals more wide-ranging than the policy outcomes.

In both wars policy proposals and outcomes were strongly influenced by pre-war attitudes and experiences. For the role of war to be understood, the wars themselves must be placed in the context of what went before. The memory of pre-war economic failure in the Second World War, of relative success in the First, the growth of government and the impact of external economic changes in both wars, had more effect upon subsequent social policies than had any tempering of internal social divisions. Nor have wars been more productive of social policy innovation in Britain than periods of international peace. The years 1906–14 and the inter-war years were as productive of proposals and action as the war periods. Such action, especially in the inter-war period, was not always in the direction of 'progress', of expanding benefits and services, but it would be wrong to define as 'social policy' only measures which improve, rather than restrict, provision.

Recognition of such difficulties has led Robert Pinker to propose another interpretation of the development of the 'idea' of state welfare. At its heart, he argues, lies nationalism and the urge for national survival, which is acute not only in wartime but in periods of economic and social crisis.[6] Pinker does not risk evaluation of the importance of nationalism in relation to other influences, but his interpretation suggests the existence of an important gap in prevailing interpretations of the history of social policy: they have emphasized the importance of ideological, political and military events but have made little systematic effort to analyse social policy in relation to the wider economy. At present, in 1981, the fortunes of the national economy and the government response to them are profoundly affecting both practice and discussion of social policy, and they have done so in the past.

The closest to Pinker's interpretation is the argument that social policies are functionally necessary at a certain stage of economic growth, especially in urban industrial societies. But there have been few attempts at systematic comparative analysis.[7] Certainly rather similar policies have emerged in many societies, not necessarily industrial, at similar stages of their economic development. But for whom have they been 'functional'? For the poor? For employers? or politicians? Or for all to some degree, and if so, to what degree? And how do we explain the rather different developments in different societies?

The structure of, and pressures upon, national economies have been important everywhere. For Britain this became an issue in the last third of the nineteenth century, when Britain's economic pre-eminence came under threat from the competition of other growing economies. We should remember, however, that the reform of the Poor Law in 1834 was also chiefly motivated by the desire to maximize the labour force and to reduce government expenditure in order to stimulate economic growth. Even then, concerns of economic and social policy were closely related. The threat to the economy in the late nineteenth century was limited; Britain's continued economic growth was not seriously at issue. It led, however, to some re-thinking of Britain's economic position, above all about how the economy could effectively compete with her new rivals. The response, as in other countries similarly facing international competition, took the form of measures to increase the efficiency of capital, by investment, by merger, by measures to increase the efficiency of human capital by improved management techniques designed to increase productivity, and by social measures to increase the efficiency of the workforce by raising standards of health, education and 'social security'. The latter measures were directed towards essential, mainly skilled, workers, rather than towards the mass of the poor. Blueprints for the resulting policies were to hand in the recommendations of reformers, including civil servants, often with quite different motives of philanthropy or administrative reform.

The impact upon government policy was limited. There was no serious doubt among the élite who made or influenced policy that the economy could continue to flourish on a free enterprise basis with only minor modifications. Rather it was believed that minor social adjustments, guided by the state, would ensure the future success of the free market. The most serious challenge to free enterprise, from the tariff reformers, was rejected, an index of the confidence of British capitalism when her major rivals had introduced similar protective measures. The challenge from labour, which did imply a threat to free enterprise, and which grew in response to the growing scale of industry and increased pressure upon the workforce, was real but as yet also limited and relatively easily contained by the recognition of trade unions, the granting of the vote, and by welfare benefits directed at the most organized sector of the workforce. The latter were modified by and generally acceptable to more politically and economically powerful groups.

This interpretation emphasizes the primacy of economic and closely related political imperatives over altruism and aspirations for redistribution. It argues that an important element in the consensus on which social policy was based before 1914 was the maximization of Britain's economic position and the maintenance of stable social and political order on which a stable economy was based.

The means by which this consensus came into being cannot, however, be understood purely on economic terms but must rest upon an understanding of the political system in the generation before 1914. It was a 'pluralist' system in that it provided channels for the expression of a wide range of views, including those of the labour movement. However, the working class vote was still restricted, excluding all women and poorer men; trades unions had little influence in the circles where high policy was made; Parliament and the civil service were dominated by members of the landed, business and professional élites. The Treasury exercised considerable and increasing control over government expenditure, as demonstrated by its influence upon the pensions and national insurance legislation; to do so was its role in the political system. It was committed to a policy of low taxation, balanced budgets and minimum social expenditure. It could be persuaded into limited social expenditure by determined politicians, such as Asquith, Churchill or Lloyd George, but their proposals also were successfully limited by Treasury action. The politicians could extend these limits only when they had strong political support for doing so. By the 1900s they had broad support for limited extension from reformers, businessmen, from the labour movement and from those anxious to contain labour. The need to maintain a balance among these often conflicting forces resulted in measures which went less far than radical reformers wanted. The outcome was compromise which supported without harming the free enterprise economy, but gave sufficient to opposition groups to maintain social order – it was a compromise which gave little to the least powerful, the very poor. This is not to argue for a conscious, malign, élite conspiracy against the masses. The élite acted rationally according to the dominant perception among them of their personal, and the national, good, often after some internal conflict. Other countries with different political and social structures responded differently to the pressures of an increasingly competitive international economy in the late nineteenth century, but all recognized the economic and political value of increased state 'welfare' provision.

The war of 1914–18 did little in the short run to upset the balance established before the war in Britain and the perceptions upon which it depended. It created certain internal problems over rent and labour conditions, but with these the government was able to deal easily enough. What is striking about the war is the degree to which élite groups emerged from it with their presuppositions intact. An influential number of businessmen, politicians and civil servants had every confidence that after the war they could return to 'business as usual'. They prevented any long-term commitment to change by the government, except in so far as this was in the direction fixed before the war, towards measures to secure economic and social harmony, e.g. housing.

But, as they were forced gradually to realize, things *had*

changed. The labour movement had become stronger and more organized during the war. Its role in the pluralist system was more powerful: more workers had the vote, trade unions had gained entry to the normal processes of political consultation. The structure of industry and of the labour force had changed as a result of mergers and mechanization, blurring the distinction between skilled and unskilled labour. Most importantly, Britain's role in the international economy had changed, her financial dominance diminished, as had her share of world trade, and the balance of the international economy had changed, partly due to the destruction of the German economy.

As a result, from 1920 Britain faced a new national crisis, more severe than that of the late nineteenth century, which required a more radical response. The immediate response of government, however, was to seek to restore the old economic equilibrium by cutting government expenditure in order to stimulate free enterprise. The capacity to do so was now, however, constrained, first by the power of labour which imposed some limitation on wage reductions and, second, by the need to maintain social order amid high unemployment, which necessitated substantial expenditure upon unemployment benefits. Nevertheless, for much of the 1920s the attempt was made, with the powerful support of the Treasury and of the business community. Both cuts and advances in social policy in the 1920s were all officially perceived as contributing to economic revival and social order: in housing, education, unemployment policy, pensions and Poor Law reform.

Occasional breaks out of this new consensus were achieved by determined politicians, such as Wheatley in the field of housing. But, in general, the inter-war changes in social policy cannot be seen as benefiting the poorest, with the exception of unemployment relief. The better-off working- and lower-middle classes benefited disproportionately from housing and education changes as groups vital to the economy and with greater organized political influence than the poorest. The unemployed were provided for as never before because they were numerous, geographically concentrated, and composed no longer of the 'residuum' but often of those with higher expectations and trade union and political experience. There was still no serious attempt to establish a universal minimum. Effectively, inter-war policies maintained existing relativities of social conditions when these were seriously threatened, e.g. by unemployment.

By the early 1930s, especially under the influence of the slump of 1929–31, awareness was growing of the need for a fundamental re-thinking of economic policy if the economy was to enjoy a sustained revival; hence the gradual and limited introduction of protectionist and interventionist economic policies in the 1930s. It was still limited, for the policies of the 1920s had had some success – there had been a revival of industry and Britain suffered less from the slump of 1929–31 than other countries. But the incomplete nature of that revival, and the obvious difficulties of expansion when world trade was at a low level, suggested that free enterprise still required substantial permanent modification in the form of stimulation of home demand. And the political problem of the depressed areas remained. Thus the progressive reforms of Labour-controlled local authorities in the 1930s, most of them in areas of high unemployment, were acceptable to Conservative central government provided that they did not seriously conflict with economic priorities. They provided for some of the more acute needs of the most depressed towns.

By the later 1930s the new economic policies appeared to be succeeding but informed observers, notably Keynes, feared that the success was temporary and that if it was to be permanent more drastic changes were necessary. This view led to the new vogue in influential circles for forms of planning, which enjoyed labour support since it coincided with established Labour aspirations for a planned economy. This took two forms: (i) Keynesian economic management and (ii) the initially more fashionable preference for physical planning and controls, as advocated by Macmillan, Beveridge and Cole. Both implied substantially redistributive social policies; the latter very considerable controls over the free market. In the late 1930s a new though limited consensus for change was beginning to emerge, whose roots lay in fears for future economic survival.

The war averted the threatened economic crisis, indeed brought major long-term changes in the economy. Influential groups entered the war in a state of greater dissatisfaction with the economy than had been felt in 1914, hence the wartime receptiveness to proposals for change. But again the receptiveness was limited. The Treasury and business organizations, with the support of leading Conservative and some Labour politicians, strove effectively and not always unreasonably to prevent radical change until the war was over and post-war economic conditions clear. However, many were prepared to accept some changes in the direction of securing economic stability and growth and political stability. The extent of the popular desire not to return to the depression and injustice of the pre-war world was expressed in the size of the Labour vote in 1945.

The Second World War, like the first, produced a wide-ranging set of blueprints for a more socially just society after the war. None of these, including the proposals of Beveridge and Keynes, was implemented in full, partly again because the central priority of the post-war government was the necessary achievement of a sound basis for the economy; this took priority over the desire for redistribution. Unlike the aftermath of the First World War, measures were taken to reconstruct the economy, in the short term by the maintenance of wartime controls, in the longer term by the nationalization of essential but unprofitable industries, railways, coal and electricity, the introduction of a version of Keynsian techniques of economic management and support for the measures to free and to stimulate international trade embodied in the Bretton Woods agreement. All of these measures, unthinkable in the 1920s, had the effective support of many but not all leading businessmen, Conservatives and the Treasury, among whom the establishment of a mixed economy, the modification of free enterprise, was, after the experience of the 1930s, seen to be essential for economic success.

There was similar support for such social measures as the introduction of the national health service and the reform of social security. Harold Macmillan, who had been involved in the administration of the war overseas rather than in internal questions during the war, and who was defeated in the 1945 General Election, stood successfully in a by-election shortly afterwards 'unashamedly on my pre-war views'.[8] As a Conservative economic spokesman through the debates of the following five years he found himself forced, in the theatre of parliamentary debate, to criticize policies with which he and his colleagues had much sympathy:

Many of us on the Conservative side had long recognized that for a variety of reasons certain undertakings – the coal-mines on historic and sentimental grounds; the railways on financial; and the public utilities and other monopolies like gas and electricity on technical – stood in a wholly different category from the great mass of productive industry and commerce.[9]

He also noted that 'even the most extreme socialists seemed very unwilling to disturb any enterprise which chiefly operated in the export market'.[10]

The Conservatives criticized the form and above all the speed of nationalization but despite opposition on their own right wing, and among some employers directly involved, offered little opposition in principle to major social and economic measures. 'We could never,' said Macmillan, 'return to the old classical *laissez-faire*.'[11]

A consensus had been born of the traditional aspirations of Labour and of Conservative recognition that certain changes were necessary for the sake of economic success. Both made compromises distasteful to their extreme wings. And there were clear limits to the compromise, as in the opposition to certain national health proposals, such as a salaried service and private beds, and to expensive subsistence level old-age pensions. There was powerful opposition to measures which diminished privilege and necessitated extensive redistribution of income. Even a Labour government with a large majority could not easily impose its wishes upon unwilling opponents.

Between 1945 and 1950 the Labour government established a viable mixed economy and filled the most serious gaps in the pre-war social services, establishing what almost amounted to a national minimum. Its actions were built upon a new middle-ground consensus of a rather less radical nature than had appeared to be emerging in 1939. The availability and viability of a limited version of the Keynesian alternative to strict centralized planning, the greater buoyancy of the international economy after the war, and the near achievement of full employment by 1950, made more drastic controls and more thorough-going redistribution of wealth and power seem less essential than some had previously thought. Demands on the Labour left for greater change were muted, due to awareness of problems of shortage of resources and to euphoria about the extent of change achieved by the government. Its social measures were indeed greatly superior to anything which had gone before, the product of an historically unprecedented and short-lived compromise among influential economic and political interests, born above all of the desire not to return to the Depression of the 1930s. When that danger was averted, it faded away.

Manual workers and the poor gained from post-war social legislation but so did the better off, most directly in the form of free health care and free education to university level, without serious compensatory losses. The legislation did not produce substantial redistribution or significant change in the relative positions of rich and poor. The greatest gain to the working class was the establishment of full employment, which resulted partly from government economic policies and partly, perhaps rather more, from revitalization of the international economy.

The history of social policy between 1870 and the end of the Second World War cannot be dissociated from that of the history of the economy and from resulting economic policies, nor from the nature of the political system within which such policies were formulated and translated into action. Policy decisions were taken within a framework which was 'pluralist', but it was a 'bounded' pluralism, within which the economically powerful had considerably greater influence than the economically weak.[12] The influence of the latter, or at least of its more organized sections, grew sufficiently within a century to enable its poorer strata to maintain their relative position in society, but not sufficiently, except on rare occasions, to enable them to improve it.

The broad consensus basis of social policies, then, throughout the period 1870–1950, was consensus less about equalization of material conditions than about the primary need to achieve economic stability, growth and political harmony. It was a consensus which included many labour leaders. It rested upon the willingness and capability of leaders of capital and of labour to make concessions, though often only after considerable discussion. Hence all legislation was the outcome of negotiation among interested groups. It was facilitated by, and also reinforced, the relative social cohesion of British society in this century, in comparison with many other European societies. Britain has had a very peaceful recent history in comparison with many of her neighbours. One effect of the growth of state welfare has been to maintain a remarkably stable distribution of material rewards and of power.

The process of policy-making whereby politicians, civil servants and the leaders of influential groups negotiated about policy proposals emanating either from among themselves or from other reformers, in accordance with their perceptions of what was desirable for the nation and for the groups they represented, led to compromises which fell short of more radical reform demands and often did not entirely satisfy anyone. One persistent strand in popular discussion of state welfare among all classes, fear of bureaucratic centralism, was largely and increasingly disregarded in this process of negotiation. It had no obvious place in a consensus whose central concern was with national economic and political stability and the efficient use of resources, priorities which conflicted with the local and individual variations in provision which resulted from decentralization of control. The relative decentralization of the inter-war period and before had created, in different localities, both greater and lesser provision than was thought centrally desirable and exacerbated political conflict. These conflicts were resolved in favour of greater central control.

The precise contribution of state welfare measures to the diminution of primary poverty is difficult to measure. The contribution of wider economic changes, guided and unguided, has been considerable in providing at certain times increased employment and new forms of employment. These have removed some from primary poverty directly, by giving them jobs, and indirectly, by enabling them to support dependents. The historically decisive decline in the numbers in primary poverty occurred during and immediately after the First World War, for reasons which are not fully clear, but had more to do with changes in the labour market than with the limited social policies of the period. The further decline during and after the Second World War was also associated with the achievement of almost full employment. Yet it does not follow that social legislation has not had important results. Its importance has lain in giving income support, though rarely above a minimal level, to those in need who were outside the labour market (the unemployed, aged, etc.); and in providing a steadily improving range of services for all. It has prevented the emergence of too substantial a gap between the low paid and dependent and the remainder of society but has done little to diminish that gap. By relating the history of social policy to the histories of the economy and of the structure of political power its outcome can be more clearly understood. It can be interpreted, according to political preference, as a story of remarkable success or of sad failure.

REFERENCES

1. P. TOWNSEND, *Poverty in the United Kingdom*, Penguin, Harmondsworth (1979).
2. *Ibid.*, p. 41.
3. R. PINKER, *The Idea of Welfare*, Heinemann, London (1979) p. 255.
4. T. H. MARSHALL, *Sociology at the Crossroads*, Heinemann, London (1963).
5. P. HALL *et al.*, *Change, Choice and Conflict in Social Policy*, Heinemann, London (1975) pp. 6ff.
6. R. PINKER, *op. cit.*

7. An important exception is G. RIMLINGER, *Welfare Policy and Industrialization in Europe, America and Russia*, John Wiley & Sons, New York (1971).
8. H. MACMILLAN, *Tides of Fortune 1945–1955*, Macmillan, London (1969) p. 35.
9. *Ibid.*, p. 74.
10. *Ibid.*, p. 75.
11. *Ibid..*, p. 81.
12. P. HALL *et al.*, *op. cit.*, pp. 140–46.

Part three
DOCUMENTS

Document one
HENRY MAYHEW ON CASUAL WORKERS IN LONDON

ACCOUNT OF THE CASUAL LABOURERS

I now proceed to give some short account of the condition and earnings of this most wretched class. On the platform surrounding the Commercial Dock basins are a number whom I have heard described as 'idlers,' 'pokers,' and 'casual labourers.' These men are waiting in hopes of a job, which they rarely obtain until all the known hands have been set to work before them. . . .

On my visits the casual labourers were less numerous than usual, as the summer is the season when such persons consider that they have the best chance in the country. But I saw groups of 10 and 20 waiting about the docks; some standing alone, and some straggling in twos and threes, as they waited, all looking dull and listless. These men, thus wearisomely waiting, could not be called ragged, for they wore mostly strong canvas or fustian suits – large, and seemingly often washed jackets, predominating; and rents, and tatters are far less common in such attire than in woollen-cloth garments. From a man dressed in a large, coarse, canvas jacket, with worn corduroy trousers, and very heavy and very brown laced-leather boots, I had the following statement, in a somewhat provincial tone:

'My father was a small farmer in Dorset-shire. I was middling educated, and may thank the parson for it. I can read the Bible and spell most of the names there. I was left destitute, and I had to shift for myself – that's nine year ago, I think. I've hungered, and I've ordered my bottle of wine since, sir . . .

I shifted my quarters every now and then till within two or three years ago, and then I tried my hand in London. At first Mr – (a second cousin of my father he was) helped me now and then, and he gave me odd jobs at portering for himself, as he was a grocer, and he got me odd jobs from other people besides. When I was a navvy I should at the best time have had my 50s. a-week, and more if it hadn't been for the tommy-shops; and I've had my 15s. a-week in portering in London for my cousin; but sometimes I came down to 10s., and sometimes to 5s. My cousin died sudden, and I was very hard up after that. I made nothing at portering some weeks. I had no one to help me; and in the spring of last year – and very cold it often was – I've walked after 10, 11, or 12 at night, many a mile to lie down and sleep in any bye-place. I never stole, but have been hard tempted. I've thought of drowning myself, and of hanging myself, but somehow a penny or two came in to stop that. Perhaps I didn't seriously intend it. I begged sometimes of an evening. I stayed at lodging-houses, for one can't sleep out in bad weather, till I heard from one lodger that he took his turn at the Commerical Dock. He worked at timber, or corn, or anything; and so I went, about the cholera time last year, and waited, and run from one dock to another, because I was new and hadn't a chance like the old hands. I've had 14s. a-week sometimes; and many's the week I've had three, and more's the week I've had nothing at all. They've said, 'I don't know you.' I've lived on penny loaves – one or two a-day, when there was no work, and then I've begged. I don't know what the other people waiting at any of the docks got. I didn't talk to them much, and they didn't talk much to me.'

From: Henry Mayhew, *London Labour and the London Poor*, vol. 3, reprinted Dover Books, New York (1968) p. 300.

Document two
POOR LAW POLICY IN 1878. MEMORANDUM FROM THE PRESIDENT OF THE LOCAL GOVERNMENT BOARD (J. SCHLATER-BOOTH) TO ALL BOARDS OF GUARDIANS

MEMORANDUM RELATING TO THE ADMINISTRATION OF OUT RELIEF

1.   It will be in the recollection of most persons who have taken an active interest in the administration of the Poor Laws that in the year 1871 a Circular was issued by the Local Government Board, calling the attention of their Inspectors, and through them of the various boards of guardians throughout the country, to certain points connected with the important subject of out-door relief.

2.   The object of the present Memorandum is to show, so far as is possible, to what extent the principles then put forward and pressed upon the attention of the guardians have operated beneficially.

3.   In the Circular of 1871 special attention was called to the following suggestions:

1.   That out-door relief should not be granted to single able-bodied men or to single able-bodied women, either with or without illegitimate children.

2.   That out-door relief should not, except in special cases, be granted to any woman deserted by her husband during the first twelve months after the desertion, or to any able-bodied widow with one child only.

3.   That in the case of any able-bodied widow with more than one child it may be desirable to take one or more of the children into the workhouse in preference to giving out-door relief.

4.   That in unions where the prohibitory order is in force the workhouse test should be strictly applied; and the guardians should be informed that the Boards will not be prepared to sanction any cases which are not reported within the time limited by the order, and in which the reports do not contain a detailed statement of the paupers to which they refer, showing the number of their respective families, with the ages and number of children employed, amount of wages of the several member of the family at work, cause of destitution, period during which they have been without employment, amount of relief, if any, given previously to the transmission of the report, and what extent of accommodation for all classes exists in the workhouse at the time.

5. That out-door relief should be granted for a fixed period only, which should not, in any case, exceed three months.

6. That all orders to able-bodied men for relief in the labour yard should be only given from week to week.

7. That out-door relief should not be granted in any case unless the relieving officer has, since the application, visited the home of the applicant, and has recorded the date of such visit in the relief application and report book. Cases in which the relieving officer has not had time to visit should be relieved by him in kind only or by an order for the workhouse.

8. That the relieving officer should be required to make at least fortnightly visits to the homes of all persons receiving relief on account of temporary sickness and of able-bodied men receiving relief in the labour yard, and to visit the old and infirm cases at least once a quarter; and the relieving officer should be required to keep a diary with the dates and results of such visits.

9. That the provisions with respect to the compulsory maintenance of paupers by relations legally liable to contribute to their support should be more generally acted upon.

10. That as the recommendations of medical officers for meat and stimulants are regarded as equivalent to orders for additional relief, they should in all cases be accompanied by a report from the medical officer in a prescribed form, setting forth the particulars of each case ascertained by personal inquiry.

11. That in the most populous unions it may be expedient to appoint one or more officers to be termed 'Inspectors of Our Relief,' whose duty it would be to act as a check upon the relieving officers, and ascertain also the circumstances connected with the recipients of relief. Such appointments have already been tried in Liverpool, and found to answer very successfully.

It is of essential importance to any sound system of out-door relief that the relief districts should not be too large or the number of relieving officers too small. If a relieving officer's district be too large it will be impossible for him, however zealous and vigilant he may be, to investigate with sufficient care the circumstances of each applicant for relief or pauper in receipt of relief; and nothing can be more objectionable than that an officer should be compelled to perform his duty in a hurried and incomplete manner.

4. The consideration and the application of these rules has not been without effect.

£

In the year 1870–71 the expenditure on out-relief was 3,663,970
In the year 1876–77 it had fallen to 2,616,465;
thus showing a decrease in six years of 1,047,505*l*., or 28.6 per cent.

The number of out-door paupers on the 1st January 1871 was 917,890
The number of 1st January 1877 was 571,982;

therefore, in the same six years, the out-door paupers decreased by 345,908, or 37.7 per cent.

. . .

6. It is especially worthy of remark that, so far as the Inspectors have been able to ascertain, the results above described have been arrived at without any real hardship to the poor, and without any, or at least with a very slight, increase in the number of in-door paupers. No alteration of the law has been requisite to enable the guardians to adopt and apply, according to their discretion, rules that appear to be stringent and efficient.

. . .

8. With respect to non-resident relief the Board are of opinion that it might be almost entirely discontinued. It is only evident to them that if the proper means were taken, no inconsiderable sums might be recovered from the relatives of paupers towards their maintenance.

. . .

12. The guardians need scarcely be reminded of the broad and general principle of the English Poor Law, viz., that no person has a claim to relief from the rates, except in case of actual destitution. To ensure relief being strictly limited to the class for whom it is intended, it is only requisite that those who are entrusted with the administration of the law should, by diligent and minute inquiry, ascertain the exact condition and circumstances of each applicant; and to enable the guardians to do this effectually, it is essential that they should have the aid of competent and painstaking relieving officers, whose districts should not be so extensive as to preclude them from visiting each recipient of relief at his own home, and at frequent intervals, in conformity with the regulations of the Board. An adherence to these simple requirements has been the main cause which has led to such gratifying results in those unions where pauperism has been so largely reduced.

From: Annual Report of the Local Government Board 1878, *Parliamentary Papers* (1878), vol. 65.

A. L. BOWLEY ON POVERTY SURVEYS AND THE
DEFINITION OF POVERTY (1937)

... Booth obtained information about every family in the County of London from which children were known to the School Attendance Officers. From this observed 'universe' he generalised with a considerable loss of precision to include other working-class families. He also took as a unit of classification a street as a whole, and compared the result with the 'universe' of families. Rowntree obtained information from every working-class family except a small margin. Neither gave an explicit definition of the working class.

In the more recent Surveys there have been three main objects: to classify the incomes of families in relation to their needs over the whole scale of working-class families; to find what proportion and what numbers were in poverty; and to make comparisons from place to place and from one year to another.

The earlier enquiries were principally directed to the second of these, and we have therefore to describe the use of the word poverty. For the third purpose, that of comparison, it is less important to labour at a theoretical definition of poverty than to make it exact and intelligible, and to keep it absolutely unchanged in comparisons. Any minimum is arbitrary and relative. Even if it were the case that the estimates of the calorie content of food as digested were precise, and if it were known what *quantities* of vitamins were present in milk, fruit, etc. and how much was required for healthy persons of different ages, it would still be true that different degrees of health and efficiency would call for different quantities. At the one extreme it is the diet that would just support an inactive life without impairment of vitality, at the other the greatest expenditure that could be applied without waste to keep a man at maximum efficiency in the most exacting work. In feeding oxen there is a point where an increase of expenditure will no longer be met by an increase in the value of the resulting meat, and no doubt practical farmers are aware of the balance; but experiments on human beings are not so easy and the objective can only be defined for sheer muscular work. Such experiments as have been made are inconclusive. It is well known that the English labourer has existed and brought up families on diets that would be regarded as semi-starvation now, and that some continental workmen and most Eastern have had, and in some cases still have, an apparently even more penurious diet.

We are not considering now an optimum diet, nor one that in present conditions should be taken as the official administrative minimum; when the wealth of a country increases that can be raised. But we must have some definite scale below which a family can certainly be said to be in want. For comparisons with the past we must take the scale of the earlier writers. For the future it would be reasonable to raise the scale.

Booth's class of 'very poor' was described by him as ill-nourished and ill-clad; his 'poor' class is neither ill-nourished nor ill-clad 'according to any standard that can reasonably be used' (Vol. I, p. 131), its members are not 'in want', though they would be much the better off for more of everything. These two classes are taken as below the line of poverty, which he defines no more accurately than this, at least in words. But this leads to a definite statement of income, viz. about 23s. weekly for a moderate-sized family in 1890 in London, and this sum can be translated with the help of the budgets of expenditure he gives in terms of food, clothing, rent, etc. Close examination of these data showed that the food gave just the minimum amount of calories that were computed by physiologists to be necessary and used to establish a minimum line by Rowntree and subsequent investigators. It is difficult to understand with modern ideas how those with less than this minimum could be described as 'neither ill-nourished nor ill-clad'.

With such difficulties in assigning food minima, it is not surprising that the standard for other classes of expenditure is purely conventional. As regards clothing, if we assume that hats, boots, and socks are necessaries, and recognise that protection against cold and wet is essential, we can make a rough estimate, based on actual habits and expenditure, of the cost of clothes as purchased by the poorer sections of the working class. Nothing is allowed for ornament. Booth gave no definite figure, but took under 2s. weekly for a moderate family; Rowntree put it at 2s. 3d. for parents and three children. The corresponding figure in the *New London Survey* was 5s., which allowed for the rise in prices.

Fuel is more definite, since the fire necessary for cooking and washing may also be sufficient for heating. Light is so small an item in a poor household that an arbitrary sum may be added for it. For soap and other household necessaries also a small sum can be assigned.

. . .

While Booth's classification was based on the impression given by all the circumstances of the family as well as on its visible income, Rowntree, and the compilers of the *New London Survey* and also of the 'five towns' enquiries, subtracted from income rent as actually paid, and compared the remainder with other minimum requirements. The justification for this method lies in the fact that a man is not free to adjust his rent to his income and needs, but must get what accommodation is available with reference to his work. When this method is used, the question of the adequacy of the accommodation can be discussed separately.

The alternative method of computing the minimum size of a tenement that would accommodate each family, and its cost when it is in a satisfactory condition, is abstract, since such houses are not always available, and it also depends on what is considered necessary in housing. The standard now aimed at is far superior to that which the poor have hitherto reached, and it is doubtful whether if expenditure was completely uncontrolled by custom or law, money would not be devoted to other objects rather than to the rent of a house that satisfies modern ideas.

The minimum as defined or described by Booth or Rowntree, and followed to ensure comparability by later investigators, is more inadequate than was formerly believed for the families where there are young children. The discrepancy is partly due to incomplete arithmetic. There is a scale of requirements by age and sex based on the amount of calories needed. The cost to an adult is computed, and that for a child is assigned by applying to this cost the smaller number of calories he is supposed to need. This process assumes that the *cost* of 1000 calories is the same for the diet of a child as for that of an adult. Now milk, reckoned in calories, is an expensive form of food. In London in 1928 one penny bought 130 calories if spent on milk, but 570 if on bread, 600 on margarine, 730 on sugar. It is therefore necessary for completeness to construct adequate dietaries at minimum cost for different ages. The protein content also needs examination, but the numerical effect is smaller, since bread is the cheapest source of protein, unless we distinguish animal from vegetable protein and emphasise the former.

A great deal depends on what quantity of milk is necessary for a child's healthy growth, and whether other foods can be substituted for it. Not enough is definitely known on this subject, but there are very good reasons for giving more than is necessary so as to be on the safe side.

. . .

When unemployment is not acute there are many families in fair circumstances who can tide over periods of illness or unemployment or short-time out of savings or credit. When unemployment is severe more and more families exhaust their resources. Also a proportion of workmen never get more than intermittent work, and the nominal full-time earnings are far above their average earnings.

. . .

Since the poverty line is descriptive rather than logical, it is well to form some idea of the standard of living reached on it. In London in 1929 the minimum for a workman with wife and two children of young school age was put at 39s. weekly. Of this 9s. 4d. was allotted to rent, nearly a quarter of income; this would pay for two rooms with a scullery, and is on the margin of overcrowding. 2s. 4d. goes for travelling to work and for unemployment and health insurance. 4s. 2d is allotted to clothes, 3s. for fuel

(1¼ cwt. weekly) 1s. 2d. for cleansing materials, etc. There is left 19s. for food. There is no surplus for beer, tobacco, amusement, trade-union subscription or voluntary expenditure of any sort. Emergency can only be met by some windfall or by stinting food or clothes. None the less it affords a living at a higher standard than has had to suffice in earlier generations for the existence of a great part of the working class. This has been chosen as the fixed basis from which to compute; and it gives a description of the poverty line and incidentally a definition of poverty.

With the minimum so computed for each family we have to compare its income. Here again we come to difficulties of definition. The unit is the family, consisting of all persons related to each other who sleep in the same tenement. The total income is the sum of the earnings of all working members, together with income from property, if any, including the value of a house owned and occupied, and pensions arising from former employment. Old-age pensions are usually included as income.

. . .

The process of comparing the aggregate of incomes of members of the family with the family needs assumes that the whole income is pooled if necessary. Where family ties are strong, or where additional earnings come from the wife or young workers, the assumption is justified; but when the income is that of elder brothers or sisters, they may not be willing to hand over all surplus above their special needs to the support of an unemployed parent or other children. The experience of the opposition to the means test affords some evidence on this point.

From: A. L. Bowley, *Wages and Income since 1860*, Cambridge University Press (1937) pp 54–63.

Document four
EVIDENCE OF THE EFFECTS OF THE POOR LAW COLLECTED FOR THE ROYAL COMMISSION OF 1905–1909

FIRST INTERIM REPORT OF INVESTIGATORS INTO THE EFFECT OF OUTDOOR RELIEF ON WAGES AND THE CONDITIONS OF EMPLOYMENT IN CERTAIN UNIONS IN LONDON.

The first effect of an examination of nearly 2,000 cases on the outdoor roll is to bewilder the reader with the infinite diversity of human nature. No theory of the Poor Law which neglects this diversity of social conditions for the sake of easy generalisation can be true. All sorts of combinations of character, skill, poverty, health, energy and hope are found in people lumped together as paupers. The good or evil effect of out-relief will vary according as certain qualities are present or absent or combined in the recipient. The other important preliminary distinction is that between immediate and remote effects on the pauper, the family and the community generally.

The objection to entering the workhouse is probably due, in the majority of cases, not to a sense of shame, but to the loss of liberty involved. Many old people, however, think of the workhouse as it was when they were growing up, not as it is now, and have a traditional horror of it. Some of the poorest hate the thought of mixing with the people found inside. The same is the case with out-relief. Under the influence of popular agitation an increasing number claim out-relief as a right and look forward to it as a matter of course when they reach sixty. But it is also true that the respectable poor – though they do not carry out their threats of starvation and suicide – make all sorts of shifts to keep off the roll. They try to qualify for a pension in a charity, under-feed and over-work themselves, and die comforted with the thought that they will not have a pauper's burial. Some men are willing to go to A Settlement to ask for help, and will not go to the parish; but they do not mind their wives applying there. Others, when out of work, will go into the workhouse temporarily as they dislike being kept by their wives. These men are paupers, but they are a higher type than many helped by Borough Council Distress Funds. On the other hand, if they remain long in the workhouse they deteriorate.

Some widows, from selfish motives, refuse to give up their children to the guardians. Their presence draws forth pity, on which the mother trades. There are widows who fear to lose touch with their children when they go to the schools. The mother looks forward to the time when the children will help her, just as do parents in all grades of society, except the well-to-do. Some widows unselfishly yield up their children to the guardians. It may be worse for the mother, but it will be better for the children.

The road to out-relief often lies through the dispensary, but there are paupers who will not call in the parish doctor. He does so much of his work by deputy; his assistants are always changing; they do things in a routine manner. Hence some of the poor try to get an outside doctor. It is not unusual to find the private practitioner with a dozen out-relief cases on his books, and we found in one case that a respectable step-cleaner had paid ordinary medical fees rather than disclose the fact that she was a pauper.

The Poor Law was once supposed to deal with destitution rather than with poverty. In practice the persons helped have few resources rather than absolutely none. They can and do possess food or clothing or lodging or health in various degrees. Similarly the Poor Law deals with the 'dissolute' and the 'deserving' and all the intermediate gradations of moral condition. And as its direct contact (in out-relief) is usually with adults whose characters are more or less fixed, its action depends on what those characteristics are. It deepens tendencies already operative. The bad will turn its help into an instrument for deeper corruption, the good into a means of sustaining the standard of life through a period of struggle

. . .

Some guardians encourage applicants to earn all they can and do not reduce the relief; others cut down the relief as wages rise, or as children begin to earn; others seem to think changes in income irrelevant to the amount of relief given. No board in the unions we have examined gives adequate relief on condition that the mother ceases to work. . . .

But often the relief given is so paltry and the earnings possible so small that even with a low standard of needs the temptation of laziness is not great. We are certain that, among many aged out-workers we visited, are to be found the most pathetically industrious workers in the community. They may be doing work which machines should do, they may be slow, but they are rarely idle or drunken. The extra 3s. or 4s. from the parish makes the difference between chronic semi-starvation and a low minimum of comfort. They would live on somehow if the relief were withdrawn. Now they are enabled to obtain fresh vegetables and a little fruit in summer and some coal and meat in winter. It would otherwise be always bread, margarine, and tea. Out-relief varies the diet and warms the single room.

We have met with two cases where, during the husband's absence at a labour colony and during the enjoyment of an allowance at home, the wives ceased to work one at shirt-making, the other at tie-making.

. . .

The conditions of home and work are such that many of these young people are too flabby to have the enterprise to leave their surroundings. Again, to cross the river to learn a trade would be to drop out of the society of the street or group or club in which they have grown up. For the girls it might lessen the chances of the marriage to which they all look forward. Besides, they often think their neighbourhood choice and superior to all others.

In other words, the poor are more idealistic than is often imagined. It is in this direction we must look for the reasons why many girls placed out in service from Poor Law schools come back to low-grade factories. And here, too, is to be found some explanation why they do not move to the trades which, it is urged, are open to them elsewhere. In domestic service they are too friendless and lonely. They chafe at having to live always with superiors. They do not get the pleasures natural to them. They are bribed on the material side only, with good food, a soft bed, and wages.

We have been able to inquire only incidentally into the comparative effects of charity and out-relief on income and character. The number of people who take the trouble to give wisely, though increasing, is still small compared with the number of givers, and the amount of wisdom required is so great that perhaps the numbers will always remain small. In some unions old endowed charities which scattered loaves and bibles broadcast are being converted into pensions and surgical aid, but despite such enlightened schemes the area of competitive philanthropy is hardly reduced nor its darkness illumined. In one church vestry we came upon a pile of packets of garments which were being doled out to the parishioners who had refrained from buying and selling on the Sabbath. In another district we asked a trained social reformer what she desired above all things to help her in her work. The reply was, 'To abolish district visitors and to educate the clergy.' Several experienced workers with whom we talked instanced the abuses after the late war. 'Compared with the soldiers' wives during the late war, the widows on outdoor relief are positively industrious.' 'Deferred pay led to dreadful orgies.'
. . .

A Camberwell witness of much experience told us that 'on the whole,' he thought, 'indiscriminate charity and drink hit the people harder than trade conditions. Others complained that creches, cheap clubs, and subsidised restaurants were enabling girls to work for less, because they obtained their food, etc., at less than cost price. But the whole subject of the economic influence of charities needs to be investigated.

The effect of out-relief on women's wages is part of the general wage question and cannot be sharply isolated. Women's work and wages have also peculiarities of their own quite apart from Poor Law influence. In most trades in which women are employed there is no competition whatever between men and women. In some occupations there is debatable land where boys and girls are contending with one another and with adults for possession. Where men and women work in similar occupations the unequal pay is usually due in part to some drawback in women's work. But the inferiority of the pay is frequently greater than the inferiority of the work. The wages paid to girls and women are generally low; the skill demanded by many occupations in which they are engaged is small and quickly acquired, the chances of promotion are few; 'woman, having an eye to marriage, is not equally wedded to her trade'; the supply of low-skilled women workers is abundant; women make low-priced goods. The whole problem is complicated by the fact that women's earnings are often subsidised by the earnings of others – those of the wife by the husband, those of the daughter by the parents, those of wives, widows, and single women by charity and out-relief.

From: Investigation by the Royal Commission on the Poor Laws and Relief of Distress, *Parliamentary Papers* (1909), vol. 43, Appendix.

D. LLOYD GEORGE & WINSTON CHURCHILL ON SOCIAL REFORM

1. LLOYD GEORGE ON OLD AGE PENSIONS, 1908

With another criticism I am rather disposed to sympathise. I think the right hon. Gentleman said that in Germany they make provision for the infirm and sick, and he seemed to attach more importance to that than to the direct provision for old age. I am disposed to agree with him. There may, I think, be many cases of young people who have broken down with family cares, which are much harder than even cases of old people; and I hope that in the future the Government – whether this Government or some other, I do not know – will take cases of that kind into account. At the present moment sufficient unto us is it to provide £6,000,000 or £7,000,000 for old-age pensions. . . . When so much has to be done in the way of social reform – and here I agree absolutely with the hon. Member for Blackburn as to the poverty, distress, and misery prevailing not merely in this country, but throughout the whole of Europe and in all the old countries – it does seem a piece of gigantic folly that we should be spending hundreds of millions a year on machinery for blowing each other's brains out.

. . .

It is simply this mad competition for which we are just as responsible as any other country in the world. I am not sure, really, that in many respects we have not forced the pace, especially in the matter of shipbuilding.

. . .

We think that Germany is preparing to attack us and Germany thinks that we are preparing to attack her. And the result is that the Press in both countries is doing its very best to work up this feeling of panic. Within the few years in the compass of my Parliamentary life, we have increased the expenditure of this country by what would be more than sufficient to provide an old-age pension for every man over sixty-five and to provide a fund for the sick and unemployed as well. Now I think really it is a very serious matter. . . . The House of Commons itself ought to take a matter of this kind in hand. If they do not – and here I agree absolutely with the hon. Member for Dulwich – there are only two ways of providing for social reform. One is reducing expenditure, the other is increasing taxation. If you do not reduce expenditure, you must inevitably provide increased taxation, and if increased taxation has to be provided, and I have some hopes that it will not be necessary, I do not agree with the criticisms of hon. Gentlemen opposite that the resources of free trade finance are at an end. The wealth of this country is enormous. It is not merely great, but it is growing at a gigantic pace, and I do not think it is too much to expect the more favoured part of the community who have got riches so great that they have really to spend a good part of their time in thinking how to spend them, to make a substantial contribution to improve the lot of the poorer members of the same community to which they belong, because it is their interest after all that they should not belong to a country where there is so much poverty and distress side by side with gigantic wealth.

From: *Hansard* 25 May 1908.

2. WINSTON CHURCHILL INTRODUCES UNEMPLOYMENT INSURANCE, 1911

It is, therefore, true to say, broadly speaking, that the compulsory provisions of this Bill are large and substantial, covering very nearly half of the whole field of unemployment; . . . there was a danger that workmen would prefer to be idle and draw unemployed benefit, we are told, instead of remaining at work, but no workman in his senses would ever exchange the regular reward of wage payment for what are, after all, the very narrowly cut grants which alone will be payable under this scheme. I should like to say that there can really be no danger of malingering in the field of unemployment insurance, because a workman who will malinger in unemployment insurance – a workman who will not work when he has the chance and prefers to draw these very exiguous benefits – is only drawing his benefit out at a period when he does not want it instead of keeping it for a period when he will be really unemployed. If he malingers he malingers against himself. I hope I have convinced the House that the danger is not a very serious one . . . To employers we say . . . : 'If your business is subjected to special regulations it will also receive substantial and special benefit,' and lastly, we say to the employer: 'Nothing is more important to you than discipline and efficient workmen and the organisation of insurance will unquestionably enable you to command superior efficiency from the insured workmen.' . . . To the superior workman . . . we say: 'Your risks are limited to sharing your comrades' burdens. You are not called upon to take mere inefficients on your back. They soon drop out of the scheme under the conditions, and you have only to share your risks with your normal comrades.' . . . People talk of the improvidence of the working man. No doubt he has to bear his responsibility, but how can you expect a working man who has few pleasures and small resources, and with the constant strain that is put upon him, to scan trade cycles and to discern with the accuracy of Board of Trade officials the indications and fluctuations of world-wide markets. His failure to do so is excusable. But what can be said of the House of Commons? We have the knowledge and the experience, and it is our duty to think of the future. It is our duty to prepare and to make provision for those for whom we are responsible. What could be said for us, and what could excuse our own improvidence, if the next depression found us all unprepared? There is something to be said for the working man who does not provide against unemployment. It may not fall upon him. The great majority of working men will not become unemployed in the insured trades. A working man may escape, but the State will not escape, and the House of Commons will not escape. The problem will come back to the House of Commons as sure as death and quite as cruel, and then it will be too late ... The penalties for misfortune and failure are terrible to-day; they are wholly disproportionate, even when they are brought on by a man's own fault, either through the culpability of the individual or neglect of what is necessary to make him try or to make him take care. A man may have neglected to make provision for unemployment; he may have neglected to make provision for sickness; he may be below the average standard as a workman; he may have contracted illness through his own folly or his own misconduct. No doubt he is a less good citizen for that reason than others who have taken more thought and trouble. But what relation is there between these weaknesses and failings and the appalling catastrophes which occasionally follow in the wake of these failures; so narrow is the margin upon which even the industrious respectable working class family rely that when sickness or unemployment come knocking at the door the whole economy and even the status of the family are imperilled. The sickness may not be severe; the unemployment may not be prolonged. The good offices of friends and neighbours may carry the family through the crisis; but they come out with an accumulated weight of debt, and with furniture and clothing scattered at ruinous rates. Privation has weakened the efficiency of the bread-winner, and poverty has set its stamp upon his appearance. If sickness and unemployment return and knock again a second time it is all over. The home is broken up; the family is scattered on the high roads, in the casual wards, in the public houses and the prisons of the country. No one can measure the suffering to individuals which this process causes. No one can measure the futile unnecessary loss which the State incurs. We do not pretend that our Bill is going to prevent these evils. Unemployment and sickness will return to the cottage of the working man, but they will not return alone. We are going to send him by this Bill other visitors to his home, visitors who will guard his fortunes and strengthen the force of his right arm against every foe.

From: *Hansard* 25 May 1911.

Document six
ASQUITH ON THE REASONS WHY THE LIBERALS
INTRODUCED OLD AGE PENSIONS IN 1908

Last year, in introducing the Budget, I said that this Parliament and this
Government had come here pledged to social reform; and I pointed to two
figures in our modern society that make an especially strong and, indeed,
an irresistable appeal, not only to our sympathy, but to something more
practical, a sympathy translated into a concrete and constructive policy of
social and financial effort. One is the figure of the child. I reminded the
House that in less than forty years – since 1870 – you have added to your
annual provision for the education of the children of this country out of
taxes and rates an annual sum of over £24,000,000 sterling. There is not
one of us who would go back upon that. The other figure is the figure of
old age, still unprovided for except by casual and unorganised effort, or,
by what is worse, invidious dependence upon Poor Law relief. I said then
that we hoped and intended this year to lay firm the foundations of a wiser
and a humaner policy. With that view . . . I propose now to show how we
intend to redeem the promises which I then made . . . His Majesty's present Government came into power and went through the last general election entirely unpledged in regard to this matter, not that they were insensi-
ble to its importance or to its urgency, but they felt it right to enter into no
binding engagement until they had had full time to survey the problem in
all its aspects, and – what is still more important – to lay a solid financial
foundation for any future structure it might be possible to raise. It was
accordingly not until we had seen our way to make some substantial provision for the reduction of the national liabilities that I found myself able to
announce in the Budget of last year that this year it was our intention to
make a beginning – and more than a beginning I never promised – in the
creation of a sound and workable scheme . . . Let me pause to say that
there is one governing consideration which in framing our proposals we
have kept steadily in view. The problem of making better provision for the
aged is only one of a group of questions the settlement of which, although
it cannot be simultaneous, should as far as possible be harmonious and
self-consistent. A Royal Commission, as the Committee is aware, has now
been at work for some time investigating the administration of the Poor
Law, and we understand that its Report may be expected before many

months. Without in any way anticipating what, of course, we do not know – namely, the character and extent of the recommendations of that Commission, I think we may assume that it will give effect in some shape or other to what has long been regarded by careful observers as the most urgent of all reforms – namely, the reclassification of that vast heterogeneous mass of persons, young and old, sound and infirm, underserving or unfortunate, who at present fall within one province or another of the area of Poor Law administration. It appears to the Government to be a preliminary specially necessary in itself – and reasonably certain not to clash with any wider proposal which the Commissioners may make to take the care of the aged and place it once for all outside both the machinery and the associations of our Poor Law system.

From: *Hansard* 7 May 1908.

RAMSAY MACDONALD, THE LEADER OF THE LABOUR PARTY, ON NATIONAL INSURANCE, 1911

... we are in favour of a contributory scheme with reference to sickness, whilst we were in favour of a non-contributory scheme in reference to old age pensions ... Each one of the cases has to be adjudged on its merits, and the reason why we were in favour of old age pensions was because the contingency of the old age of seventy was so very remote that nobody who held our views could have suggested for a moment that it was an intelligent proposition to suggest that a man should insure himself against such a contingency. The fact of insurance must be determined by the nearness or possibility of the risk which is theoretical becoming a risk which is actual ... But when we agree to the contributory basis, then the question arises, is the distribution fair. So far as I am concerned I do not think this contribution is fair. The distribution of two-ninths from the State and seven-ninths from the employers and workpeople, I think, is a very unfair distribution. I do not think that the distribution means that the State is going to do its duty under the circumstances. Why? Let me remind the Government of this point. The Chancellor of the Exchequer, in his Bill, proposes to give very substantial benefits to those who are to become beneficiaries under the Bill. It is perfectly true that so far as those benefits are concerned the working class contributor is getting full value for his money. But then the difficulty in which the working class contributor is placed is this. If he was in a position to pay 4*d.* for sickness insurance, and having paid the 4*d.*, to deal with the same fulness with all his other responsibilities that have to be placed upon his income, then it would be all right ... man's income was sufficiently large to enable him to meet all his contingencies, then the Chancellor of the Exchequer would be perfectly right, but until his income is sufficiently large, to expect him to meet all those contingencies as fully as the one contingency, then the Chancellor of the Exchequer ought not to impose upon him such a large percentage as 4d. He is running a grave risk, and I am sure he must recognise it, by making a person insure himself against sickness at the cost of his standard of life.

When a man is sick and receiving his benefit, then undoubtedly he is far better off under this Bill than he would be if there were no Bill at all. Whilst a man is not sick, and whilst a man is struggling and striving to make ends meet week in and week out, the proportion of 4*d.* taken from him compulsorily is too large a proportion in a great many instances to enable him to fulfil his other responsibilities . . . The Chancellor is going to start a system, which I hope will be efficient and well equipped, of experimental medicine. To charge the cost of a system and experimental medicine upon personal income is altogether wrong, because any system of experimental medicine which is going to be carried on on a proper scale must be a State system. You might just as well tell us that he should impose a personal charge upon us for London University or for Oxford or Cambridge. Experimental medicine must be organised by the State, must be staffed by the State, must be kept going by the State, and to impose one single brass farthing of the cost of the system upon individual insurance is a very wrong and a very unjust system. All that ought to have come from the State . . . If you allow slums to exist in your midst and the vitality of your people to be low it is unfair to ask those people to insure themselves against that part of the sickness which ought to be a public charge and ought to be a communal charge, and the State ought to bear the expense of it. I do not say altogether. I admit, the Chancellor of the Exchequer has done some of it, but it is not my case at all that he has not done anything. My case is that if he classifies all the activities which he contemplates in his Bill, and for which he is making financial provision, more than two-ninths of them are social in their origin, social in their character, and therefore ought to be social in the source from which they ought to be paid. . . If you take Part II., unemployment, the case is far worse. As a matter of fact a very good case can be made out under Part II. for no contribution from the workmen at all. . . If a small contribution from the workman is going to lubricate the matter, so that the State will do its duty and give us an opportunity of starting a very important experiment, I am not going to quarrel with the Chancellor of the Exchequer for asking for a small contribution. But what has happened? The actuarial return shows that to the income of the unemployment fund the workman will contribute 9*s.* 2*d.*, whilst the employer contributes 7*s.* 6*d.*, and the State contributes 5*s.* 6*d.* and two-thirds of a penny. That is not fair. . . Unemployment is mainly a social disease. You have said that over and over again in this House, and we shall have to say so often again. It is caused very largely by inefficient industrial organisation for which the employer is responsible. If there is any cause at all which calls for a contribution from the workman it is a cause very slightly indeed due to the workman by anything he has done or can do in our very complicated industrial organisation. . . If you insist upon the workman contributing something, it should be a minimum, the very minimum, just enough to be a contribution at all.

From: *Hansard* 6 July 1911.

ILL-HEALTH AMONG WOMEN REVEALED IN THE ADMINISTRATION OF NATIONAL HEALTH INSURANCE

REPORT OF THE DEPARTMENTAL COMMITTEE ON SICKNESS BENEFIT CLAIMS UNDER THE NATIONAL INSURANCE ACT 1914

... secretaries of societies have expressed themselves as astounded by their realisation for the first time, on the coming into operation of the Act, of the kind of work done by women in certain occupations, and of the amount of sickness entailed by the conditions under which they live. More especially with regard to women this view of the question is emphasised by those witnesses who have appeared before us, and have given evidence from a standpoint other than that of those engaged in the administration of the Act. By these witnesses it is contended that there is in fact more sickness than was expected when the Act came into operation, and that the excessive sickness among married women is a common experience due to illnesses connected with and consequent upon childbirth. The evidence of medical practitioners is overwhelmingly in support of the view that the effect of the Act has been to disclose, especially among industrial women, an enormous amount of unsuspected sickness and disease, and to afford treatment to many who have hitherto been without medical attendance during sickness. It may be permissible to quote the words of one witness practising in an area which would not ordinarily be regarded as unhealthy, 'I thought I knew how much illness there was in my neighbourhood, but I had no conception of the amount of real illness that existed until I was brought in contact with it through the Act. ... I had no idea that it existed, and was going unrelieved, and that people were dragging along with such illness.' ...

Some hopes appear to be entertained that some of this disease, though of a nature to demand immediate treatment and to justify the statement that those who are suffering from it are incapable of work, will yield to treatment, and that within a time which may be foreseen but cannot be defined, there will result a healthier population and a diminished demand on the funds of approved societies. Already there are indications that as a result of the rest obtained under the Act a better condition of health has in certain cases been attained than has been experienced for many years.

'They have been in bed for a month, and they say now that they have never been so well in their lives. It is represented that in some of the cases treated the ravages of the past will never be repaired, although under the conditions now in force a further worsening may be prevented, but that in other cases there will be a real recoupment, and that in time the general standard of health will tend to improve.

The chief danger in these circumstances appears to lie, not so much in any undue eagerness on the part of the insured to obtain benefits to which they are not entitled, as in a valetudinarian habit of mind which may be induced from over-attention to health and to disease. Medical practitioners who have appeared in evidence before us have repeatedly referred to the fact that in a large number of cases persons suffering from only trivial ailments have attended for treatment. . . .

It has been repeatedly stated that the attitude of women towards insurance differs from that of men, and that there is among women a more wide-spread ignorance of what is involved in insurance. This is attributed largely to their previous lack of training in insurance and to the fact that the overwhelming majority of insured women have now entered into insurance for the first time. The words of one witness may be quoted as representative of many who professed this view. 'A woman on the other hand would clearly feel, and does feel, that if she does not get out more than she has paid in she is losing something. I think that it is a result of a misunderstanding of the principle of insurance, and a want of that education which a man has had for many years. It is her natural desire to do the best she can for herself.'

PROPORTION OF ILL-PAID AND ILL-FED AMONG WOMEN

The higher rate of claims among women is also largely attributed to the fact that the total number of insured women includes a very large proportion of ill-paid and ill-fed persons, who have had little education in the care of their health, and who, in most cases, have no one to prepare the meal which should be ready for them on their return from work, and, therefore, live on unsuitable food.

APPROXIMATION OF SICKNESS BENEFIT TO AVERAGE EARNINGS

There is the further fact that 7s. 6d. a week bears a larger proportion to the average woman's wage than 10s. does to the average man's wage, and that among a very large class of women engaged in poorly paid industries or in casual occupation, the benefit under the Act represents a sum as large as, or larger than, the average weekly earnings. Over-insurance in the case of men generally arises from multiple insurance and thus, as has been indicated in an earlier paragraph of this Report, in many cases affects the more prudent and consequently the more healthy class of working man, but in the case of the women now referred to, large numbers, even when capable of work, are at all times in an unsatisfactory state of health.

The excessive sickness claims paid in the case of women, and above all, in the case of married women, are further increased by the difficulty of supervising the behaviour of women who are in receipt of benefit. The principle of sickness insurance has always been that the grant of benefit must be made under slightly deterrent conditions, and that certain restrictions must be placed on the freedom of the person in receipt of benefit if he is to be induced to return to work. The witnesses have all been impressed by the very great temptation under which a woman in receipt of sickness benefit labours to take part in ordinary household occupations. In the case of men, enforced idleness often becomes irksome, and leads to a return to work, whereas the possibility of doing ordinary housework, or, at appropriate seasons, extraordinary housework, may induce women to stay on the funds longer than they otherwise would or may even retard recovery. . .

Another reason for the heavy drains made on the funds of women's societies is to be found in the illnesses accompanying pregnancy. The difficulty of providing insurance to cover periods of pregnancy has led in the past, among societies which undertook the insurance of women, to a very general exclusion of liability during pregnancy. . . . As a means of lessening these difficulties, we suggest that in the last month of pregnancy, when it may be assumed, as a general rule, without further inquiry, that the woman should not go to her work, it should be assumed that she is in fact incapacitated, and that an automatic payment should be made to her in respect of the last month upon the statement, supported by a medical certificate, that she is at that stage of pregnancy. . . . . The Act of 1911 specifically required that women in receipt of sickness benefit should only be visited by women. It appears to the Committee that the principle thus laid down by the statute is capable of extension, and that a smoother administration of the Act would be secured, if the claims of women under the Act were more extensively dealt with by women officials. If it is necessary that women's certificates should be handled locally by men in some cases, a feeling of unpleasantness would at least be avoided if steps were taken to secure that any discussion arising between the woman and the society should be conducted on their side by women. Where the claims are handled locally in the office, every care should be taken to narrow the possibilities of unpleasant gossip, to emphasise the confidential nature of the information upon the certificate, and to increase the sense of responsibility for silence upon those in charge, whether men or women. A doctor who had issued a certificate for 'internal trouble' informed the Committee that 'a day or two later the patient came and told me that when she took the certificate to the office, which was full of men, the man in authority had said, 'Oh, internal trouble; we know what that means. There will be inquiry made into this.' Of course he had no idea of what it meant, but the suggestion was offensive.' Another witness, a secretary of a society, gave evidence to the effect that he found it a source of embarrassment in certain cases to have to deal with women's certificates. 'When a woman brings a certificate with 'gastritis,' and I ask her, is she pregnant, she tells me to mind my own business. I was told that twice in one week.'

From: Report of the Departmental Committee on Sickness Benefit claims under the National Insurance Act 1914, *Parliamentary Papers* (1914–16) vol. 30.

SYLVIA PANKHURST ON THE CONDITIONS OF WOMEN IN EAST LONDON AT THE BEGINNING OF WORLD WAR I

Up and down the Old Ford Road under my windows, women were wont to hurry past, pushing the battered old perambulators of children, or packing cases on wheels, laden with garments for the factories. Now, with their little conveyances all empty, they lingered hopeless. 'Any work?' Always they asked each other that question; the answer, so obvious from the downcast face and the empty vehicle, was always: 'No.' I gazed on them mournfully, tenderly, feeling as though the wings of a great pity enfolded me. The absence of work, the cost of food – these were the burden of every talk, floating up to my window, passing me on the road.

Across a neighbouring street a rudely lettered calico banner hung:

Please, landlord, don't be offended,
Don't come for the rent till the War is ended.

Was it a product of our Suffragette call for a No Vote, No Rent strike?

Women gathered about our door asking for 'Sylvia.' They had followed and fought with her in the hectic Suffragette struggles; they turned to her now in these hours of desperate hardship; poor wan, white-faced mothers, clasping their wasted babies, whose pain-filled eyes seemed older than their own. Their breasts gone dry, they had no milk to give their infants, no food for the elder children, no money for the landlord.

Their faith in me seemed a sacred charge, their sorrows stirred me – I girded myself to fight for their interests. I had no thought, as yet, of collecting charitable donations for them. On the contrary, I wanted the need for such charity abolished, by the Community taking the responsibility for the well-being of its members; for the unemployed, not doles, but work at a living wage; for the men drafted away to fight, pay at least not worse than the best obtainable in industry; nationalisation of food to keep down prices and insure that the incidence of shortage should be equally shared; such measures as steps toward the goal of plenty for all by mutual aid. . .

Yet public assistance tarried; the plight of the distressed weighted heavily on me. Under pressure of the need, daily confronting us, I announced an employment bureau, with Maud Joachim as secretary, and appealed for work for brushmakers, shoemakers and others. In the following issue I had thrown away reserves, and was pleading for funds to buy milk, for eggs to provide albumen water for infants too ill to digest milk, for other invalid necessities, and announcing that a nurse to advise mothers whose babies had fallen ill would attend every afternoon at the Women's Hall. Henceforth every week Dr Lilian Simpson was in attendance, and a regular clinic was established in the Old Ford Road, and soon at five other centres.

How could one face a starving family with nothing to offer save milk for the baby? Orders for the various sorts of home work our distressed people could do, we gave out, as they came to us, through the employment bureau; but these were miserably few, as compared with our numbers. Expectant mothers were unable to provide for their confinements. We purchased material, cut out garments for mothers and babies, and older children, and paid our starving applicants for employment to make them up.

From the first we laid it down rigidly that we should pay no woman less than 5d. per hour, the district minimum wage of the unskilled labouring man. To pay a woman less, and call it charity, was to connive at sweating; and cost what it might, we were resolved not to depart from that standard.

A member, whose husband was out of work, came with her four months baby in her arms; a child of two and a half was ill at home, and she had eight of them under the age for leaving school. The wife of an unemployed stevedore, expecting another baby in three months time, fainted on our doorstep. She had an infant of twelve months in her arms, and another of three years clutching to her skirts. 'Everything pawned and nothing coming in,' was the common condition. Mrs Walker, in her canvassing, called on a woman with six children under thirteen years. Her twins, only two months old, she was feeding on boiled bread, having no other food in the house, and but little of that. A mother came pleading for work, already worn down by toil for her eight children, whose ages ranged from four months to just under fourteen years. The wife of a ship's greaser told us the Government had taken over her husband's ship, since when she had had no money from him, nor any tidings of his whereabouts. She and her six children had gone four days without food. Starving householders, whose lodgers were thrown out of work and unable to pay any rent, forgave them this default in the large charity of the very poor. A girl of nineteen, the sole support of her mother and four little brothers and sisters, was unemployed. She was flagging from anaemia and debility; if her plight were prolonged she might never be fit to work again. More fortunate than many, they got 8s. a week and four loaves from the Guardians, 'and a job to get that!' In a household of ten children, all the breadwinners, and the lodger also, had lost their work. A widow supporting three children by brushmaking was unemployed. Her fifteen-year-old daughter had been bedridden five months, as the result of a street accident, and was still incapacitated; her action for compensation was suspended, as two of the witnesses had been called to the War.

There was terrible confusion. Masses of women did not know how, or where to apply for their allowances, and waited long and vainly for them to come through automatically. Some in their destitute condition had not money to purchase their marriage certificates and the birth certificates of their children, which were demanded as an essential preliminary to any allowance. The price even of the certificates had been raised, the children's from 3*d*. to 7*d*. each, a hardship indeed to people lacking pence to buy bread! There was doubt and confusion as to whether the certificates should be sent to the War Office or the Army Paymaster. Often the certificates were lost by the officials who handled them, and had to be supplied a second time.

Often for some reason the woman failed to discover, the money did not come through. Sometimes it was because the soldiers forgot to fill up the forms for separation allowance and allotment; or, as the men themselves insisted, the forms were not forthcoming. Entire companies of men had often to complain that no forms had been supplied. If, as often happened, men were late in responding to the summons to the colours, or tardy in returning from leave, or if they committed some other veniality – an offence according to military standards, which might be no offence at all in civilian life – their families were punished by the stoppage of allotment and separation allowance for weeks or even months. Weeks of privation were frequently endured before the unfortunate wives learnt why they and their children had thus been plunged into destitution.

From: Sylvia Pankhurst, *The Home Front*, Hutchinson, London (1932) pp. 18–25.

THE LIVING STANDARDS OF OLD AGE PENSIONERS IN 1919

Budgets of old-age pensioners who live on pensions, pp. 332–3.

Budgets of those who do not live on the old-age pension, pp. 334–5.

Budgets of old-age pensioners who live on pension

	Widow, 76 years, Wallesley, Cheshire	Finchley	Hove	Old Woman, 78 years, Horbury, lives alone.	Biddulph	Ann Owen, Wednesbury, lives with a widow.	78 years
	s. d.	s. d.	s. d.	s. d.	s. d.	s. d.	s. d.
Rent	2 6	2 6	3 0	1 8	3 6	2 6 (includes Lodging and Fire).	1 8
Coal	—	2 0	0 3½	2 0	—	—	2 0
Gas	—	—	—	—	—	—	—
Wood	—	—	—	—	—	—	—
Matches	—	0 9	—	—	—	0 3½ (Candles).	—
Oil	—	—	—	—	—	—	—
Soap	0 3	—	—	0 8½	0 7½	0 4½	0 7
Meat	—	—	—	—	—	1 1 (Bacon).	0 8½ (includes Laundry).
Fish	—	0 4½ (Herrings).	—	—	—	—	—
Bread	0 9	1 1½	0 4¾	0 9	—	0 9	0 9
Milk	—	—	1 9	1 0	—	0 5	1 0
Margarine	1 0	0 6	0 6	0 7	0 6	0 3 (5½d. Lard).	0 5½

Eggs	0 6	—	—	0 4	0 9	0 8	0 4
Tea	1 3	—	} 1 1	0 5½	0 6	0 5½	—
Sugar	0 3	0 3	0 6	—	0 8½	0 3	—
Potatoes	0 6	—	—	—	0 3	—	—
Insurance	—	—	—	—	—	—	—
Sundries	0 6	—	—	—	—	—	—
Total	7 6	7 6	7 6	7 6	7 6	7 6	7 6

Budgets of those who do not live on the old-age pension

	Mrs A. Leney, Battersea. Pension, 7s. 6d. From son, 2s. 6d. Total 10s.		Old Woman at Thornaby-on-Tees. No sons or grandsons to support her.		Kingswood		Mr and Mrs H., aged 90 and 81, Taunton. Daughter pays 7s. or 8s. for keep.		Bournemouth	
	s.	d.	s.	d.	s.	d.	s.	d.	s.	d.
Rent	2	9	2	6	2	6	3	6	3	0
Coal	1	2½	1	10½	2	6	2	4	2	6
									(fire and light).	
Wood	0	3¾	—		—		0	6	—	
Matches	—		—		0	1	—		—	
Oil	0	8½	—		—		1	0	—	
							(no gas).			
Soap	—		—		—		1	0	0	4
Meat	0	9	1	2	1	3	1	0	3	0
			(Bacon).				(Bacon).			
Fish	0	6	—		—		—		—	
Bread and Flour	1	1½	0	9	1	1½	2	10½	1	1½
			(Flour and Yeast).							
Milk	1	1	1	6	1	0¾	2	11	1	4
	(tinned).						(1 pint daily).		(includes Tea and Sugar).	
Margarine	0	6	0	4	0	3¾	0	6	1	0
									(includes Cheese).	
Tea	0	8	0	4½	0	7	0	7	—	
							(and Cocoa).			
Eggs	—		—		—		0	6	—	
Vegetables	0	6	—		—		—		0	6

Sugar	0 7	0 7	0 5½	0 10	—
Rice	0 3	—	—	—	—
Jam	—	—	—	0 10½	—
Oats	0 6	0 5½	—	—	—
Insurance	—	1 0	—	0 6	0 4
Sundries	—			3 6	
		(Clothes Club).		(for woman to wash and clean).	
Total	11 5½	10 6½	9 10	£1 4 1	13 1½

Collected by the Joint Committees of Industrial Women's Organizations from members of Women's Section of the Labour Party, Branches of the Women's Co-operative Guild, Branches of the Railway Women's Guild, Labour Poor Law Guardians, Labour members of Old-Age Pensions Committees, Labour Town Councillors, Labour members of War Pensions Committees and 37 other individuals, and presented as evidence to the Departmental Committee on Old-Age Pensions, Minutes of Evidence, *Parliamentary Papers* (1919) vol. 27, pp. 224–5.

THE SECRETARY TO THE TREASURY'S VIEWS ON
PUBLIC EXPENDITURE AND OLD AGE PENSIONS, 1919

It is perfectly true that owing to the de-valuation of money which may be temporary these people have suffered. The question is whether you should compensate them completely for that suffering or only partially, and put them back relatively into the position they were in before the war. I suggest that you should only do it partially because I think that everyone in the community must necessarily be poorer and have his standard of living reduced as the result of the war. I would like it to be understood that I would apply that principle much more drastically to the wealthy than the poor, and I think myself that when the real economic effect of the taxation that we have to impose to meet the interest charges of the new necessary social services, war pensions and so on comes to be felt the wealthy will realise what has happened to them to a degree of which they do not dream at the present moment. ... A certain number of sanguine people say that we ought, with improvements of industrial organisation, and so on, to produce twice what we did before the war. If we do that, well and good. We all then would be very much wealthier in a very short time and everybody would be better off, but as I read the signs of the times instead of producing more we shall produce less, owing to labour unrest and so forth, and therefore everybody has to go more or less short. The question is what kind of cut are you to make with regard to different classes of the community. You cannot put everybody into as favourable a position under the circumstances as he was before the war, and I do not think you can do so in the case of anybody. You have the active industrial classes insisting not only on a pre-war standard of comfort, but on something more, or doing their best to do so. Owing to the rise in prices their efforts are defeated at every turn. I doubt whether the active working classes short of a social revolution will be content with a lower standard of comfort. You must therefore make economy elsewhere, and I want to make the economy principally at the expense of the wealthier classes. I want to prevent people riding in motor cars; I want to prevent people wearing expensive furs; I want to prevent people buying unnecessary clothing, and very soon the Income Tax will have that effect I think. I think it quite impossible to restore people like Old Age Pensioners who are not part of the industrial machine to as favourable a position as they occupied before the war.

From: Evidence of Sir John Bradbury to the Report of the Departmental Committee on Old-Age Pensions, Minutes of Evidence, *Parliamentary Papers* (1919), vol. 27, p. 311

Industry is not seeking the Special Areas; therefore, it must be attracted to those districts of the Areas which are endowed with suitable economic facilities, and many are available. How can this be effected? My recommendation is that by means of *State-provided inducements* a determined attempt should be made to attract industrialists to the Special Areas. The failure of these Areas to attract cannot be simply explained away by lack of opportunity for economic expansion. Fear is the dominant deterrent which holds back industrialists from taking risks in the Areas; fear that their very distress makes them unsuitable for the development of industrial activity; fear of labour unrest and of further increases of already high rates. However well or ill founded these fears may be, they not only prevail but often engender a habit of mind which is wholly prejudicial to any favourable consideration of the Special Areas. This mental attitude can be considerably changed if new conditions which challenge attention are set up in the Areas and make industrialists seeking expansion feel that, unless they study them, opportunity may be lost. It is sought by means of State-provided inducements to supply the required incentive. Unless something is done to banish fear, its influence will continue to rule out consideration of the possibilities of the Special Areas.

To get those journeying downstream to change their course and make for the Special Areas, these must be endowed with compelling attractiveness. Faint-hearted measures will prove ineffective. The effort, to be successful, requires bold action. A magnet must be fixed in the Special Areas which will overcome such attractions of London and the South as are not based on their essential requirements or on well-founded economic considerations. A powerful initial pull will be required, but it must be under control so that it can be relaxed should the tide turn strongly towards the Special Areas and more normal industrial conditions be there enjoyed.

State-provided inducements can supply this magnetic attraction.

From: 3rd Report of the Commission for the Special Areas (England and Wales), Cmnd 5303 (1936).

A most disturbing feature of the British health services at present is the extent to which profit-making concerns take advantage of the ignorance and credulity of the man in the street. No doubt many of the proprietary health foods are admirable, but it is obvious that those products which have behind them a vigorous and well-conducted advertising campaign claim an excessive share of the attention and expenditure of all classes. With the exception of a few of the voluntary hospitals the basic health services which are carrying the real burden of the work have only just begun to achieve the volume and skill of publicity which would be given to a new laxative or a rupture appliance. Official and scientific announcements and advice on health matters are promptly seized by commercial interests to make capital for products the consumption of which may be directly opposed to the advice quoted. In the same way the work of great chemists and inventors is misused with an ease which should be impossible in a civilised country. The making of unlimited profits from the exploitation of ill-health by such methods has long since been barred in Sweden and other countries. This misuse of advertising, too, makes necessary costly large scale publicity for elementary products such as milk and basic services which might otherwise be taken for granted.

In the past two or three generations a bewildering variety of agencies have been created to work for health mainly by attacking specific diseases and disabilities as they occur and by maintaining the sufferers. To a lesser extent successful efforts have been made to eradicate the social and economic causes of sickness and disability such as bad housing, sanitation and water supply, and dangerous or unhealthy working conditions.

Although these efforts have had remarkable results they have failed to give the nation an acceptable measure of good health or satisfactorily to reduce the economic burden of sickness and accidents. Perhaps the most fundamental defect in the existing system is that it is overwhelmingly preoccupied with manifest and advanced diseases or disabilities and is more interested in enabling the sufferers to go on functioning in society somehow than in studying the nature of health and the means of producing and maintaining it. From this it naturally follows that millions of pounds are spent in looking after and trying to cure the victims of accidents and illnesses which need never have occurred if a fraction of this amount of intelligence and money had been devoted to tracing the social and economic causes of the trouble and making the necessary adjustments.

While everyone knows that cholera, bubonic plague, malaria, scurvy and other scourges have been eliminated by the engineer or through raising the standard of living rather than by medical treatment, we are all apt to think of health in terms of curing and treating disease, and to ignore or under-rate the extent to which habits of life, the lay-out of our towns and buildings, labour management, transport, food manufacturing and distribution and so forth can and must be brought into the campaign for fitness.

From: S. M. Herbert, *Britain's Health*, Penguin, Harmondsworth (1937).

NEVILLE CHAMBERLAIN AND JOHN WHEATLEY
DEBATE THE HOUSING QUESTION IN 1924

MR N. CHAMBERLAIN: I do not think it can be denied, at any rate, that the Act of 1923 has actually produced proposals from the local authorities for a larger number of houses than the industry itself can supply. I know it was the case until very recently that the Ministry, who had, very properly, to examine every scheme to see whether it could be carried out, were obliged to reject a number of schemes, and in many other cases were obliged to cut down the number of houses which the local authorities had proposed to build, because when they came to ask what labour was available, they found that the locality could not produce the necessary labour, and that, if it were to be forthcoming, it would have to be by robbing some other locality where, very likely, the needs were just as great. Of course, it was that very consideration which caused that tremendous rise in prices under the Addison scheme, when the houses on paper for which contracts were let were so much more numerous than the houses which the industry could supply, that builders and others were enabled to ask higher and higher prices for their work. In fact, it would appear that the limitations upon the amount of housing that has been done under the 1923 Act were due, not to the defects in the Act itself, but to the shortage of skilled labour. There has been no shortage in unskilled labour, but the unskilled men are dependent on a proportionate supply of skilled men, and if the skilled men are not forthcoming it means that there is no work for the unskilled. . . . I remember warning the House at the time that, if you were to increase the superficial area of houses, one of two things would follow, either that the poorer classes of people for whom I had desired to provide would have to sublet in order to be able to afford the rents which would be attached to those houses, or that you would have another class, rather higher in the social scale, earning more money per week, who would take advantage of the subsidy and take those houses to the exclusion of the poorer classes for whom I had desired to provide in the first instance. I believe that is exactly what has happened. The increase in the superficial area has enabled a good number of people who, on the whole and comparatively speaking, are fairly well off – I do not mean to say that they are the upper middle-class but they are equal to our well-paid artisans, clerks and others – by slightly reducing the standard of the houses that they them-selves would have chosen have been enabled to take advantage of this sub-sidy and to occupy houses which we hoped would have been occupied by another class of persons. . . . But I would be very glad to know what the Minister himself thinks about encouraging people to own their own houses. I remember that he was asked how he would define 'houses for the working classes'. He gave then a curious, and I think an original definition of the working classes, as those who could not afford to buy their own houses. I will return to that in a moment. I want to put it to him that, whether these people are members of the working classes or whether, if you like, by buying their own houses they have ceased to be members of the working class, in any case it is a good thing that as many people as possible should own their own houses. I say that for many reasons. I be-lieve it is a very strong incentive to thrift. I believe it is a thing that appeals to the best instincts of the working classes, and I am quite certain that the man who owns his own house is generally a good citizen also. As to whether the working classes are capable of owning their own houses I would like to tell the Minister that in my own city there is an institution called the Municipal Savings Bank.

Perhaps I may be pardoned for taking some personal pride in it, because I had some responsibility for its foundation. One of the functions of this municipal bank is to use its deposits for the purpose of making advances to people who desire to purchase their own houses. . . . Since the War – and, of course, you can hardly find a period in history when you would suppose there was less inducement to purchase a house than within recent years, when the values of houses first rose to a tremendous height and afterwards fell with extraordinary rapidity – the total number of people who have purchased their houses through the bank is 2,226, and out of those I find that a class which I call definitely manual workers amounted to 773, just about one-third of the whole; shopkeepers accounted for 92, the clerical classes for 529, professors and teachers for 208 and then comes a miscel-laneous lot. . . .

I want again to suggest to the Minister of Health that it is in the in-terests of the housing problem as a whole that he should try and lighten, as far as he can, the burden, which in any case is going to be very heavy, which lies upon the local authorities. I know he holds very strongly the view that, so far as houses for the working classes are concerned, private enterprise will never function again. Well, at any rate, even if he holds that view, is it not desirable to take out of the residuum, whatever it is – and I agree that there must be a residuum which cannot be provided for by private enterprise and which must be provided for by the local authorities – as many as he possibly can? [An HON. MEMBER: 'Why?'] Because the financial burden on the municipalities is going to be so great that, if they have to take the whole of it upon their own shoulders, it is going finally to break their backs. I suggest to him that it is his duty to foster and to encourage, by every means in his power, this question of occupying house ownership.

MR WHEATLEY: Let us see what is the actual housing difficulty which I inherited when I took over the Ministry of Health. There is, undoubtedly, a shortage of houses numbering hundreds of thousands, on which I should not care to put a figure; but perhaps, if I turn to the city which the right hon. Gentleman himself so worthily represents, I may get there some indication of the extent of that shortage. The right hon. Gentleman told us with a good deal of pride that 773 manual workers in the city of Birmingham had succeeded, through his municipal banking system, in purchasing the houses which they occupy. I congratulate him on that result, but may I remind him that 773 constitutes but a very small percentage of the total number of manual workers in the city of Birmingham, and is he aware that the Corporation of Birmingham has a waiting list of no less than 19,000 workers waiting for dwelling-houses? Does he suggest that there is anything to gloat over in the fact that 773 have become thirled to a city which has 19,000 families who cannot find housing accommodation, and who are probably contributing to terrible overcrowding and the dissemination of disease in the city which the right hon. Gentleman represents?

On the question of the owner-occupier, may I ask him how he can expect men who are in receipt to-day of something in the neighbourhood of 40s. a week to become the owners of their dwellings? He knows that we are threatened with a miners' strike, and he knows, I am quite sure, that the average wage of the miner, against which he is in revolt, is something in the neighbourhood of 8s. a day.

I had a deputation from Birmingham waiting on me the other day, and I put a question to them which I have put to every deputation on housing, or indeed on anything akin to housing, which has called at the Ministry of Health during my period of office. I asked them: 'Is there any indication in your district which would lead you to believe that individuals or companies are prepared to invest capital for the provision of working-class houses at rents?' and I got an emphatic 'No' from Birmingham and permission to announce it as the opinion of leading members of the municipality ... if you go on suggesting that private enterprise, in the sense of an investor for rented houses, may be expected to return to this branch of industry you are postponing the activities of the local authorities in doing their duty and you are making conditions worse and worse every day that passes over our heads. I wish I could convince hon. Members opposite that there is no district in the country in which there is any likelihood at all of men investing their money in these houses in the hope of getting a return from them out of rents in the future.

While I am on this point, may I contest the statement which is frequently made, that somehow or other Labour's policy in housing is directed to the destruction of private enterprise in houses. Nothing of the kind. We have not driven these people out of the investing field. They have gone out. We have to deal with facts as we find them. Labour does not propose to interfere with private enterprise in the building of houses. Labour does not propose to interfere with private enterprise in the manufacturing of building material. Labour only touches private enterprise here at one point, and that is in the investment of private capital in the ownership of these rented houses... The Labour party's programme on housing is not a Socialist programme at all I wish it were. I wish this country were ready to receive a Socialist programme, and we would show you how much easier it is to solve the housing problem along those lines than in trying to patch up the capitalist system, of which you yourselves have made such a mess... It is not merely that we are short of houses. We are short of men to build the houses, and we are short of the materials and the means of producing the materials for the building of houses. We are short of these things because of the continued instability of the building industry. That is the root cause of the whole thing. ...

From: *Hansard* 26 March 1926.

A large proportion of our population is living in conditions of poverty. Their incomes are not sufficient to enable them to buy the elementary necessities of life. A still larger proportion, including the great majority of the people, suffer the anxieties of insecurity. . . . The urgent need is undoubtedly that we should find a means by which the incomes of the population may be raised as soon as possible to a level which represents at least the minimum standard of nutrition, of clothing, and of shelter necessary for the maintenance of physical efficiency and health. . . .

The dynamic of social change, the driving power towards the achievement of these ends, resides in our discontent with things as they are. If that discontent is shared by the comfortable as well as the unfortunate, then these changes can be accomplished by a process of peaceful evolution throughout which we shall continue to preserve the heritage of our liberty. If, however, it is not shared by all classes in society, if our political views are merely to be a reflection of the money in our pockets, if the poor are to do the driving, and the rich stubbornly to resist, if, at this critical moment, we hesitate to be guided by the British tradition of peaceful change, then we shall move stage by stage towards the embitterment of class antagonism and the decay and destruction of our democratic institutions.

The reply to the menace of political tyranny is to be made not when hatred has fanned the flames of popular discontent to revolutionary fervour, but in the period when it is still possible to achieve economic reconstruction and social amelioration by peaceful means. Such a consummation would rob the revolutionary movements of their meaning, and apparent justification, by eliminating the social despair upon which alone they can be fostered.

At other periods of history the conflict of class interests may have been more difficult to avoid. In an age of relative scarcity it might reasonably have been felt that improvements in the standard of life of the poor would only be possible by curtailment of the incomes of other classes. In the society of today this is obviously not true. It is not necessary to reduce the incomes of one class in order to increase the incomes of another. If we could unleash the latent productive possibilities which are now being held in check, we could easily increase the production of wealth to a level more than sufficient to satisfy the demand for a tolerable standard of life. .... If the progressive elements in society will respond to the need for an imaginative policy of reconstruction *now*, we can safeguard Democracy by lifting the conditions of our people to a higher level of material well-being and cultural opportunity. .... These are not matters of party politics. They are profound and fundamental issues, demanding the surrender of prejudice and the attention and combined effort of a united nation. Democracy is being revealed as much more than a political system; it is a way of life. Upon its preservation depends the future of civilisation as we have been taught to regard it. We owe it to ourselves and to posterity, as our contribution to the history of human progress, so to strengthen, enlarge, and reconstruct the very groundwork of this way of life as to enable it to endure unshaken the inner strains and external perils of the anxious days that seem to lie ahead.

From: Harold Macmillan, *The Middle Way*, Macmillan, London (1938) pp. 373–6.

J. M. KEYNES: HOW TO PAY FOR THE WAR 1940

It is not easy for a free community to organise for war. We are not accustomed to listen to experts or prophets. Our strength lies in an ability to improvise. Yet an open mind to untried ideas is also necessary. . . . Courage will be forthcoming if the leaders of opinion in all parties will summon out of the fatigue and confusion of war enough lucidity of mind to understand for themselves and to explain to the public what is required; and then propose a plan conceived in a spirit of social justice, a plan which uses a time of general sacrifice, not as an excuse for postponing desirable reforms, but as an opportunity for moving further than we have moved hitherto towards reducing inequalities. . .

The first provision in our radical plan is . . . to determine a proportion of each man's earnings which must be deferred; – withdrawn, that is to say, from immediate consumption and only made available as a right to consume after the war is over. If the proportion can be fixed fairly for each income group, this device will have a double advantage. It means that rights to immediate consumption during the war can be allotted with a closer regard to relative sacrifice than under any other plan. It also means that rights to deferred consumption after the war, which is another name for the National Debt, will be widely distributed amongst all those who are foregoing immediate consumption, instead of being mainly concentrated, as they were last time, in the hands of the capitalist class.

The second provision is to provide for this deferred consumption without increasing the National Debt by a general capital levy after the war.

The third provision is to protect from any reductions in current consumption those whose standard of life offers no sufficient margin. This is effected by an exempt minimum, a sharply progressive scale and a system of family allowances. The net result of these proposals is, to increase the consumption of young families with less than 75s. a week, to leave the *aggregate* consumption of the lower income group having £5 a week or less nearly as high as before the war (whilst at the same time giving them rights, in return for extra work, to deferred consumption after the war), and to reduce the aggregate consumption of the higher income group with more than £5 a week by about a third on the average.

The fourth provision, rendered possible by the previous provisions but not itself essential to them, is to link further changes in money-rates of wages, pensions and other allowances to changes in the cost of a limited range of rationed articles of consumption, an iron ration as it has been called, which the authorities will endeavour to prevent, one way or another, from rising in price.

A general plan like this, to which all are required to conform, is like a rule of the road – everyone gains and no one can lose. To regard such a rule as an infringement of liberty is somewhat silly. If the rule of the road is imposed, people will travel as much as before. Under this plan people will consume as much as before. The rule of the road allows people as much choice, as they would have without it, along which roads to travel. This plan would allow people as much choice as before what goods they consume.

From: J. M. Keynes, *How to Pay for the War*, Macmillan, London (1940) pp. 1, 10–12.

Document seventeen
THE VIEWS OF TRADE UNIONS AND EMPLOYERS GIVEN TO THE BEVERIDGE COMMITTEE, 1942

1. MEMORANDUM BY THE BRITISH EMPLOYERS' CONFEDERATION

The Committee's Survey makes manifest the many anomalies in our present system of Social Services – anomalies which are the inevitable result of the various Services having been instituted and developed from time to time without relation to each other.

Notwithstanding these anomalies, however, it is not open to question that the Social Service system of Great Britain is the most comprehensive and highly developed in the whole world and that this country has, for many years, devoted to the Social Services a larger part of its national income and public expenditure than any other country has ever done...

In the building up of our State insurance systems for Unemployment, Health and Pensions, the Confederation has supported the principle of a national compulsory contributory system as an integral part of our industrial life.

In its evidence before the various Commissions and Committees, the Confederation has often had occasion to criticise the operation and development of these systems but it has never failed to recognise the beneficial part which these Services, under proper safeguards, are qualified to play in the welfare of this industrial country.

The Confederation has throughout, however, maintained that it is imperative that the expenditure on these Services, and the other Social Services, must be directly related to the industrial performance of the country on which they ultimately depend for their continuance, and that the benefits they provide should not be such as to weaken the incentive of the population to play their full part in maintaining the productivity and exporting ability of the country at its highest level...

In the light of these considerations, the Confederation regards it as essential in the first place that any proposals for a new or revised Social Services system to operate after the present war should be framed with due regard to the potential post-war economic position of the country.

The Confederation realises that it must inevitably be some time yet before any reliable forecast can be made on that aspect of the problem. Much must depend on unknown factors such as the length of the war and the devastation it causes throughout the world; the extent of our war casualties; the extent of the physical destruction of plant and materials which may be caused in this country by enemy action before the war is over; the nature of our post-war political and trading relationships with other countries; the burden of our War Debt; and the financial and fiscal policies of our own and other countries, including, in particular, the USA.

What does seem clear is that the world as a whole will emerge from the present war even more impoverished than it was by the last war, and that the first call which the nations of the world will have to meet at the end of this war may well be the relieving – not only in their own countries but also in other countries – of the distress of those whose homes and livelihoods have been shattered by the war.

It also seems clear that this country will emerge from the war as a debtor instead of a creditor country . . .

It is in these circumstances that the Confederation has suggested that this problem of the post-war reconstruction of the Social Services should be entrusted to a small war-time Commission which would not only leave Employers and their Organisations free to devote their whole energies to the immediate prosecution of the war, but would also give to the country the assurance that this highly important question was receiving the fullest and most constant attention. . .

In conclusion, in justice to the wider perspective of this subject and without in any way minimising its importance, we think it right to say – and we feel sure the Committee will agree – that, however desirable it may be to give assurances at this time regarding the Social Services, there are some broader considerations which hold a prior and deeper place in the minds of the people of this country, and that the anxieties and hopes round which their minds are centred are, not the Social Services, but that victory shall be achieved as speedily as possible and their freedom preserved; that future generations shall not be subjected to the human sacrifice and sufferings of another war; and that when this war is won, in a post-war world with new problems and new opportunities, they shall not be exposed to the mass unemployment with all its frustrations and hopelessness and demoralisation which followed in the wake of our last victory.

11 May 1942

2. MEMORANDUM BY THE TUC

The General Council took the view that from the workers' angle the problem of social security was one of securing an adequate income at all times and efficient treatment in case of illness. The present social services do not provide either of these things and the position is intensified because the sums provided are at varying levels which have no justification from the workers' standpoint however justifiable they may be on actuarial or other considerations. . .

The General Council, therefore, as a result of their detailed consideration, submit that the following should be the governing principles for reconstruction of Social Insurance and Allied Services:

(1) Cash benefit in respect of industrial accidents and industrial diseases should be dealt with and administered under separate and specific workmen's compensation legislation.

(2) There should be an inclusive scheme to cover unemployment, sickness, maternity, non-compensatable accidents, invalidity, old age, blindness, death and widowhood and orphanhood. The scheme should cover all gainfully occupied persons irrespective of income as defined in the Personal Injuries (Civilians) Scheme: viz., 'a person who is engaged in any trade, business, profession, office, employment or vocation and is wholly or substantially dependent thereon for a livelihood, or a person, who though temporarily unemployed, is normally so engaged and dependent'.

(3) There should be a flat rate of benefit which for a commencement should be £2 per week plus dependants' allowances, this to be the amount payable to adults in respect of unemployment, sickness, maternity, invalidity, non-compensatable accidents, widowhood, blindness and old age.

Persons not entitled to benefit should be provided for by a body like the present Assistance Board, properly constituted and remodelled to meet the situation and operating on a personal means test. This would involve the abolition of Local Authority Public Assistance Committees.

(4) There should be a flat rate of contribution and the proportion might be 25 per cent from insured persons, 25 per cent from employers and 50 per cent from the State. Contributions should only be payable in respect of the present contribution schemes including death benefit. This proposal would ensure that contributions would not be paid for benefits not now on a contributory basis, e.g., blindness.

(5) The Scheme should come under the direction of one Ministry with special arrangements for health services.

(6) A comprehensive national medical service covering everything that medical science can command for prevention and cure of sickness should be provided by the nation and be made available to everybody in the State. This service should include a statistical department for the provision of occupational and geographical records necessary to safeguard the health of the people. There should also be associated with the medical services a complete rehabilitation service on up-to-date lines.

3. MEMORANDUM OF EVIDENCE BY THE SHIPPING FEDERATION AND THE LIVERPOOL STEAM SHIP OWNERS' ASSOCIATION·

GENERAL

1. This country is entitled to feel proud of its Social Services as a whole.

The individual Services have come in for a good deal of criticism. Much of this is because they have grown up piece-meal, and have been allowed to develop in an apparently haphazard fashion. One of the compensations of this method of development is that it has enabled many experiments to be made. But the experimental stage is now over and for some years employers have urged that, instead of individual reviews in watertight compartments, the Social Services should be surveyed as a whole. We therefore welcome this opportunity of putting their suggestions before the Inter-Departmental Committee.

2. It seems to us that the present Social Services are like an industry in need of rationalisation. They are wastefully competitive: their products are not sufficiently standardised: their plants are too numerous and some are out-of-date.

3. Our main proposal is that there should be a single national compulsory contributory industrial social insurance scheme embracing the industrial risks now covered by the following four separate schemes:

(a) Unemployment;
(b) Health Insurance;
(c) Workmen's Compensation;
(d) Widows, Orphans and Old-Age Pensions.

The new scheme should be financed by equal contributions from employers and employees and by at least an equal third from the Exchequer. There should be a single combined weekly contribution from employer and employed covering all four services.

The cash benefits should be the same for the first three risks and (unless a more general scheme of family allowances finds favour) should provide for family benefits.

The medical benefits should be the same for accident, disease and illness, wherever they occur, i.e., irrespective of whether or not they are due to the fact of employment and should be available to the dependants of the insured. There should be a single administrative collecting agency and, probably, just a single payment agency.

There should continue to be separate administrative agencies for placing in employment and for administering medical benefits.

To supervise the Scheme as a whole there should be a special Statutory Committee or body of Social Service Commissioners.

4. To avoid a morass of detail this Memorandum is confined to broad general outlines.

On finance, in particular, it is only possible to deal in general principles, because we cannot foretell what we will be able to afford for the Social Services after the war.

4. MEMORANDUM BY THE NATIONAL COUNCIL OF WOMEN

(4) Women are at a disadvantage in all the schemes. In National Health Insurance and Unemployment Insurance they receive a lower rate of benefit, although their basic needs are no less than those of men. In

unemployment insurance there is a single fund from which all benefits are drawn. Since women's claims are lighter than those of men, women's contributions in effect assist in the payment of men's claims. In National Health Insurance on the other hand where it is women's claims (heavier largely on account of the excess sickness of Married Women) which are the larger burden, men's and women's funds are separated so that men reap the benefit of their lighter sickness experience. In Workmen's Compensation, the rate of compensation is linked to wages, and the present inequality of rates of wage between men and women prejudices the amount of compensation. Inadequate provision is made for the maintenance of income of the woman, married or unmarried, during pregnancy, confinement and the early infancy of her baby.

From: Report of Committee on Social Insurance and Allied Services 1942 (Beveridge Report), Memorandum of Evidence, *Parliamentary Papers* (1942–43) vol. 6.

WILLIAM BEVERIDGE ON FULL EMPLOYMENT

THE PURPOSE OF EMPLOYMENT
Idleness is not the same as Want, but a separate evil, which men do not escape by having an income. They must also have the chance of rendering useful service and of feeling that they are doing so. This means that employment is not wanted for the sake of employment, irrespective of what it produces. The material end of all human activity is consumption. Employment is wanted as a means to more consumption or more leisure, as a means to a higher standard of life. Employment which is merely time-wasting, equivalent to digging holes and filling them again, or merely destructive, like war and preparing for war, will not serve that purpose. Nor will it be felt worth while. It must be productive and progressive... though the Report assumes the continuance of some unemployment and suggests a figure of 3 per cent, it is the essence of the proposals made in the Report that this 3 per cent should be unemployed only because there is industrial friction, and not because there are no vacant jobs. For men to have value and a sense of value there must always be useful things waiting to be done, with money to pay for doing them. Jobs, rather than men, should wait.

PRESERVATION OF ESSENTIAL LIBERTIES
The labour market in the past has invariably, or all but invariably, been a buyer's market rather than a seller's market, with more unemployed men – generally many more unemployed men – than unfilled jobs. To reverse this and make the labour market always a seller's rather than a buyer's market, to remove not only unemployment but the fear of unemployment, would affect the working of many existing institutions. It would change and is meant to change fundamentally the conditions of living and working in Britain, to make Britain again a land of opportunity for all. There are some things in Britain which neither full employment nor the means of achieving it should be allowed to change.

The Report, as its title indicates, is not concerned simply with the problem of full employment. It is concerned with the necessity, possibility and methods of achieving full employment in a free society, that is to say, subject to the proviso that all essential citizen liberties are preserved. The precise effect of the proviso depends on the list of essential citizen liberties. For the purpose of this Report they are taken as freedom of worship, speech, writing, study and teaching; freedom of assembly and of association for political and other purposes, including the bringing about of a peaceful change of the governing authority; freedom in choice of occupation; and freedom in the management of a personal income. The proviso excludes the totalitarian solution of full employment in a society completely planned and regimented by an irremovable dictator. It makes the problem of full employment more complex in many ways . . .

The list of essential liberties given above does not include liberty of a private citizen to own means of production and to employ other citizens in operating them at a wage. Whether private ownership of means of production to be operated by others is a good economic device or not, it must be judged as a device. It is not an essential citizen liberty in Britain, because it is not and never has been enjoyed by more than a very small proportion of the British people. It cannot even be suggested that any considerable proportion of the people have any lively hope of gaining such ownership later.

On the view taken in this Report, full employment is in fact attainable while leaving the conduct of industry in the main to private enterprise, and the proposals made in the Report are based on this view. But if, contrary to this view, it should be shown by experience or by argument that abolition of private property in the means of production was necessary for full employment, this abolition would have to be undertaken.

From: William Beveridge, *Full Employment in a Free Society*, George Allen & Unwin, London (1944) pp. 20–23.

LABOUR (ANEURIN BEVAN) AND CONSERVATIVES (RICHARD LAW) DEBATE THE INTRODUCTION OF THE NATIONAL HEALTH SERVICE

MR BEVAN: The first reason why a health scheme of this sort is necessary at all is because it has been the firm conclusion of all parties that money ought not to be permitted to stand in the way of obtaining an efficient health service. Although it is true that the national health insurance system provides a general practitioner service and caters for something like 21 million of the population, the rest of the population have to pay whenever they desire the services of a doctor. It is cardinal to a proper health organisation that a person ought not to be financially deterred from seeking medical assistance at the earliest possible stage. It is one of the evils of having to buy medical advice that, in addition to the natural anxiety that may arise because people do not like to hear unpleasant things about themselves, and therefore tend to postpone consultation as long as possible, there is the financial anxiety caused by having to pay doctors' bills. Therefore, the first evil that we must deal with is that which exists as a consequence of the fact that the whole thing is the wrong way round. A person ought to be able to receive medical and hospital help without being involved in financial anxiety.

In the second place, the national health insurance scheme does not provide for the self-employed, nor, of course, for the families of dependants. It depends on insurance qualification, and no matter how ill you are; if you cease to be insured you cease to have free doctoring. Furthermore, it gives no backing to the doctor in the form of specialist services. The doctor has to provide himself, he has to use his own discretion and his own personal connections, in order to obtain hospital treatment for his patients and in order to get them specialists, and in very many cases, of course – in an overwhelming number of cases – the services of a specialist are not available to poor people.

Not only is this the case, but our hospital organisation has grown up with no plan, with no system; it is unevenly distributed over the country and indeed it is one of the tragedies of the situation, that very often the best hospital facilities are available where they are least needed. In the older industrial districts of Great Britain hospital facilities are inadequate. Many of the hospitals are too small – very much too small.

Furthermore – I want to be quite frank with the House – I believe it is repugnant to a civilised community for hospitals to have to rely upon private charity. I believe we ought to have left hospital flag days behind. I have always felt a shudder of repulsion when I have seen nurses and sisters who ought to be at their work, and students who ought to be at their work, going about the streets collecting money for the hospitals. I do not believe there is an hon. Member of this House who approves that system. It is repugnant, and we must leave it behind – entirely. But the implications of doing this are very considerable.

I have been forming some estimates of what might happen to voluntary hospital finance when the all-in insurance contributions fall to be paid by the people of Great Britain, when the Bill is passed and becomes an Act, and they are entitled to free hospital services. The estimates I have go to show that between 80 per cent and 90 per cent of the revenues of the voluntary hospitals in these circumstances will be provided by public funds, by national or rate funds. [An HON. MEMBER: 'By workers' contributions.'] And, of course, as the hon. Member reminds me, in very many parts of the country it is a travesty to call them voluntary hospitals. In the mining districts, in the textile districts, in the districts where there are heavy industries it is the industrial population who pay the weekly contributions for the maintenance of the hospitals. When I was a miner I used to find that situation, when I was on the hospital committee. We had an annual meeting and a cordial vote of thanks was moved and passed with great enthusiasm to the managing director of the colliery company for his generosity towards the hospital; and when I looked at the balance sheet, I saw that 97½ per cent of the revenues were provided by the miners' own contributions; but nobody passed a vote of thanks to the miners. . .

MR LAW: . . . We accept the principle, and we accept the consequences that flow from it. We understand, for example, that once we are committed, as we are gladly committed, to the principle of a 100 per cent, service, we require an enormous expansion and development in the health services as a whole. We understand, once we accept the principle, that we are committed to a far greater degree of coordination, or planning as it is usually called, than we have ever known before . . . if my right hon. and learned Friend the Member for North Croydon (Mr Willink) had still been Minister of Health, had the General Election result gone another way, I do not doubt that he would have introduced, before this, a Bill which would have differed from this Bill only in that my right hon. and learned Friend would not have attempted to control, own and direct the hospital service of this country or to interfere with that age-old relationship which exists, always has existed, and in our view ought to continue to exist, between a doctor and his patient. Therefore, the right hon. Gentleman is not entitled to say – he has not said it, but he might – that we will the end without the means. We will both the end and the means. We will this end, a comprehensive and efficient health service. We are willing to support any practicable means that will give us that end.

357

But we differ from the right hon. Gentleman on this issue. We believe that the right hon. Gentleman could have reached his end, and a better end, by other means, and by better means. We believe that he could have established a health service, equally comprehensive, better coordinated and far more efficient, if he had not been determined to sweep away the voluntary hospitals; if he had not been determined to weaken the whole structure of English local government by removing from the field of local government one of the most important and vital responsibilities of local authorities; and if he had not sought to impose upon the medical profession a form of discipline which, in our view and in theirs, is totally unsuited to the practice of medicine, an art, a vocation, however you like to call it, which depends above all else upon individual responsibility, individual devotion and individual sympathy.

From: *Hansard*, 30 April 1946.

TABLE OF STATUTES

1911	Shops Act
1911	National Insurance Act
1914	Education (Provision of Meals) Act
1915	Notification of Births (Extension) Act
1915	Rent and Mortgage Interest (Rent Restriction) Act
1915	Milk and Dairies Consolidation Act
1916	Midwives (Amendment) Act
1918	Maternity and Child Welfare Act
1918	Wages (Temporary Regulation) Act
1918	Education Act
1919	Housing and Town Planning Act
1919	Housing Act
1919	Old Age Pensions Act
1920	Blind Persons Act
1920	Adoption Act
1920	Unemployment Insurance Act
1920	National Health Insurance Act
1921	Unemployment Insurance (Amendment I) Act
1921	Unemployment Insurance (Amendment II) Act
1921	Unemployed Workers' Dependants (Temporary Provision) Act
1921	Trade Facilities Act
1923	Housing Act
1924	Housing (Financial Provisions) Act
1924	Old Age Pensions Act
1925	Old Age and Widows and Orphans Contributory Pensions Act
1926	Board of Guardians (Default) Act
1926	Economy (Miscellaneous Provisions) Act
1926	Adoption Act
1926	Legitimacy Act
1927	Unemployment Insurance Act
1929	Local Government Act
1930	Housing Act
1933	Housing Act
1933	Children and Young Persons' Act
1933	Rent and Mortgage Interest Restrictions (Amendment) Act
1934	Special Areas (Development and Improvement) Act
1934	Unemployment Act
1935	Housing Act
1935	Unemployment Assistance (Temporary Provisions) Act
1936	Midwives Act

1937	Special Areas (Amendment) Act
1938	Factories Act
1938	Increase of Tenant and Mortgage Interest (Restrictions) Act
1938	Holidays with Pay Act
1944	Education Act
1944	Disabled Persons Employment Act
1945	Family Allowances Act
1946	National Insurance Act
1946	National Insurance (Industrial Injuries) Act
1946	National Health Service Act
1946	Town and Country Planning Act
1948	Children Act
1948	National Assistance Act

COMMONWEALTH AND OTHER TERRITORIES

Australia

| 1908 | Juvenile Delinquents Act |

Germany

| 1911 | Social Insurance Act |

Japan

| 1911 | Factory Law |

USA

1906	Food and Drug Act
1906	Federal Employee's Liability Act
1935	Social Security Act
1946	Employment Act

TABLE OF REPORTS OF ROYAL COMMISSIONS, SELECT COMMITTEES ETC.

nection with the provision of dwellings for the working-class (Tudor-Walters committee)

1918   Ministry of Reconstruction Local Government sub-committee on the transfer of functions of the Poor Law Authorities of England and Wales (Maclean Committee)

1922   Committee on National Expenditure (Geddes Committee)

1922–3 Departmental Committee on Health and Unemployment Insurance (Anderson Committee)

1926   Royal Commission on National Health Insurance

1926   Consultative Committee to the Board of Education: Report on the Education of the Adolescent (Hadow Report)

1927   Unemployment Insurance Committee (Blanesburgh Committee)

1931   Committee on National Expenditure (May Committee)

1931   Royal Commission on Unemployment Insurance (Gregory Committee)

1932   Departmental Committee on Private Schools (Chuter Ede Committee)

1938   Consultative Committee to the Board of Education: Report on Secondary Education with special reference to Grammar Schools and Technical High Schools (Spens Committee)

1940   Royal Commission on the Distribution of the Industrial Population (Barlow Commission)

1941   Interdepartmental Committee on the Rehabilitation and Resettlement of the Disabled (Tomlinson Committee)

1942   Committee on Social Insurance and Allied Services (Beveridge Committee)

1943   Secondary Schools Examination Council: Report on Curriculum and Examinations in Secondary Schools (Norwood Committee)

1946   Interdepartmental Committee on the care of children (Curtis Committee)

All dates are those of the publication of the Report.

SELECT BIBLIOGRAPHY

BACKGROUND

HOBSBAWM, E. J., *Industry and Empire*, Penguin, Harmondsworth (1970).
MATHIAS, P., *The First Industrial Nation*, Methuen, London (1969).
MOWAT, C. L., *Britain Between the Wars*, Methuen, London (1955).
BARKER, R., *Political Ideas in Modern Britain*, Methuen, London (1978).

SOCIAL POLICY: GENERAL

FRASER, D., *The Evolution of the British Welfare State*, Macmillan, London (1973).
ROSE, M. E., *The Relief of Poverty 1834–1914*, Macmillan, London (1972).
HAY, J. R., *The Origins of the Liberal Welfare Reforms 1906–1914*, Macmillan, London (1975).
HALL, P., *et al*, *Change, Choice and Conflict in Social Policy*, Heinemann, London (1975).
RIMLINGER, G., *Welfare Policy and Industrialization in Europe, America, and Russia*, John Wiley & Sons, New York (1971).
PROCHASKA, F., *Women and Philanthropy in 19th Century England*, Oxford University Press (1980).

SOCIAL POLICIES

GILBERT, B. B., *The Origins of National Insurance*, Michael Joseph, London (1966).

GAULDIE E., *Cruel Habitations*, George Allen & Unwin, London (1974).

STEDMAN JONES, G., *Outcast London*, Oxford University Press (1971).

HARRIS, J., *Unemployment and Politics 1886–1914*, Oxford University Press (1972).

HARRIS, J., *William Beveridge*, Oxford University Press (1977).

LEWIS, J., *The Politics of Motherhood*, Croom Helm, London (1980).

ADDISON, P., *The Road to 1945*, Jonathan Cape, London (1975).

SOURCES AND SELECTIONS FROM SOURCES

KEATING, P., (ed.), *Into Unknown England, 1866–1913*, Selections from the social explorers, Fontana, London (1976).

EVANS, E. J., *Social Policy 1830–1913*, Routledge & Kegan Paul, London (1978).

HAY, J. R., *The Development of the British Welfare State 1880–1975*, Edward Arnold, London (1978).

STEVENSON, J., *Social Conditions in Britain between the Wars*, Penguin, Harmondsworth (1977).

PEMBER REEVES, M., *Round About a Pound a Week* (1913), reprinted Virago, London (1979).

LLEWELLYN DAVIES, M., (ed.), *Maternity – Letters from working women* (1915) reprinted Virago, London (1978).

SPRING RICE, M., *Working Class Wives* (1939), reprinted Virago, London 1981.

SILVER, H., (ed.) *Equal Opportunity in Education*, Methuen, London (1973).

INDEX

Abercrombie, Patrick, 259
abortion, as element of maternal
    mortality, 195
absenteeism from school by children, 41
Addison, Christopher, 137–8, 141,
    143–4, 190, 289; as first Minister of
    Health, 138; becomes President of
    Local Government Board, 145;
    dismissed from Ministry of Health,
    146, 190
Adkins, Sir Ryland, 142
Adoption Act 1926, 200
aged: care of, 37; 'comforts' allowed in
    workhouse, 37; government
    investigation into conditions of, 38
Aliens Act 1905, 60
altruism, growth of, 289, 294
American Medical Association, 279
Amery, Leopold, 241
Anderson, Sir John, see Waverley, John
    Anderson, 1st viscount
Anti-Sweating League, 94
anti-waste campaign organized, 153
Arch, Joseph, attempt to organize
    agricultural labourers, 8
armed services, allowances paid to
    127–8
Asquith, Herbert Henry, 1st earl of
    Oxford and Asquith, 80, 81, 90,
    137, 295: introduces graduated
    income tax, 80, 87; introduces
    different rates of tax for earned and
    unearned incomes, 80; and old-age
    pensioners, 82; doc 6
Astor, Lady, 192
Atholl, Duchess of, 205; asserts need

for 'small hands' in textile industry,
    205
Attlee, Clement Richard, earl, 178, 237;
    welcomes Beveridge social service
    reform plan, 252
Australia: reform measures in, 113;
    introduces non-contributory
    invalidity pension, 113; reasonable
    standard wage for workers ordered,
    113–14; fails to tackle
    unemployment, 114; provisions of
    federal legislation, 115; selective in
    encouraging population growth and
    immigration, 115; leading world in
    some social policy fields, 116, 160;
    economy's benefit from war, 160;
    near stasis in social policy, 160;
    gains in international trade during
    war, 272; economic stability in, 274;
    national development as post-war
    priority, 274; strong measures taken
    against strikers, 274; international
    slump, effects on, 275; changes of
    government in, 275; policy changes
    implemented during war, 275;
    establishes minimum means-tested
    provision, 276; post-war success of
    economy, 276
Austro-Hungarian Empire,
    disintegration of, 157

Baldwin of Bewdley, earl, 178
Balfour, Arthur James, Earl of, 64, 72;
    disinterest in social issues, 64–5
Barlow Commission on Distribution of

Henderson, Arthur, 177

Hill, Charles, baron H. of Luton, 231

Hill, Octavia, 26, 73; initiates building of low-cost apartments for poor families, 26; founder-member of COS, 26; an energetic propagandist, 26

Hilton, Professor John, 153, 169

Hitler, Adolf, 280–1; no clear economic policy of, 281

Hobhouse, L. T., 57; theorist of compromise view between 'collectivism' and 'individualism', 57–8; demands for state action, 58

Holidays with Pay Act 1939, 163

'home colonization', 24–5

hospital services, poorness of in rural areas, 192

housing: lower rural density, 7; government subsidies for, 25; major crisis in cities, 26; problems of rural, 27; reluctance of state to intervene in market, 42; little improvement in, 97; continuing closure of unfit dwellings, 97; shortage of in First World War, 131–2; programme cut, 146; ending of subsidies, 146; substantial number of council houses built, 206–7; and overcrowding, 212–13; number built between 1931–39, 213; poor state of rural, 213

Housing Act 1885, 43

Housing Act 1890, 43

Housing Act 1919, 206, 213; building diminished under, 207

Housing Act 1923, 207

Housing Act 1924, 208

Housing Act 1930, 209; as means of attempting to solve housing problem of poorest, 209

Housing Act 1935, 211; provisions of, 211; definition of 'slums', 212

Housing and Town Planning Act 1909, 97–8; purpose of Act, 98

Housing and Town Planning Act 1919, 145; number of houses built under, 145

Howard Association for Penal Reform, 78

Howard, Ebenezer, 97, 214; advocate of 'garden cities', 97

hunger marches, 183, 184

'hygienic milk depots', 67

ill-health: high levels of, 189–90; poverty as central cause of, 190

income: limited redistribution of, 262; rising of fully employed households in Second World War, 263

income support system, ideas for improvement in, 245–6

income tax: graduated as means of raising revenue, 45; increase in, 178; reduction in, 179; increase in, 240

Independent Labour Party (ILP): foundations of, 18; views on municipalization, 47; demands for 'endowment of motherhood', 67; demonstrations by, 70

'individualism', 11, 57

industries: decline of staple, 163; development of new, 163

infant education, limiting school provision for children under 5, 76

Infant Health Society, 68

infant mortality: variations in regional and social class, 56; reasons for decline in, 56–7; higher rate of male over female, 59; high rate of in Germany, 110; downward trend of, 134, 135–6, 166, 194

infant welfare, continuation and expansion of, 135

Infant Welfare Propaganda Fund, 135

infants and children, pressure to improve health and survival rates of, 68

infirmaries, 36; improvement of, 36

insurance benefits, pressure exerted for extension to dependents, 231

insurance companies, commercial, growth of, 29

inter-war years, 163ff.

International Monetary Fund, 257

Italy: severe poverty in, 158; severe recession in, 272

Japan: rise in literacy rate in, 103; social provision in, 106; provision of social benefits in, 111; government

World War, Second: devastation of, 283;
    blueprints produced for more
    socially just society after, 298;
    measures taken to reconstruct
    economy, 298

YMCA, 20
Yokoyama, Gennosuke, 112
Young, Sir Hilton, 211